THE PELICAN HISTORY OF ART

EDITED BY NIKOLAUS PEVSNER

Z 12

ARCHITECTURE IN BRITAIN : THE MIDDLE AGES

GEOFFREY WEBB

Lady Chapel. Wells Cathedral,
Somerset. *c.* 1300 (photograph by
Rodney Todd-White)

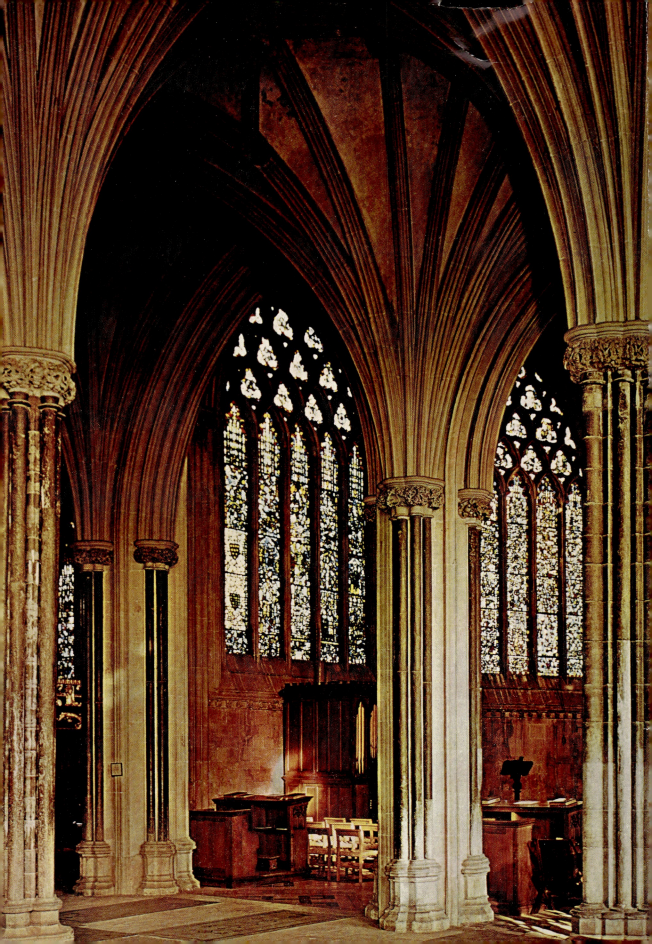

GEOFFREY WEBB

ARCHITECTURE IN BRITAIN

THE MIDDLE AGES

PUBLISHED BY PENGUIN BOOKS

Penguin Books Ltd, Harmondsworth, Middlesex
Penguin Books Inc., Baltimore, Maryland, U.S.A.
Penguin Books Pty Ltd, Ringwood, Victoria, Australia

★

Printed by Richard Clay (The Chaucer Press) Ltd,
Bungay, Suffolk
Made and printed in Great Britain

★

TO

M.I.W.

★

CONTENTS

The Plates

LIST OF FIGURES

Indications of vaulting on plans are diagrammatic only

ix

LIST OF FIGURES

LIST OF PLATES

xi

720 WGB

9753

Thanks are due to the Society of Antiquaries of London for permission to reproduce Plates 119A and B. The permission of the Controller of H.M. Stationery Office has been obtained to reproduce plates 74B, 76, 77, 150B, 151 A and B, 152 A and B, 153 A and B, 156B, and 189B.

FOREWORD

In a book which covers such a long period of time as this the most important problem for the writer to decide is what to leave out. The most obvious omission from this book is that of military architecture. There is in it no discussion of the development of fortification – a particularly important omission in regard to England, where examples of motte and bailey castles, twelfth-century keeps of various forms, and of later thirteenth-century castles, culminating in the splendid and well documented examples erected at the end of the thirteenth and beginning of the fourteenth centuries, especially in Wales, form a series of the greatest importance to the history of this subject. The decision to omit these monuments, or only to discuss parts of them such as the great halls and reception-rooms which they contain, was a difficult one, for clearly the quality of the work of the masters who carried out the greatest castles – and they were often the same men who built the great churches – gave to the result characteristics which are occasionally of the highest architectural interest. I decided, however, that the test of what should be included should be whether the appearance of the building was primarily dictated by non-material considerations, one might almost say by an appeal to the imagination. This is clearly true of the great ecclesiastical buildings, and in an only slightly lesser degree of the great halls of castles or houses and the comparable buildings of monastic establishments, which were built to impress quite as much as to provide the necessary physical accommodation, for worldly splendour is also an appeal to the imagination.

There are, however, other omissions less obviously striking than that of military architecture, which are in these days perhaps more difficult to defend. The character of modern historical study has been much influenced by economic preoccupations, deriving not only from the studies of the economists themselves, properly so called, but also from the nature of modern methods in archaeology, a field where the nature of the material available has dictated a largely economic approach. It would be possible to write a history of medieval architecture in the British Isles which was founded entirely on the examination of the social and economic forces which brought about the erection of buildings of different types, and it is to be hoped that this will one day be done. Equally, the subject could be treated from the point of view of the materials used and their regional distribution, the techniques employed and the structure of the building trade itself, as well as the sequence of technical devices. From the later nineteenth century onwards much work has been put in along these various lines, and it will be clear to the reader of this book that some of this accumulated knowledge has been drawn upon in the pages that follow; particularly of recent years, our knowledge of building accounts and documents of all sorts giving evidence of how building enterprises were organized has been greatly increased, especially for the period from the mid thirteenth century onwards. From the time of Henry III's rebuilding of Westminster Abbey we are abundantly provided in this country with documentary material of this kind, and it can quite frequently be related to surviving monuments. Before the middle of the thirteenth century, however, the documentary material is generally of a rather different character, and the prospect that we shall be able to relate the immensely important technical and architectural changes which took place in the twelfth and early thirteenth centuries to changes in the structure of the building industry is not very hopeful. This is not in any way to denigrate the importance of the study of building documents in any period; it has already added immensely to our understanding of medieval architecture, quite apart from its interest to economic historians, which was admirably pointed out by Professors Knoop and Jones when they said that a great medieval building enterprise was the only form of industrial activity in which the society of the Middle Ages was working on a scale in any way comparable to the modern world, and that the way the men of the Middle Ages tackled the problem of a large-scale enterprise had therefore, for the historian, an outstanding interest.

It is perhaps even more indefensible to have treated parish-church building as shortly as I have been compelled to do in this book, but until the mid thirteenth century, and indeed until considerably later, the parish churches are, for the most part, modest in scale, and their architectural interest is mainly in details and individual features rather than in the total effect. This omission is to be the more regretted in that England is exceptionally rich in this kind of building.

Of recent years a number of scholars have devoted attention to the typology of smaller medieval houses, and it is clear that in the next few years our understanding of the evidence which still remains to us on this aspect of medieval building is likely to be very greatly increased. The impetus of this study has ultimately come from men whose training has been in early archaeology, and unquestionably their work will immensely enlarge our understanding of the social history and technology of the Middle Ages; but I felt that, this volume being one of a series which dealt primarily with the history of art all over the world, the point of view which should govern the selection of material must be one which was at any rate related to that of the continental art historians, some of whom would be contributing to the series. The typological approach to the history of medieval architecture in England was well understood in the nineteenth century, and such works as those of the late Francis Bond or Greening Lamborne are fundamentally concerned with this aspect of the subject. One of the first attempts to write a history of English architecture in the Middle Ages which was not primarily a history of building technique, was that of the late Professor Prior, whose *Gothic Art in England* appeared in 1901, and which represented a summing up of the accumulated learning which had grown up with the Gothic revival of the two generations which preceded him. Prior reinterpreted this accumulated knowledge in the light of the point of view of the German scholars of his time, who were themselves the founders of present-day art historical method. Since Prior's time the work of such remarkable medievalists as the late Sir Alfred Clapham and Professor Hamilton Thompson has put the dating of many important monuments on to a new footing, and the chief defect of Professor Prior's great work is that in many cases his dating is extremely uncertain. In addition, Sir Alfred Clapham has shown in quite a new light the relations of this early material to continental work, and Professor Hamilton Thompson's knowledge of documentary evidence has advanced far beyond anything available to Prior at the beginning of this century.

Every few generations it is necessary, in the light of such accumulated scholarship, not only to revise our views of such great subjects as these, but to rewrite the history of an art in the light of the preoccupations of a new generation. These preoccupations are nowadays somewhat divergent, and it has been necessary to come to a decision as to which should be allowed to predominate. The decision in this instance has been to attempt to write of architecture as an art historian, in spite of the well-reasoned claims of other methods of approach and the inherent difficulties of applying to architectural history a discipline which has been developed mainly in the study of painting and sculpture.

Three friends to whom I am most especially grateful are Dr Joan Evans, Director of the Society of Antiquaries, and Professor Wormald of the University of London, who have read the typescript in whole or in part, and Mrs Parry of the National Buildings Record, whose help with the illustrations has been beyond estimation. My wife has not only endured much discussion of a subject remote from her own with exemplary patience, but crowned her generosity by doing her best with the proofs.

G. F. W.

CHAPTER I

THE EARLIEST CHURCHES

IT seems reasonable to begin the history of medieval architecture in the British Isles with the seventh century and the importation into England by the Christian missionaries of a new kind of building from the Mediterranean and Gaul. It is likely that pagan Saxon architecture in England was entirely a timber one and that the most revolutionary feature of the imported style was the use of brick and stone.[1] This is not to suggest that timber buildings are unworthy to be considered as architecture. At a later stage in this book we shall have to give considerable attention to monumental buildings for which the carpenter deserves even more credit than the mason, and it is in every way likely that timber buildings of considerable size were erected in pre-Christian Anglo-Saxon times.

The evidence of the Great Hall at Tara [2] shows that buildings of the grandest scale were constructed in timber in Ireland at an early period, and though the most famous Irish building – the oratory of Gallerus, with its extremely accomplished dry stone-walling technique, including an oversailing vault – seems to show continuity with a building technique reaching back to very remote times, there is every reason to suppose that the majority of the earlier Irish church buildings, including the most ambitious, were in wood. The fact that the *Vetusta Ecclesia* at Glastonbury, destroyed in 1185, was made of wood suggests that in places where the influence of Irish Christianity was strongly felt timber was the natural building material.

England is fortunate in possessing extensive remains of the church buildings of the seventh and eighth centuries. In a number of cases there are considerable parts of the structures still standing, and in others the plan is in large measure recoverable. A distinction has been drawn between the churches of south-eastern England and those of the north. The south-eastern churches most probably derive their form in the main from Gaul, and there is indeed evidence of the importation of craftsmen, to Northumbria as well as to Kent, in the early stages of the establishment of the Christian Church in Saxon England. The remains of at least eight churches of the earliest age of English Christianity are known in the south: four at Canterbury – St Peter and St Paul, St Mary, St Pancras, and St Martin – one at Rochester, one at Lyminge, and one at Reculver, all in Kent, and one at Bradwell-juxta-Mare, in Essex.[3]

All these churches consisted of a rectangular body with an apse towards the east. In most cases the two parts were separated by an arcade of three arches. In one case – that of St Martin, Canterbury – a small presbytery appears to intervene between the main body of the church and the apse, but this is probably due to a longer nave having been added at an early date to the original small building. In addition to these two main components, many of the churches had rectangular extensions built out to the north and south and, more rarely, to the west. These are called Porticus in the early documents.

The earliest of this group of buildings – St Peter and St Paul, Canterbury – formed the chief church of the Abbey founded by St Augustine himself in 597, and is known to have been in process of building at the time of his death in 604. Excavations made in 1904 and 1924 have recovered considerable evidence of the church (Figure 9), though the eastern parts have been obliterated by the additions made to it in the eleventh century. The remains recovered by excavation show that the body of the church was 27 feet wide and was flanked by two rectangular chapels to the north and two to the south. The north chapels were 12 feet wide and 29 and 24 feet from east to west respectively. In addition, there was a narthex or porch 11 feet deep to the west. The north-east chapel contained the tombs of St Augustine and his earliest successors, remains of which

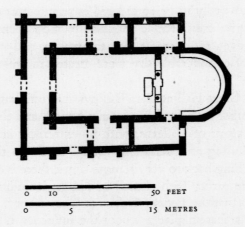

Figure 1. Reculver church: Plan

were found *in situ*. The corresponding chapel to the south contained the tombs of King Ethelbert, his wife Bertha, and others. St Peter and St Paul appears to have been the most complex of the early churches at Canterbury, though St Pancras also appears to have had rectangular chapels to the north and south and a square porch to the west, in addition to the usual component parts. A considerable part of the walls of this church remains standing. They are built mainly of Roman brick re-used, and are about 1 foot 10 inches in thickness.

The somewhat later church at Reculver[4] is dated by a reference in the *Anglo-Saxon Chronicle*, which says that in 669 King Egbert of Kent gave Reculver to Bassa, his Mass priest, to build a minster. When excavated, very complete evidence of the church plan and some detail of its architectural fittings were found (Figure 1). The church consisted of a body or nave 37½ by 24 feet, and an apse with a bench running round the inside of the curve; there were two rectangular chapels, which overlapped the junction of the nave and the apsidal chancel to the north and south. There were also traces of slightly later (probably eighth-century) chapels which completely surrounded the nave walls of the church to the north, south, and west. We are fortunate in possessing an early nineteenth-century picture of the Reculver church which shows that the nave and chancel were separated by an arcade of three arches, supported in the middle on columns of a distinctly antique character. Remains of these columns have been preserved and are now at Canterbury. Reculver, in the form which it assumed after the eighth-century additions, has the most complex plan of any of these early churches. It also possessed the peculiarity of a great carved standing cross, placed before the central opening of the arcade which divides the nave and apse on the nave side. The base of the cross was found *in situ*, and the floor, of a concrete composition, was so stopped against it as to indicate that the cross was either an original feature of the church or possibly had even preceded the building of the church around it.

The example of these early churches of which most survives, and to which little or no modern restoration has been applied, is that of St Peter's, Bradwell-juxta-Mare (Plate 1). It is almost certainly to be identified with the church built at Ythancester by St Cedd shortly after 653. The walls, which are mostly of re-used Roman material and are supported by boldly projecting buttresses at regular intervals, survive to their full height. The apse, however, and any chapels of the kind we have described above, have disappeared, but there is evidence in the east wall of the original triple arcade now walled up. The building is also remarkable in that the plain square windows and wide west doorway are largely original. There are sufficient traces to make it certain that square chapels did exist to the north and south of the line of the triple arcade, and these must have overlapped the nave and chancel, as in the example at Reculver. It seems likely that the west door was covered by a porch.

Architecturally considered, the plans of this group of buildings seem to consist of two motifs: the ceremonial part of the church, which we will call the main body with the chancel, and the surrounding chapels or porticus. The source of the ceremonial part is almost certainly Mediterranean. Comparable plans, with the main body separated from the chancel by a triple arcade, have been found in North Africa and on the east coast of the Adriatic, but the extreme scarcity of remains from the sixth and early seventh centuries on the continent, except for grandiose Byzantine buildings such as those at Ravenna, makes it difficult to trace any real connexion with the English group. The porticus motif is even more obscure. It seems that the earliest church at Como possessed such features, and there is a reference in the letters of St Paulinus of Nola describing the new church of St Felix there (*c.* 400) as having 'four cubicula' on each side of the nave within the aisles, 'made for those who desired to pray or meditate the word of God and as memorials to the departed'. This seems to fit very well with the fact of the burial of the early archbishops in the north porticus of St Peter and St Paul, Canterbury, and of King Ethelbert and his wife in the corresponding one to the south. There is also evidence that St Ethelburga was buried in a similar position on the north side of Lyminge church and a bishop at the end of the seventh century in the same position at Rochester. Where there are only two porticus and they overlap the main body and the chancel on each side, the feature seems to derive from the *prothesis* and *diaconicon* familiar in Byzantine churches, but the multiplication of these lateral annexes constitutes the interesting feature of the plans of these early churches in southern England.

The second group of early stone churches in England is the northern one, and dates from the last quarter of the seventh century when the Roman mission had definitely established its authority over the Irish-converted areas in Northumbria. The actual remains consist of the church at Monkwearmouth, probably part of the small church at Jarrow, Escomb church, all three in County Durham, and the crypts at Hexham in Northumberland and Ripon in Yorkshire. The monastery of Jarrow [5] contained two

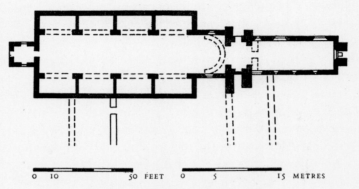

Figure 2. Monastery of Jarrow: Plan

churches sited axially; the easternmost one (about 39 ft by 15 ft internally) was a simple rectangle, possibly with an apsidal sanctuary, and of this three sides dating from the seventh century remain, though the eastern end has been so patched and altered as to leave the existence and form of the sanctuary uncertain (Figure 2). There are three surviving windows of the early church, two of them with their original pierced stone infilling. An eighteenth-century drawing in the British Museum shows that to the west of this building there was a larger church (some 80 ft by 20 ft) having four porticus on each side and a projecting western porch. This was presumably the 'basilica' of St Paul built by Benedict Biscop, of which an inscription recording the dedication in A.D. 685 still survives. In the late eleventh century the two churches were joined together by a building in the form of a tower, and this involved the destruction of the adjacent ends of the early buildings. The most important remains at Monkwearmouth, where two churches are also recorded, are the two-storied western porch and the remains of sculptured decorations and fittings (see below). The porch (Plate 2A) has a barrel vault to the first storey and there are considerable remains of the original decorative treatment. The round-headed western archway has responds consisting of two stones running through the thickness of the walls carved with intertwined beaked animals and these are surmounted on either side by turned stone balusters which support the heavy impost blocks. Above the archway are the remains of a carved frieze and in the gable of the upper storey is the much-weathered remnant of a large standing figure in relief. The upper storey of the porch connected with the nave of the church by a door. The church at Escomb (Plate 2B) has a long narrow nave with a small rectangular chancel. This has been thought to represent a continuation of the Celtic, ultimately Irish, timber building tradition, in contrast to the work of the masons brought by Benedict Biscop from Gaul to build 'more Romanorum' at Jarrow and Monkwearmouth, according to Bede. Both at Escomb and at Corbridge in Northumberland there are details of arch construction which seem to derive from neighbouring Roman sites, and indeed the chancel arch at Escomb has been claimed as a re-use of Roman work.

The two crypts at Hexham and Ripon are the remains of the churches built by St Wilfrid (d. 709), and we have descriptions of them. They seem to have been relatively ambitious buildings. Hexham is described as having colonnaded aisles with galleries above, and the Ripon church as having numerous columns and porticus. Apart from the crypt, the remains which have been discovered at Hexham are very ambiguous, though it seems possible to establish the total width of the church as some 62 feet.[6] It is likely that the crypt (Figure 3) stood in both cases under the eastern parts of the nave, but the form of the transepts, if they existed, is extremely doubtful. Wilfrid also built a church at York and a second church at Hexham; the latter is described as built in the form of a tower having porticus on four sides. This seems to indicate a centrally planned building, and the biographer of St Wilfrid particularly stresses the fineness of the masonry in these buildings.

The only building of which enough survives to give any real idea, by its scale and quality, of the class of these foundations of St Wilfrid is the parish church at Brixworth in Northamptonshire (Plates 3 and 4, A and B), which was founded by the monks of Peterborough not long after 675. Brixworth was an aisled basilica of four bays, or rather, had a nave of four bays with arches opening into porticus on each side giving the effect of aisles (Figure 4). It had a triple arcade, of which vestiges remain, separating the nave from a square presbytery beyond which is an apse, round inside and polygonal outside, reached by an arch from the presbytery.

Two further porticus aligned with those of the nave, but separated from them and

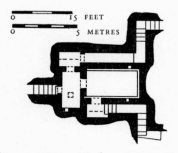

Figure 3. Crypt, Hexham Priory: Plan

possibly taller, flanked the western part of the presbytery from which they were entered through narrow doors. At the west end of the church was a two-storied porch flanked by porticus also of two stories, and there is evidence that the upper storey of the porch was entered by a door in its eastern wall, as at Monkwearmouth, which seems to imply some form of timber western gallery. All the porticus, including those flanking the porch, have been removed, or possibly they were destroyed in the later ninth century and not rebuilt. Considerable alterations were made to the church in the late eighth or early ninth century when a subterranean ambulatory was added round the apse, and again in the tenth and early eleventh century when the porch was increased in height to form a tower and a room contrived in it reached by a circular turret stair against its western face. This tower room opened into the nave by a three-light window with turned baluster shafts. The purpose of these later alterations seems to have been to provide a 'state pew' for some local person of importance.

The nave is some 60 by 30 feet internal measurement, without the aisles, and the presbytery is about 30 feet square. The arcades are turned in three rings of Roman brick, with a course of brick laid on the curve of the arch as a border. At the springing of the arch the bricks are laid at an acute angle with the radial line, which produces a very disorderly effect. This characteristic links them closely with work of the fifth and sixth

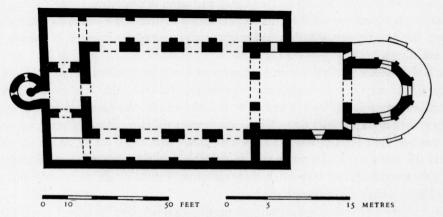

Figure 4. Brixworth church: Plan

centuries in Italy, notably at S. Pietro in Vincoli at Rome, and is even found at S. Vitale at Ravenna. In recent years an arch of rather similar construction has been found at All Hallows Barking.

Though in point of scale and architectural ambition Brixworth is the nearest that we have to Wilfrid's great churches, it will be seen that in plan it belongs to the southeastern group. There are evidences, however, that the western portions which flanked the porch had upper storeys, as had the porch itself, and these remind us again of the description of Wilfrid's building at Hexham, with its galleries and spiral staircase. The most important thing about Brixworth, however, is the scale of the building, and even in its truncated condition it remains the first building of serious architectural pretension that comes within the scope of this book.[7]

The churches of Mediterranean inspiration, to use a comprehensive expression, as we know them from actual remains in the south and mainly written accounts in Northumbria, make up almost all there is of architecture surviving from the early Dark Ages, if the word 'architecture' is to be used in a way that can be at all consistent throughout this book. There are, however, the problems of the types of building and techniques employed in the British Isles independently of these imported examples. Of recent years a number of sites have been excavated: Llantwit Major,[8] Tintagel,[9] and Whitby,[10] where considerable remains of early monastic establishments have been found, and at Whithorn in Galloway some remains of St Ninian's church of the first half of the fifth century. Perhaps the most important aspect of these discoveries is the picture they present of the layout and general arrangement of these early communities. At Whitby a large number of stone-built cells was discovered, and one larger building, the refectory. The ground between the separate cell buildings was roughly paved, and there were stone-paved roads as a means of getting about from one part of the monastery to another. At Tintagel the excavations also showed an arrangement of scattered cells, on this site apparently disposed in groups. One group included a building with a simple form of hypocaust and seemed to be an example of the survival of Roman ideas of comfort: later groups showed a considerable falling off in this respect.

The evidence of the *Abingdon Chronicle*, which tells of the early monastery there (founded in 675) as consisting of the church, a building of considerable pretension (120 feet in length and with apses at both ends), and twelve cells each with an oratory attached, states that instead of a cloister, in the sense that the later writer of the *Chronicle* understood the word, there was a high surrounding wall which served for a cloister. This rather mysterious statement may be explained by the discovery at the early monastic site at Nendrum [11] in County Down, excavated in 1924, of a paved walk along a large part of the inner enclosing wall of the monastery, and it seems clear from the sites excavated and from this passage in the *Abingdon Chronicle* that no formal centre of communal life corresponding to the later cloister existed in early times, and that the monks foregathered, as might be expected, on the broader paved walks, much as soldiers in an improvised hutted camp naturally do. No buildings that could be identified as churches were found at any of the sites excavated, but it seems likely that there were, both at Whitby and at Llantwit Major, churches now concealed by later church buildings. At Tintagel it may well have been that the churches were not distinguishable by their foundations from the other small rectangular buildings of which the establishment seems to have consisted. As to the building technique of these remains, they are all simple rectangular constructions, and vary considerably in quality of masonry. The stonework of the Whitby buildings was noticeably poor, but at Llantwit Major much better. It has been suggested that in South Wales a tradition from antique times had survived to account for this superiority. At Tintagel there is a marked deterioration in the quality of the stonework from the earliest sub-antique structures, such as the building with the hypocaust mentioned above, to the later mid Dark Age cells.

The comparison made above between the account in the *Abingdon Chronicle* and the monastic site at Nendrum, suggests that the most illuminating parallels with these very early sites in Great Britain are to be found in Ireland, where there are considerable remains of Christian buildings of very early Dark Age date. The most distinguished of these is certainly the Oratory of Gallerus (Plate 5A) in County Kerry, a rectangular building measuring 22 by 18½ feet externally and covered with an oversailing stone vault, i.e. built in oversailing courses and not a true arch; there is a round-headed window in the east wall. The whole building is very finely finished, and the stones of the dry walling are most carefully cut and fitted and brought to a very smooth finish inside. It has a special quality, as of the culmination of an extremely primitive technique used in the service of the new religion. The Oratory of Gallerus is only the finest among many examples of this type of building in Ireland, and there are a number of early monastic sites, all of which seem to have been of the nature of those already discussed. Amongst the most famous is Skellig Michael, an assemblage of cells romantically placed on the cliffs overlooking the Atlantic. It has been plausibly suggested that the survival of examples like Skellig Michael is due to the fact that they happen to have been built in dry-stone technique in treeless regions and isolated positions, and that the greater monasteries in the more hospitable parts of Ireland were almost certainly built of wood, and have in consequence perished.

The churches of these early monastic establishments both in Ireland and in Great Britain seem often to have been quite small, and sometimes several in one monastery. There are traces of this tradition, which has survived to a considerable extent in the Greek Orthodox Church, at various sites in Great Britain: for example, St Augustine's, Canterbury, and Glastonbury and Malmesbury. All early monasteries, however, did not follow this tradition of a number of small churches, and just as there were monasteries with comparatively large churches, as at Brixworth and Abingdon in England, so literary evidence suggests that monastic churches of considerable size existed from early times in Ireland. As has been suggested, these were most probably built of timber, even the most ambitious of them. That timber was used for buildings of the highest pretension is shown from the accounts of the Great Hall of Tara, the foundations of which are said to indicate a building 759 feet long by 46 feet wide. There are references to this early Irish timber-work, 'opus Scotorum', at Iona and at Lindisfarne, where the early church is described as 'built in the Irish fashion, not of stone but of cut oak and thatched with reeds'. The most remarkable account of this Irish timber-work is to be found in Cogitosus's life of St Bridget.[12]

Cogitosus gives an account of the church in which the bodies of Bishop Conleagh and St Bridget were buried on the right and on the left side in magnificent monuments variously adorned with gold and silver, jewels and precious stones, and having crowns (coronis) of gold and silver hanging over them.[13] The church, he says, owing to the growing number of the faithful of both sexes, was laid out on a broad site and was raised to a towering height and had painted boardings. Inside there were three spacious chapels divided from each other by partitions, but under the one roof of the great church, across the eastern part of which a decorated screen adorned with painted images and covered with linen cloths extended from one wall to the other. There was a door at each end of this screen; through that on the right the bishop and his attendant company could enter the sanctuary for the celebration of the Office, while through the door in the left-hand end of the screen across the church the abbess and her maidens and women entered to partake of the Sacraments. Moreover, another screen extended from the west end as far as the transverse screen. The church had many windows, and one magnificent door on the right for the priests and men of the congregation to come in at, and one on the left for the maidens and women. 'And so in one great basilica a great multitude, mixed in degree, rank, and sex, from different places and of different vocations, though of different orders yet of one mind, prayed to Almighty God.'

The interest of this account showing the arrangement of a double monastery, the dividing wall down the middle of the church, and so on, has attracted attention, but the details given of the ritual arrangements and the decorations of the building are quite as important as the other rather more exceptional features. It has been suggested that this timber-building tradition would militate against the adoption of the apse, the most notable feature of the imported architecture of south England and essentially a feature deriving from a sophisticated architectural tradition founded on a stone or brick building technique, and it is worth observing that though we have good reason to believe that the more ambitious buildings in Northumbria, such as those associated with Wilfrid, would be in every way abreast of the new imported fashions, the surviving examples of the earliest buildings in the north, such as Escomb in Durham, have strictly rectangular plans, including small rectangular chancels. Bede contrasts the 'More Scotorum' with stone building, but there was equally a widespread timber tradition in England. There is the evidence of the early Saxon poems, and though excavation has shown us no actual remains of important timber structures of the pagan Saxon period, it is surely reasonable to assume that such a king as he whose cenotaph was found at Sutton Hoo inhabited a building of considerable splendour, and there is every reason to suppose that it was a timber one. It would, however, be rash to attempt to distinguish Anglo-Saxon timber technique from that of Ireland on the strength of Bede's contrast of Irish building as against Roman stone or brick, as Strygowski attempted to do by founding his distinction on the expression 'cut oak' which he contrasted with log building technique. The other example of the use of timber in early times for church building in England is of course the famous *Vetusta Ecclesia* at Glastonbury, which is described as made with wattle and daub on a timber frame, and this fits well with other references in early literary sources.[13a]

Except for the fragments of the cross-shaft from Reculver and the details of the columns from the same church now at Canterbury, we know nothing of the decorative fittings of the early churches of the south. There is, however, evidence from documents of this aspect of some of the Northumbrian churches, and a few fragments survive at Monkwearmouth (Plate 5B). The most important of these are two sculptured lion-like beasts, one of which seems to have been the north-west end of a bench round the chancel, and the other the left-hand (i.e. north side) support of a throne like those surviving at Hexham (Plate 5C) and Beverley. The lions are very much worn and damaged, but the boldness of the relief seems to link them with other northern sculptures of this epoch, such as the great crosses, notably that of Ruthwell. As already mentioned, a very much weathered and battered figure, probably Christ, survives *in situ* with some fragments of frieze above the west door at Monkwearmouth, though all that it is possible to conclude from the remains of the figure is that sculpture of considerable size in high relief was employed in these churches. At Hovingham in Yorkshire there is part of a frieze with vine-scroll decoration of a type considered to be even earlier than the Bewcastle and Ruthwell crosses. This is thought to have formed part of a reredos, and at South Kyme (Plate 6A) in Lincolnshire there are fragments of decorative panels which are best explained as pieces of a low screen, such as the *Cancelli* of early Roman churches. The documentary evidence includes that of Bede, who tells us that Benedict Biscop brought back paintings from Italy which he placed in the church at Monkwearmouth, and a late description of St Wilfrid's church at Hexham which speaks of the sculptured relief decoration on the walls, the capitals, and the sanctuary arch, and suggests that these decorations included both pictorial relief and single figures *(historiis et imaginibus)*; painted decoration in colour is also implied. All this is enough, with the many examples of the sculpture of that age that have survived on cross-shafts, to enable us to get some idea of the character of the internal finish of (at any rate) the Northumbrian churches of the late seventh and early eighth centuries.

The immediately succeeding period, the later eighth and early ninth centuries, is strangely devoid of evidence of the planning and structural character of the churches. We hear of a great church at York dating from between 766 and 782, described as having columns and arches and being surrounded by porticus; a large number of upper storey apartments and no fewer than thirty altars are also mentioned. In 1927 some remains of the eighth-century buildings attributed to King Ine (*c.* 700) at Glastonbury were found, sufficient to show that with its narthex and porticus it was very considerably larger than the wooden *Vetusta Ecclesia*, itself a building 60 by 26 feet.[14] The Glastonbury discoveries do not imply a real change in the type of structure from that of the churches already described. There are, however, features both at Britford (Plate 6B), which may belong to the early ninth century, and in the York description, which may be held to foreshadow the architecture of the succeeding age and will have to be discussed in connexion with it.[15]

If evidence of the plan and structure of the eighth and ninth centuries is lacking, we at least know something of the decorative character of the buildings. At Breedon in Leicestershire about 60 feet of frieze with a great variety of decorative motifs and figure and animal carvings have survived, built into the later church. There are other examples of similar work at Fletton which may have come from the early church at Peterborough nearby, and at Castor in the same district there is another fragment of later carving. Part of the Breedon friezes and the fragment at Castor are possibly from reredoses, but the large amount of the surviving carved work at Breedon implies that the church as a whole must have been extremely richly decorated. The quality of this work is of a very high order, notably the figures [16] of mounted men; all this implies a church of great distinction and is perhaps the most tantalizing survival of our early architecture. At Britford in Wiltshire, which may belong to the early ninth century, the arch belonging to a porticus or other annexe on the north side has survived with its decorated soffit. The arch was decorated with a kind of stone framework, the lower members of which are enriched with vine-scroll of a type which takes its place in the typological development at about 800.

Irish Dark Age architecture remained dominated by a pre-Benedictine monasticism until the twelfth century. We do not know when a masonry technique employing mortar was introduced into Ireland, but it is suggested that 'by the seventh century' is a conservative estimate. The earlier surviving examples of such buildings show no other sign of influence from more sophisticated building traditions, and maintain the rectangular forms which come naturally in timber. It seems likely that the stone building consisting of a rectangular nave and a rectangular chancel is as early as the simpler single-cell-type plan, for, as the Cogitosus quotation implies, such a form was carried out in timber, and it is important to bear in mind that the larger and more ambitious churches were probably built in that material. The existing examples are so small and simple that there is little to be said of their features, except that their windows are round-headed with wide internal splays. Their doors are made with inclined jambs and a lintel which sometimes has a relieving arch over it. There is often a simple chancel, and good examples are the churches at Reffert and the Trinity at Glendalough,[17] both probably of the eighth century. It is at first sight a paradox that the chief remains of early Irish architecture date from the period when the ravages of the Viking invaders were at their worst. But it is presumable that the very circumstance of the raids caused the greater monasteries to substitute stone for timber as less liable to destruction by fire, and hence the appearance of stone buildings of considerable pretensions, though still very small in size, during the ninth and tenth centuries.

This is also the age of the much-discussed round towers,[18] the earliest of which are ascribed to c. 850 to c. 900 (Plate 7). They continued to be built until well into the twelfth century. These structures are for the most part detached from the churches they accompany, but seem to be definitely related to them. For example, the doorway is generally facing toward the church. They attain, in the largest examples, to a height of over 100 feet, and are built of very slender proportions with a pronounced taper. The doors are placed at some considerable height from the ground, and there seems good reason to believe that one of the main motives for building them was to provide a place of safe-keeping for relics and other valuables. At the same time, as the form of the structures and the name bell-tower in the early Irish documents imply, this can hardly have been the primary intention, though there is no reason to suppose that they were ever intended to contain bells as we know church bells from later epochs. It is, however, worth observing that the early church of Ireland appears to have attached an altogether unusual importance to bells. St Patrick is especially mentioned in the Book of Armagh as having brought with him across the Shannon fifty bells, fifty patens, and fifty chalices, as well as other church furniture. Moreover it is certain that bells of great sanctity, which were preserved from early times, were provided with richly decorated housings. Bell reliquaries were a type of cult object which is peculiar to the Celtic church. The bell is mentioned, with the crozier and other insignia, at the consecration of a bishop. These bells were all handbells, the larger ones being only just over a foot in height. The earlier examples were of iron, being made in the manner of a sheep-bell. Later examples were of iron coated with bronze, and later still they were cast of bronze in the shape of the iron types. It is tempting to associate the special Irish reverence for bells with the otherwise

C

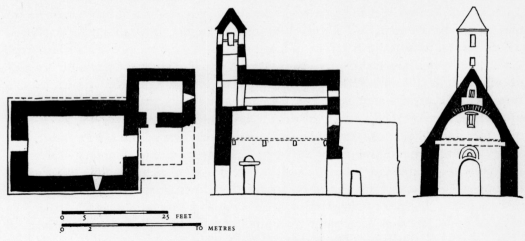

Figure 5. St Kevin's Kitchen, Glendalough: Plan and section

not wholly explicable fashion for building these round towers. Two of the most interesting structures of this age that have remained to us are the House of St Columba at Kells in County Meath, and St Kevin's Kitchen at Glendalough. St Columba's House (Plate 8) dates probably from the period 800–16, when the relics of the Saint and his early followers were brought over from Iona to Ireland. This building is made with a roof of corbelled vaulting in oversailing courses, but has within a true arched segmental vault which acts as an internal prop or buttress to the approaching corbelled slopes. The building is thus divided into two storeys, the space above the buttress vault being subdivided into small chambers by transverse walls with arches through them. There was a further division into upper and lower storeys by a wooden floor below the buttress vault, making three storeys in all. There is no evidence that the building was ever a church. St Kevin's Kitchen (Plate 9), however, was certainly a church. Its original form was similar to that of St Columba's House, but a chancel and sacristy were added later (Figure 5). A bell-tower of the usual form, except that it springs from the end of the roof of the building, is an unusual feature. The tower communicates with the space above the buttress vault. St Kevin's Kitchen also had a wooden floor, as in St Columba's House, below the buttress vault. Another noteworthy feature of many of these early Irish buildings is the use of *antae*; that is, prolongations of the side walls to form small piers or pilasters at either side of the end wall. That these antae carried an external roof-truss in timber is perhaps confirmed by the form of the tops of the antae at Rossden, Tipperary, a tenth-century building of comparative elaboration.[19] In one instance, however, on St Macdara's Island (Plate 10A) off the coast of Galway, these antae piers are carried up the slopes of the gable itself, as it were the raking sides of a pediment. Later examples – the motif survived as late as the twelfth century – are said to have carried some form of timber-roof members, but it is hard to visualize them, in view of their position in front of the gable wall. There are also at Glendalough examples where, though there are no antae piers, corbel stones of considerable size flank the angles of the gables as though to support such raking members either of wood or of stone.

Possibly the earliest Irish building where carved stone decoration on any considerable scale has survived is at Rahan, in Offaly, an example of the early tenth century (Plate 10B). From that time onwards it is increasingly used, and has a very characteristic quality of delicate linear low-relief surface enrichment. This characteristic distinguishes what may be called Irish Romanesque as it develops in the course of the eleventh century. A favourite motif is the chevron, more delicately used than in Anglo-Norman Romanesque. Ireland has a strong claim to have originated this motif.

The affinities between the early medieval architecture of Ireland and Scotland extend beyond the use of round towers in both countries (the best known Scottish example is at Brechin; Plate 11), for the vogue of the great monumental church did not reach Scotland until the Romanesque style was not only established but mature. Beneath the existing building of the mid twelfth century at Dunfermline the foundations of a church, presumably that of St Margaret, have been discovered, showing it to have had a small aisleless rectangular nave with a little square chancel. The most important survival of this immediately pre-Romanesque phase of architecture in Scotland is the church of St Rule at St Andrews (Plate 12, A and B; Figure 6). Here again the church consists of an aisleless nave of very tall and slender proportions with a small square chancel and a western tower. It was built between 1133 and 1140. Details of the tower have been shown by Dr Bilson [20] to be so close to the tower of Wharram-le-Street in Yorkshire as to make it almost certain that St Rule was the work of the same builders. The mid-wall shafts in the belfry windows provide very striking resemblances and are a notable survival of pre-Conquest practice, for the church at Wharram-le-Street dates from the early twelfth century. The Yorkshire church belonged to the Augustinians of Nostell, from which canons were imported to Scotland, first to Scone and then later migrating to St Andrews where they built the surviving church of St Rule.

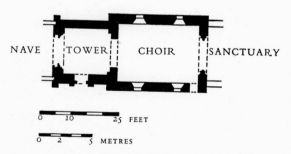

Figure 6. St Rule, St Andrews: Plan

CHAPTER 2

THE CAROLINGIAN TRADITION

THE ninth century is a period of which the architectural history has hitherto been almost completely obscure. The remains of Britford, with its remarkably decorated arch, leading, it seems, to a porticus on the north side of the nave, date from the very beginning of the century and seem to belong in character to the type of church of the preceding period. From the end of the century comes the church at Athelney, described by William of Malmesbury in terms that leave little doubt that it was of the same planform as Germigny-des-Prés, that is, a square centralized plan with four internal supports and four apsidal extensions, one in the middle of each side. The relation of Athelney to Germigny may be more than merely an analogy, for that church was founded about 810 by Theodulph, Abbot of Fleury and Bishop of Orleans, and may well have been the actual example from which King Alfred derived his new church. That the king should turn to Frankish examples fits well with the observed signs of Frankish (Carolingian) influence in the drawing, carving, and decorative arts of the ninth century. It is only to be supposed that there may have been other buildings reflecting this Carolingian influence erected in Wessex, but we have no knowledge of them. Even the description of the position of the tomb of St Swithin at Winchester, as being before the west door between the nave and the great tower which stood over the entrance to the holy temple, which fits so well with what we know of the great Carolingian-type churches of the tenth century, may indeed refer to a rebuilding at Winchester of that time.

All this is little and vague enough, and the real effect of the influence of the Carolingian Renaissance on English architecture was appropriately reserved for the monastic revival of the tenth century, associated with the names of St Dunstan, St Oswald, and St Ethelwold. The revival had a very considerable architectural achievement to its credit, though for the most part only buildings of the second rank have survived, and our knowledge of the greater churches must be derived from documents, from the few sites which have been excavated, and by analogy from the lesser churches.

These buildings, and particularly the greater churches, have a special importance as the first group of buildings to embody the new spirit of order and magnificence and, above all, monumental scale, which produced such astonishing achievements a century later under the stimulus of the closer association with continental monasticism after the Norman Conquest. The very words order, magnificence, monumental scale, suffice to indicate the ultimate source of this spirit, Rome, as the representative of that tradition which was summed up for the church of the Dark Ages in the figure of St Gregory the Great. Indeed, the only buildings in England which foreshadowed these great works of the tenth-century revival are the group of churches built for St Wilfrid at Hexham, York, and Ripon, and these equally represented a conscious importation of the Gregorian Roman ideas of magnificence: perhaps Brixworth may be added to their number.

The type of monumental church and the standard scheme for the arrangement of the domestic and administrative buildings of a monastery, which are the most important contribution of the Carolingian Renaissance to the development of European architecture, not least in England, presumably owe their origin to the reform movement associated with the name of St Benedict of Aniane (d. 829), but, except in two particulars, they hardly recall to modern eyes the architecture of antique Rome itself. The particulars are, however, important. They are the introduction of the cloister in the form we know it – a court round which the monastic buildings were grouped – and the use of the architectural scheme of the aisled hall with clerestory lighting for the naves of the larger churches. It is true that within the influence of the Court circle of Charlemagne himself some churches were built which clearly imitated the great Roman basilicas of the age of Constantine, and some of these included details of an antiquarian revivalist quality.

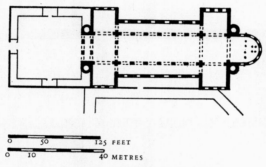

Figure 7. St Riquier (Centula): Plan

Moreover the capitals of St Dunstan's narthex, excavated at St Augustine's, Canterbury, suggest that this antiquarian feeling was also present in England in the tenth century, but the essential architectural contribution of the continent to English architecture at that time derived from the layout of the great monasteries of the Empire and central France. The type of church that had been developed there is well illustrated by the famous St Gall plan and by a number of actual churches known to us from documents or remains at Cologne, Corvey, Chartres, and, most important of all, St Riquier (Centula) near Amiens. This last was not only perfectly placed to have a special significance in relation to England, but as the result of learned and intensive study is better known to us than almost any other great Carolingian monastic establishment.

The church at St Riquier (Figure 7) consisted of transepts, crossing, presbytery, and main apse to the east, and an arcaded atrium, one side of which was formed by a portico flanked by staircase towers leading to the upper levels of a transept and crossing on the west; these eastern and western complexes were linked by an aisled nave, and both crossings were surmounted by towers of open arcaded stages, each stage set back from the face of the stage below. The church was entered on the ground level from the western portico in the atrium through the western crossing, on the upper floor of which was the western choir. It is an ingenious adaptation of the St Gall scheme with its two apses, one at each end, to afford entrance to the church on its main east and west axis.

Evidence of churches built on this scheme with variations is known in England at Canterbury, Winchester (probably), Sherborne, Durham, North Elmham in Norfolk, Deerhurst (Figure 8), Ely, Ramsey, Thorney, Breamore in Hampshire, and St Mary's, Dover. Few, if any, of these are known possessors of all the characteristics mentioned in connexion with St Riquier; Canterbury had certainly a western choir as well as an eastern one; Winchester seems to have had an atrium at the west, and the position of St Swithin's grave suggests a treatment like that of St Angilbert, whose tomb at St Riquier was placed at the entrance from the atrium to the western crossing, but it is worth remarking

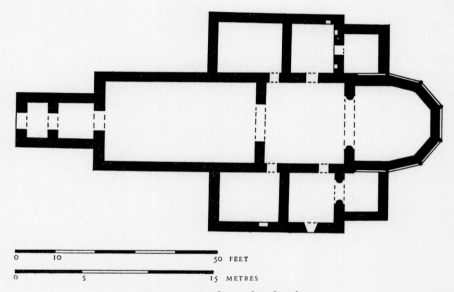

0   10   50 FEET

0   5   15 METRES

Figure 8. Deerhurst church: Plan

that at St Augustine's, Canterbury, various important persons were buried under a tower at the western side of the atrium, and this may be the real analogy with St Swithin's tomb. Sherborne certainly had a western tower axial with that over the crossing, and almost certainly a gallery in the tower giving on to the nave by arches in its eastern face; it is possible that there were small north and south annexes to the tower: Thorney had an altar at the west: Durham, Elmham, Ramsey, and Ely all had two axial towers, and the last seems to have had a western transept. Other features derived from Carolingian examples are the timber arcaded lantern towers which are shown on the well-known Chichester seal and which most probably existed at other places, such as Stow in Lincolnshire, Great Paxton in Huntingdonshire, and elsewhere. The timber upper parts of the tower at the crossing of Breamore may very well represent a renewal of something like the original treatment, and the three-storeyed timber belfries at Blackmore in Essex, and Pembridge in Herefordshire, though belonging to the later Middle Ages, may represent a survival of a mode of construction which can give us some idea of these late Dark Age towers. The small round stair towers which appear at St Riquier are to be found at St Augustine's, Canterbury, Brigstock, Brixworth (as an addition), and North Elmham. At this last church there are also small square stair towers placed at the re-entrant angles of the nave and transepts.

One of the most striking differences between the English series and their continental prototypes is the rarity of aisled naves among the English examples: of the major churches set out on the double-ended plan, only at Canterbury, Sherborne, and Ely is there any evidence of aisled naves, and in the last instance the south aisle is mentioned in a document as an addition to the original plan. A possible explanation of this lack of evidence for aisled churches of the tenth and earlier eleventh centuries, is that when a new monastic church was begun the essential parts to be built were not, as in the twelfth century and later, the eastern limb, transepts, and crossing – that is, the parts containing the monks' choir, main altars, and shrines – but the two ends – that is, the western as well as the eastern choirs and the nave which links them. Aisles could be added to this link-piece as opportunity offered, but were not essential in the first setting out, just as prolonged naves and elaborate west fronts were things to be left till later in the building projects of the twelfth and thirteenth centuries. This suggestion would help to account for the comparatively short naves of the churches of this period, as compared with their Romanesque successors. Further, the grandest churches, such as Canterbury, Winchester, or Malmesbury, where aisles might have been expected to have been built from the outset, are just those whose earlier forms were most completely obliterated by later rebuilding; indeed, our knowledge of the existence of aisles at Canterbury rests on a written record and not on actual remains.

As far as the particular relations of the English churches with their continental exemplars are concerned, we can get little help from the two great buildings which have been most thoroughly studied and excavated: Glastonbury and St Augustine's, Canterbury. In these instances the sites were so venerable that the reformers (St Dunstan was connected with both) seem to have been concerned to preserve and incorporate the earlier buildings with their own work. At Glastonbury, where the *Vetusta Ecclesia* was believed to have been miraculously dedicated by Christ Himself, there was naturally no question of replacing the early wooden building until it was burnt down in 1184, and even then the original dimensions (60 by 26 feet) are said to have been preserved. The work of about 950 has been identified at the east end of the eighth-century church, and may have included a tower, but the date of the main building campaign, during which Ine's church of about 700 was enlarged and linked with the *Vetusta Ecclesia*, is obscure. All that can be said is that it was later than Ine's, and before St Dunstan's time. At St Augustine's, Canterbury (Figure 9), the tenth-century work consisted in the addition of a new narthex to the west of the early church of St Peter and St Paul, the burial-place of St Augustine and his early successors, and a large porch extending the building still further to the west and leading down, by two flights of steps, to the level of the forecourt or atrium: at the same time the space of the original narthex was thrown into the nave. In the mid eleventh century the eastern end of St Peter and St Paul was pulled

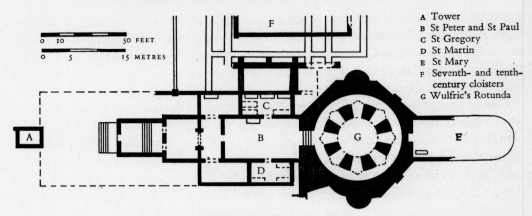

A Tower
B St Peter and St Paul
C St Gregory
D St Martin
E St Mary
F Seventh- and tenth-
   century cloisters
G Wulfric's Rotunda

Figure 9. St Augustine's Priory, Canterbury: Plan

down and the western end of St Mary's, another church of the seventh century which stood to the east of it, and the two buildings were linked by a rotunda, rather after the manner of S. Bénigne at Dijon. The total length of the two churches thus prolonged is about 230 feet. It will therefore be appreciated that both these churches were special cases and, apart from such characteristics as the processional quality of the western additions made by St Dunstan to St Peter and St Paul and the nature of the rotunda itself with its round stair towers to north and south, the most important thing these schemes owe to Carolingian example is the attempt, made both at Glastonbury and Canterbury, to make a single large building out of a group of small early sanctuaries. It is significant that after the Conquest all these makeshifts were swept away at St Augustine's, and the work of the seventh, eighth, tenth, and eleventh centuries swallowed up in a single great Romanesque church.[1]

There seem to be only three surviving examples of later Anglo-Saxon aisled naves, Lydd in Kent, Wing in Buckinghamshire (Figure 10), and Great Paxton in Huntingdonshire, for Ickleton in Cambridgeshire is certainly of the later eleventh century. Of these,

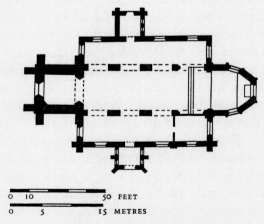

Figure 10. Wing church: Plan

Lydd has only indications of its early arcades, and at Great Paxton they have been cut short by the building of the later medieval western tower. The north aisle at Wing is some 12 feet wide and the nave itself about 62 by 21 feet in four bays: the church has an apse which is polygonal both inside and out, such as once existed at Deerhurst. Great Paxton (Plates 13A and 20B) is an even more interesting church, in spite of fourteenth-century alterations, as two and a half bays of each arcade survive to their full height with their walls and clerestory above them, together with the arch into the north transept and its responds. The main arcades are in two orders of simple rectangular section supported on compound piers consisting of a rectangular core set diagonally with a very substantial

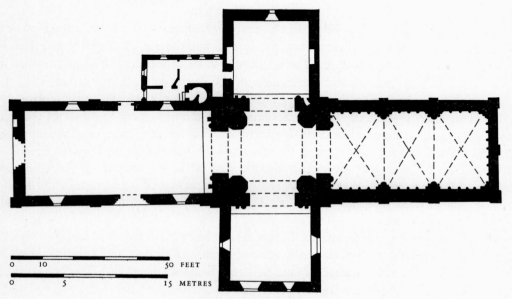

Figure 11. Stow church: Plan

shaft on each face; the shafts have large bulbous capitals and bases with rudimentary spurs. The responds of the transept arch, which is of a single plain order, have four very thin shafts with smaller capitals of the same bulbous form. All this is very ambitious when compared with the plain rectangular piers of the smaller arches of Lydd and Wing. Another unusual feature of Great Paxton is the width and height of the transept arch, which is of an even wider and taller proportion than those of Hadstock in Essex and Stow in Lincolnshire, both of which date from earlier in the eleventh century. When all is said, however, the most remarkable thing about Great Paxton is the preservation of the full height of the nave clerestory, which enables one to get a more striking impression of the interior proportions and space effect of a mid eleventh-century aisled church than anywhere else in England.[2]

The planning of other churches of this age, even those of some scale by pre-Conquest standards, as St Mary in Castro at Dover (with a total length of some 117 feet), or

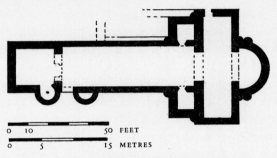

Figure 12. North Elmham church: Plan

Breamore in Hampshire (about 97 feet), generally resolves itself into an assemblage of rectangular boxes, the nave, the crossing, the chancel, and the north and south extensions – that is, the transepts and porches. The effect of a series of distinct rectangular spaces is emphasized by the comparative narrowness of the openings from one to another, especially those giving on to the transepts, and even where the chancel arch is relatively wide the chancel is generally considerably narrower than the nave or crossing, though not so markedly as the north and south extensions. This leaves the angles of the crossing itself as salients between the chancel and the transepts externally. At Stow in Lincolnshire (Figure 11), this may have been also the case with the junction of the nave and crossing.[3] It seems certain that these plans represent a process of emergence of the cross-shaped plan formula from the early Dark Age system of surrounding the main body of the church with porticus.

Two exceptional churches are the Cathedral at North Elmham,[4] in Norfolk (Figure 12), whose unusual system of towers has already been mentioned, and South Elmham,[5] in Suffolk. The former, a cathedral church, had a T-shaped plan, that is, transepts that formed a single rectangular vessel, whose main axis crossed the nave at right angles with a shallow apse opposite the point of crossing. This seems to be a reminiscence of the Roman type of plan of the age of Constantine and may well be another example, with St Dunstan's capitals at Canterbury, of deliberate antiquarianism deriving very likely through Germany, where similar plans had been used for the same reason in Carolingian times. South Elmham church (Figure 13), which has also been claimed as the seat of the

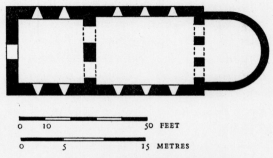

Figure 13. South Elmham church: Plan

Anglo-Saxon bishopric – though this is unlikely in view of the special character of the North Elmham church – has an extremely unusual plan. It consists of a nave about 69 feet long, of which the western part forms a vestibule some 26 feet square with a western door, and communicates with the eastern part of the nave proper by two wide openings; the chancel was apsidal and there was a sleeper wall across the wide opening between the nave and the apse. A similar western vestibule seems to have existed at Boarhunt in Hampshire, and it is possible that at South Elmham it was the ground storey of a tower. The only parallel to this arrangement is possibly to be found in the twelfth-century tower at Finchingfield in Essex, which has an internal wall arcade and two recesses, as though for altars, flanking the archway into the nave on the ground level.

Almost the most imposing remains of church building in the tenth and eleventh centuries are the towers. These were, for the most part, western towers, but at Barton-on-Humber in Lincolnshire (Figure 14), and perhaps at Barnack and Broughton, there were

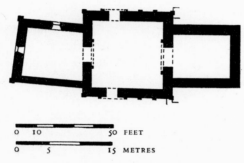

Figure 14. Barton-on-Humber church: Plan

'tower-naves' with a short eastern extension for the presbytery opening directly from the tower, and in the first-mentioned instance a western extension also. Langford in Oxfordshire has a central tower of the mid eleventh century of some considerable architectural pretensions, and the west tower of Sompting (Plate 14) retains its top finish of a type well known in the Rhineland, in which the ridges of the pyramidal capping rise from the apexes of the high-pitched gables of the tower, while the faces of the pyramid are continued down on to the angle spaces between the gables; there are signs that the tower of St Benet's, Cambridge, was also finished in this way. Some of these towers, such as Deerhurst and Clapham in Bedfordshire, are severely plain with no horizontal divisions. At Sompting there is one horizontal division, and pilaster strips, comparable to those used elsewhere on Saxon buildings, are carried up the centre of each face of the tower and combined with those at the angles to give it some sort of decorative character. At Sompting this character seems very restrained, however, by comparison with the use of the pilaster strips on the faces of the towers of Earls Barton, Barnack, and Barton-on-Humber. On these the strips are arranged not only vertically and horizontally, but also in half circles, producing as it were arcaded forms, and in short inclined strips giving the effect of triangular arcading, and also as short inclined struts to the vertical strips. The whole effect at Earls Barton (Plate 15) and Barton-on-Humber is strongly reminiscent of timber frame building, and this is especially true of Earls Barton, where the curved forms employed rather enhance the timbered effect than otherwise. A similar form of decoration is found along the upper part of the north wall above the arcades at Geddington in Northamptonshire. This was originally an external wall, and the pre-Conquest decoration has been preserved by the addition of a north aisle later in the Middle Ages.

The nature of pre-Conquest timber building is necessarily a matter of speculation, and only one fragment, at Greenstead in Essex, is known to have survived, and that consists only of the outer walls of the church, which are formed of a series of vertical timber supports looking, as it were, like a fence made of railway sleepers. So far excavation has yielded us nothing, but the evidence for the importance of timber building is strong, as is shown by the towers just described and the nature of many of the mouldings of stone buildings which, in the words of Sir Alfred Clapham, 'with their acutely pointed projections and the collection of insignificant members indicate the hand of the worker in wood rather than the stonemason'. It seems very likely that the tower-nave type of church is itself a translation into stone of a timber type, and it has been suggested that some of the timber church towers of Essex reflect this early tradition not only in their material but to some extent in their technique. The towers in question are western tower belfries, all the examples of which seem to be works of the later Middle Ages. They are, however, built on a structural system which has a relation to the timber churches of Norway, where the great vertical posts are framed into sleeper walls and tied above where the lean-to roofs of the outer aisles abut. Most of the Essex belfries built on this system have four bays, though one of them has six bays with major and minor supports alternating, which certainly suggests the possibility of descent from a type of building which constituted a timber tower church and not an *ad hoc* device for hanging bells; examples are at Blackmore (Plate 174B) and Margaretting.

The arches of the tenth- and eleventh-century churches are generally of simple rectangular section, but at Bosham in Hampshire (Plate 18B), and Wittering in Northamptonshire (Plate 13B), the soffit is formed with a big simple roll. There is evidence of a fondness for this big roll motif in the sections of the responds of Deerhurst and Stow in Lincolnshire, and similar responds almost certainly existed at Sherborne and at Langford in Oxfordshire, where there is some sign of a similar motif in the design of the belfry windows. This usage has a special interest as a possible precursor of the treatment of the soffits of late eleventh- and twelfth-century arcades, such as those at Durham and Gloucester, which is so distinctively an Anglo-Norman development in contrast to the practice in continental schools.

The most important motif of architectural decoration is the pilaster strip and its variations. This was very widely used in very varying degrees of elaboration. One of the most frequent variants is to frame an arch or doorway with a pilaster strip that follows the curve of the arch and is intercepted by a horizontal strip at the impost. Sir Alfred Clapham remarks that this is the most frequent of all Anglo-Saxon features and is found in almost every church of importance. The source of the pilaster strip motif, including the triangular arcading noticed above on the late Northamptonshire and Lincolnshire churches, has long been accepted as from Carolingian Germany [6] – where the *lisenen* are ultimately derived from Roman antiquity in Italy. The effect of timbering which we have already mentioned in connexion with the towers is difficult to ignore, however; it has been suggested that the exploitation of the motif in a timber-framing way was first done in Germany, but found a ready welcome in England where there were equally strong traditions of timber building.[7]

Another inheritance from Carolingian Germany is the use of mid-wall shafts in windows. The normal late Saxon window is the simple round-headed type set midway in the wall with equal splays both inside and out. There are also circular windows which are used both as sound-holes in belfries, and as windows in the clerestories at Avebury and Bosham. Triangular heads for both doors and windows, as at Deerhurst (Plate 16) and elsewhere, are fairly common, and windows with two or more openings, as in the nave of Worth – a very simple example – or used more elaborately in some of the towers, are divided by short round columns set in the middle of the wall and accommodated to its thickness by bracket capitals reaching out to the internal and external faces. The short columns themselves are generally of the baluster type, often with a very exaggerated bulge or entasis. Simple examples of such shafts, though without the bulging profile, have survived from the seventh century at Monkwearmouth, but the late examples are quite distinctive not only in their general profile but in the multiplicity of their mouldings. The most remarkable assemblage of them is on the tower at Earls Barton, where, including those used as responds, there are rows of six shafts forming five-light windows in the upper stages of the tower. The triforium of the great post-Conquest church at St Albans shows others, apparently re-used from a pre-Conquest building scheme. A few examples remain to indicate that window openings were also filled with ornamental pierced panels: three in stone are at Barnack, and the remains of a wooden one is to be seen at Birstall in Leicestershire.

Of purely decorative motifs, other than the pilaster strip and its variants, the most obviously architectural is the blind arcade. The triangular-headed arcade at Geddington has already been mentioned in connexion with pilaster strips, and the tall external round arch examples on the apse at Wing in Buckinghamshire are also linked by a series of pilaster strips. At Bradford-on-Avon (Plate 17), a church remodelled in the earlier tenth century, there are, however, examples of a different kind; these are shallow recessed arcades, and the arches spring from broad, flat pilasters with both capitals and bases. They are a true brick or stone motif without any of the timber feeling of the pilaster strip varieties, and at the same time their breadth and comparative shallowness of relief contrast clearly with the usual type of pre-Conquest wall arcading. Of carved architectural decoration there are not many surviving examples from this period, and certainly nothing of the quality or suggesting the abundance of the Breedon friezes, but there is a good deal of evidence of decorative carving in stone on individual objects such as grave-slabs and crosses, and a few instances of such decoration applied to buildings, notably both capitals and friezes at Sompting, the narthex capitals from St Augustine's, Canterbury, and the palmette decoration on capitals and strings at Hadstock; [8] there are other examples, not many, but too numerous to warrant listing here.

More important than these relatively scanty examples of purely architectural decorative carving is the problem of major figure sculpture and its employment on buildings. The dating of the more ambitious pieces is still in some cases a matter of much controversy. The discussion of this problem has taken place very largely on the grounds of internal characteristics of style, as if the sculptures were isolated museum exhibits, and the question of the architectural context of the sculptures has hardly been considered except by the late Sir Alfred Clapham. In this connexion the angels at Bradford-on-Avon (Plate 18A), the remains of carving at Barton-on-Humber, and the Breamore and Headbourne Worthy (Plate 20A) crucifixion groups are of special importance, for they all appear to be *in situ*. At Bradford-on-Avon and Barton-on-Humber it seems very probable that the remaining stone carvings formed parts of groups the rest of which were executed in stucco.[9] Many fragments of stucco were found in the excavations at Glastonbury, and at Milborne Port in Somerset the capitals of the crossing piers are said to be in this material, the use of which is well known in Germany and Italy. The loss of the work in stucco is one of the major difficulties in the way of our solution of this problem of late Anglo-Saxon architectural sculpture. The Bradford-on-Avon and Barton-on-Humber groups were set on the walls above the chancel arches, and at Breamore and Headbourne Worthy the stone groups that survive, though in a very damaged condition, are similarly set in walls above arches, at Breamore over the south door and at Headbourne Worthy over the west door. At Deerhurst[10] the polygonal apse had a gable head on each external face, and in the one which survives to its full height there are the remains of a fine sculptured angel *in situ*. The Deerhurst angel is of about the same date as those at Bradford-on-Avon, and another, now displaced, at Winterbourne Steepleton in Dorset presumably formed part of a similar composition to that at Bradford, all three belonging to the first half of the tenth century. The placing of these sculptures in their plain areas of wall is in marked contrast to the Romanesque practice of the twelfth century, when, as Sir Thomas Kendrick says of the decoration of the west doors of Lincoln, 'It [the carved decoration] was strictly systematized and employed simply as a disciplined emphasis to the architectural scheme.' [11]

Professor Focillon [12] has called attention to a similar development in the uses of French architectural sculpture from the eleventh to the twelfth century. The placing of these early tenth-century sculptures in relation to the walls which they adorn provides a possible context for some of the more important disputed carvings, such as the Romsey Rood and the Langford Draped Rood, both of which are placed in most improbable positions for large-scale sculpture, which suggests that they have been moved at a period of reconstruction.[13] There certainly seems to have been a phase, represented by some eleventh-century examples on the continent, when sculpture was used for architectural adornment in friezes or self-sufficient groups applied to plain areas of wall in lieu of the more normal painted subjects and, of course, reserved rather for the focal points of the building, as over chancel arches or main entrances. This way of using sculpture survived in some cases, as Professor Focillon has shown, into the twelfth century, and it is to be presumed that the early tenth-century examples that we have cited in England had also their continental fellows. An English instance of the late survival of this earlier way of relating sculpture to architecture is to be found in the frieze of figure-slabs placed across the west front of Lincoln, above the doors, presumably by Bishop Alexander, who did so much to embellish that remarkable building. If the Lincoln frieze is indeed of 1140 it must be very close in date to a somewhat similar survival in France on the apse at Selles-sur-Cher, which is dated 1145, and there are indications of other instances, dated in some places to the eleventh century, in Spain. The Selles-sur-Cher sculptures are cited by Professor Focillon as a good, though late, example to contrast with the more disciplined Romanesque use which was already coming into fashion and required the carvings to be far more closely linked with the structural lines of the building.

In the years immediately preceding the Conquest a number of examples of carved tympana seem to have been made, presumably a further instance of those renewed continental influences, particularly Norman, which are to be observed in other architectural details of that time. The examples at Knook in Wiltshire and at Ipswich are very markedly barbaric in character, and seem to represent a different current of decorative art to that of the sophisticated continental-type figures of the groups we have been discussing. Carvings of an equally barbaric character appear as head-stops at Deerhurst; these also have a very Scandinavian look about them, compared with which the lions carved as stops to the pilaster strips round the tower arch of St Benet's, Cambridge, have an almost sophisticated southern air.

Some of the buildings we have been discussing date from the middle years of the eleventh century, and there are, indeed, a considerable number of examples which cannot be dated with certainty either before or after the Norman invasion. It is known that Edward the Confessor's church at Westminster was strongly Norman in character, deriving, as we know from excavation, an alternate system of large compound and smaller cylindrical piers from Jumièges (though the plan of its eastern parts is closer to that of the church at Bernay), and there are other examples of this influence.

The question of the so-called Saxo-Norman overlap is rendered very obscure by the total disappearance of the greater buildings of the years immediately preceding the Conquest, at any rate as far as their decorative finish is concerned. The whole problem derives its special interest from the importance of the architecture of the late years of the century, not only in actual achievement, but in paving the way for even greater things in the generation that succeeded. An instance of this is the problem of the cubical capital; this form is characteristic of west German architecture from a relatively early date and is indeed found in England before the Conquest. It is very rarely found in Normandy before the twelfth century, but it is not only the most frequent form of capital in the Anglo-Norman usage, but is developed in England in special ways, notably the scalloped capital. The presumption is either that there was a strong influence from Germany, or more probably from the Low Countries, into England immediately preceding or following the Conquest – this is certainly true, though it seems hardly likely to have been greater in the years preceding the invasion – or that the cubical capital was in more frequent and familiar use in the earlier part of the century than the surviving examples would suggest.

The last thirty years of the eleventh century pose some of the most obscure and inter-esting problems in the history of English architecture. By the end of that period a num-ber of outstanding buildings were already begun, notable among them Durham and Tewkesbury, and England had entered on one of the most splendid periods of its archi-tecture, splendid not only in the scale of the work undertaken, but also in the quality. It is generally agreed nowadays to call these buildings by the name of the Anglo-Norman school, in recognition of the fact that at an early date England became the predominant partner in the school, and that the nineteenth-century custom of calling them all simply Norman is misleading. But the difficulty of determining how the predominance of Eng-land came about is very considerable. In the first place, the remains of English buildings in the first half of the eleventh century are very fragmentary and, except for such things as the remains of Wulfric's Rotunda at Canterbury – and that is hardly more than evi-dence of a plan – do not belong to buildings of any great pretensions. Equally, though Normandy in the mid eleventh century was enjoying a period of splendid architectural achievement, and the surviving remains are considerable, so much has perished by re-building – for example at Rouen and Fécamp, where we know just enough to suggest what we have lost – that we are heavily handicapped in trying to estimate the Norman contribution at all closely.

There is, however, no doubt about the fact of the importance of the revolution after 1066. From the very first there is perceptible an ambition for greatness of scale and a cer-tainty of handling in the architecture of that age which make late pre-Conquest building, as far as we know it, seem rather tentative by comparison. The source of this contrast is not far to seek in the monastic reform movement, for which the name of Cluny can stand as a symbol, though there were other sources of the reform. Fécamp and Jumièges in Normandy had been reformed under Cluniac influence, and indeed the whole re-forming monastic movement in Normandy was largely of Cluniac inspiration. The new reforming Norman bishops and abbots in England,[14] though they were apparently arro-gant enough, had a real task to perform, for the effects of the tenth-century English re-form had in some degree spent themselves. Perhaps it had been from the beginning more the personal influence of a few men and their immediate followers, affecting only a limited number of monastic houses, rather than a broadly based movement, and it may be significant that Abbot Serlo, who began the rebuilding of the existing Gloucester Cathedral, found there only two monks and eight small boys when he took over the abbey, a circumstance which can hardly have been due to lack of endowment. An important aspect of the Cluniac reform was its emphasis on outward and visible signs, including among them the scale of church building. The third church at Cluny was one of the largest churches ever built, and it is more than possible that two of the general characteristics of the great Anglo-Norman churches in England derived in a quite direct way from Cluny itself, the very long naves, noticeable as early as St Albans, begun in 1077, and rather later the double transept plan which began at Canterbury about 1100. The former characteristic can hardly have derived from the third church of Cluny, which was almost exactly contemporary with St Albans, but the latter almost certainly did.

In planning, the post-Conquest architecture seems to have been quite revolutionary so far as the eastern parts of the larger churches were concerned. The eleventh-century examples already show that two main ways of treating this part of the building were introduced at the same time: the three-apsed plan with two additional apses projecting eastwards from the transepts, and the apse and ambulatory plan in which the aisles of the eastern limb, instead of finishing in apses, are returned round the apsidal end of the main vessel which opens into them by arcades. The three-apse plan is found in the churches of Caen of the time of the Conquest, and may very probably derive from the second church at Cluny, which began to be replaced by the great third church in 1088. There is a more elaborate version of the three-apsed plan in which two chapels are provided on the eastern sides of each transept, the inner ones having a greater projection, so as to give the effect of a group of seven apses in *échelon*. The apse and ambulatory plan is generally accepted as originating in central France rather than Normandy, and appears in England first at Battle Abbey, which was begun *c*. 1070 and was well advanced as far as the east end was concerned by 1076. Battle was colonized by monks from Tours who are specially recorded as having concerned themselves with the superintendence of the buildings. There were, however, important examples of this type of plan in Normandy itself, at Jumièges and Rouen.

Sir Alfred Clapham has pointed out that it is not possible to distinguish any regional usage in the distribution of these two main plan-types, except perhaps in the special case of the three-sided apse with ambulatory found at Gloucester and Tewkesbury; at Canterbury, for instance, Lanfranc's Cathedral, begun at the same time as Battle (1070), had the three-apsed plan, while St Augustine's only a few years later had an ambulatory and three radiating chapels. In a number of eleventh-century examples of the three-apsed type, including Edward the Confessor's at Westminster,[15] St Albans,[16] and Bishop Remigius's at Lincoln,[17] the aisles of the eastern limb were separated from the main vessel of the presbytery by solid walls.

All these eleventh-century plans of greater churches, with the exception of Old Sarum, made provision for a central lantern tower which was not, however, completed in some cases till the following century. This feature, which persisted throughout the Middle Ages in the greater English churches,[18] may be accepted as of Norman origin, for though some similar feature, generally in wood, was certainly the normal usage in pre-Conquest Saxon building of any pretension, we have no evidence as to how it was treated internally and whether it made any great contribution to the space effect of the buildings. The central lantern tower is the Anglo-Norman variant of the dome over the crossing which is found in some continental Romanesque schools. Its continued popularity in England may well be in large part the effect of the lasting monastic influence over our architecture, for the monastic church, in which the monks' choir occupied the crossing and eastern bays of the nave, gave to the crossings an importance and dignity which the canons' church did not require at that point. The number of cathedral churches in this country which were situated in monasteries – an unusual practice on the continent – and above all the prestige of the great cathedral monastery at Canterbury, had a strong and enduring effect on the whole character of our medieval architecture.

From before the Conquest there is apparent at Westminster another characteristic of the English churches of the Anglo-Norman school – the tendency to increase the length of the buildings as compared with continental examples. The Confessor's church at Westminster had a nave of twelve bays and western towers in addition. Of the post-Conquest churches, St Alban's nave had ten bays, and at Norwich and Ely there were naves of fourteen and thirteen bays respectively. Some of these extreme examples may not have been intended from the outset, and may represent increases of scale in the early twelfth century. Perhaps even more striking are the lengthenings of the eastern limbs from the normal two bays of Normandy to three at Worcester, Gloucester, Chichester, Lincoln, and Christchurch, and four at St Albans, Ely, Norwich, and Durham.[19]

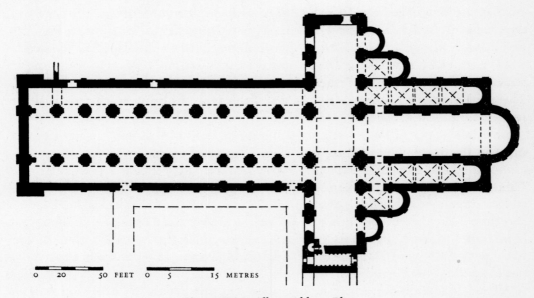

Figure 15. St Albans Abbey: Plan

The greatest surviving monuments of the generation following the Conquest are St Albans, Blyth, parts of the west front of Lincoln, the transepts of Winchester and Ely, the crypts at Winchester, Worcester (Plate 19), and Gloucester, and parts of the super-structure of the last (Plate 29B). To these must be added the beginnings of Durham and Tewkesbury – the eastern parts which date from the last decade of the eleventh century. St Albans (Figure 15), with its lantern tower, transepts, and much of its north nave arcade (Plates 21 and 22A), gives us more of the general appearance of a church of that age on the largest scale than any other, but the nature of its materials – flint and Roman bricks from nearby Verulamium, together with some re-use of pre-Conquest materials in the triforium openings – sets it rather apart from other churches as lacking the masonry de-tails in which much of the character of a building of that time inevitably consists.[20] The remains of Blyth, though a relatively small building, have great interest, as it is almost the most completely Norman-looking building in this country, both in its details and its general proportions (Plate 22B). The transepts of Winchester (Plate 23) and Ely – buildings that are clearly related to each other – have perhaps an even greater importance. They are clearly derived from Normandy itself, with their large transeptal galleries at tribune level – surviving at Winchester and later reduced in size at Ely – the simplicity of their great unmoulded arch orders, their bold division into vertical bays, and their galleried clerestories. Of these features the transeptal galleries which link the tribunes of the western parts of the church – both Winchester and Ely have aisles on both sides of their transepts – with those on the east were a fashion in Normandy in the early and middle years of the century, and in some cases, as Jumièges, Bayeux, and in England Christchurch, near Bournemouth, extended to cover the whole area of the transepts. It has been suggested that this type of transept derives from the great church of St Martin at Tours, and that the Winchester and Ely transepts, with their two aisles and tribunes, also derive from that famous church in the general character of their elevation.

The transeptal gallery was not a fashion of long duration in England, but the division into vertical bays by substantial half-round shafts rising the whole height of the internal elevation, and the galleried clerestories, were innovations in England of far greater importance. The origin in Normandy of these half-round shafts seems to be as part of a system for strengthening the upper walls of the building, in combination with buttresses on the outer faces of the walls and occasionally diaphragm arches thrown across the main vessel of the church to stiffen still further the whole upper part.[21] These diaphragm arches were built in alternate bays, and this involved an alternating scheme of pier design which affected the whole elevational treatment of the interior; such diaphragm arches were certainly used at St Vigor, a monastery near Bayeux, where they occur between every three bays, probably originally at Cerisy-le-Forêt, and very possibly at Jumièges. This is the consistent statement of the origin and purpose of these tall shaftings, but inevitably it is an over-simplification. The theory dissociates these tall shafts from the intention to build stone vaults over the main spans of the churches, and therefore allows for their presence in so many English as well as Norman buildings where no such intention is credible. It does not, however, explain why the tall shafts were retained, and indeed often applied to every bay, in buildings whose structural system was of a kind which did not need external strengthening applied to either the inner or outer faces of the walls. This structural system has been called by Monsieur Bony, who first called attention to it and its importance, that of the 'thick wall'.[22] In the churches of St Étienne at Caen, and at Cerisy, a new structural system was produced in which the upper walls were much thicker above the level of the great arcades. At St Étienne they were built so as to oversail the piers on their outer (i.e. aisle) sides, and at clerestory level are provided with galleries on the internal face linked by low vaulted tunnels from bay to bay (Figure 16). The object was to provide a series of solid masses of masonry in the upper parts of the building in lieu of buttresses and attached shaftings. Logically this should have

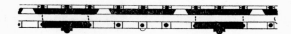

Figure 16. 'Thick Walls' at Caen: Plan at clerestory level

entailed the disappearance of these unnecessary features,[23] but though the buttresses do disappear from the exteriors of a number of clerestories, in general the half-round shafts are retained, presumably because the division into vertical bays was valued for aesthetic reasons. The desire to break up an all-over effect by subdivision or punctuation is a characteristic of the newly emerging Romanesque, which distinguishes it from the Carolingian tradition that preceded it widely over Europe.

At Winchester [24] the clerestory galleries (Plates 23 and 24) are treated in units of three features: a large stilted arch framing the window, flanked by two much smaller arches, a scheme which became popular in England, though it is rarely found with the difference between the size of the arches so exaggerated. The effect at Winchester is to increase the area and importance of the plain wall surface in this part of the building as compared with the Norman examples. In the middle of the double bay at Winchester the adjacent small arches share a central column, and the pair are united under a relieving arch which produces a curiously ambiguous effect. If this system was carried out in the choir and in the nave especially, the repeated effect must have been strikingly dissimilar to the almost classic simplicity of the clerestory galleries of St Étienne, Caen, and Cerisy. At Ely the transepts do not seem to have been carried up as high as the clerestory in the first building campaign, and the treatment of the clerestory gallery hardly differs in the transept and the nave. It again consists of three arches to a bay, the wider central arch, however, being only slightly taller than its two neighbours, and all springing from the same level, an effect that is much lighter and more like Cerisy than Winchester.

The other important survivals of the major church buildings of the eleventh century are the crypts of Winchester (begun 1079), Worcester [25] (begun 1084), and Gloucester [26] (begun 1089). These great crypts underlying the whole area of the eastern limbs of their churches are unusual on the continent, though the early eleventh-century example at Rouen may have provided a precedent for the English use, and it may be significant in this connexion that all the English examples are in churches of the apse and ambulatory plan like Rouen (Figures 17 and 18). The chief interest of these great crypts, apart from

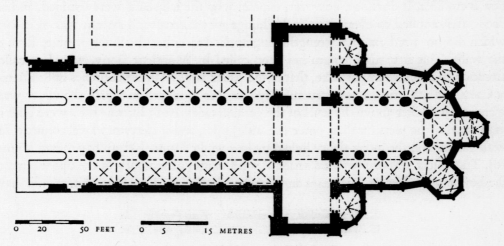

0 20 50 FEET   0 5 15 METRES

Figure 17. Gloucester Cathedral: Plan

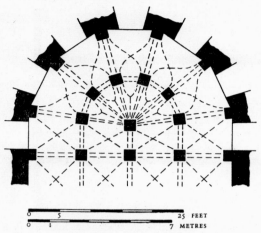

Figure 18. Worcester Cathedral: Plan of crypt

the evidence they afford at Winchester and Worcester of the planning of the eleventh-century superstructures which have disappeared, is in the treatment of the capitals, and especially in the management of the groined vaults with which they are covered. The cubical capital is the rule in these crypts, except at Gloucester, where indeed it is used but not exclusively, and in the new crypt at Canterbury (begun about 1100) the capitals are of this form, though enriched with sculpture later in the twelfth century. The importance of this lies in the fact that the cushion capital is very rare in Normandy as early as these crypts, and its source must be sought in those continental schools – notably of the western parts of Germany and the Empire – where it prevailed, and with which later pre-Conquest architecture had most affinity. As to the vaults, they are chiefly remarkable for the virtuosity with which the builders have exploited the character of the roughly coursed stonework brought to a smooth finish by rendering. Both at Winchester and Worcester the triangular and trapezoidal-shaped bays, occasioned by the apses and the ambulatories, have been managed quite simply and straightforwardly, thanks to the adaptability of the moulded concrete technique employed.[27]

The remarkable western block which encloses the bases of the towers and forms the core of the later western buildings at Lincoln (Plate 25) was also completed in the last decade of the eleventh century. This building, which forms a most striking and original design, is unparalleled in England or, as far as we know, in Normandy, though there is evidence that the eleventh-century church at Fécamp – whence Bishop Remigius the building patron came – had some kind of elaborate western treatment, the early accounts of which are tantalizingly obscure. In the details of the capitals the Lincoln work is very close to the Caen group of churches, and it is possible that our ideas as to the variety of planning current in Normandy in the eleventh century are unduly restricted. The Lincoln building consists of a block standing bold from the bases of the towers on three sides (Figure 19): on the western side are three great arched recesses and to the left and right of them two small semi-domed niches. A similar great recess is on the return to the south. The nearest parallels to this remarkable design are the west blocks at Liège and

31

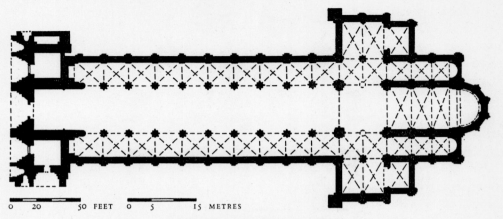

Figure 19. Eleventh-century church, Lincoln: Plan

Maastricht, which have a similar relation to the western towers, but there are one or two details of the niches at the western angles of the building, which have a strange resemblance to the original forms of St Mark's at Venice, which is an almost contemporary building.[28]

The Lincoln front was altered in the mid twelfth century, when the towers were carried up to about half their present height (Plate 47B), rows of blind arcading were added above the great recesses, and gables faced with a close mesh pattern of small arches were built, probably three to the west and one each to the north and south: at the same time the doors and lower parts of the composition were enriched with sculpture. There seems to be no evidence how the eleventh-century design was finished at the top, whether with gables, as later, or with the horizontal line of an eaves cornice, as at Liège and Maastricht, or a combination of both. But even allowing for the twelfth-century alterations and the still larger additions made to the front in the thirteenth and fourteenth centuries, the surviving eleventh-century parts form one of the most striking and original works of their age.

The last years of the eleventh century saw the beginnings of the most remarkable Romanesque buildings in the country, Tewkesbury [29] and Durham. The monks were moved from their original home at Cranborne to the new establishment at Tewkesbury in 1102, and it may be presumed that a considerable part of the great church was usable by then, at any rate the eastern parts. The building consists of an eastern limb of two bays with a three-sided apse and an ambulatory, transepts with eastern chapels and a nave of eight bays (Figure 20). Presumably the work on the nave continued throughout most of the first quarter of the twelfth century, but its early characteristics, as compared with Gloucester which was finished in the main by 1128 – the date of consecration – suggests that the work was fairly continuous and speedy, helped on as it was by a rich patron who died in 1107.[30] The plan of the eastern arm, which is similar to that of Gloucester though smaller, is exceptional in the form of the apse of three bays. The internal elevation of this part of the church was also remarkable: it has been shown to have consisted of a colossal order of round piers rising on the inside to support arches above the tribune openings, the lower arches into the aisles being set back from the face of the piers in the manner

32

afterwards followed at Romsey, Jedburgh, Oxford, and elsewhere. Above the tribune was a triforium opening on to the main space of the church, with two pairs of small arches having a short column between each pair. The small arches have no impost moulding or other break on their outer sides, but the column in the middle has, in the nave examples, an enriched capital. The upper parts of the eastern limb have been completely destroyed, but evidence for the existence of the colossal order remains in the lower parts of the piers and in the transept, and for the triforium and the clerestory above it, making a four-storeyed internal elevation, on the eastern wall of the transept [31] only (Plate 26). The nave design omits the tribune, and the colossal order of arches on cylindrical piers rises to the full height of aisle and tribune combined (Plate 27). The proportions suggested by the transepts and nave are very different from anything we know in Normandy, where the four-storeyed internal elevation is unknown. The height of the two top storeys in the transept suggests such a church as Vignory in eastern France, and the whole effect seems to link the building with Germany, the Low Countries, and eastern France.[32] The form of the triforium openings reinforces this impression very strongly. If, as the late Dr John Bilson suggested, the eastern parts of Gloucester also had a four-storeyed system, the effect of the tall upper storeys above the tribune openings would have been strikingly 'late Carolingian'.[33]

Gloucester, Tewkesbury, and Pershore form part of a group of churches, the nearest approximation to a regional school that can be identified in England at this time. At Pershore there was also a four-storeyed treatment in the eastern limb, and the colossal cylindrical pier was used in the nave. Cylindrical piers of comparable diameter but of normal height are to be found in a number of other churches in the west, as Hereford (Plate 28),

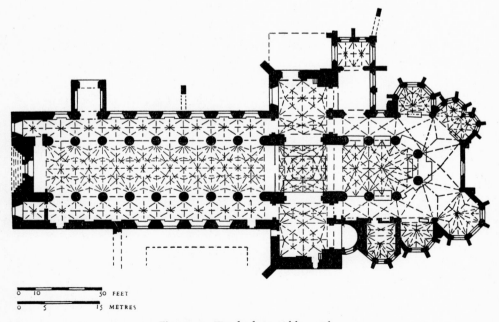

0 10   50 FEET
0   5   15 METRES

Figure 20. Tewkesbury Abbey: Plan

33

Malvern, and elsewhere.[34] It seems likely that the earliest example of their use was in the nave of Evesham, a building which was well advanced in the early years of William II, but we have no evidence of the height of the Evesham piers. It is perhaps significant that in this part of England the Anglo-Saxon church was in a peculiarly strong position in the early years after the Conquest, notably in the abbeys of Evesham, Winchcombe, and the cathedral monastery of Worcester, where the outstanding figure of St Wulfstan was present as Bishop. The traditional Anglo-Saxon links with Ottonian and late Carolingian Germany may well have survived in those parts, and the presence of a succession of Lorrainers as bishops and abbots – a tradition which links the early twelfth-century Reinhelm at Hereford with the mid eleventh-century appointments of Edward the Confessor – is suggestive in this connexion. Reinhelm's predecessor, Robert de Losinga (1079–95), is recorded to have built a church after the manner of Aachen at Hereford, and this almost certainly refers to the two-storeyed chapel to the south of the cloister. This chapel was destroyed in the eighteenth century, but some vestiges survive, and its plan and general external appearance are known from engravings. It seems to have been a square building (Figure 21) with a projecting rectangular chancel and four internal piers forming an inner square which was carried up through an upper storey to form a clerestory. It was, in short, a *Doppelkapelle* of a type well known in the Rhineland. It is perhaps indicative of the enduring character of this German influence in the west that the new Cathedral at Hereford, begun about the end of the first decade of the twelfth century by Bishop Reinhelm, was designed with two eastern towers flanking the apse.[35]

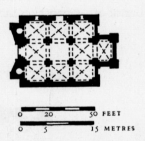

Figure 21. Hereford Cathedral,
Bishop's Chapel: Plan

CHAPTER 3

ANGLO-NORMAN ROMANESQUE

In 1093 the new church was begun at Durham,[1] starting from the east, and by 1099 the work had reached the nave. Durham is the most important work of the Anglo-Norman school, both historically and aesthetically. Historically because it is vaulted throughout with ribbed vaults and, as Dr Bilson established, those over the aisles of the eastern limb were complete by 1096, the high vaults[2] by 1107 (Plate 33B), those over the north transept by about 1110, and those over the south transept and nave by about 1130 (Plate 29A). These dates show that in the matter of ribbed vaulting Durham was extremely precocious – there are, indeed, no surviving examples of importance in France for some fifteen years after the completion of the eastern parts of Durham. It has been reasonably suggested that though the eastern aisle vaults at Durham have the early depressed curve which connects them with the groined vaults from which they evolved, they are too mature to be the actual first experiments. Outside Italy they seem, however, to be the earliest surviving examples.

The problems of the origin of the ribbed vault, and the priority of different examples, have naturally been much canvassed in view of the astonishing developments which took place in France from about 1130 onwards. Whether the immediate ancestors of the Durham vaults were in England or Normandy we have at present no evidence; there are, however, a larger number and more complicated groined vaults in England in the years immediately before Durham than overseas, and not only in the great crypts but notably in the chapels opening from the ambulatory at Gloucester, where instead of the apses having semi-domes, they are treated with a series of groined cells which seem to anticipate the form of the later French chevet vaults but without ribs.[3] Dr Bilson has shown the possibility of a development from the more complex groined vaults of the great crypts to the early ribbed vaults at Durham, and it is very likely a mere accident of survival that has given him his examples from England rather than from Normandy, though the great outburst of building activity in England in the last quarter of the eleventh century may have given the Norman builders their opportunity in England instead of Normandy.

The earliest closely dated examples of ribbed vaults after Durham are also in England, built in the transepts of Winchester when these were repaired after the fall of the tower in 1107. The next important step in the development of the ribbed vault, though there was considerable progress in the refinement of technique in England, is certainly found in Normandy, where the sexpartite vault appears in the two great Caen churches about the end of the first quarter of the twelfth century. The sexpartite vault is so called to distinguish it from the quadripartite, where, in addition to transverse and diagonal ribs dividing the surface of the vault into four, an extra transverse rib springs from the middle of the bay and passes through the point where the diagonals cross, thus dividing the surface into six. It is a system that is rare in England before the last quarter of the twelfth century, but was taken up by the builders of the Île-de-France and carried out in regularly worked courses of well-cut stone, as contrasted with the plaster-covered rubble technique which for long continued to be the method used in Normandy and England. The

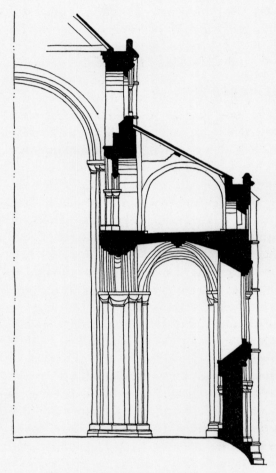

Figure 22. Durham Cathedral: Section of choir

importance of this change of material and technique is often overlooked in discussions of the origin of the Gothic vault in favour of questions of the geometry of the vaults which, though of great importance, are not the only factors.

The historical importance of the vaults of Durham has perhaps tended to divert attention from other qualities of the building which are hardly less remarkable (Figures 22, 23, 24, and 25). The plan had the normal three apses to the east, the transepts have eastern aisles but no apsidal chapels, and the nave is of eight bays. The most remarkable thing about the plan is the length of the eastern limb, four full bays, and a narrower one before the main apse. The four bays to the east of the crossing and the six immediately

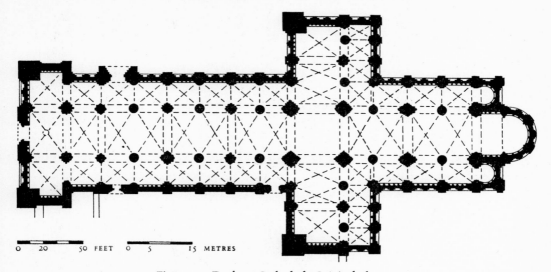

O 20   50 FEET   O   5   15 METRES

Figure 23. Durham Cathedral: Original plan

to the west of it (Plate 30) form part of a scheme of double bays on an alternating system of compound and cylindrical [4] piers after the manner deriving from Jumièges and the Confessor's church at Westminster. The internal elevations of the eastern limb and transepts consist of the main arcades spaced as described, tribunes of about half their height and clerestory: but it is the decorative system of these elevations that is perhaps their most striking characteristic (Plate 31). The compound piers are of course sufficiently diversified by their shaftings, but the cylindrical piers are enriched by incised spiral mouldings, and the arches are elaborately moulded both on their outer orders and their soffits. The tribune arches are subdivided into smaller arches supported on a central column, all being outlined with roll mouldings and the two smaller openings having bold rolls on their soffits. In the nave the main lines and proportions of the design are similar, except that there is greater variety of enrichment on the cylindrical columns, and the chevron ornament, which is an innovation of the early twelfth century, is used on the outer order of the main arcade and the two outer orders of the main arches of the tribune, which is provided with an additional order in this part of the church (Plate 32). Unlike the eastern limb, the transepts and nave have clerestory galleries, and in the latter the middle arch in each bay has chevron ornament, but the greatest display of this enrichment appears in the vault ribs, which in the nave and south transept are all enriched in this way. There is also a string course of this motif at the clerestory level. In addition to this decorative elaboration of the interior of the main vessels, the aisle walls below the windows are treated with intersecting blind arcading (Plate 33A).[5]

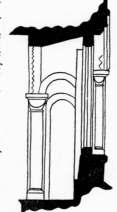

Figure 24. Durham Cathedral: Section of clerestory

In all this Durham interior, both in the management of the proportions and in the disposition of the ornament, there is an impression of mastery that distinguishes it from all its near contemporaries, which can only be enhanced rather than finally explained by analysis of sources and development. Durham is a building which looks towards the future, not only in its structural achievement, for in it for the first time, as far as we know, an all-over linear pattern covering the whole interior was consistently maintained; this effect was to be the almost consistent aim of the major architecture of England to the end of the Middle Ages and beyond, and is not in the same degree characteristic of any continental school. It is interesting to speculate whether this all-over linear effect which is so marked at Durham, may not be the firstfruits of the fusion of Anglo-Saxon and Norman tradition. Not only was the monastery of Durham predominantly Anglo-Saxon in personnel at this time, but it is known as the centre of a school of illuminated manuscripts which carried on the general tradition of English pre-Conquest linear design till well into the twelfth century.[6] This survival of Anglo-Saxon taste and tradition at Durham may be further connected with the source of the monastic recolonization of the holy sites of Northumbria by monks from Evesham and Winchcombe in the years after the Conquest, for these monasteries were prominent as parts of that enclave of Anglo-Saxon monastic tradition in the west.

This is not to suggest that the merits of Durham are Anglo-Saxon rather than Norman, for we know of nothing in late pre-Conquest architecture to prepare us for such a masterpiece, and little in the west of England after the Conquest except the virtuosity of the groined vaulting and the originality of a building such as Tewkesbury; indeed, the alternate system of bay design was, as far as we know, conspicuously absent from that area. There is, however, one important detail at Durham which seems very likely to be of Anglo-Saxon derivation – the elaboration of the soffits of the arches, and especially the big soffit roll. This is only very occasionally found in Normandy – at Bernay in the early eleventh century, for example – but not at all in the Caen churches and Cerisy, though it is a well-known characteristic of late Anglo-Saxon buildings of which Wittering, Bosham, and Langford show conspicuous examples (Plates 13B and 18B). In the early twelfth century it is found in Gloucester nave (where the use of the chevron ornament also recalls Durham (Plate 34, A and B), though it is less profuse) at Romsey and at Peterborough, and the elaboration of soffits with moulding became in the course of the twelfth century one of the most characteristically English habits of design. Another

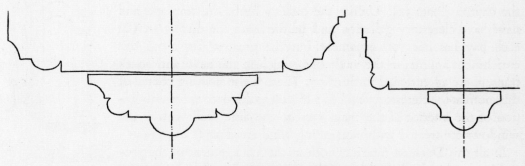

Figure 25. Durham Cathedral: Profiles Arcade and Triforium

detail which may be significant of an Anglo-Saxon contribution to the Durham design, or at least of an English rather than an overseas experience on the part of its builder, is the employment throughout the building of the cushion capital and its derivatives, forms, as we have said, little used in Normandy at that date.

In claiming Durham as an early example of the striving for the all-over linear pattern in English medieval architecture it is necessary to make reservations. This characteristic is present at Durham, and plays an increasingly large part in the total internal effect from the earliest built parts to the latest, but Durham is above all a Romanesque building and, except for the enrichment of the cylindrical piers and the intersecting arcading below the aisle windows, all the elaboration of moulding and, when it comes, the chevron ornament as well, is made to follow the structural lines of the building. Moreover, the large slow rhythm of the double bays divided by their strong vertical lines brings out the articulated quality of the design in a way that suggests a continental parentage. And further, the design of the vaults, though contributing notably to the consistency of the linear pattern of the whole interior, by its omission of the alternate transverse arches above the cylindrical piers strongly emphasizes that rhythm. There is at Durham a quality of consistency and purpose, the integrity of the later medieval writers, which is hardly to be found in any other English Romanesque church.[7]

The search for decorative effect of a linear character can be traced in a number of monuments in progress as the great era of Anglo-Norman building opened out with the twelfth century. Some of them, such as Ely,[8] are instances of the comparatively leisurely completion of works undertaken at the same time as Durham or even a few years before (Plate 36). Ely was begun between 1087 and 1093 and was carried on consistently till about 1107, after which things moved more slowly. It is interesting to compare the early design, as far as we know it from the transepts, with what it became in the nave. The arcade storey of the transepts shows an alternating system carried out with great simplicity of detail and strongly reminiscent of Winchester. Above, the tribunes and clerestory have the same mouldings and comparative elaboration as the nave. In general the nave seems to derive from Cerisy-le-Forêt, a church which also shows signs of having been altered from an alternating to a uniform system of bay design. In the Ely nave (Plates 35A and 38B) the alternating system survives only as a decorative motif; every bay is divided from its neighbour by shafts rising the full height of the building, and in consequence every pier is compound, though every other pier, both in arcade and tribune, is a combination of the cylindrical motif with the compound in which the cylinder emerges as a segmentally curved surface to support the inner orders of the arches. Moreover, the orders themselves have been increased in the arcade from two to three, and the compound piers have increased the number of their shafts from eight to twelve. The effect of the quicker rhythm of the narrower bays, as compared with Durham, repeated in a nave of such length as Ely, and the proportion of the three storeys all about equal in height, by multiplicity and repetition of similar units, gives the effect of a close-mesh all-over pattern far more strongly than Durham.

Norwich Cathedral, begun on an apse and ambulatory plan in 1096 and finished before 1145, is said to have reached to four or five bays west of the crossing by 1119 (Figure

26; Plate 37). This church is an even more remarkable example of the same kind of effect as Ely: here again there is a nave of great length (fourteen bays) designed with an alternate system which is more stressed in the arcades than in the tribunes. The latter have no subordinate arches, and the effect of complexity is gained by mouldings and ornament (chevron and billet), and by the extravagant elaboration of the piers which have sixteen shafts in the major piers of the nave. Peterborough, another church of the largest size, was begun on a three-apse plan in 1118, and work continued till late in the century, the two western bays of the nave and the western transepts being built after 1175. The eastern limb and main transepts were begun on a scheme of alternating cylindrical and octagonal piers with elaborately moulded arches with soffit rolls: the octagonal piers have four attached shafts. The tribune alternation is of a more usual kind and consists of

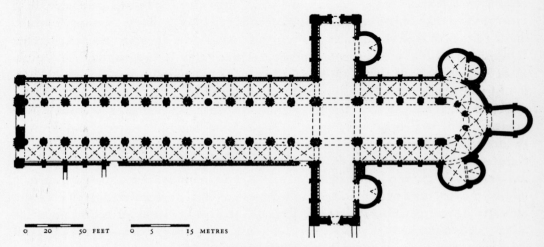

Figure 26. Norwich Cathedral: Plan

compound piers with twelve shafts and compound-cylindrical piers with four shafts, one to each cardinal face. All the bays are divided by half-round shafts rising the full height of the interior, and in the eastern limb these form part of the arcade piers, including the cylindrical ones, but in the transepts they rise from corbels just above the springing of the arches. The continually growing taste for an all-over effect, to be attained by breaking up the piers with a multiplicity of shafts, is very evident in the nave to the west of the two first bays nearest the crossing. This is the natural point for a pause in the building work when the actual accommodation for the monks, whose stalls extended under the lantern tower and into the eastern bays of the nave, had been provided. In all the churches we have been discussing, the normal procedure of building was from east to west, and accounts for the paradox that the naves were often more rich in effect than the eastern parts.

Norwich and Peterborough are good examples of another development which becomes apparent in the early years of the twelfth century and increases in importance.

This is the desire to reduce the mass of the walls. The tendency is visible in Normandy also, and the methods employed are similar on both sides of the Channel. The wall passage and gallery, originally a device for localizing the masses of masonry in the clerestory wall, is now used in other parts of the building. Already at St Étienne, Caen (*c.* 1080), there is a wall passage and gallery across the west end of the nave which serves to link the tribunes in lieu of the elaborate west works of such a church as Jumièges. At Lessay, about 1090, and at La Trinité, Caen, some ten years later, the apses also have galleries at the tribune level, and at the latter church there is a sort of rudimentary ambulatory on the ground level, for four slender piers stand bold from the outer wall of the apse. In England, where the walls were generally even more massive than in Normandy – in some instances perhaps to economize freestone where that had to be brought from a distance, and perhaps also to economize skilled labour in the earlier days of the great outburst of building which, in both numbers and scale of the churches, greatly exceeded Normandy – this extension of the principle of the galleried wall is very marked indeed. The effect of the multiplication of arches in giving vitality to large areas of internal wall where there were no arcades or tribunes, as for example in the transepts, and in linking them in character with the rest of the interior, is a factor possibly even more important. The western walls of the Norwich transepts are notable examples which date from early in the twelfth century (Plate 38A), and at Hereford there is a curious composition of two wall galleries as well as two storeys of blind arcading. The Norwich transept also shows the result of abandoning the broad gallery carrying the tribune across the end of the transept, in the manner found at Winchester, in favour of a narrow wall gallery. This led easily to the use of three windows instead of two on each storey of the transept end, and the development of such admirable compositions both inside and out as the transept ends of Peterborough. But the most remarkable effect of the vogue of the galleried wall in England was in its application to the apse. At Peterborough the galleries pass round the main apse at both tribune and clerestory level, and this involved the abandonment of the semi-dome vault which was always used for the covering of apses in Normandy. The effect of employing two gallery passages while retaining the semi-dome can be seen in Normandy at Cerisy, where a curious change in scale is produced in the apse. Unfortunately there are no other surviving examples in England of the main apses of the three-apsed-type plan, for the requirements of the more elaborate services and the accommodation of the shrines of the saints have led in almost every church of importance to the enlargement of the east end at a later period: even at Peterborough the original appearance of the apse has been obscured by the sixteenth-century additions which have converted it to an ambulatory plan.

The first half of the twelfth century saw the appearance of a variety of new ways of treating the east end of a major church. All of these showed a tendency to reduce the importance of the apse as a main feature of the church or to abandon it in favour of a rectangular treatment. A simple early example was Southwell (Figure 27), begun before 1114, where the main vessel projected almost two bays to the east beyond the apses of the aisles and finished square. At Hereford, begun before 1115, the main apse was entered through an arch no higher than the main arcades, and the aisle apses were square externally;[9] the aisle bays next to the apses formed the bases of substantial towers, the remains of which can still be traced. Thus the external effect of the east end of the church became like a western façade, with the main apse reduced to the proportion of a central porch and the high roofs presumably finishing in a gable [10] between the towers. Except for the existence of the towers, we have no evidence of how the upper parts of the composition were treated, and one wonders especially about the roofs of the aisle apses be-

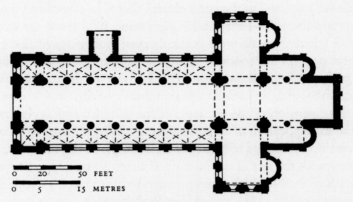

O   20   50 FEET
O   5   15 METRES

Figure 27. Southwell Minster: Plan

yond the face of the towers, but all three apses were swept away in the eastern enlargement at the end of the twelfth century. A similar treatment of the arch into the main apse is found at Llandaff, begun in 1120, and on a large scale at St John's, Chester (1130–40), where the choir was one or possibly two bays longer than Hereford; but little remains at either church except the eastern arches themselves. Another early twelfth-century variation of the treatment of the east end was at Chertsey, begun in 1110, where the eastern arm of the main vessel had a single arch in a square east end and there were three apsidal chapels opening from an ambulatory beyond. About the end of the first quarter of the century two buildings show a much less tentative handling of the problem of the square east end: Romsey (c. 1120) and the extensions at Old Sarum (probably 1125–30): in both churches the aisle is returned round the gable end of the main vessel to form an ambulatory with one chapel at Romsey and three at Sarum opening off to the east. This was a scheme, anticipated it seems at Chertsey, which was to have a great future in the later twelfth and thirteenth centuries, and at Salisbury and Wells was to produce two of the most remarkable architectural achievements in medieval England. The Old Sarum work was an enlargement of the eleventh-century church which was begun in 1075–8 and consecrated in 1092. This church had three eastern apses, the aisles of the presbytery were divided from the main vessel by walls, and there was no central tower or crossing but transepts in the form of towers, as at Exeter. When the celebrated minister of Henry I, Bishop Roger, enlarged this church in about 1125–30, he rebuilt all the eastern parts, making a presbytery of four bays with its aisles returned to form a rectangular ambulatory with three chapels opening from it to the east (Figure

28). These were apsidal inside but finished square outside, the central chapel projecting further to the east than the two at the ends of the aisles. At the same time enlarged transepts were built with east and west aisles, and a crossing was formed on the site of the earlier presbytery.

The most notable later examples of the Old Sarum type of plan are Wells (1180–90), Glastonbury (of about the same date), Lichfield (1170–1200), possibly York (1160), and Ripon, and among the known Cistercian churches, Byland (begun *c.* 1175), and Dore (*c.* 1200). Byland is a particularly interesting example, as it seems to be earlier than the adoption of this plan for the fourth church at Citeaux, which was consecrated in 1193. In the thirteenth century there are Winchester, St Saviour's at Southwark, the new church at Salisbury, Exeter, the reconstruction at Wells, Glasgow Cathedral, and St Patrick's, Dublin. Some of these later examples have reasonably been attributed directly to the adoption of the liturgy according to the Use of Sarum by the chapter concerned.[11]

We are on much surer ground in attributing the growth in popularity of the square east end to the example of the churches of the Cistercian order, the first English house

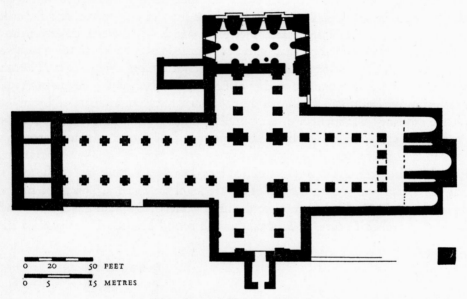

Figure 28. Old Sarum: Plan

of which was founded at Waverley in 1128. Three characteristics distinguish the Cistercians among religious orders from the point of view of architectural history: the prodigious success of the movement both in numbers and size of the houses, and the prestige that this implies, spiritual as well as worldly; the close-knit unity of the organization so that its continental contacts were maintained; and the extreme severity of the attitude towards art of the generation of St Bernard and St Ailred of Rievaulx. This puritan attitude towards art was not merely a question of forgoing sculptured decoration; the

E 43

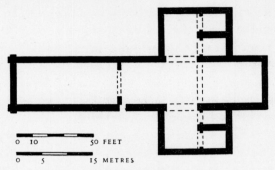

Figure 29. Tintern, early church: Plan

mid twelfth-century Cistercian churches give an impression of severity which is a conscious effect beyond a merely negative attitude toward decoration. Excavations have given us the plans of the early churches at both Waverley and Tintern (Figure 29): buildings with naves without aisles, transepts with one and two square eastern chapels respectively, and short rectangular presbyteries, also without aisles, projecting only a short way beyond the transept chapels. There is no provision for a central tower, and the crossing of the transepts is quite unemphasized. This plan, which was the earliest Cistercian type known, was soon superseded by that with a long aisled nave, of which the transepts and the foundations of the nave remain at Rievaulx, founded in 1132 (Figure 30). The scheme of the early Rievaulx is very close to that of Fontenay in Burgundy, begun in 1139, and, as in the primitive examples, the line of the roof ran through uninterrupted by any structure at the crossing. The manner of the building at Rievaulx is clearly a direct importation from Burgundy, which was the home country of the Order; the main arcades were all pointed, a characteristic of the Romanesque of that region, and – also a Burgundian device – the aisles were covered with pointed barrel vaults set transverse to the axis of the church, the vaults being continuations of the arches of the arcades. This is the first use of the pointed arch in England, except for the high vaults of Durham nave. The windows and the other arched features at Rievaulx are all round-headed. There was no middle

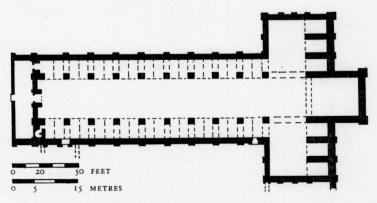

Figure 30. Rievaulx, early church: Plan

storey, but a blank wall between the top of the main arcade and the line of the clerestory windows.[12] There were wooden roofs over the transepts and the main vessel of the nave. The eastern parts of Rievaulx were of the same plan-form as Waverley and Tintern, except that the transepts were enlarged to take three chapels on each of their eastern sides.

The nave survives, though roofless, at the mid twelfth-century church at Fountains Abbey (Plate 39) (begun about 1135), and shows pointed arches and transverse barrel vaults similar to those at Rievaulx, and a similar blank wall in lieu of a middle storey. Both churches were provided at the west end with lean-to porches with small arcades like a cloister on their outer sides: this survives at Fountains, can be traced at Rievaulx, and is also a Burgundian feature. There are at Fountains, however, interesting modifications of the purely Burgundian characteristics of Rievaulx. The piers are cylindrical rather than square and have scalloped capitals, the main arcades are moulded, and there are two string courses, one below the clerestory windows and the other linking them at impost level and returning over each rounded head. Moreover, the church is designed with a marked structural emphasis at the crossing of the transepts in the form of a tower. All these are Anglo-Norman features, and the central towers are especially remarkable departures from Cistercian orthodoxy, as they are the only architectural features singled out for particular prohibition in the regulations.

Buildwas, a smaller building than Fountains, dating from about 1157, shows a similar Anglo-Norman character in its details, and also has a central tower at the crossing. The pointed barrel vaults over the aisles have, however, been abandoned, and there are traces of a ribbed vault over the presbytery. The projecting eastern bay of Buildwas presbytery is lit by three very tall, narrow, round-headed windows, which, however, appear to have been lengthened. At Kirkstall, near Leeds, which was begun two or three years before Buildwas, the pointed barrel vaults over the transeptal chapels have been retained, but there is a ribbed vault over the presbytery. This vault has a special importance in the study of early Gothic vaulting, as it seems to be technically in the Anglo-Norman descent from the Durham vaults and, in its combination of the vault rib and the pointed arch, to suggest a development parallel to that of the Île-de-France but independent of it.[13] Apart from its vault, Kirkstall shows as clearly as Fountains and Buildwas the early adoption of Anglo-Norman details and practice in Cistercian building after the very first examples.

The Cistercian order was active very early in Ireland, but unfortunately nothing has survived of the churches of the earliest period, except the plan of the transepts at Mellifont, which was consecrated in 1152. These had three chapels in each transept, the middle one square-ended and the two flanking it apsidal. The apse is otherwise unknown in Ireland at any date, and this must be an importation.[14]

The middle years of the twelfth century, which in northern France, and especially in the *Domaine Royale*, saw such revolutionary developments in architecture, are more difficult to characterize in the British Isles. Scholars have been somewhat at a loss to account for the apparent failure to exploit the precocious structural experiments of the beginning of the century. Durham has few real successors on the road to Gothic. A variety of factors has over-simplified and over-dramatized this contrast, and especially the concentration on the problem of the development of the high vault and its abutment, which, however important as the most readily isolated of all aspects of twelfth- and thirteenth-century architectural history, can seriously distort our understanding of every region other than northern France, and has even on occasion blinded students to important aspects of the Parisian achievement itself: for example, the tendency to a concentration of space in the design of great buildings, which was made possible by the new methods and the desire for which may have in part prompted them. The French development of vaulting technique was occasioned, no doubt, by the political and economic situation of the towns of the *Domaine Royale* that gave the wealth and confidence to embark on such ambitious projects, and ultimately the position of Paris as an intellectual centre for all Europe tended to spread French fashions far and wide; but apart from these large general factors, there are others of purely architectural character.

This outburst of French building coincides with developments in the technique of stone-cutting involving the use of improved tools and making possible greater precision and economy in the handling of material.[15] The Île-de-France was a region of notable urban development at this time, and these rising towns were situated in a country well endowed geologically with fine building-stones. It is not easy to be precise about this technical improvement in stone-cutting, which is a problem calling for study, but it is one of the most hopeful ways in which the economic approach to architectural history can be applied. It seems clear even now that, important as it was in northern France, the technical change was a widespread one and can be traced in Italy and also in England. Throughout Europe there was this increase in the economy of material, implying better technical methods or a higher proportion of skilled labour employed on any one job. In England the change in the character of plain ashlar, from the wide-jointed work of the late eleventh century to the more sophisticated work which appears in the early years of the twelfth, is well known, and William of Malmesbury's comment on the quality of the fine-jointed stonework of Bishop Roger of Sarum's buildings has often been quoted. A specimen of Bishop Roger's building illustrating this survives in the gatehouse of Sherborne Castle, which was built in about 1120. This is only of interest as an extreme example, which was remarkable in its day perhaps as much for the extent to which fine-jointed ashlar was used as for the quality of the work. The more obvious evidences of the change are in the increasing use of moulded work and its increased complexity, the introduction of new ornamental motifs, and the development of decorative and figure carving, especially on capitals. A general date round about 1120–25 seems to suit a number of early signs of this fashion, as for example the decorated crossing capitals of Southwell and those of the crypt at Canterbury (Plates 40, A and B, 41A); by the 1130s the movement is in full swing, as for instance the newly-discovered capitals of Reading cloister, the capitals on the porch at Durham, and those of the eastern parts of Romsey.[16] The more ambitious figure compositions which are mostly on doorways, such as those on the doorway from the cloister into the church at Ely and the celebrated compositions round the doors at Malmesbury and at Glastonbury, are of the middle and later years of the century, though the Ely door may date from about 1140. An exceptional group of figure sculptures of about that date has also survived at Lincoln, where it forms a large-scale frieze or band inserted by Bishop Alexander across the eleventh-century west front, just above the main doorways which the bishop had altered and enriched. He also heightened the whole composition, including the western towers, in a highly elaborate fashion about the same time.

In addition to such main fields for sculptural enrichment as capitals, doorways, etc., a tradition was established of enriching the corbel tables which supported the eaves with sculptured heads and other carvings (Plates 40B, 41B). These are a feature common in the Anglo-Norman school and in many regions of French Romanesque, as contrasted with the Lombardic and German system of small arches linking the tops of the pilaster strips. In twelfth-century practice in Italy and Germany these arches have become formalized into rows of small-scale arcade brackets, with pilaster strips appearing only at intervals. Examples of this can be found in Anglo-Norman buildings, as for example at Southwell. A peculiarly English feature, however, is the carved heads, often of monsters, used as stops to the ends of hood-moulds both on exteriors and interiors. These stand at the beginning of a long tradition, continuing into the thirteenth century and later. The appearance of chevron ornament and intersecting wall arcading at Durham has already been mentioned. These were the first additions to what may be called the original post-Conquest repertory of ornament, consisting of elementary diaper and billet ornament and cable-moulding.

It is not claimed that these motifs originated on this side of the Channel, only that they were exploited here with an unprecedented enthusiasm, first evident at Durham. Another precocious example is on the exterior of the transeptal chapels of Christchurch in Hampshire, where a variety of diapers and intersecting arcading was used in the first years of the twelfth century to produce a very rich effect. Throughout the first three-quarters of the century the ornamental work increased in variety and precision of execution with the technical advance in stone-cutting. The chevron itself develops its own variations, and there are all manner of discs, reels, beadings, and interlaces, the last-named on occasion recalling pre-Conquest motifs, which in some remote places can be found surviving into the new century.

In the third quarter of the century there is evidence which suggests a definite revival of Anglo-Saxon motifs in the decoration of capitals, notably at Kirkstall in Yorkshire and St Frideswide's in Oxford, both places where such ornament is rather specially striking, Kirkstall being a Cistercian building of the end of what may be called the first phase, and Oxford one of the most sophisticated Romanesque buildings in the country. A development of the middle and later decades of the century is the overlaying of one motif by another, of which the beak-head is the earliest and most frequent and striking example. The 'classic' beak-head consists of a series of pointed monster heads which grasp the roll moulding: generally they are set radially to an arch, but sometimes they continue round the jambs of a doorway, their heads being set at right angles to the roll which they grasp. In pure beak-head the monsters are birdlike, as the name implies, but in some developed examples – for example, at Kilpeck – a variety of types of creature appear. There is also a special use of a double chevron clasping or overlaying a roll moulding which relates to beak-head in that one motif overlays another. A curious late example of this at New Shoreham has a small roll which breaks in towards the centre of the arch in V-shaped points on alternate voussoirs, the centres of the Vs being filled with leaf carving. Beak-head seems to be an English invention and, though it spread to Normandy and elsewhere, it is perhaps significant that it is not found in Essex, Kent, or Surrey, where continental influence is naturally strongest. It is chiefly found in the smaller churches rather than in the great buildings, a point which tends to confirm its native origin, though an exception is the great doorway of the west front of Lincoln (dated about 1140). The Scandinavian affinities of the beak-head motif have often been remarked, but this is rather a visual impression than anything more 'documented', and, as Sir Alfred Clapham has pointed out, its architectural application is probably English. To the writer it seems to suggest a borrowing from the repertory of the timber builder, and this impression is reinforced by its presence at Kilpeck in Herefordshire (Plate 41B), where a curious kind of far-projecting monster head is found at the upper angles of the nave walls. These seem to be a translation into stone of the ornamental ends of wooden wall-plates. Scandinavian influences are unlikely at Kilpeck, and in the absence of early timber buildings of any decorative pretension this possible explanation, which would account for the Scandinavian look, must be the purest speculation.

The placing of this decoration, with its expanding repertory of motifs, in relation to the total architectural effect, is the aspect of it which gives to the Anglo-Norman school one of its most distinctive characteristics. Put very broadly, there seems to be a progress from the extreme severity of the early post-Conquest buildings through a phase in which the ornament is used lavishly but subject to a discipline which confined it fairly strictly to the enrichment of the structural lines of the building, to a mid twelfth-century use of all-over effects of surface enrichment, which in extreme cases shows a remarkable disregard for such structural considerations. This is, of course, an over-simplification: for example, the decorative patterns on the cylindrical piers at Durham are an exception to the severely structural placing of the chevron ornament of the nave; but the increasing tendency at Ely and elsewhere as the buildings progressed to break up the main forms so as to produce a closer-mesh pattern supports the generalization, and so does the structural propriety of the decorative treatment of the nave of Gloucester. Naturally enough, the designs in which one finds the greatest disregard of structural propriety are those features which are themselves largely decorative in intention, such as west fronts and towers. The mid twelfth-century front at Castle Acre (Plate 42A) is an outstanding example, in which almost every decorative motif known to the age is spread thickly and fairly evenly over the whole area, and there seems to be a conscious intention to disguise the fact that the front consists of two towers and the end wall of the nave. Even at Durham (Plate 42B), where these fundamental structural divisions between the towers at the ends of the aisles and the end wall of the main vessel of the nave are indeed clearly marked by buttresses of shallow projection, the buttresses are tied into the centre division at the top by a band of enriched arcading which goes across the end gable and the inner buttresses with a complete disregard of the structural line. Melbourne in Derbyshire is another example of a two-towered front which disregards the form of the church behind and develops as an independent composition, though in this case the effect is not gained by spread of ornament but by the emphasis given to the outer buttresses. The placing of the western towers outside the line of the aisles to north and south, which was to produce such a remarkable effect at Wells in the thirteenth century, is foreshadowed at St Botolph's, Colchester, where, though the state of the monument makes it difficult to reconstruct the decorative effect intended, the general intention is clear enough. At Malmesbury (Plate 43A) the remains of the front show a frankly screen-like treatment, which completely disregards the sectional form of the church behind it, being carried across the ends of the aisle roofs at the height of the main vessel and returning round so that the screen-like character of the design is quite visible from the side elevation. In this respect it is most probably the ancestor of the thirteenth-century treatment at Salisbury. The front at Rochester (Plate 43B) had no western towers, but only angle turrets carried well above the aisle roofs to make a composition with the two slighter turrets flanking the main western gable of the church. The whole front was treated with arcading, and hardly any other motif is used except in the main western doorway. The arcading, however, is very evenly and closely set, and very good use has been made of the contrast of surfaces between the upper and lower parts and of the slight recession of the aisle doors behind the line of the main vessel and the angle turrets. Hereford seems to have had a similar though less monumental scheme with slighter and shorter angle turrets. In these designs, especially at Rochester, there is a tension between the expression of the structural divisions of the front and the treatment of the surface in which much of the quality of the design consists. This is a fundamental problem in the design of the end elevation of aisled buildings with clerestories, common to church architecture all over Europe, except where an independent western mass, as at Lincoln, Ely, etc., or a screen treatment such as Malmesbury, completely disguises the issue. It is a problem of special importance in the medieval architecture of Great Britain, where the adoption of the square east end and the importance given to transepts supplied numerous opportunities for façade design.

The surviving examples of Romanesque towers, with few exceptions, of which St Alban's is the most important (Plate 46A), are of the mid twelfth century. This is partly because the builders of the great churches, especially the monastic churches, built the essential working parts of the church before proceeding to the upper parts of the towers and the finishing of the western ends; and partly perhaps because we have lost a number of examples by accident. Romanesque builders seem often to have let zeal outrun discretion in this feature, and the number of disasters is remarkable. These mid twelfth-century towers, both inside and out, are outstanding examples of the taste for rich surface decoration, notably at Norwich (Plates 44 and 45), where a remarkable variety of motifs is employed in addition to the usual arcading, plain or enriched, which forms the basis of the surface treatment of Tewkesbury (Plate 46B) and the simpler towers of Southwell (Plate 47A) and Wimborne. The upper storeys of Norwich consist, first, of a tall stage having three narrow windows separated by four panels filled with a kind of relief treillage and small arches linking vertical strips;[17] above this is a shorter stage having two rows of five round windows, the lower row blind and the upper pierced. The tower has strongly marked angle turrets, where the vertical lines are emphasized by a number of attached strips or shafts; the circular window features are also found in the lantern space inside the tower at Norwich and on the transeptal towers at Exeter. The stages of the western towers at Lincoln (Plate 47B), which come above the eleventh-century western work and form the bases of the famous fourteenth-century compositions, were built as part of the general embellishment of the west front by Bishop Alexander in the mid twelfth century and included the decoration of the doorways, the frieze of figure sculptures above them, and the enrichment of the whole upper part of the western building with three rows of arcading and a reticulated trellis pattern in the gables. These last are visible on the return gables to the north and south. The trellis pattern at Lincoln is similar to that on the larger gables on the transept ends at Southwell (Plate 47A), which have perhaps the largest spread of twelfth-century ornamented surface in the country. The two towers at Lincoln are not an exact pair, but they have the form of their angle turrets in common. This is polygonal – part octagon – in plan, and determined the treatment of the fourteenth-century towers. The angles of the polygonal form give a strong vertical line to these turrets, an effect obtained at Norwich by purely decorative means.

The Lincoln treatment started a fashion in the east of England which can be traced through the thirteenth century, becoming part of the common stock of architectural motifs in later medieval times. Polygonally planned turrets are also used both at the angles of the late twelfth-century tower at Ely, and in the pair which form the southern terminations of the western transept (Plate 48). Indeed, the whole treatment of this crossing and transept, both inside (Plate 35B) and out, is as good an example as could be found of the decorative tendencies we have been discussing.

In the great churches of eastern England – Ely, Norwich, and Peterborough – one can trace the gradual elaboration with some degree of refinement of motifs which had already established themselves in the first half of the century, until at Ely and Peterborough the western transepts with their pointed arches and banded shafts pass almost imperceptibly into the new phase, which is, by general consent, called Gothic.[18] Elsewhere we can equally trace back the new designs to experiments of Henry I's time, or earlier, and the contrast is often found to be more marked.

St Frideswide's at Oxford, a church of the Augustinians, is one of the most remarkable designs of its time – that is, about 1170–80 (Plate 49). It is a development of the system first employed at Tewkesbury, a colossal arcade order embracing the middle storey which is supported by a sub-arch springing from half-capitals on the outer side of the main piers. The Oxford piers in the choir and north transept can almost be described as columns in the classical antique sense, an effect due to their proportions, including those of the capitals with their rectangular abaci, and to a use of entasis which is sufficiently marked and yet subtle enough to suggest a knowledge of antique practice. This can be best appreciated in the north transept, where the sixteenth-century vaulting was never carried out and the evidences of the Romanesque vaulting are still clear. Moreover, some of the clerestory windows have been left unaltered. The whole quality of the work is of a very high order in its details, notably in the handling of the traditional triplet clerestory arches and the moulding of the main arcade. The total effect is of extreme intellectual sophistication, and this impression is confirmed by comparison with the other buildings which share this type of internal elevation. Of these, Romsey, Dunstable, and Jedburgh (Plate 51A), which are earlier than Oxford, though Jedburgh is not much earlier, all have important middle storeys treated as tribunes with large arches, those at Romsey being subdivided into two sub-arches. Oxford and the two latest examples, Glastonbury and Waterford [19] (thirteenth century), emphasize the effect of this feature by reducing the middle storey to a mere triforium opening – two arches at Oxford, and three at Glastonbury and Waterford – in the tympanum of the colossal arcade, thus making the whole into what is essentially a two-storey composition. There is a further contrast between Oxford and its fellows; at Romsey, in the two eastward bays of the nave an alternating system is used, which was changed to a uniform system farther west. The effect of the colossal order is much weaker in the compound piers, where the shafts of the main faces carry up the whole height of the elevation past the springing of the arch above the tribune. A similar compromise with the more usual bay treatment is found at Dunstable, where all the piers are compound and have a pilaster as well as a vertical shaft on the main face, and the latter again is carried above the springing of the tribune arches. Both at Romsey in the westernmost Romanesque bays and at Dunstable throughout, the arches into the aisles are given mouldings and enrichment which lend them an importance almost equal to those of the tribune, and further reduce the effect of the colossal order as compared with the severe subordination of the lower to the upper arches at Oxford. Jedburgh seems to be closest to Romsey in this and other respects. The Glastonbury design also has compound piers with triple vaulting shafts rising to the clerestory; the reduction of the middle storey to a slight and elegant triforium of three arches, and the concentration of enrichment in the great arch, while that opening into the aisle is left severely plain, again emphasizes the two-storey nature of the scheme while keeping the bay division. There is no sign of antiquity here, however, close as the design is in general conception to Oxford: the west-country details and the pointed arches see to that.

The fragmentary remains of the great church of Malmesbury consist of parts of the nave (Plate 50B) and west front, and of the western walls of the transept. The church was begun in 1145, not earlier, and the nave presumably dates from about 1160. As we see it the building is of more interest for its individual features than for any special felicity or even enterprise in its general composition. The nave arcade is of bluntly pointed arches on short cylindrical piers with scalloped capitals, and the middle storey has wide enriched arch orders embracing four sub-arches. The clerestory has been so much altered in the late fourteenth century as to give no evidence of its original effect internally. The aisles are vaulted, and represent a phase in the development of the Anglo-Norman ribbed vault similar to those of Kirkstall. Of the individual features, the west front with its frankly screen-like character has already been referred to, and the great south porch, which may be dated c. 1160, belongs rather to the history of figure sculpture than of architecture. Some of the detailed motifs employed in the building are, however, of great interest. Mr Brakspear has called attention to some of them as the first examples

of those building mannerisms which can be traced in a number of west-country buildings in the last years of the twelfth century and first years of the thirteenth, and give
them a very special character. Of these, the arch with a plain roll-moulding uninterrupted by a capital or other break at the impost is one of the most important; the trick
of enclosing a sub-arch of a similar radius below another – a very distinctive and curious
habit – and the remains of a scheme of decoration round the windows consisting of large
isolated roundels, also have an interest in this connexion. The distinctive quality of this
last ornament at Malmesbury consists in its placing as a series of discreet points of
enrichment set in an area of very finely worked ashlar, from which they gain their importance and which they in turn set off. The affinities of this rosette ornament at Malmesbury are with similar isolated points of decoration, not always rosettes: squares and
lozenges at Worcester and Glastonbury and, the latest example of all, the carvings of
dragons in rectangular frames in the spandrels of the north porch of Wells.

All these share this common quality, that their *raison d'être* lies in their relation to the
surrounding field. Such a motif could only arise in a countryside with a fine stone building tradition, and it is perhaps permissible to speculate on the possibility that the tradition of well-cut ashlar in this district goes back to Bishop Roger's fine stonework, to
which William of Malmesbury refers. A last detail at Malmesbury which is worth men-
tioning is the bold use of hood-moulds above the main arches of the arcade. This peculiarly illogical practice of using an exterior feature as an internal decoration, which
became common in England, appears here in its frankest form.[20] Moreover, not only are
the hood-moulds specially enriched, but their sculptured stops and the masks at their
apexes, and the distance of the hood-moulding from the outer order of the arch, combine to give them a special decorative prominence.

One of the most remarkable of late Romanesque interior designs is the nave at Worksop Priory (Plate 50A), which dates from about 1180. The piers, which are almost slight
enough to be called columns, are alternately octagonal and round, and the arches of
both the arcade and the tribune are elaborately enriched, a distinctive feature being the
outlining of the arches by another enriched motif and the use of an enrichment of similar
scale on the abaci of the arcade capitals, thus strongly emphasizing the linear character of
the composition. There is a heavily marked string at tribune level, and a second enriched
string below the clerestory windows. The line of the clerestory string is interrupted by
the tops of the tribune arches, and the clerestory windows are, in consequence, displaced
to positions above the main piers. Small and narrow arches are placed below the clerestory windows and between the main arches of the tribune. This extraordinary scheme is
a most extreme development of a type of composition which almost ignores the vertical
division into bays. The most important earlier example is Southwell, where the nave
dates from at least a generation before (Plate 52A). There is no such eccentricity in
the placing of the windows at Southwell, but the broad, low proportions of the arches
of all three storeys, the absence of any vertical division by shafts or other members
between the bays, and the emphasis given to the unbroken strings between the
storeys, tend strongly to make one read the design in a horizontal rather than a vertical
sense.

Southwell has other qualities of its own, such as the exploitation of broad, uninterrupted surfaces of ashlar on the short, cylindrical piers, the spandrels of the arcade and tribune arches, and notably in the clerestory, though there are evidences that this impression would not be so strong had the intention to fill the heads of the tribune arches with some device in open-work arcading been carried out. The evidences suggest something in the nature of the skeleton arches of the tribune at Romsey.

The absence of division into vertical bays is common enough on the continent, though generally in designs which are more or less frankly descended from the arcaded basilicas of the Ravenna type, in which the middle storey is left plain or, very rarely, treated with a continuous row of small arches. The nearest continental example to the Southwell scheme and effect is the nave of Tournai, where, though the detail is very different and the elevation is one of four storeys, the 'aqueduct' impression of continuous rows of superimposed arches is very marked. In Great Britain it is hardly easier to find related buildings, though Shrewsbury Abbey, where the cylindrical piers of the arcade are repeated in the tribune and the strings between the storeys are uninterrupted, has more than a hint of this system, though the taller proportions of the church and the suggestion that it was intended to divide the bays vertically into groups of three give a very different effect.

All the most important Romanesque buildings in Scotland, however, share this characteristic of ignoring the vertical divisions, notably the nave of Dunfermline (Plates 51B and 52B), which in its lower parts must be about contemporary with Southwell and in its upper parts almost with Worksop. Dunfermline has often been compared with Durham, from which, like various other places in the north, it derives its cylindrical piers decorated with incised linear patterns, but in the nave there is little of Durham above the arcade storey, except perhaps the curiously timid use of a roll-moulding on the soffit of the small and almost primitively plain arches of the tribune, which otherwise have only one order and no enrichment of any kind, not even at the imposts.[21] It seems clear that there was a pause in the building at Dunfermline above the arcade and again before the clerestory was undertaken.[22] This last is much more sophisticated work than the tribune and, indeed, recalls Southwell in the proportions of its single rather squat openings: these are given angle shafts which look slight as compared with the bold respond-like shafts in the jambs of the openings at Southwell, though the inner wall of the Dunfermline clerestory is the thicker of the two. Moreover, the clerestory windows at Dunfermline are of the normal round-headed type, and not circular as at Southwell. A further difference is that the Dunfermline clerestory has a third string course in addition to those above the arcades of the tribunes, at the level of the imposts of the clerestory openings, which greatly emphasizes the horizontal effect of the composition.

To judge from the surviving fragments of the western crossing, with its forebuilding and transepts and two bays of the nave, Kelso[23] was the most splendid Romanesque building in Scotland (Figure 31; Plates 53 and 54A). Moreover it has a special interest in that the western complex was completed in one consistent manner, unlike Ely where the Galilee Porch is a later addition and different in character from the crossing and the transept. At Kelso sufficient of the building at the west end survives to give an idea of the effect both inside and out. The date is in the last quarter of the twelfth century, and in the upper parts the influence of the Cistercian early Gothic, which was strong in Scotland at that time, can be seen in the details of the clerestory arcades. The nave system consists of squat compound cylindrical piers, which have pilasters and shafts to take the inner arch orders, and, above, two rows of small but elaborate arcades forming the triforium and clerestory, the former supported on single, the latter on triple shafts. There are strings between each storey, and the upper arcades are continuous, producing a strongly emphasized horizontal effect. These upper arcades contrast very vividly with the long, slow rhythm of the main arches below them, and suggest the effect of an elegant linear decorated box, raised up in this case on an arcade of the main arches, the nearest parallel to which is at St John's, Chester, where the triforium and clerestory, though of a later date than Kelso, make a similar contrast with the main arches below

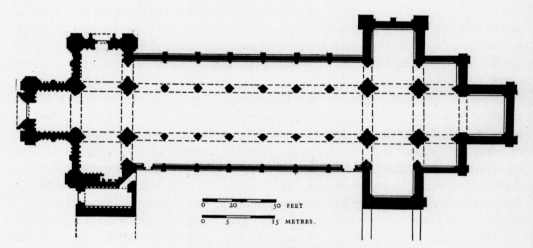

Figure 31. Kelso Abbey: Plan

them. At St John's, however, the contrast represents the work of two periods, and there are slender vertical divisions marking off the elevation into a bay design of four of the upper arches to one of the main arcade. This is about the numerical ratio also at Kelso. It is possible that the Kelso nave design is an ancestor of the treatment of the choirs at Coldingham and Darlington, where the system is simplified and adapted to a two-storey elevation by the omission of the main arcades.

Apart from the special character of the nave and tower, the other surviving parts of Kelso deserve detailed attention. The shortness of the north, south, and western arms of the crossing, combined with their great height and the even loftier lantern, imply an effect of space at once centralized and soaring, of which some idea can still be gained at Ely, though Kelso must always have been the more successful arrangement. The contrast between this space experience on entering the building, and the strong horizontal emphasis of the nave, is a reconstruction amply supported by the surviving evidence. Internally the elevations of the arms of the western crossing, their three tiers of shafted and galleried windows above a wall enriched with intersecting arcading, are extremely effective, and, with the transept ends of Peterborough and Norwich, are the finest examples of what can be done with the tradition of the galleried wall. Externally the strongly marked vertical bays and the angle turrets grouped about the central lantern tower are equally effective. In detail the ends of the northern and western arms and the form of the enriched doorway features enclosed in gabled projections on the main faces of the building set a fashion which was followed with great success in later Scottish buildings.

CHAPTER 4

ROMANESQUE AND EARLY GOTHIC BUILDINGS
OTHER THAN CHURCHES

THE domestic, ceremonial, and administrative buildings of the great monasteries offer us the best examples of the versatility of the early medieval architects and of the flexibility of their way of building. The number and wealth of these institutions, the continuity of their life throughout the Middle Ages and, even in the case of some of the greater monasteries, to some degree the abruptness with which that life ended, thus saving them from seventeenth- and eighteenth-century adaptations, have left to us far more monastic examples than there are domestic buildings made for laymen, even including those in castles. Bishops' palaces have generally been rebuilt, and of the kings' palaces little that is medieval remains except Westminster Hall and as much of Clarendon as has been revealed by excavation.[1]

The change from the diffused and apparently unorganized layout of the Dark Age monasteries to the standardized plan, with the main buildings grouped round a rectangular cloister court, is likely to be due to the reforms of Benedict of Aniane (d. 822) in the time of Charlemagne. The architectural effects of these reforms may have reached England as early as the ninth century, and almost certainly did in the tenth, but, as with the tendency to develop the 'great church' which dominated or even absorbed the smaller churches of a monastery, the movement to systematize the layout of monastic buildings probably took some generations to establish itself completely, though we have little or no evidence of the stages of this process, at any rate in England.

Though there is little evidence of the tenth- and early eleventh-century pre-Conquest monastic buildings in England,[2] there is abundance of material from the late eleventh century and from the twelfth, though there is curiously little evidence of the appearance of the cloister arcades. In many of the richer monasteries the cloisters were reconstructed in the new vaulted and tracery-lighted form, of which the north-eastern bays of Westminster Abbey cloister are among the earliest surviving examples. The earliest type of cloister was roofed with a wooden lean-to, and this was supported on the courtyard side by arcades of coupled columns set at right angles to the line of the arcades so as to give greater strength to take the thrust of the roof (Plate 54B).[3] In some instances the lines of arcades were divided up into bays, as if in anticipation of the future traceried window systems: a possible example of this was at Westminster. A number of fragments of capitals, bases, shafts, and arch voussoirs have survived at Westminster, Winchester, Norwich, Bridlington (Plate 55A), and from Reading Abbey; at Fountains the arcading of the narthex shows the type of early Cistercian cloister arcade,[4] and at Canterbury a fragment of an arcade of the type employed for cloisters has survived *in situ* by the treasury. There are, of course, plenty of examples to show the treatment of the walls of the buildings round the cloister, as these formed parts of very substantial works which have often survived the disappearance of the lightly built arcades. The fragments mentioned above, especially those from Westminster, Winchester, Reading, and Bridlington, give some idea of the richness of sculptural decoration, both grotesque and figured, that was lavished on this part of the monastic buildings in England no less than in southern France or Spain.

All these examples date from the mid twelfth century, at the earliest from the second quarter of the century, and they are scanty enough as compared with what has been

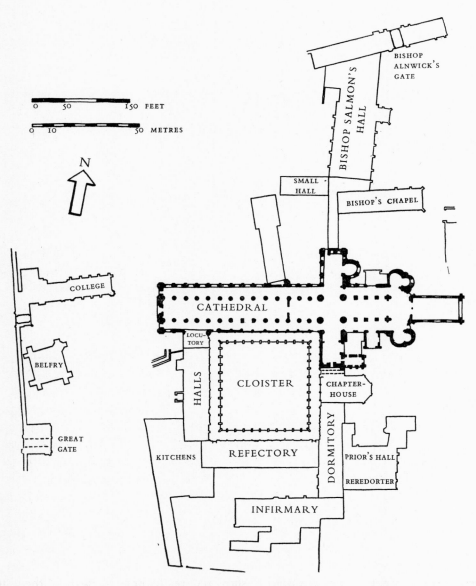

Figure 32. Norwich Cathedral: Plan of layout

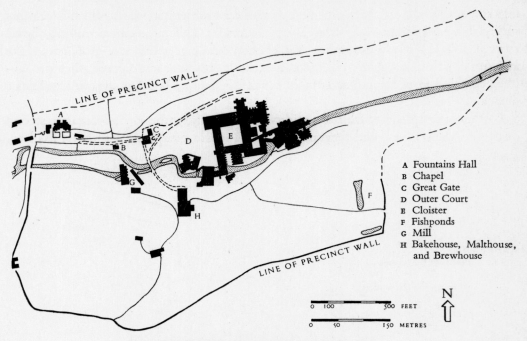

A Fountains Hall
B Chapel
C Great Gate
D Outer Court
E Cloister
F Fishponds
G Mill
H Bakehouse, Malthouse, and Brewhouse

Figure 33. Fountains Abbey: Plan of layout

lost: little more has survived from the early Gothic period. At Newminster [5] in Northumberland (Plate 55B) there are considerable remains; at Southwark some caps and bases
from the cloister of about 1190 are extant; and at Forde Abbey in Dorset the wall arcade
on the north wall of the north walk has been exposed. The Southwark examples are very
French in the character of their carved foliage capitals, and share the same system of twin
columns as in Romanesque times. Fragments were also found at Butley Priory in Suffolk
of twin capitals and bases and some lengths of shafting dating from about 1200. These
were all of Purbeck marble and very interesting examples of their time; the bases stood
on a dwarf wall. Similar fragments, also in Purbeck but rather later in date and having
rounded abaci and plain moulded capitals as against the rectangular abaci and carved
capitals of Butley, were found at Lacock Abbey. Perhaps as good an impression of the
general effect of these early Gothic cloisters as can be obtained is to be seen at Mont S.
Michel, where an early thirteenth-century example with markedly English affinities in
detail has survived. The open arcade leading to the chapter-house at Southwell, though
a classic example of advanced thirteenth-century naturalistic detail, preserves some of the
effect of these earlier cloister arcades.

The arrangement of the buildings round the cloister court admitted of considerable
variety, but the positions of certain important buildings were fixed by custom (Figures
32 and 33). The chapter-house was always on the eastern side in line with the transept of
the church, and the frater or refectory, the common eating-hall of the monks, on the
side opposite to the church and generally raised up on an undercroft. The dormitory was
usually also on the east side in line with the transept, and also raised on an undercroft.

The western side of the cloister was used for a variety of purposes – the abbot's or prior's lodging might be there, as at Westminster, or special apartments for distinguished functionaries, as at Norwich, or sometimes merely offices. In Cistercian houses the lay brothers' dormitory was usually to the west of the cloister. Of all these buildings, the cloister itself, the chapter-house, and the refectory are those most to our purpose as offering the most distinctive architectural opportunities, and these three buildings were by custom the most strictly fixed as to their positions. The other domestic buildings, such as the abbot's lodgings and the accommodation for guests, were linked in kind with the grander domestic architecture of the world outside the monastery, though there are probably as fine or finer examples to be found in the great monasteries as in any of the royal castles or palaces. This is especially true of Ely,[6] where a series of splendid halls remains buried in the accretions of post-dissolution building. The infirmaries of the great monasteries are in a category all to themselves. They were not part of the essential buildings grouped round the cloister itself, the very centre of the monastic organism, but were often placed to the east of the main group. They take their place rather in the history of the development of other hospital buildings, though certainly the great monastic infirmaries are the earliest examples in the series.

Of the peculiarly monastic buildings, the chapter-house is the most important, ranking only after the church itself. The church belonged to God and the Saints whom the monks served, but the chapter-house belonged to the community in a special sense: in it their solemn business was transacted, and in it, hardly less than in the choir itself, their intense corporate feeling was concentrated. Partly because they are not very big buildings, and partly because their practical space requirements were often not very complicated, chapter-houses have not been much studied out of England, where the problem of the centrally planned chapter-houses has attracted some attention. They are, however, almost always buildings of some architectural pretension, and even those which retained the original simple rectangular plan, or rectangular with an apse to the east, have generally some quality of architectural ambition often shown in the relation of the chapter-house itself to the vestibule between it and the cloister walk.

In many monasteries the monks' dormitory ran the whole length of the east side of the cloister at first-floor level, and this prevented the chapter-house on the floor below from being given any adequate height. This position for the dormitory was sanctioned by tradition as well as practical convenience for the service of the church, and in the ideal scheme for a monastic layout, known as the St Gall plan of the early ninth century, the dormitory occupies this position with a series of apartments – one of which is described as the 'warming house' – in the undercroft beneath it: it is noteworthy that the St Gall plan shows no special chapter-house, but indicates by an inscription that its place was taken by the north walk of the cloister, that is over against the church. It is clear, however, that the desire for a chapter-house of appropriate size and splendour soon became stronger than any tradition as to the placing of the dormitory. At Canterbury and Winchester buildings of such size, and particularly height, were built that the dormitory was cut off from the transept of the church. The Canterbury and Winchester chapter-houses, of the same size, 90 by 40 feet approximately, are large rectangular buildings leading directly off the east cloister walk; but in most examples of the twelfth century, where height and splendour were required, the direct communication of the dormitory with the transept was preserved by a compromise whereby the chapter-house was entered through a vestibule which occupied the undercroft of the dormitory, the chapter-house proper being built out to its full height to the east. This provided an opportunity for very effective dramatic contrast between the vestibule, low and broken up with columns supporting a vault in small bays, and the hall itself, which was lofty and covered in a single

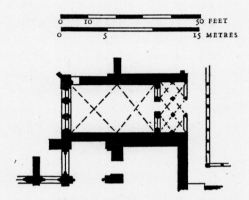

Figure 34. Chapter-house, Bristol Cathedral: Plan

unbroken span. Good examples are at Bristol, Hexham, and Chester. Some of the greater chapter-houses of the twelfth century had vaults of up to as much as a 35-foot span, as at Durham, Gloucester, and Reading.[7] The Bristol chapter-house is a remarkably interesting example (Plate 57); the low vestibule (Figure 34) with its spaces much broken up by internal supports leading to a splendid chamber which, even in its restored condition, provides as good an example as could be wished of the linear pattern-making taste of the English twelfth century, the wall arcadings and diapers being of extraordinary variety and richness and covering every inch of the wall surfaces. The fragments of the chapter-house at Much Wenlock show a similar treatment.

In the Cistercian houses of the north a different type of rectangular chapter-house was developed, having vaulting piers dividing it into three aisles and preceded by a shallow vestibule only one bay deep, over which a passage led from the dormitory to the night stairs in the transept. The details of these northern buildings are of remarkable elegance, and Fountains, Furness, Jervaulx, and Dundrennan are all good examples. The chapter-houses at Fountains and Furness measure 55 by 40 feet, and 61 by 45 feet respectively, and with their twelve bays of steeply pointed quadripartite vaulting on slender piers make an impressive effect both as space arrangements and as linear patterns. They are examples of a type of effect, of which the eastern extension of the churches at Abbey Dore (Plate 88) and Southwark are others, which can best be described as the fragmentation of space, the main area being broken up by the columns, and this subdivision being expressed in terms of volume by the sharply pointed vaults. The use of the ribbed vault to produce this type of effect is characteristic of the late twelfth and first half of the thirteenth century, and can be found appearing with many variations, as in the chapels at Chichester and at the west end of Lincoln, the sacristy (now called the chapter-house) at Llandaff, and in a very original form in the porch added to the south transept at Lincoln where the breaking up and complicating of the spaces is achieved by the addition of shallow vaulted bays on each side of the main vessel of the porch and the use of a combination of quadripartite and sexpartite vaulting (Plate 106; Figure 46). A comparison of these thirteenth-century effects with their steeply pointed vaultings, and such earlier examples as the chapter-house at Buildwas, where the rhythm of the vault pattern is much broader and shallower, is instructive as showing how the more developed type of vaulting enabled a more lively and stimulating effect to be obtained.

Architecturally the most interesting form of chapter-house is the polygonal: this is a peculiarly English development, and there are some thirty known examples in Great Britain ranging in date from the twelfth to the fifteenth centuries, and varying in size from 59 and 58 feet diameter at Lincoln and Westminster, to 18 feet at Manchester. The earliest example is at Worcester which is a circular building of 56 feet in diameter:

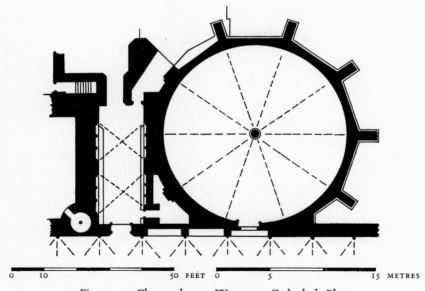

0   10   50 FEET   0   5   15 METRES

Figure 35. Chapter-house, Worcester Cathedral: Plan

it is vaulted to a central column with groined vaults in the bays divided by radial arches (Plate 58A; Figure 35). The vaults have been altered towards the perimeter to accommodate the enlarged windows made in the fifteenth century. The internal walls are divided into four zones: first a bench, above which is a series of shallow round-headed niches, next a zone of elaborate intersecting arcading, and finally the zone of the windows. The two upper zones are divided into ten bays by the responds of the arches from

61

the central column and the springing of the vaults. The masonry of the lower zones and of the responds is carried out in polychrome bands of green and white stone. The building appears to date from the first half of the twelfth century. The question naturally arises as to the source of this novel design, but we can do little more than speculate. Structurally the vaulting to a central column is a development of the vaulting of the crypt of the great church of Worcester, which was completed, as far as the relevant parts are concerned, by 1092, when St Wulfstan held a Synod in it. It is tempting to see in the prestige of St Wulfstan and of this Synod a possible impulse to designing chapter-houses by doubling the apse form of the place where the Saint had held his famous meeting. The Worcester chapter-house [8] opens directly off the east cloister walk without the need of any vestibule, as the dormitory there is placed most unusually on the west side of the cloister.

Two other chapter-houses belonging to Cistercian houses in the west country are most probably derived from Worcester, Abbey Dore and Margam. Both of these date from the late twelfth century or first years of the thirteenth, and both are polygons of twelve sides, Abbey Dore having a diameter of 45 feet and Margam of 49 feet. We know only the plan of the Abbey Dore chapter-house, but considerable remains exist at Margam which, together with its vestibule, show the distinctive signs of the western school of design discussed above. It had a ribbed vault which is on record in a late eighteenth-century engraving, and one rather broad lancet window in each bay, but otherwise it showed the rather prim Cistercian elegance. The many-sided polygon form was used again at Lincoln about 1220, where it is preceded by a fine vestibule of unusual form.

The Lincoln chapter-house is the earliest example we have of a great polygonal chapter-house built for a community of secular canons (Plate 58B). As such it is the first of a splendid series which includes such examples as Salisbury, York, and Wells. These chapter-houses attached to canons' churches were conceived on a scale and of a magnificence that only the very greatest monasteries could approach, and were, of course, unhampered by any strict tradition as to position such as we have discussed above. This led to great variety in the treatment of the approaches to the chapter-house proper, and though at Wells, Beverley, Lichfield, York, and Southwell they are all placed, as at Lincoln, to the north of the eastern limb of the great church, the approach to each of them is managed differently. At Lincoln the chapter-house is preceded by an unusually ambitious vestibule rising to the full height of the building, and opening on to it direct without any effect of a door. The result is to incorporate the space of the vestibule with that of the polygon with some loss of dramatic contrast, but a fine sense of great spaciousness. The whole interior is characterized by a free use of Purbeck shafting and the typically Lincoln acutely pointed arcading. The vestibule is covered in two sexpartite bays of vaulting, the vault of the polygon being rather more complex, and with its intermediate ribs and ridge ribs relating more to the nave and later vaults of the great church.

After Lincoln the more important chapter-houses were generally octagonal in plan, though the polygon with more than eight sides was used in some instances into the fourteenth century, for example at Hexham and Evesham. The reason for this preference for the octagon, apart from the effect of the prestige of the Westminster builders, is to be sought in the scope which it offered for the extended use of the great tracery windows which had captured the imagination of designers in the middle of the century, and as such belongs to a later phase of Gothic art than that under discussion here. One interesting instance remains of an octagonal scheme which in its inception dates from early in the thirteenth century. At Wells the undercroft of the chapter-house dates from the earlier building campaign, and can hardly be later than 1220. The building was, however, left unfinished and the original scheme of the chapter-house and its approaches occasioned one of the most important and successful works of English late thirteenth- and early fourteenth-century design. At Beverley, an octagonal chapter-house was built about 1230 on a comparatively modest scale, measuring 31 feet internal diameter. The building itself has perished and its character is only known from the excavation of its foundations. These show that it almost certainly was vaulted without a central column, as that found in the centre of the undercroft was too slight to support anything but its immediate load. The building was approached by an ingenious and effective arcaded double staircase (Plate 59) from the north aisle of the choir, a memorable example of the virtuosity of the thirteenth-century builders and of that curious attitude to the arch mouldings, whereby they were treated quite freely as lines to be drawn out or distorted at will without regard to the structural form of the arch. Other striking examples of this treatment of mouldings are to be found in the eastern lancets of the choir of Salisbury and Ely and on the east windows of Wimborne Minster.

This discussion of the chapter-house and the remarkable development it attained at the hands of the secular canons has outrun the treatment of monastic buildings proper. Of these the refectory and infirmary buildings are the only ones that can usefully be discussed as types. There are a number of specialized buildings to be found in the great monastic complexes which have a special interest as showing the aims and methods of twelfth-century building applied to a variety of purposes: such are the treasury, the lavatory tower, and the great covered staircase leading to part of the guest-house accommodation at Canterbury. There are also a number of gatehouses, of which the Bury St Edmunds gate is the most complete example of an ambitious design for this purpose remaining from the twelfth century (Plate 56). Gloucester, Bristol, and Peterborough all have fine examples of the vaulted passage-way of their gates, but none of these is as unaltered as the Bury gate. The monastic gatehouse was a feature with a remarkable future in the later Middle Ages, when the accommodation above the gateway was exploited for a variety of purposes – administrative offices for instance at Ely, or more purely domestic purposes at Thornton in Lincolnshire: in some instances a chapel was placed in this position.

The earliest infirmary buildings of which we have substantial remains, at Canterbury, Westminster, and Ely, were all in the form of long aisled halls lit either by windows in the aisles only, or by a clerestory, or by both. The halls themselves formed the 'wards' and were generally orientated so that the infirmary chapel projected to the east as if it were the chancel of a church. The scale of these buildings was very considerable; at Canterbury the total length including the chapel is 240 feet, and at Fountains, where the main infirmary building runs north and south and the chapel in consequence projects from one of the long sides, the hall is 170 by 70 feet.[9] At Westminster the infirmary chapel is known to us from considerable fragments: it was clearly a building some 75 feet long, dating from about 1160, and consisting of a nave of five bays supported on alternate round and octagonal piers and richly decorated; a small chancel projected to the east. The form and dimensions of the hall itself are matters of dispute, thanks to the later medieval arrangements of what is now the 'Little Cloister'. The Ely infirmary, of about the same date as Westminster, though less elaborate in detail, has left more appreciable remains (Figure 36). One of the best surviving buildings of this type from which an impression of the internal effect can be gained is the hospital-type building outside the great gate at Ramsey Abbey in Huntingdonshire. It is now used as a parish church, and is 44 feet wide and about 113 feet long including a square-vaulted chancel; it has notably

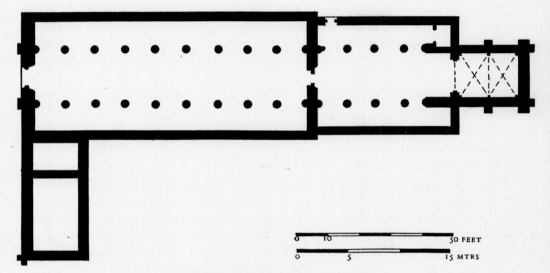

Figure 36. Infirmary, Ely Cathedral: Plan

elegant capitals to its pointed arcade of about 1180. Originally the chancel appears to have been flanked by chambers to the north and south which may have been extra chapels. It is possible that the transformation of this building to a parish church was made as early as the fourteenth century.

The refectories of the great monasteries present specially interesting problems. They were often of great size and splendour as at Fountains (110 by 47 feet), Rievaulx (124 by 38 feet), and Byland (100 by 31 feet). Peterborough, a typical Benedictine example remodelled in the mid thirteenth century, was 145 by 37 feet 8 inches, and Westminster 130 by 37 feet. In general the Cistercian refectories stand with their gable ends to the cloister walk opposite the church, that is lying north and south, whereas the Benedictine refectories lay east and west, parallel to the church along the side of the cloister. The elements from which these great buildings derived their character were primarily the management of the roof, the positions and character of the windows and the presence of an elaborate pulpit, contrived as part of the structure, from which the readings were given during meals. Only two great refectories survive roofed and well enough preserved in detail to allow one to appreciate something of the internal effect; these are at Chester, and Beaulieu in Hampshire, and both are of the mid thirteenth century. Beaulieu (Plate 60A) is now a parish church, and Chester (90 by 54 feet) (Plate 60B) is used as an auxiliary hall attached to the Cathedral. Both have preserved their pulpits, splendidly enriched works approached by arcaded staircases in the thickness of the walls, the Beaulieu stair, the earlier of the two, having Purbeck marble shafts. The Beaulieu pulpit, which is more spacious than the one at Chester, consists of a projecting portion corbelled out into the hall, and behind this a rib-vaulted recess is lit by a traceried window. At Chester the pulpit consists only of the depth of the approach stair and a modest corbelled projection surmounted by a prettily contrived canopy.[10] Apart from the pulpit features, the character of these interiors depends on their windows. Both Beaulieu and Chester have fine groups of shafted lancets at the daïs end, but the most striking of all refectory windows are at Rievaulx: there the great lancets of the northern school make a monumental effect both inside and out, particularly the latter, as, owing to the fall in the ground, the refectory appears from the south raised upon its undercroft, and the lancets and buttresses combine to give a magnificent vertical composition comparable with the east end of Tynemouth Abbey Church which is of about the same date. At Westminster and Peterborough the refectories were enriched with wall arcading below the level of the windows, which, by reason of the traditional position parallel with the cloister walk, had to be kept high. At Westminster, where the remains date from the late eleventh century, the wall arcading is carried out in alternate voussoirs of yellow and white stone.

Historically the most interesting aspect of this type of building is the question of the roofs. Fountains, the widest example that we know, was provided with a central arcade dividing the hall into two broad aisles. This is very rare in England but common enough in France, where examples such as the thirteenth-century Salle des États in the château of Blois, and later the great halls in the Palais des Papes at Avignon, may be cited apart from monastic examples.[11] The use of this system at Fountains is surely a further example of the strength of French influence on the second Cistercian building period of the later twelfth century. That this influence was enduring in only a limited number of aspects is suggested by the great refectory at Rievaulx, which also belongs to the twelfth century though to the very end of it. There the width of 38 feet was covered in a single span in timber, and this seems to have been the normal treatment. It may be that internal supports in wood were employed in some instances, but we have no evidence of them. The Peterborough plan suggests that the arrangement of the refectory there was with two tables running lengthwise and one, the High Table, across the end: if this were usual it would almost rule out the three-aisled arrangement in timber or stone that seems to be the earliest form of the large domestic hall. The problem of these great refectory roofs is one that needs further study, for it may well be that among them are to be found the precursors of the great halls of the fourteenth century with their wide-span timber roofs.[12]

The State apartments of the great houses of the twelfth and early thirteenth centuries, palaces and castles, are the aspect of domestic and military architecture which primarily concerns this book. Apart from the rooms in the White Tower in the Tower of London (Figure 37), almost the earliest of these is Westminster Hall,[13] which was begun and probably completed before the beginning of the twelfth century. This building, which was of the same internal dimensions as at present – that is, 237½ by 67½ feet – was built with three aisles in twelve bays (Figure 38). We do not know whether the internal supports were in wood or stone, most likely the latter, but enough has survived, built into the fourteenth-century reconstructions of the long walls, to enable us to know their original

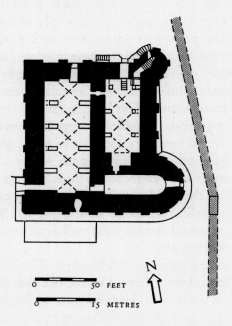

Figure 37. White Tower, Tower of London: Plan

treatment. There was a wall passage at a height of some 25 feet above floor level, arcaded internally in a rhythm of two small arches divided by one tall stilted arch opposite the windows, the stilted arches being some 15 feet high. It was a scheme very like the clerestory of the transept of Winchester Cathedral of the 1080s and also appears in the clerestory of St Étienne at Caen. The other halls of the eleventh century of which we have remains are all parts of large castles, as Chepstow, Richmond, and possibly Corfe, and have not retained any very remarkable characteristic qualities except that, unlike Westminster, they are all raised on undercrofts, and compare in this way with the well-known illustration of Harold's Hall at Bosham in the Bayeux Tapestry.

Of the surviving aisled halls of the twelfth century the most splendid is Oakham (Plate 61). A late example and perhaps the most interesting, though very much damaged and obscured by later alterations, is the timber hall of the Bishop's Palace at Hereford; it is 49 feet wide, the aisles being 10 feet wide and the central vessel 23½ feet.[14] There were three or probably five bays, of which the central one is 22 feet in the clear. The whole work is in wood. The details, wooden scalloped capitals and arches enriched with dog-tooth, are very rare examples of the handling of large-scale timber-work in the late twelfth century, and may be compared with the early thirteenth-century frames of the great west doors at Peterborough Cathedral. It is clear that this is the survival of a large class of buildings of which the halls at Hertford and Havering Castles, as known to us from sixteenth-century survey plans, may be mentioned. The Oakham hall is a stone-built structure of about 65 by 43 feet, built in four bays and carried out in the most sumptuous late Romanesque just becoming Gothic: it has very notable capitals and other sculptured

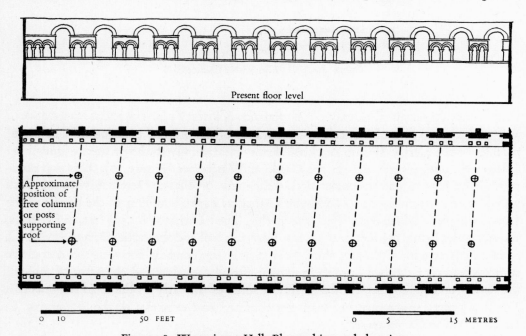

Figure 38. Westminster Hall: Plan and internal elevation

enrichments. At each end of the building the round arches spring from corbels instead of responds, presumably to increase the space for serving both at the screens end and behind the High Table. The aisles are only 7 feet wide in the clear, and were presumably also intended mainly for communication and service. There is no clerestory, light being derived from a two-light window in the east wall at the service end of the building, and from four two-light windows in each aisle wall. These windows are extremely elaborate, pointed externally and round inside, having richly carved capitals to their outside shafts as well as much dog-tooth enrichment and carved foliage in their tympana.

Bishop Pudsey's Hall at Bishop Auckland, though less richly decorated, is rather larger than Oakham and of about the same date (last quarter of the twelfth century). Alterations later in the Middle Ages, and above all the transformation of this hall into a chapel by Bishop Cosin after the Restoration, by enlarging the windows and providing a clerestory, have so altered the character of this building both inside and out that the fine arcade

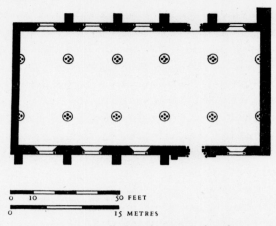

0   10   50 FEET

0   15 METRES

Figure 39. Hall, Winchester Castle: Plan

with its marble piers is effectively all that remains of Pudsey's Hall: but this is a great deal, and gives a good idea of the scale and splendour of the original conception. The use of marble for the piers at Bishop Auckland leads one naturally to the greatest of surviving aisled halls, undoubtedly that in the Castle at Winchester (Figure 39). This was completed[15] by 1235-6, and the association of the name of Elias de Dereham with the work reinforces the resemblance to Salisbury Cathedral in the handling of the details of the arcade and piers, which are of Purbeck marble. The hall is 111¼ by 55¾ feet, in five bays, the side aisles being 17½ feet in the clear. Both this hall and the earlier Bishop Auckland, in comparison with Oakham, show very clearly the contrast between the decorative sumptuousness of the late Romanesque taste, for all the advanced character of some of the details, and the sophisticated restraint of some of the early Gothic, and suggests that this is a general movement of taste not confined to the circles of the 'Religious' in the technical medieval sense.

If Bishop Pudsey's Hall at Bishop Auckland shows signs of the elegant simplicity that has been noticed in other buildings of the late twelfth century in the north, his earlier buildings at Durham Castle are in the most ornate Romanesque manner. These cons st of a great hall raised on an undercroft partly formed of the earlier (eleventh-century) chapel, and on a second floor above the great hall another large apartment known as the Constables' Hall. Both these halls have been so divided up into a variety of rooms that their effect as spaces is completely lost. The splendid door of the lower hall survives (Plates 62B and 63A), however, and the arcaded wall and window treatment of the Constables' Hall (Plate 62A). These Durham halls are very grandiose representatives of the type of state apartment built in the great castles, of which King John's fine hall and chapel block at Corfe is a slightly smaller but exquisitely finished example.[16] Both hall and chapel are raised on an undercroft, and from their details of leaf-carving and the uninterrupted roll-mouldings round their doors are closely related to the Wells Cathedral work of the very first years of the thirteenth century. The windows of this hall with their window-seats and signs of some form of early tracery are also of exceptional

interest. A later phase of Wells thirteenth-century work applied to grand 'domestic' purposes is in the earlier part of the Bishop's Palace [17] at Wells itself, which may be dated
1220–30. This, perhaps the finest piece of thirteenth-century domestic architecture still
extant in England, is a most surprising design; for the main block (97 by 45 feet) was
built two rooms thick (Figure 40). The ground floor is occupied by a vaulted undercroft,
running approximately north and south, and separated from the central and eastern bays
by a party wall the whole length of the building, and the vault-ribs spring from corbels
in this wall. These western bays, which now form a long vaulted passage, were originally divided into two, the northern part apparently forming the original entrance. To
the east of the party wall is the undercroft of the hall and solar, ten bays divided by four
columns, and four bays vaulted to a central column respectively and divided by a cross
wall at the second bay from the north. The main state apartments on the first floor
correspond to these subdivisions of the undercroft. The hall is to the south and is 68 by
28 feet internal measurement, and the solar some 28 feet square at the north end, having
a garderobe tower opening off to the east. The hall is lit by a series of fine traceried windows on the east side, and a pair of similar but rather more elaborate windows surmounted by a quatrefoil window to the south. The solar has a similar group on its north
wall, but is even more richly treated as to the rear-arches and jamb-shafts. Above the
western undercroft bays is an upper gallery running the entire length of the two main
apartments, lit by seven good two-light windows in its western wall and one in the
south wall. It is believed that this upper gallery was subdivided into rooms, as its undercroft certainly was, but the original arrangement is lost. There seems no parallel to this

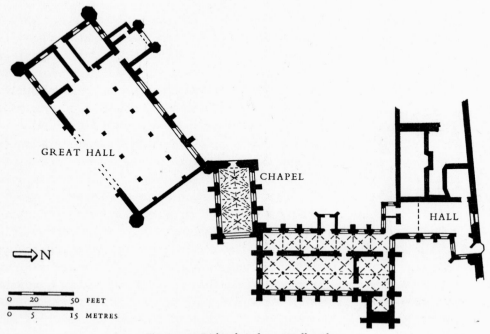

GREAT HALL

CHAPEL

HALL

⇒N

0   20   50 FEET

0   5   15 METRES

Figure 40. Bishop's Palace, Wells: Plan

very interesting scheme, which, contrary to all
usage, involved having the whole of one long side of
the hall without windows.

Apart from the aisled halls and the other state
apartments built as parts of castle *ensembles*, there is
one other category of palatial accommodation of
the twelfth century which includes some of the
finest surviving examples, the apartments in the
great tower keeps. The exigencies of the defensive
character of the tower keeps give these rooms a
special character, but in spite of this a better idea of
the effect of the dignity and splendour required of
the living accommodation of a great twelfth-century
household can be obtained from Castle Hedingham
in Essex, or Newcastle-on-Tyne, than anywhere else
(Figures 41 and 42).

The earliest of the great stone keeps, the White
Tower in the Tower of London, and at Colchester,

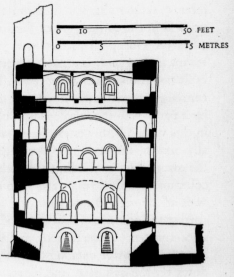

Figure 41. Castle Hedingham Keep:
Section

were certainly intended as residences as well as military works, and the chapel in the
White Tower is a building of notable architectural quality. It is aisled, and the aisles
are returned round an apse. There is a tribune, duplicating the aisles in an upper
storey, but no clerestory, and the building is covered with a barrel vault and a
semi-dome over the apse. The rest of the internal space on each floor of the keep is
divided into two unequal rooms by a longitudinal wall. The smaller rooms on each
floor do not seem to have been inner chambers, but rather ante-rooms to the great hall-
spaces alongside them, for the main staircase leads directly into the smaller room. The
London and Colchester arrangements are similar, and distinguished by the exceptional
amount of space devoted to the chapel, as well as by their size, the London chapel being
60 by 35 feet and the larger living-space 95 by 40 feet. Elsewhere in the later examples,

such as Rochester (before 1140) and the still later works
at Dover and Newcastle, the chapels are on a much more
intimate scale, though very richly executed with elaborately moulded vault ribs, decorated capitals, wall arcading, and so forth. These smaller chapels are generally
contrived in the 'fore-buildings', annexes projecting
from one face of the keep and providing, in addition to
the chapel spaces, for an elaborate covered entrance
stairway. The most splendid of these stairways is at Castle
Rising in Norfolk (Figure 43), where there is a small
vaulted room at the top of the stairs corresponding to
the chapels elsewhere. It is not certain whether this room
was intended as a chapel, as we have evidence of a detached chapel building in the courtyard of the castle.

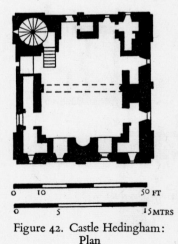

Figure 42. Castle Hedingham:
Plan

The system whereby the living-space on each floor of the stone keep was divided into two by a longitudinal wall persists in the larger examples of the twelfth century, of which Rochester and Castle Rising, Norfolk, are among the finest. The purpose was presumably to economize timber for floor-joists. At Rochester the main apartments were divided by an arcade, thus providing a single great hall divided into two equal parts by an arcade down the middle. This is a form of state apartment which is unusual in England, though common enough in France as late as the thirteenth and fourteenth centuries. An English example in a non-military building is the refectory of Rievaulx mentioned above. The great apartment at Rochester occupies two storeys of the keep, and is surrounded by a clerestory gallery above the main windows at floor level. The splendid apartment in the keep at Hedingham is treated as one space (Plate 63B), the difficulty of providing for economy of timber in the floor-joists of the storey above being solved by a single great moulded arch which spans the whole internal width of the keep. This great hall also occupies the space of two floors and has a gallery in the upper part of the walls. The rear-arches of the lower window embrasures have angle-shafts and two orders of chevron enrichment, and there are bold shafts and roll mouldings to the arches of the upper gallery.

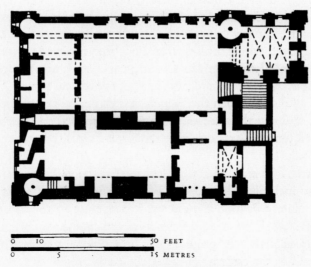

Figure 43. Castle Rising Keep: Plan

CHAPTER 5

EARLY GOTHIC

IT seems almost artificially appropriate that the building to which the origins of the English Gothic style of the thirteenth century are by general agreement to be traced should be the Metropolitan Cathedral of Christchurch, Canterbury.[1] The eastern parts of that church were rebuilt in the years 1174–85 after a fire. It is also extremely fortunate that, of all building enterprises of the twelfth century in Europe, this one should have the fullest and most trustworthy documentation. Gervase's account of the building is not only that of a contemporary member of the monastic community, but also is quite exceptional in the straightforward and business-like character of its narrative of the progress of the work from year to year. The fire occurred in the afternoon of 5 September 1174, and damaged everything to the east of the central tower. The ensuing twelve months were devoted to preparations for the rebuilding and to pulling down those parts of the old work which on the advice of the master mason, William of Sens, it was considered impossible to preserve. These included the arcades of the choir and all that they supported, and left only the crypt, the lower parts of the aisle walls, the eastern transepts and the two chapels of the chevet, which took the form of three-storeyed towers set tangentially to the curve of the ambulatory. In the second year a start was made with the actual building, beginning at the western end over against the central tower (Plate 64A). Work continued steadily until 1178 when the French master mason fell off the scaffolding and was badly injured, and shortly afterwards he was compelled to return to France. The work was continued for the next five years under an English master mason also named William.

Before his accident William of Sens had completed the work of the choir itself with the vaults up to and including the crossing of the eastern transepts. He had also carried on the work immediately beyond the eastern transepts up to the top of the triforium. There is every reason to believe that the further eastern extension, comprising the Trinity Chapel and the Corona, had been projected by him. The new master mason's work included the outer bays of the eastern transepts, the clerestory of the easternmost parts of the choir (the presbytery), and all the Trinity Chapel and the Corona, which is a circular chapel at the extreme end of the church (Figure 44). Much of his work was conditioned by what his predecessor had already built, and very probably by the accumulation of cut stone and moulded work and other details prepared in advance. In consequence there is no very marked change in style from the French master's work to the Englishman's.

It is often claimed that the eastern parts of Canterbury Cathedral represent an example of Metropolitan French Gothic which takes its place in the general picture of the development of that school in an orderly and natural way (Plates 64B and 65A). This is true of certain aspects of the design and certain details, notably the capitals (Plates 65B and 66), but there are two very important points which deserve further consideration; these are

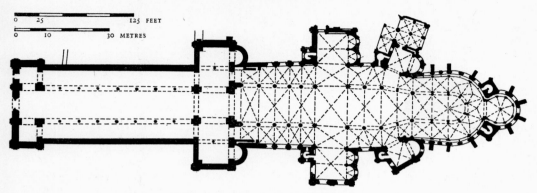

Figure 44. Canterbury Cathedral: Plan

the use of Purbeck marble shafting, and the treatment of the clerestory with all that it implies for the general constructional system of the building. It has been suggested by Monsieur Bony that the use of marble shafting probably derives from the great church at Valenciennes, now destroyed, where Tournai marble is believed to have been used, and there may well have been other precedents in north-eastern France and the Low Countries.[2] Certainly it is not a characteristic of Île-de-France architecture of that time or any other. Whatever the source of this idea, the example set at Canterbury led to an exploitation of marble for strings, and especially for shafting, that was taken up and developed in England on a scale for which there is no continental parallel.[3]

It is difficult to lay too much stress on this use of marble in the Canterbury interiors. Other imported features of the design, such as the French treatment of the capitals and the sexpartite vaults, had a comparatively restricted future in England, but the use of contrasting marble shafting against a light background, appealing as it did to the native desire for a strongly marked linear pattern, enjoyed an immediate and enduring success (Plate 64). Before Canterbury the only known English example of the use of marble shafting, and that not a very significant one, is in the responds of the chancel arch at Iffley near Oxford; after Canterbury it was taken up at Chichester, at the Temple Church, and then on a splendid scale at Lincoln: thereafter it spread far and wide, and in the great churches of the thirteenth century became almost the most characteristic feature of the Early English style. The parts of the Canterbury design where the use of marble seems most clearly to foreshadow later developments are the eastern transepts. It is tempting to see an Anglo-Norman tradition in these, which were most probably built by the English mason, but the special circumstances of this work should be borne in mind, and how far the interior effect of the eastern transepts is due to the preferences of their author and how far to the fact that his job was to clothe an earlier structure in a way that would fit the design of the new choir, it would be hard to decide.

One of the most curious aspects of the late twelfth-century work at Canterbury is the management of the clerestory and the whole system of buttressing (Figure 45). The system is essentially that of the thick upper wall that we have discussed as one of the most characteristic devices of the Anglo-Norman school, which, as Monsieur Bony has pointed out, was already disappearing in Normandy itself in favour of the Île-de-France system of external buttresses, including flyers. At Canterbury the thickening of the upper walls involved an oversailing by the upper structure of the aisle vaults, both above each main pier of the arcade and above the outer responds of the transverse arches of the aisle vaults.[4] These transverse arches are thus heavily loaded by buttress masses on their haunches, and these buttress masses are linked by arches across the space within the aisle roofs, like those at Durham and intended at Norwich. In addition there are at Canterbury rudimentary flyers above these transverse arches, though from their form they must be of limited value as abutments. The concomitant of the heavy upper wall system is the arcaded clerestory gallery: at Canterbury this exists in fully developed form in the western bays of the choir, that is the part built by William of Sens and throughout the eastern transepts and the parts built by his successor, except in those parts where the bays are not wide enough to allow of it. The total effect is of a building essentially different from any extant contemporary work in northern France in spite of many and important French traits, not only in matters of detail but even in vaulting technique.

It may be suggested that though a French mason of 1175 might not naturally build in the Canterbury manner if he had a free choice and was building a town church on a free site, when he was remodelling a great Benedictine abbey church of strong traditional sanctity, he was not hampered in his choice of means by an overwhelming prejudice in favour of any structural system; and French Gothic of the late twelfth century probably seems to us much more consciously consistent and exclusive than it did to the masters who were developing it. This suggestion is perhaps reinforced by consideration of the interior treatment of the late twelfth-century parts of the church as a whole. There is a marked tendency to differentiate parts of the building from each other so that the whole eastern extension, while having a unity of decorative manner, gives the effect of a series of related spaces divided according to their function: the monks' choir, extending from the western crossing to the eastern, is designed with an alternating system of round and octagonal piers that gives it a unity in itself, as compared with the more varied piers of the presbytery and the coupled columns of the Trinity Chapel to the east. This is surely a reflection of the differentiation of the various parts of a great monastic church according to their functions, as compared with the emphasis on spatial unity that already seems to be the object of the French builders in their great town churches. This additive system of spaces, whatever its origin, was to remain a feature of English church design for generations to come, showing itself generally in the importance given to the transepts as compared with French usage. The parts of Canterbury where the detail treatment seems to point forward most clearly, particularly to Lincoln, are the eastern transepts. Partly no doubt because there were more storeys to be accounted for – the original number of the earlier church and the new clerestory added – there is an effect of a complicated pattern of arcading over the interior surfaces of these transepts far more strongly marked than in the main vessel of the choir. It is possible to attach too much importance to this as the work of the native mason, but at least it can be said that it would have been possible to minimize this effect had there been the desire; but the builders showed no such inclination.

The buildings immediately deriving from Canterbury are Chichester and Lincoln. Chichester (Plate 67) was very seriously damaged by fire in 1186, and the reconstruction most likely began within about a year after the disaster. This makes it very nearly contemporary with the new Lincoln of 1192. It seems reasonable to assume that the eastern arm of the church, including the two eastern bays which form the end of the presbytery and the ambulatory, was begun at once. There was a consecration in 1199 which, vague as these dates are and often misleading, may be held to imply that by that date the remodelled eastern arm was ready for use. In the main the Chichester work consists of an embellishment of the Anglo-Norman structure with Purbeck marble shaftings and strings, and the rebuilding of the clerestory. The whole church was eventually vaulted, and in the eastern arm this work may belong to the end of the twelfth or very beginning of the thirteenth century. The completely new work of this period at Chichester consists of an eastern extension of two bays, providing an ambulatory and giving access to the Lady Chapel which had already been built before the fire and alterations. The aisles were extended so as to overlap the western end of the Lady Chapel,

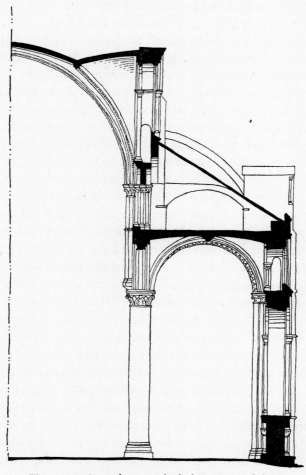

Figure 45. Canterbury Cathedral: Section of choir

forming two small eastern chapels. In general proportions this new work corresponds with the old, and in the arcade and triforium storeys the main arches are round. The subordinate arches of the triforium and the clerestory are, however, pointed. The most remarkable features of the work are the arcade piers, with their free standing marble shafts and their very French treatment of the capitals, varying in depth according to the diameter of the pier and shafts. The eastern end is treated with a single arch opening to the Lady Chapel, and two round arches in the triforium divided into pointed sub-arches through which can be seen a wall arcade the spacing of which alternates with the sub-arches and further complicates the effect. Above, the gable is filled with three tall graduated lancets. The use of decorative sculpture in the triforium at Chichester, especially figures, seems very precocious, and if genuinely of so early a date would foreshadow such developments as those at Worcester. Some of this figure sculpture at Chichester, however, seems to have been added to this part of the church at the Translation of St Richard in 1276.

The new work on the cathedral of Lincoln was begun in 1192.[5] The arrangement of the choir and presbytery as then begun has been partly obliterated by the great eastward extension undertaken shortly after 1255. There remain, however, two eastern transepts and three of the four bays of the choir itself west of the eastern crossing; traces of the plan of the early east end were found by excavation in the nineteenth century (Figure 46). The westernmost bay of the choir was rebuilt after being damaged by the fall of the central tower in 1237–9. The original layout, as far as it can be reconstructed, consisted of a chevet with an ambulatory of a curious three-sided form. This ambulatory gave access to a polygonal chapel on the axis of the church and there were two round chapels on each side. Between these side chapels and the axial chapel were two round spaces, rather too small to be chapels and rather too large to be staircase turrets.

The interpretation of this plan is full of difficulty, for in addition to the unusual features already mentioned it is hard to see how the eastern opening into the ambulatory was contrived, as there is not height enough to take so wide an arch in view of the known proportions of the interior as shown in the surviving parts. A single wide arch, as at Chichester, may have been the solution, and the eastern part of the tribune may have been stepped up to take it, as at Pershore, but this would have had to be done on a very large scale. It has often been pointed out that the eastern transepts at Lincoln are presumably derived from those at Canterbury, and it may be that in the arrangement of the original east end the polygonal chapel reflects the corona. In the handling of the detail there are also many reminiscences of Canterbury, as for instance the depth of the capitals as proportioned to the diameter of the shafts and piers such as we have noted at Chichester, the scheme of the triforium and clerestory, and indeed the whole constructional system, and the quinquepartite vaulting of the aisles which is found in the compartment of the aisle just east of the south-east transept at Canterbury. The sexpartite vaults at Lincoln which are used in the eastern transepts and in the great transept (probably shortly after 1205) form another link with Canterbury, but the problem of the Lincoln vaults is a difficult one and their chronology has been much disputed. Some authorities are inclined to believe that the whole of the vaulting of the central vessel of the choir as far east as the eastern crossing was renewed after the tower disaster in 1237–9, but this seems extremely unlikely. This choir vault is of a most unusual character. The bays, which include a narrow one (with sexpartite vaulting) just east of the central tower and a broad one over the eastern crossing, are of very varying dimensions (Plate 68A). The rib system may be described as consisting of a longitudinal ridge rib which is divided into three in each bay, instead of into two as would be the case with a normal quadripartite or sexpartite system. In addition to the transverse rib, three ribs spring from each side to the two points on the ridge rib, thus dividing the vault surface into eight severies, six small and two large ones.

This system seems to be unique and has caused much speculation as to its purpose, which seems to have been entirely one of effect. The sexpartite system of Canterbury, which is employed elsewhere in the early parts of Lincoln, meant that in the eastern limb there was perforce a change to a quadripartite system of vaulting at the eastern crossing, beyond which the sexpartite vaults were resumed, with a consequent interruption of the pattern made by the ribs, and larger unbroken vault surfaces in the crossing bay than in the others. The Lincoln choir vault seems intended to avoid this contrast and maintain the continuity of the vault pattern in length, at the same time avoiding the emphasis on the eastern crossing which a more orthodox treatment would have given.[6] If this be accepted it is a striking example of the preoccupation with the effect of the linear pattern made by the vault ribs, which indicates a point of view, if not radically different from that of the Île de France masters themselves, at any rate different from that of their modern expositors. This preoccupation with linear pattern is evident throughout the work at Lincoln to a far greater degree than at Canterbury. Resemblances between Lincoln and Canterbury are so clear and so far-reaching, including as they do both fundamentals of planning and structure and details of piers and capitals, that it is interesting to dwell on the differences. Lincoln is some fifteen years younger than Canterbury – half a generation – yet, except for the complete acceptance of the pointed arch – and it is a large exception – there is little sign of structural advance (Figure 47); indeed the structure of both churches is very similar, and even the much-debated little arches that appear above the clerestory string at Lincoln have their forebears at Canterbury.[7] Some of the differences are clearly the consequence of the Lincoln programme, which, unlike that of Canterbury, clearly envisaged a complete rebuilding, including the main transepts (Plate 68B) which are indeed almost the grandest feature of the church, whereas the eastern limb as originally built was some 100 feet shorter than the new work at Canterbury; but the real difference which makes the two buildings so utterly unlike each other is in the far more elaborate decorative character of Lincoln. The normal pier at Lincoln derives from the specially elaborate ones in the presbytery at Canterbury; the quinquepartite vaults which were devised for a special position at Canterbury are the normal aisle vaults of Lincoln; the wall arcading of Lincoln is in two planes, as though the twelfth-century type of intersecting arcading had taken on a third dimension (Plate 96). The tribune openings, though derived from Canterbury, have increased the number of their marble shafts, and the clerestory has exploited all the Anglo-Norman tricks of arcaded gallery in the interior (more modestly used at Canterbury) and blind arcading on the

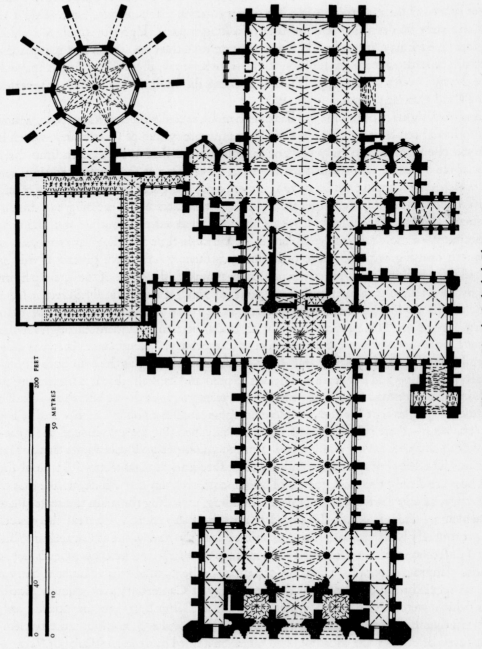

Figure 46. Lincoln Cathedral: Plan

exterior. The twelfth-century designers of Lincoln, for all their Canterbury mannerisms, had not forgotten their Anglo-Norman predecessors, and they produced a design whose festal quality foreshadows the Angel Choir which was to be added to it, and even the characteristics of the Lady Chapel at Ely.

Two other works of the end of the twelfth and beginning of the thirteenth century in south-east England deserve special description – Rochester [8] and Peterborough. The

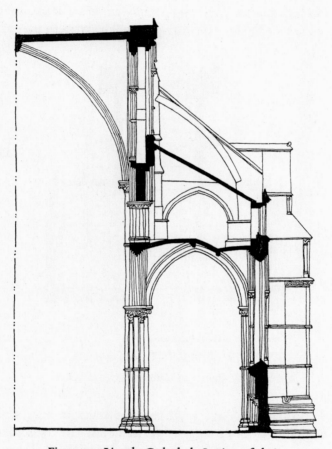

Figure 47. Lincoln Cathedral: Section of choir

eastern extension of the cathedral at Rochester was begun about 1200, and seems to have been completed by 1227 (Figure 48): the evidence for the earlier form of the eastern part of the church is ambiguous, though it is clear that some extension was built in the course of the twelfth century. The new work took the form of an aisleless presbytery of two sexpartite vaulted bays and to the west of them an eastern transept having aisles forming two chapels on each of its eastern sides; the choir of the church was aisled, but the central vessel was enclosed by solid walls in the manner already noticed as the original form at St Albans. The work is distinguished for the immense solidity of its construction. The eastern angles of the presbytery externally are buttressed by great rectangular masses of stone so large as to give the appearance of small towers (Plate 69). Similar buttressing masses containing stairs appear on the northern side of the eastern transept, and there are in addition heavy buttresses at the mid-points of the presbytery walls. Internally the presbytery is treated with a galleried clerestory surmounting four deep arched recesses in the lower parts of the north and south walls (Plate 70). The corresponding recesses in the east wall contain short broad lancets, which thus form a composition of two tiers of windows. The line of the vaulting shafts is carried down to the floor level: they are substantial shafts of Purbeck marble, logically grouped in threes at the division of the bays with similar single shafts at the intermediate points. The western part of the presbytery,

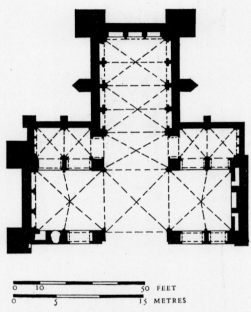

Figure 48. Rochester Cathedral, east end: Plan

which has arches opening north and south into the transept aisles, has a quadripartite vault, and there is another at the crossing of the transepts. The transepts themselves have irregular sexpartite vaults occasioned by the unequal spacing of the east and west bays. The whole effect is a curious mixture, having a solidity and massiveness of construction which is greater even than that of the earlier Romanesque parts of the church, while at the same time the sexpartite vaulting, which must surely derive from Canterbury, and the logic with which its lines are carried to the ground level, give it an extremely French appearance. The design is extremely effective and the proportions good, but no scholar has yet suggested any satisfactory explanation for the highly individual character of this work, which is typical of contemporary practice neither in England nor, as far as we know, anywhere on the continent.

Another exceptional work of this age is the western completion of the great church at Peterborough.[9] The early and mid twelfth-century church was to have been finished with two western towers which were in part erected, but in the course of the last quarter of the century these were pulled down and two further bays added to the nave, and a western transept, extending one bay to north and south, was begun. The arms of the transept are vaulted and there is evidence of the intention to vault the whole length of the nave. The abandonment of this has left us with the only early example of a wooden painted ceiling to a great Romanesque church that remains to us. The first phase of the work at the west end of the nave is distinguished by the continued use of diagonal tooling on the masonry, but this changes to vertical tooling in the west wall of the transept and in the great porch and towers to the west of it. The date of this change cannot be fixed with any certainty. Sir Charles Peers suggested a date in the 1190s which would be a good fifteen years before the time at which Dr Bilson considered the change from diagonal to vertical tooling took place at Wells. The highly individual character of the Peterborough western work (Plate 72) belongs to the second phase of the building, when it was decided to complete the church to the west with a great loggia or portico. In general conception the scheme was founded on the west work at Lincoln as it then existed, that is the eleventh-century design with its three great arched recesses, as they were left by Bishop Alexander's alterations, with the enrichment at the top and three gables to the westward and two return gables to the north and south.

The difference between Peterborough and Lincoln, however, resides in the fact that whereas at Lincoln the three great recesses correspond with the internal divisions of the nave of the church, at Peterborough the portico backs against a transept which rises to the full height of the church, and it was therefore decided to give the western loggia a character of its own as a self-sufficient design. This involves a curious discrepancy between the inside and the outside of the west wall of the transept. On the inside the wall is divided into bays corresponding with the main vessel of the nave, the aisles and tribunes, and the north and south transept bays themselves (Plate 71). On the outside these divisions have been completely ignored, and instead of the wall and the vault above it being divided into five bays it is divided into seven in such a way that they fall into three groups, of which the middle group is equal to one and a half of the side groups, or, in the words of Sir Charles Peers, 'The width of the middle bay plus that of the narrow bays on each side of it is three times that of each of the other four bays.' In order to achieve this spacing the two side doorways have had to be displaced inwards so that they are noticeably off-centre in the bay division of the interior face of the wall, a clear indication of the independent character of the design. This placing also governs the positions of the piers of the three great external arches of the portico which rise to the full height of the church (Plate 72). The internal wall of the portico and the two flanking towers are covered with an elaborate system of blind arcading, and are provided with brackets for figure sculptures. The great arches themselves are elaborately moulded and their piers shafted, while above them the upper part of the composition is extremely richly decorated. This top storey consists of three main gables each adorned with a rose window below which is an arcade partly blind and partly containing windows, the blind arches forming frames for figure sculptures. At the base of the gables is an enriched string course, and the spandrels of the great arches are decorated with figures standing before blind arcades, and large roundels containing heads. The shafts between the great arches rise up to the full height of the string, but the elaborate pinnacle-turrets above them are curiously displaced outwards, so as to compose in the skyline of the building with the two intended western towers which were to rise above the bays of the transept opposite the aisles of the church. Of these towers only the northern one was completed (Plate 73A). There is reason to believe that all four towers, the slender ones which flank the arches of the portico and now have late medieval stone spires, and the two transept towers, were intended originally to have wooden spires.[10]

There has been much speculation as to the intention of this design, occasioned by the offence given to a classically trained sense of architectural propriety by the fact that the centre arch of the portico is narrower than the two side arches. The design, by reason of its incompleteness, lacking the south transept tower which was not carried up high enough to tell in the external view, and by reason of the late fourteenth-century porch which was inserted in the middle arch and grievously interrupts its lines, is very difficult to judge, but it seems that the central feature of the composition was conceived in terms of void rather than solid, and that the line of the central arch was to be continued and broadened up into the space between the towers with their spires. The problem is complicated by the question of the use of 2:3 and 3:4 ratios in determining the spacing of the features of the composition. There is reason to believe that these, and similar simple arithmetical ratios, were applied throughout the design, and it is curious to note that these are the ratios which had a special prestige, descending through the *Timaeus* of Plato from Pythagoras and resting on the basis of the musical intervals. These ratios were extremely familiar to educated men in the age of the Peterborough west building through the *Boethius de Musica*, a work in the possession of almost every great ecclesiastical establishment.

*

The early development of Gothic in the north presents at first sight a simpler appearance than in other parts of the country. The Cistercian Order had attained a position of especial prestige and influence in the archdiocese of York, and the first signs of the new influence of north French Gothic are appropriately to be found at Roche Abbey, in south Yorkshire, and date from about 1170[11] (Plate 73B). At Kirkstall near Leeds, begun shortly after 1150, the Anglo-Norman building technique had advanced a long way towards Gothic, but there is a definite distinction between Roche and Kirkstall: the one is as clearly an importation as the other is an Anglo-Norman development of the ideas that the early Cistercians brought from Burgundy. At Roche there are vaulting shafts descending to the ground, piers with grouped shafts the centre one having a pointed section,[12] a triforium storey with two blind pointed arches, and a clerestory with a single round-headed lancet to each bay. There is no clerestory passage or arcaded gallery. Roche is a very early example of the exploitation of the middle storey in a Cistercian building; there is said to be no earlier surviving example in France, though it seems likely from the general character of the Roche work that some Cistercian prototypes may have existed in Picardy. In the work at Ripon, of *c.* 1179, and Byland, begun about

1175, the effect of this new French importation is clearly visible, but in both, the Anglo-Norman galleried clerestory has come back and the triforium arcading has been elaborated. The effect is to emphasize the general decorative effect at the expense of the distinct division into bays. At Ripon (Figure 50), where a group of five shafts is provided at arcade and triforium level, there is every evidence of a change of intention at the level of the clerestory string, where the shaftings of the arcaded gallery seem to correspond well enough with the grouped shafts for the intended vaulting in number but hardly in magnitude.[13] Though this return to the Anglo-Norman tradition of linear surface decoration at Byland and Ripon is in some degree a backsliding from the strict tradition of Cistercian asceticism in architecture, it is done with such restraint and almost fastidious grace that, in comparison with the massive primitive Puritanism of Rievaulx or the nave of Fountains, these churches seem to reflect a different aspect of the Cistercian movement, its humane and at times almost romantic quality. These buildings belong to the generation immediately after St Ailred, but there is often a natural time-lag

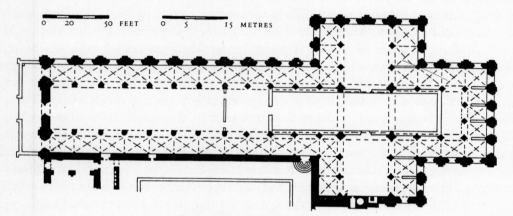

Figure 49. Byland Abbey: Plan

in the expression of such a mood in architecture. Ripon was a church of Canons and not a Cistercian monastery, but a comparison with the detail of the vestibule to the chapter-house of the Benedictines of St Mary's, York, only a little later in date, brings home to one the widely pervading influence of Cistercian example on other types of religious bodies. It would not be difficult to cite other examples in the north.

Roche and Byland are only the best preserved for our purposes of a group of great Cistercian churches of the last quarter of the twelfth century in the north, and with them must be reckoned Jervaulx, Furness, and, a little later, Dundrennan in south-west Scotland. All these buildings have strong family resemblances, though there are considerable variations, especially in planning. At Byland, a church of some 330 feet internal length (Figure 49). there are aisled transepts, and the aisles of the eastern limb are returned round the presbytery in the form of an ambulatory into which the presbytery opens by three arches. At Jervaulx, where the presbytery was also aisled, the arcades are carried to the extreme east end, giving a single great cliff-like façade, a motif that was to have a great future in the north. Considerable evidence was found at Byland of the internal decoration of the building, which seems to have been whitewashed and the walls lined with a masonry pattern in red. Fragments found during excavation by the Ministry of Works show that the carved foliage capitals, which are of extremely high quality, were also picked out in red.

Apart from the Cistercians, the late twelfth and early thirteenth century was a great building period in the north. Ripon choir, where the influence of Roche seems especially marked, was given a nave without aisles, 40 feet in span. The walls of this nave are designed in three zones: the lowest is plain ashlar, the middle zone contains an arcaded passage gallery, and there is a second gallery at the top at what corresponds to clerestory level. The two upper zones are divided into alternate broad and narrow bays by slender shafts. The broad bays consist of a wide round arch enclosing a graduated group of four pointed arches which are shafted. At the top of each broad bay is a round arched window flanked by two smaller pointed arches. The narrow bays have in the middle zone one tall pointed arch containing two sub-arches, and a group of three small pointed arches in the zone above. The neighbouring church of Nun Monkton clearly derives from this Ripon nave scheme (Plate 74A), and, to judge from the surviving parts, the two churches must have been remarkable and highly successful examples of the linear organization of such large wall spaces. The nave of Ripon was of course wooden-roofed, and the choir, which was certainly designed for vaulting as at Roche,[14] was finished off with a clerestory having an arcaded gallery passage divided into bays by single slender shafts, which seems to indicate a change of intention from stone vaulting to a wooden covering in that part of the church also. There seems little difference in the handling of detail in the work of this clerestory from that immediately below it, and hardly any long interval in the actual building is implied. Ripon's nave and Nun Monkton had, as far as we know, no imitators, and the later unaisled choir of Coldingham, which was only some 25 feet in breadth, though attempting to solve a somewhat analogous problem in design, seems to link with other buildings such as Kelso.

In the last years of the twelfth and first years of the thirteenth century a series of notable buildings were carried out in Scotland and the English Border country. These include St Andrews Cathedral and Arbroath[15] Abbey Church, Lanercost, Hexham, and parts of Jedburgh and Tynemouth.[16] St Andrews Cathedral and Arbroath are both buildings of great size: the former was at its original laying out 392 feet from east to west, including a nave of fourteen bays as compared with twelve bays at Byland, eleven at Fountains, and nine at Rievaulx; Arbroath, which measures about 280 feet internally, has nine bays to its nave. Both churches have aisled choirs with the central vessel projecting to the east beyond the aisles to form a presbytery. This is a scheme which is also found at Jedburgh, Tynemouth, and Lanercost. Attempts have been made to associate this plan with the Austin Canons, but it seems improbable that any one type of plan can be strictly associated with that Order except in a local or regional way by dint of imitation and example. Of the churches mentioned above, St Andrews, Jedburgh, and Lanercost were Augustinian Houses, Arbroath was of the Order of Tiron, and Tynemouth, a dependency of St Albans, Benedictine. It is possible that this treatment of the east end

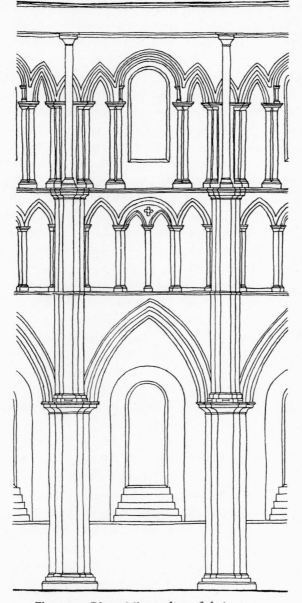

Figure 50. Ripon Minster, bay of choir

was a compromise between the aisled choir and the earlier Cistercian type of Kirkstall, Roche, Dundrennan, etc., and was adopted by Orders which were influenced – and not only in an architectural sense – by Cistercian example; but no satisfactory explanation of the source and popularity of this type of plan has been worked out, though, as we have seen, Southwell was possibly the earliest example.

Arbroath (Plate 74B) was founded by William the Lion, King of Scotland, shortly after 1176, and he was buried there in 1214. Some part of the building was dedicated as early as 1178, but it would be rash to assign any part of the existing church to so early a date. The remains of the great church consist of the east wall of the presbytery to a height above the first tier of lancets, the south and west walls of the south transept to full height, and the west front again very nearly to full height. The building seems to have many characteristics of detail and important architectural features which link it with Byland. The bay design, as far as it can be reconstructed from the fragments of the west end and the south-east corner of the transept, seems very close to Byland, in that it has a clerestory passage and a second passage at triforium level. The most notable features of the transept are the window compositions of both the south and west walls. The lower part of the south wall is composed of two tiers of blind arcading, the upper one having shafts in pairs: above this is an arcaded gallery of round-headed arches, and above this again the deep splays of two great shafted lancets. Two even larger lancets, rising the full height of the wall from the level of the springing of the second tier of blind arcading, fill the west wall; these again are very deeply splayed and have round-headed rear-arches. An unusual feature is that the upper parts of these tall splays seem to have been crossed by wooden bridges at the level of the clerestory passage. The east end treatment at Arbroath, as far as it can be reconstructed, seems to have been in three tiers of pointed lancets, a development probably of the east end of St Andrews. The west end, however, was much more unusual. Two western towers, the northern and only surviving one having two lancets in the second stage, flanked a central feature of great interest. A tall and handsome round-headed door, with shafted jambs and richly moulded capitals and orders, stands deeply recessed below a gallery lit by three pointed arches under three gables. This gallery extended rather more than 20 feet from west to east, and opened by an arcade of six pointed arches into the central vessel of the nave. Within the gallery are two pairs of internal supports, one a pair of pillars and the other a pair of square piers. Above the gallery the west wall of the nave was filled by a large circular window strongly reminiscent in this position of Byland. The function of this western gallery is a matter for conjecture, but it is perhaps worth while recalling that the Tironensian monks who colonized Arbroath came from Kelso, where the western parts of the church have also an unusually developed form. Interesting as the problem of the western gallery at Arbroath may be, it is the design of the south transept which raises the most curious speculation. If this extremely striking composition belongs to the last years of the twelfth century it assumes a special interest in relation to the whole development of Gothic in the north, where the use of lancets was developed on a scale hardly equalled elsewhere, and seems to take its place very early in the great series that runs through the north transept at Hexham (Plate 75) and the east front at Tynemouth (Plates 76 and 77) to the Five Sisters at York. Even if, in spite of a number of early motifs such as the circular opening in the gable or the form of the rear-arches, the date must be brought as late as the end of the first quarter of the thirteenth century, the Arbroath transept lancets have an interest not only for themselves but as the forerunners of such remarkable lancet developments as the western windows of Dunblane.

★

The beginnings of Gothic in the west of England [17] are to be found in the following group of works: Worcester Cathedral west bays (c. 1175), Glastonbury Lady Chapel (1184–86), the great church of Glastonbury (begun 1185), Wells Cathedral (begun about the same date), and St David's Cathedral nave (c. 1180) and choir and transepts (1190–1200). Of these, only the Glastonbury Lady Chapel is securely dated by documents. These buildings are very different from one another in general design but show certain clearly definable motifs which are enough to suggest a regional school. Contemporary with them, but not sharing fully in the special motifs, are the transepts of Abbey Dore, a Cistercian building of c. 1175. Abbey Dore and almost all the buildings in the group show many evidences of French influence in detail, though it seems more difficult to determine the sources of these details than in the buildings of south-east England, which appear to fit more or less into the known sequences of French building. The special motifs include a fondness for an arch order, a member of which, whether a plain roll or a decorated moulding, passes round the arch opening without any capital or impost to interrupt it; also the use of applied plaques, discs, or rectangular panels of ornament set in a field of carefully wrought ashlar (Plate 81), and certain details of capitals. There is also a system whereby a subordinate arch is placed within a main arch which acts almost as a relieving arch to it. Some of these motifs – the continuous roll, the applied plaques of decorative relief, and the small sub-arches – are to be found in the transepts and western parts of Malmesbury Abbey, a building of 1150–60 which, for all its pointed nave arches and advanced Anglo-Norman aisle vaults, is purely Romanesque in character. The plaque-like discs are also found in the earliest (Romanesque) part of Llandaff Cathedral, a building which exhibits others of the special western motifs in its later (early thirteenth-century) parts. Between the work at Malmesbury and the outburst of building in the 1180s and 90s come the west bays of Worcester, which show the continuous roll, the small sub-arches, and the plaque type of ornament, together with evidence of an advanced and more French type of vaulting. This survives in the aisle and seems to have existed over the main spans.

The rebuilding of the Lady Chapel at Glastonbury was begun in 1184 and completed in 1186 (Plates 78, A and B, 79). In addition to being the only firmly dated example of the school, it is also the most sumptuous in intention and exquisite in finish. It is a small building, some 59 by 25 feet, placed to the west of the great church to which it was eventually linked by a vestibule built in the thirteenth century. It stands upon the site and perpetuates the memory of the *Vetusta Ecclesia*,[18] which was built of wood and by tradition in miraculous circumstances, and the most venerable part of the whole great complex of buildings. On this Lady Chapel the whole resources of the school, both constructional and decorative, were lavished without stint. It is an admirable summing up of that moment in the history of architecture in England when the major structural discoveries which went to make Early English Gothic had been made, but the compositional changes which followed from them had not yet become apparent. The Lady Chapel is a rectangular building with four square corner turrets: internally the walls are divided into two zones of very nearly equal height. The lower and shorter zone is faced with interlacing arcading supported on detached shafts banded in the middle; these shafts are missing, and whether they were made of some marble or other specially decorative stone is not known. The interlacing arches are enriched with zigzags, and there are sculptured bosses (related to the plaques we have mentioned) in the tympana of the arches. The upper zone is divided by the springing of the vault which is in four bays, each bay containing a round-headed window and enriched arch heads and hood-moulds with head stops. In the tympana, formed between the round-headed tops of the windows and the pointed arches of the wall ribs of the vaulting, are further carved bosses. The transverse ribs of the vaulting are enriched with an elaborate double chevron. Indeed the whole interior composition is a fascinating blend of up-to-date structural devices with a super-abundant decorative enrichment which links it with other late Romanesque examples of the Anglo-Norman school. Externally the bays are divided by buttresses and topped by a corbel table; the windows are shafted and have enriched heads, as on the inside, and there is a similar interlacing arcade in the lower zone. The north and south doors are enriched with figure sculpture of a very high quality disposed in a similar way to that on the outer orders of the Malmesbury south porch, which may date as much as a generation before.[19]

At or about the time of the building of the Lady Chapel the great church at Glastonbury was begun from the eastern end (Figure 51). In spite of destruction and later medieval alterations enough remains of this building, especially enough of the eastern bays of the transept, to give the general lines of the internal composition. This was a pointed arch version of the type of bay design already noticed at Tewkesbury, Romsey, Jedburgh, Oxford, and elsewhere, in which the triforium and main arcade opening are embraced by a colossal arch order. At Glastonbury the colossal arch is pointed and the detail motifs belong to the special group that we have been discussing. Except for an early thirteenth-century version of the same scheme at Waterford in Ireland, which presumably derived from Glastonbury, the Glastonbury bay design is the latest and most developed example of the type known.

The west bays of Worcester with their high and elaborate triforium (Plate 80), the Lady Chapel at Glastonbury and the great church there are all designs that have clearly developed from mature Anglo-Norman Romanesque. The general adoption of the pointed arch gives to the last of these a more consistent character than can be found in the other two, though in the earlier parts of Glastonbury the windows are still round-headed. The proportions of the Worcester bays were probably determined by those of the Norman nave to which they were added, and the Tewkesbury–Oxford scheme adopted at Glastonbury certainly gives a greater emphasis to the vertical proportions of the bay. Both Worcester and Glastonbury rely internally on the exploitation of broad easy expanses of fine ashlar wall surface, against which the main lines of the moulded parts make a splendid but, compared with Canterbury and Lincoln, a reticent pattern; the typical west-country surface enrichments – lozenges and squares and foliage ornament in the triforium gallery spandrels – are used with much more restraint at Glastonbury than at Worcester. The exterior of the Glastonbury Lady Chapel has something of the same qualities, in spite of the elaboration of the wall arcading in the lower zone. As at Canterbury and Lincoln it is a design based on the idea of linear patterning of

Figure 51. Glastonbury Abbey, bay of choir

wall surfaces, but in these western examples, especially Glastonbury great church, the pattern is an open rather than a closely meshed one. The characteristic Malmesbury type of enrichment, that is the ornamental plaques and discs, which relies for its effect on the placing of these spots of ornament in a plain field, is an essential element in this type of design. The Glastonbury fragments in particular suggest a special trend of Gothic design differing in intention from that of south-eastern England and from any continental school, although there are a number of details which suggest an awareness of French practice.

About the same time as the beginning of the great church at Glastonbury (i.e. 1185–90), a new cathedral church was begun at Wells.[20] In the handling of detail the two buildings were clearly very closely allied, and the evidence goes to show that the original plans of the eastern limbs of the two churches were also alike. Both churches had their choir aisles returned round their eastern ends to form an ambulatory, with chapels beyond them to the east (Figure 52). The internal elevation of the main vessel of Wells choir has been drastically altered in the early fourteenth century, and only the three westernmost bays of the main arcade remain from the twelfth century. Sufficient evidence, however, exists concealed at the triforium level to show that the system was similar to that of the transepts, where it is in the main unaltered, except that the choir bays were slightly broader (Figures 53 and 54). Wells was a church of secular canons, Glastonbury one

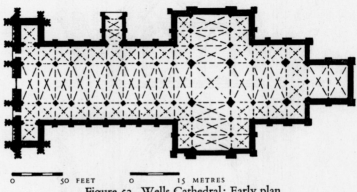

0   50 FEET   0   15 METRES

Figure 52. Wells Cathedral: Early plan

of the greatest houses of the Order of St Benedict in England, and it may be that this affected the manner of the building at Glastonbury, with its derivation from the Tewkesbury, Romsey, Oxford group, whereas the Wells work shows definite signs of the influence of the type of Cistercian design employed at Roche. The bay at Wells consists of the arcade, a triforium of two heavily moulded lancet arches, and a single rather broad lancet window in the clerestory. The vaulting shafts rise from corbels just above the triforium string. There is no obvious Cistercian tradition in the west country from which this influence could be derived, but it seems to be unquestionable. In addition to the general arrangement of the bay design, as Dr Bilson has pointed out, the forms of the lancet windows, both of the aisles and the clerestory, show marked Cistercian influence, and it is interesting to note that, though there is a clerestory passage and the constructional system is essentially advanced Anglo-Norman rather than French, there is no exploitation of this feature as an internal arcaded gallery, and indeed the level of the passage is kept well down below the sill of the window so as to tell as little as possible in the general internal effect. The detail of the main arcade with its attached shaftings in groups of three, its arch mouldings multiplied beyond all precedent, and the multiple and continuous roll mouldings of the triforium and of the rear-arches of the clerestory, all combine to make this Wells interior an outstanding example of the close-mesh linear-pattern type of design. In the choir and transept bays this all-over pattern is given a definite vertical division by the management of the vault shafts, though this is not as clearly marked

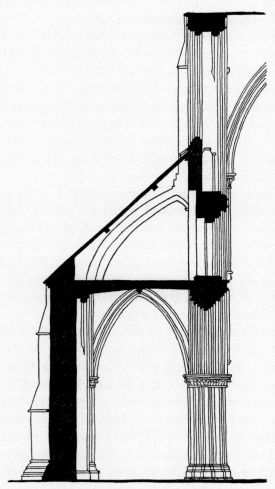

Figure 53. Wells Cathedral: Section of transept

as in such a scheme as Roche or even the Worcester west bays, and the all-over effect is also somewhat marred by the relative simplicity of the quadripartite vaults, again presumably the result of a French example.

As the work progressed at Wells a change came over the design. This change shows itself in certain details and one major alteration in design, though the general character of the piers, mouldings, triforium openings, and clerestory remains the same and gives a quality of unity to the whole work of the transepts and nave. The chief change appears

H
91

in the treatment of the triforium: in the nave the vaulting shafts are very much reduced in length and spring from the corbels in the spandrels of the triforium arches, these arches forming a continuous band the whole length of the nave and working out to three arches to each bay of the arcade and clerestory. The result of this change is to lessen the appearance of the division into vertical bays, while the effect of all-over linear pattern is greatly increased, with the result that the inconsistency of the simplicity of the vaulting system with the rich linear pattern below is more marked than ever.[21] Besides this major change, which, it has been suggested, may have derived from the effect of the continuous band of triforium arches carried across the transept ends, there are also detail changes of some importance which again show themselves in the triforium. The lancet arches of the nave triforium are of the Malmesbury–Worcester type, having a subordinate arch within them, the apex of which is level with the springing of the main moulded lancet. The tympana so formed are enriched with foliage and arabesques, and disc-like bosses appear in the spandrels of two out of three arches, that is two to a bay, the third being occupied by the corbel of the vaulting shafts. In addition, the arches of the nave triforium have hood-moulds with head stops.

The total effect of these changes is of course greatly to heighten the decorative effect of the interior. It is as though one could watch the impetus of the original French–Cistercian influence again dying away in face of the Anglo-Norman desire for splendour of surface treatment; this tendency reaches its climax in the north porch, which is a work of extraordinary elaboration dating from about 1210–15 (Plates 81 and 83). Both internally and externally the porch shows the clearest evidence of its relation to the Lady Chapel at Glastonbury of almost a generation earlier. It is the most sumptuous of the later works of the Malmesbury–Worcester group.

The nave of St David's is a work very close in date to the Lady Chapel at Glastonbury (Plates 84 and 85A): it is generally considered to have been begun about 1180, and the church was certainly in the course of building in 1189 when Giraldus Cambrensis and the Bishop were excused from going to the Holy Land on condition that they 'should bestow their labour and their aid upon the repair of the church of Myniw [St David's]'. The main parts of the church are designed in two storeys and are of no very great height. In the nave an arcade of wide round arches is supported on piers alternately round and octagonal each with four attached shafts. The arches themselves are elaborately moulded, including one heavily enriched member. Above, a pair of clerestory windows to each bay has enriched mouldings to the rear-arches, and these are carried down to the string above the arcade so as to embrace the clerestory and triforium in one design: they are uninterrupted at the imposts. The triforium itself consists of small lancet openings with plain uninterrupted roll mouldings: these are disposed in pairs within the rear-arches of each clerestory window, giving four to each bay of the arcade. Between each pair of triforium openings is a circular panel of enrichment, reminding one of the carved panels and bosses noted elsewhere in the west. The capitals of the main piers are of great interest as showing a remarkable variety of forms of early foliage carving. Indeed, the whole scheme is distinguished for the intricacy and variety of its enrichment. Short vaulting shafts are provided between each clerestory window, as though for a sexpartite system, but whether any stone vaulting was ever contemplated is open to question.[22] The choir and presbytery at St David's occupy the crossing and an eastern limb of four bays: this latter is again of two storeys and consists of a pointed arcade on alternate round and octagonal piers with one clerestory window to each bay. There is no tri-

Figure 54. Wells Cathedral, bays of transept (*left*), nave (*right*)

forium. The eastern wall has three very richly moulded graduated lancets with four smaller reconstructed lancets above. There is clearly a continuity in the character of the enriched arch mouldings of the nave and presbytery, but the reconstruction recorded after the fall of the tower in 1220 has given to the whole eastern work a somewhat later character, as the new eastern wall itself seems to show in the use of banded shafts between the lancets. These seem to be due to an influence from outside the western region.

The ruins of the church of Austin Canons at Llanthony[23] in Monmouthshire seem to date from the very end of the twelfth century, and it is particularly unfortunate that we have no documentary evidence to corroborate this as it is a building of extreme interest.[24] The plan consists of an unaisled presbytery, flanked by chapels, but extending one bay clear to the east of them, transepts and crossing, and a nave of seven bays with two western towers in addition. The eastern parts of the building give a strong impression of their Cistercian parentage, reminding one of a more refined and advanced Buildwas. The nave (Plates 85B and 86) reinforces this impression, as it is of two storeys; this is not effected in the primitive Cistercian way, but by a system of including the triforium within the rear-arches of the clerestory windows after the manner of St David's, though at Llanthony there is only one clerestory and triforium group to each bay of the arcade. The arcades themselves are also noteworthy, having a plain roll moulding without any capital or impost. This is the extreme example of this trick of the western builders, and produces an effect almost more like a late Gothic design than one of this date. The west front (Plate 87), though lacking its central feature, is an outstanding example of the two-towered type, and it is interesting to note that the system of blind arcading with which it is enriched is carried out without regard for the structural divisions of the front. The contrast between the elegant severity of the treatment of Llanthony and the richness of the St David's work, so clearly related to it and yet so completely different in spirit, seems another example of the two contrasting spirits in the architecture of this age that we have already encountered in the north: the spirit which found expression in the sumptuous late Romanesque, of which the most notable example in the north is the entrance to the chapter-house of St Mary's, York,[25] and the spirit of fastidious elegance which we found at Ripon and in some Cistercian houses and in the great late twelfth-century buildings in Scotland, a spirit owing much, no doubt, to Cistercian example, but which is far from being confined to that Order. Apart from its significance as an example of this special architectural taste and of the religious spirit behind it, Llanthony has a purely architectural importance as a link in the series of west-country buildings which achieve a two-storeyed internal elevation by absorbing the triforium into a single composition with the clerestory. St David's is the earliest, but after Llanthony the fashion continued in such examples as Pershore, in the second quarter of the thirteenth century, and Christ Church, Dublin, of about the same time, and may well have affected the design of Southwell a little later.[26]

The two-storeyed internal elevation was also achieved in the remodelled presbytery and eastern chapels at Abbey Dore [27] in Herefordshire, dating also from the very end of the twelfth or first years of the thirteenth century (Plates 88 and 89). Here the effect is gained by carrying down the multiple mouldings and shaftings of the rear-arches of the clerestory windows till they reach a string immediately above the main arcade of three arches at the end of the presbytery and giving upon the ambulatory. At the time of these alterations an ambulatory of the Wells and Glastonbury type with five chapels beyond was added to the church (Figure 55). The roof of these eastern extensions abuts against the main building below the clerestory windows, which have exaggerated lower splays reaching down to the string above the arcade openings.

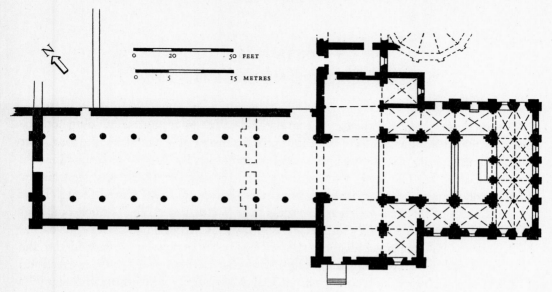

Figure 55. Abbey Dore: Plan

All these western buildings already discussed, and other works such as the late twelfth-century parts of Hereford Cathedral, the nave of Llandaff,[28] and, further north, St Mary's, Shrewsbury, parts of Lichfield Cathedral, and the Cluniac church at Much Wenlock all show remarkable resemblances in detail. The quality of the capitals at St David's, Llandaff, Abbey Dore, and Hereford, the variety of the chevron, double chevron, and other enrichments of arch mouldings at Glastonbury, St David's, Bredon (Gloucestershire), Abbey Dore, Lichfield, and elsewhere all combine to reinforce the impression of a strongly marked regional school. Attempts have been made to trace actual bands of masons working in these related buildings, and where there are so many and so various resemblances [29] it is tempting to do so.

CHAPTER 6

DEVELOPED ENGLISH GOTHIC

THE second quarter of the thirteenth century was a time of very great building activity beginning with Salisbury in 1220 and the eastern extension of Worcester some four years later, and continuing with Beverley and the east end of Ely; all this time work at Lincoln continued steadily. The latter part of the period saw the beginning of Westminster Abbey, and signs of a change in architectural taste became clearly marked though there are indications of that change in earlier works than Westminster. The London buildings of the time are not large or very important: Southwark Cathedral had been begun earlier in the century and continued till about the middle 30s, and a new choir was added to the Temple Church which was finished in 1240. Though it has been enormously restored and now, since its damage in the 1939–45 war, has had to be largely rebuilt, the main lines of the Temple Church choir are authentic. It was a large three-aisled design, without a clerestory to the central vessel which is of the same height as the side aisles. The piers were of Purbeck marble of remarkable attenuation, recalling in this the earliest parts of Salisbury, i.e. the Lady Chapel and adjacent parts of the ambulatory which were finished in 1225. The elegance of the Temple Church choir is in marked contrast to the similar three-aisled extension at the east end of Winchester.[1] The date of this is a matter of some difficulty, and certainly whatever was built in the earliest years of the century was modified in the period we are discussing, but these modifications are mainly apparent in the handling of the vaulting, and do not seem to have affected the main lines of the design. The Temple Church choir, the eastern extension of Winchester, and the Lady Chapel at Salisbury have a special interest as the only early examples in this country of the hall church type of design, that is, with the aisles and central vessel at the same height throughout. Mr Harvey has suggested that the source of this type of building is to be sought in Angers and Poitiers, citing St Hilaire at Poitiers and St Serge at Angers. This seems a reasonable suggestion, and is made the more likely if an earlier example once existed in the choir of St John of Jerusalem at Clerkenwell, of about 1180, as there seems reason to suppose. The later developments of this type of design, which belong mainly to the fourteenth century, at any rate as far as large buildings are concerned, do not seem to be directly related to these early thirteenth-century examples. In parish churches the system is often to be met with, sometimes on a great scale, notably at Rye and possibly at King's Lynn, and from the former descends the fine later example at Winchelsea.

The work begun at Salisbury in 1220 was on a new site, so that the building was un-prejudiced by any earlier work, and the enterprise was carried on steadily during a period of over forty years:[2] the building has in consequence a unity of manner which distinguishes it from all other major English medieval churches. With the exception of the central tower and spire, which were added in the fourteenth century, and allowing for the disappearance in the eighteenth century of a fine detached bell-tower to the north-west, the building as we see it now is the design of the second quarter of the thirteenth century. Apart from the treatment of the east end, the plan of the church has the long nave and the two pairs of transepts which show the influence of Canterbury and Lincoln (Figure 56). The east end consists of a returned aisle forming an ambulatory, and a Lady Chapel of the same height as the ambulatory projecting to the east (Plate 90).

The Lady Chapel has narrow aisles of its own and in consequence three parallel vaults springing from the same height, one broad and two narrow, supported on extremely

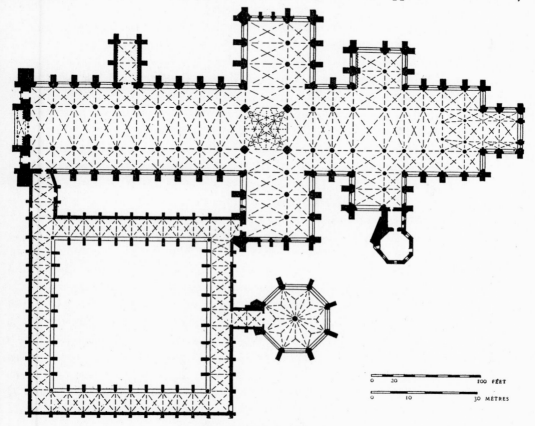

Figure 56. Salisbury Cathedral: Plan

slender marble shafts (Plate 92). This little hall church interpenetrates the ambulatory with a very picturesque effect, in a way that anticipates the remarkable developments at Wells. Externally the ends of the aisles and the Lady Chapel build up magnificently with the gable of the presbytery and the eastern transepts to the central mass of the main transepts and crossing, an effect later to be consummated by the addition of the tower and spire. It is an architectural conception both internally and externally of a very high order. Internally the main arcade is supported on piers entirely of Purbeck marble; both the core and the eight attached shafts and the moulded capitals are of the same material. The arcade is unusually high, and so is the clerestory which has a gallery of three graduated arches supported on groups of slender Purbeck marble shafts. These gallery arches correspond to the grouped lancets of the clerestory windows. In consequence of the unusually tall proportions of the arcade and clerestory, the middle storey is rather squat in its proportions. It is a 'false tribune', that is it extends in depth the full width of the aisle, but has no external wall with windows and is covered by a simple lean-to roof. The design of the middle storey is of broad low arches enclosing four cusped sub-arches in pairs, the three tympana so formed all pierced with quatrefoils. The emphasis that is given to the broad enclosing arches and the shortness and slightness of the Purbeck marble vaulting shafts, all tend to stress the stong longitudinal rhythm of this part of the design in contrast to the vertical emphasis of the arcade and clerestory. There is a curious sense of discomfort in the way the enclosing arches of the middle storey are sprung, which is possibly a personal idiosyncrasy of the designer; for this type of arch appears in other parts of the building. It is possible that this has contributed to the slightly dis-agreeable effect that some critics have found in this interior, though that is certainly largely due to the coldness of the general colour effect, the result of scraping and restoration, and can hardly be attributed to the thirteenth-century intention.

The west end of the church is finished with a broad screen wall reaching to the height of the top of the clerestory, and finished to the north and south with square turrets hardly massive enough to qualify for the dignity of towers (Plate 91). The screen crosses above the ends of the aisles and has a returned eastern side above the aisle roofs, a wall-space adorned with a false clerestory window to match the row of real ones which it adjoins. On the west side the screen has a three-gabled porch of no great size in the centre, and three lancets set in blind arcading above. The spaces of the screen flanking these central windows were adorned by rows of images which were continued round the angles of the corner turrets. The state entrance to the church was provided by a great north porch almost equal in magnificence to that already built at Wells. The source of this unusual conception of a shallow screen wall disguising the awkward section of the aisled basilica form of the nave, seems to be the mid twelfth-century treatment at Malmesbury where the remains of a similar screen exist, and where also the state en-trance to the church is through a magnificent lateral porch. At Wells, where the western bays of the nave and the west transept were certainly finished long before the Salisbury builders reached that part of their work, the scheme is fundamentally similar but much happier in effect, because the western towers are placed to north and south of the aisles and give not only greater breadth to the effect but much more substance to the screen.

Salisbury was in continuous building from 1220 to the 1260s, when there followed a pause in the later thirteenth century until work was resumed on the great spire in the middle years of the fourteenth century. Contemporary with the first building period, work was proceeding at Wells on the western towers and the front, and one can see the influence of the new style with its love of slender shafting, as often as not in special stone, generally Purbeck, though this was not used at Wells, and indeed there are examples of other local stones being used for their colour in the same manner as Purbeck. It seems most likely that this vogue for the use of special stone for shafting derived through Lin-coln as much as direct from Canterbury, and can be traced spreading both northward and westward in the period with which we are dealing.

At Wells the contrast of the new manner with the adjacent parts of the church, which embody so strongly the west-country characteristics of the earlier part of the century, is particularly striking. The most remarkable example in the west of this new Purbeck shafting manner is the eastern extension of Worcester, which consists of a presbytery projecting to the east of the aisle ends, eastern transepts and choir (Plates 93 and 94A). It is said to have been begun in 1224 and was certainly completed, or very nearly so, by 1232, when the body of King John was placed in the choir with great ceremony in the presence of his son. Eight years seems rather a short time for such an enterprise, though not impossibly so in view of the speed at which great buildings could be erected; for example, the whole of the eastern extension at Canterbury was completed in nine years. There are, however, indications that some work was proceeding at Worcester which was dedicated in 1218, though it is generally agreed that this is rather too early a date for the eastern parts. The Worcester work has suffered very gravely from restoration, and much of its quality and detail has been lost. It is the more to be regretted, as it is a work of great decorative elaboration, relying considerably on sculptural enrichment, much of which has lost its original quality, though where it survives it is of great interest.

Two characteristics are of particular interest: first the use of wall galleries below the windows of the eastern transepts and presbytery, in a manner which foreshadows the same feature at Westminster Abbey where the idea has generally been considered to have been derived from Rheims; secondly, the treatment of the middle storey as a triforium in the French sense of the word, that is a galleried wall and not an upper storey to the aisles. The triforium at Worcester consists of two elaborately moulded and shafted arches, divided into two sub-arches resting on a single Purbeck shaft in the middle. The tympanum between the sub-arches is filled with figure carvings; few if any of these seem to have survived the hand of the restorer. The wall on the outer side of the triforium gallery is also arcaded, with the arches alternating with those of the main face of the feature, a motif presumably derived from the double wall arcades of the aisles of the Lincoln choir. The wall arcades round the aisles and transept ends of the Worcester eastern limb have in their spandrels figure groups in relief, some of which have certainly survived without re-cutting – another feature which seems to look forward to Westminster Abbey. There is no sign in this part of Worcester of the characteristic west-country tricks that we have found so consistently elsewhere, but the tradition of the west-country school of the early part of the century was not entirely lost; for it may reasonably be claimed that the design of Pershore and of Christ Church, Dublin, where the middle storey is united with the clerestory into one composition, derives from Llanthony and St David's, both of them admirable examples of the school.

At Lincoln itself work must have been fairly continuous. The nave seems to have been in building from about 1225, not long after the great transepts had been completed: it seems to have been nearing completion in 1233. In 1237 (or 1239) an accident to the central tower led to its reconstruction and considerable repairs in the parts of the building immediately to the east. The character of the decorative work in the lantern seems very close to the work on the west front made necessary by the height of the new work on the nave. This is plainly seen in the treatment of the central western gable in comparison with the lower parts of the lantern, and is usually attributed to the early years of Bishop Grosseteste, i.e. post 1235 (Plate 107).

The Lincoln nave design is clearly a development of the work of St Hugh's choir (Plate 94B). The bays, however, are wider and have three sub-arches to each of the main arches of the middle storey; moreover the treatment of the clerestory is more open, with three almost equal lancets as compared with one broader and two narrower lancets in the choir. In general the work is a little more elaborately decorated, there are three orders to the main arcade compared with two in the choir, and the tympana of the tribune arches are pierced with two large and one small quatrefoil; there is a cinquefoil in the spandrel between them. The proportions are changed by the greater width of the arches, which remain of the same height as those in the earlier work. The great innovation of the nave of Lincoln, however, is in the vaulting, where a system has been devised which would have surmounted the difficulty which caused builders of the choir so much trouble. The vault consists of a longitudinal ridge rib, at the centre points of which the diagonal ribs intersect; two extra ribs are provided which meet on each side of the intersection (Plate 95, A and B). Two short ribs spring from the centre point of the bay at right angles to the ridge rib, but they do not continue to the top of the clerestory walls, for they stop off at a point where they encounter two further ribs which spring from the clerestory string. Thus there are seven ribs springing together between each bay. In the usual English way the longitudinal wall ribs are not stilted in the French fashion, and in consequence the whole vault system presents a broad bearing surface to the clerestory wall. It is the first sign of the system of vaulting which largely transformed the whole conception of vault technique from a skeleton system of ribs to a series of half-conoidal brackets, a process which was only completed by the development of the lierne vault in the course of the thirteenth century.

At Lincoln the effect of this new type of vaulting was already to make the linear enrichment of the vault consistently elaborate with the design of the walls below it, the very quality in which the Wells design had so signally failed. In contrast with the Lincoln nave the four-part vaults at Worcester, though equally presenting a broad bearing surface to the clerestory, almost giving the effect of solid brackets, have their surface much less broken up, thus producing an effect which is less consistent than the Lincoln examples. This was to some extent related to the greater areas of plain wall, especially in the spandrels of the main arcade and the middle storey in the Worcester design.

The influence of Lincoln is seen very clearly at Beverley, the rebuilding of which was begun about 1225.[3] The Beverley design is distinguished for its unusual internal proportions, being much taller in relation to its width than most English churches of its age. This characteristic, which gives it a somewhat French effect, is largely obtained by the height from which the main vault springs. There had been a tendency to spring vaults from higher up the building, observable at Salisbury and at Worcester, but whereas the vaults of these two churches spring from the base of the clerestory, at Beverley they spring from the height of the impost of the clerestory gallery arches. The decorative treatment of Beverley is extremely elaborate. Purbeck marble is used only from above the imposts of the main arcade; the main piers are largely of freestone, with Purbeck marble used in the abacus of the moulded capitals. The arches, however, are of three orders and very elaborately moulded, and the middle storey, which is treated as a triforium in the French sense, is an even more elaborate derivation of the Lincoln double-arcaded motifs than we found at Worcester (Plates 96 and 97). The outer row of arcading, which is supported on triple Purbeck shafting, is trefoil-shaped, heavily moulded, and includes sculptures. The alternating arcade behind it stands on very short shafts, so contrived that the spandrels form the tympana of the outer arches which are adorned with very elaborate foliated trefoils. The clerestory gallery, which had four arches to a bay supported on very slender Purbeck shafts, again recalls the Lincoln choir design, though carried out with far greater elegance and assurance. The fondness for steeply pointed arches which appears in the clerestory and in the blind arcading on the facing of the crossing piers of the eastern transept is also very close to the Lincoln manner.

The eastern part of Beverley is one of the best examples we possess of an exterior composition of this age (Plate 98A), for it is more complete than Salisbury where the scale of the building involved a much longer building period. The composition at Beverley comprises the plan of a presbytery projecting towards the east, eastern transepts with eastern aisles, and double aisles to the main transepts. The transept ends form a remarkable independent contribution with tiers of lancets and bold shafted buttresses with gable tops. The main gables of the transepts are flanked by octagonal arcaded turrets, and that of the main transept is filled with a wheel window. Indeed, the use of circular window-forms is a very noticeable characteristic of the Beverley design, and this again may derive from the rose windows of the transept ends of Lincoln. The Beverley examples are very close to the almost exactly contemporary roses in the western gables of Peterborough. The Beverley transept ends are fine examples of a composition made out of the elements of wall arcading, lancets, and circular windows which we have seen as characteristics of north-country architecture in the early years of the century. The most southerly example of this is the eastern front of Ely, where the church was extended five bays to the east of the Romanesque apse by Bishop Northwold. Accounts have survived which date this work very closely, and the building operations were in full swing by 1238. The eastern front, which has suffered somewhat from alterations in the later fourteenth century, still retains enough of its original character for us to appreciate its intention (Plate 98B). The end of the central vessel is composed of three tiers of lancets, the uppermost lighting the space above the vault. The middle tier of five lights graduated to the vault inside has elaborate blind arches above the low outermost lancets and deeply sunk foil figures in the spandrels on either side of the central lancet. Similar foil figures enrich the points of the gable above the topmost tier. These arches and foil figures were fitted with brackets to support images, and are so deeply sunk as almost to constitute niches. Similar arch treatments are found on the upper parts of the two main buttresses corresponding to the lines of the internal arcades. Above the eastern windows of the aisles are the remains of the arcaded treatment, partly blind, partly pierced, of the tribune storey, and the evidences of one bay on the north side shows that this treatment was carried right round the eastern limb of the building. The outer angles of the composition are formed by two buttresses set at right angles, which combine to form octagonal spire pinnacles at the top and build up well to the central gable and its flanking pinnacles. Internally the proportions of the elevation were determined by those of the Romanesque choir to which it was attached, and this meant that the middle storey was of unusual height and importance. The effect of this was somewhat mitigated by the lancet composition of the east end, for the lowest tier of lancets rises to the full height of the arcade and tribune combined. The most remarkable feature of the design, however, is the extraordinary richness of its decorative treatment (Plate 99). The piers have boldly detached shaftings and the arch mouldings are of exceptional richness; the spandrels of the arches are filled by unusually large corbels enriched with a leaf carving, which support the triple vaulting shafts and are flanked by sunk trefoils. The combination of these elements, together with the hood-moulds of the main arcades and their leaf-stops, leaves comparatively little bare wall in these spandrels. The middle storey is even more sumptuously decorated. It is treated with one richly moulded arch to each bay subdivided into two trefoil sub-arches, with a quatrefoil in the tympanum. The Purbeck shaftings supporting the main and sub-arches, three on each side, have between them vertical rows of leaf carvings, and the desire to fill every space with some sort of decorative enrichment has led to the use of complicated applied leaf carvings to fill in the spaces on either side of the quatrefoil in the tympanum. In the spandrels of the tribune arches there are further foil figures flanking the vaulting shafts which finish on the clerestory string with a foliage capital. The clerestory itself, which consists of three lights, has a gallery supported on two piers composed of four marble shafts with dog-tooth enrichment between them. The vaulting has a longitudinal ridge rib and two extra ribs in addition to the diagonals in each bay; the total effect is by far the most sumptuous of any design since the late twelfth century.

A remarkable group of buildings illustrates this phase of Gothic design in the north; the great transept of York, begun on the south side of the church c. 1242, the new choir and transepts at Whitby, about 1220, and the new choir at Rievaulx, about 1230. In addition to these major works, eastern transepts were added to Fountains Abbey before 1240, and to Durham where they were begun in 1242. These took the unusual form of a T-shaped crossing to the east end of the church presenting a broad front of nine bays to the east and affording nine additional chapels internally. The building at Fountains has been gravely damaged and has lost all its attached shaftings, though the evidence for their presence is clear enough. The work at Durham was rather slow in progress and not completely finished till about 1280; in consequence its final effect illustrates in part the new taste which developed in the middle years of the century. There seems little doubt that the York transept was inspired by the example of Lincoln. The width of these great aisled halls is equal to the main eastern and western limbs of their churches, and creates a spatial effect entirely different from the normal continental type of church design, where the transepts at most are mere appendages to the main east and west extension.

The Whitby choir, which is seven bays long, was designed to have a wooden ceiling and no stone vault; in view of this, the bays are divided by triple shafts rising from corbels in the spandrels of the main arcade and reaching to the wall-plate in the manner of a mid twelfth-century Anglo-Norman design. The design is in three storeys, a richly moulded arcade on freestone piers of grouped shafts, above this a middle storey of two pointed arches to each bay enclosed by a half round main arch enriched with dog-tooth and having a hood-mould, the pointed arches are further subdivided into two, and there are quatrefoils in the tympana of both main and sub-arches. The elaborately treated middle storey is a false tribune, that is it is open to the whole width of the aisle roof but is covered by a lean-to roof and has no external windows of its own. The clerestory string is enriched with dog-tooth, and the clerestory itself consists of one small pointed window with elaborately moulded and enriched rear-arch in each bay, flanked by blind arcading of two narrower arches on each side. This clerestory arcading has hood-moulds enriched with dog-tooth, and there are two quatrefoils in the innermost spandrels. A notable feature of the design is the use of moulded rather than carved capitals throughout, the only leaf carving being on the corbels of the shafts between the bays and on the stops to the hood-moulds.

The Rievaulx scheme is very similar to that of Whitby, but designed for vaulting and rather lighter and more elegant in effect. The piers have more numerous and slighter attached shafts, and in the middle storey, though it consists of two pointed arches each with two sub-arches, these are not enclosed in a single half round, as at Whitby, and can therefore be larger. The clerestory, by reason of the vaulting, is entirely different from that at Whitby, and consists of a pair of pointed windows enclosed in an elaborately moulded and very broad rear-arch flanked by a single low blind arch on each side.

The York transept is curiously like a more sumptuous version of the Whitby design carried out with marble shafting and no lack of leaf carving for capitals and corbels [4] (Plate IIIA). The resemblance is increased by the nature of the clerestory, which became a continuous arcade after the intention to vault the transept had been abandoned. It has been suggested that these Yorkshire interiors with their elaborately treated middle storeys owe this feature to the influence of Scotland. Certainly the immediate forebears of these buildings can best be sought in such designs as the Jedburgh nave and the Hexham transepts, and they represent the more southerly buildings of the northern school in other respects than their exploitation of the possibilities of lancets. The decorative innovations of the York transept are the only important signs of the influence of Beverley, Lincoln, and the south. The Fountains and Durham eastern extensions equally show the use of shafts of special stone, and at Durham there is a wealth of leaf carving on capitals which may also be an importation from the south.

The example of the Puritan elegance which was part of the inheritance of the great Cistercian movement in the north and west, but which affected at least the taste of other communities, combined with inevitable destruction, and the circumstance that much of the first Gothic building of the late twelfth and first half of the thirteenth centuries took the form of the reconstruction of the eastern rather than the western parts of the great churches, has made the evidence of the architectural use of sculpture in that age discontinuous both in time and place, and hard to assemble. There is, however, more of it than might appear on first reflection. It is especially unfortunate that, of the two great monuments of the first years of the thirteenth century, the splendid assembly of figures from St Mary's, York, are completely without evidence of their architectural context, and the great west front of Peterborough, in building in the first third of the century, has for the most part lost its figures. The evidence of their presence, however, is clear enough, for corbel brackets are provided to support figures in the tympana of the blind arcading on the wall within the porch and on the faces of the flanking towers. The positions suggest figures of rather short proportions, and the surviving pieces in the arcades at the base of the gables bear this out and contrast strongly with those we are accustomed to in thinking of early Gothic sculpture. The positions provided for sculpture on the extension of the Lincoln front, which dates from about the time Peterborough was finishing, imply figures much taller in proportion (Plate 100). Here the long lancet arcadings are provided with two tiers of brackets for figures with canopies to shelter the lower tier. At both Peterborough and Lincoln the brackets imply that the figures stood bold from the wall, the shafts and arcading of which act as a linear frame with little or no suggestion of the recession of a niche. At Peterborough certainly, at Lincoln less markedly, the figures were kept subordinate to the pattern of the shafts and mouldings of the arches. In the spandrels of the great arches of the Peterborough front there are boldly moulded and deeply sunk quatrefoils in which are set colossal heads. These, in relation to their settings, seem to be a transition stage between the vanished figures of the lower part and the free standing figures between the shafts of the arcades at the base of the gables.

The sculptured head has a long twelfth-century pedigree in England. Generally, both early and late, it is used as a stop to the hood-moulds that the English desire for increasing the number of arch lines needed both inside and outside their buildings. It is also applied at the junction of the arch moulding of wall arcades and on occasion, as at Oxford, as part of a respond capital. The motif occurs within a quatrefoil on an early thirteenth-century tomb at Canterbury, and a tomb of similar date at Exeter has little seated figures deeply recessed, also in quatrefoils, which seem to prefigure the astonishing use of deep-set quatrefoil frames to sculptured scenes in the spandrels and tympana of the lowest range of arcading on Wells west front.[5]

Wells west front is rightly the most celebrated assemblage of architectural sculpture in England (Plate 101A). On it the figures themselves are a predominating interest in a way that can never have been the case at Peterborough, and scarcely so at Lincoln. At Peterborough the main architectural lines of the front are so original and imposing that the sculpture is hardly missed. The form of this front is occasioned by the western transept, and it may be considered as the last of the great west fronts which descended through Bury, Ely, and Lincoln (the last is its immediate parent) from late Carolingian tradition. Lincoln is a great screen framing the original eleventh-century west front and concealing the new western chapels. At both Peterborough and Lincoln the composition had to incorporate the main ceremonial entrance to the building, but at Wells, as at Malmesbury before it and at Salisbury after it, the main entrance to the church was by a lateral porch of great magnificence, and the designer of the west front has exploited his relief from this responsibility by keeping the western doors so low that those leading into the aisles are not as high as the plinth, and the main central door only reaches to about the springing of the first row of arcading. This gives an extraordinary importance to the two great zones of decoration above, an effect which is increased by the way in which the arcading and sculpture are returned round the buttresses, both of the end of the nave and of the flanking towers, so that the vertical lines of the structure and the surface treatment of the terminal walls are kept balanced in interest.

The central feature of the Wells front with its stepped gable screen and flanking turrets remains (Plate 101B), but this makes all the more tantalizing the speculation as to how it was intended to treat the upper stages of the western towers. William of Wynford's great design of 1392 for completing them has, however, obliterated all evidence. The architectural detail handling of the Wells west front with its attached shafting and vertical lines of crockets has been claimed as the result of the importation of Lincoln ideas into the west country, and this seems true enough, but there is still much that links it with the earlier Wells work, notably at the north porch. The new devices are, in addition to the free standing shafts of special stone and the vertical lines of crockets – both known as Lincoln devices – the heavily moulded quatrefoil sinkings and other foiled and moulded figures, which are to be found equally at Peterborough, and the angle of a gable line straddling an arch, which is much in evidence at Wells. This last is a motif which tends to break up the continuity of wall arcadings into a row of individual features, and so leads on to the niche forms of the later thirteenth century: it seems to derive ultimately from the association of arch and gable in doorways, such as on the gate at Bury or the north and south doors of the Glastonbury Lady Chapel.[6] The Wells front is, however, the first example of its use as a repetitive motif playing a major part in a whole composition, and it is a very long step from the single large-scale examples to the Wells use of the gable line.

The Wells west front was in building in the 1230s, and may not have been brought to a finish until after 1240, but the earlier building period at Wells, which culminated in about 1210–15 with the north porch, was notable for the way in which the typical sculptural enrichments of the west-country manner were developed and exploited. These earlier sculptures are for the most part foliage and grotesques, the latter notably on the lower string courses of the interior of the north porch and framed in moulded rectangles in the spandrels of its external arch; but in addition to foliage and grotesques there are a series of genre subjects on foliage capitals and corbels at Wells which are outstanding among English early Gothic architectural sculptures, both for enterprise and accomplishment (Plate 82, A and B).

The arch and gable housings of the images set in the arcadings of the Wells west front appear again some twenty years later on the west front of Salisbury, a very interesting if not altogether successful composition (Plate 91). Its frankly screen-like character, which the slight angle turrets rather emphasize than disguise, seems to be derived from a similar treatment part of which survives at Malmesbury; at both places, and also at Wells, a great lateral porch was provided as a state entrance, but the Salisbury designer has made more of his western doors than his predecessor at Wells, placing a lean-to porch and three gabled arches between the middle buttresses of his front. The side arches of the porch are acutely pointed and have tympana supported on low, broad arches springing from just above the impost capitals. In the tympana are images in shafted arch and gable housings, and a triple version of the same fills the tympanum of the central inner door. It may be that earlier examples of these little tabernacle forms are to be found over the door of the south transept front at York, but the whole of this York front has been so much restored that it is dangerous to cite it as an example except on grounds of general composition; however this may be, the York transept front, owing to the size of the transept, which has both east and west aisles, is an important and somewhat neglected example of the English façade treatment. It is a design on the largest scale, and comparable to a west front, though without towers. In addition to the three arch-gable mouldings above the door to the central aisle, this motif is also used on the buttresses which flank the façade, though in that position it appears in a rather rudimentary form, and on two of the buttresses the gable line is a structural one. The front is provided with three tiers of corbel brackets for figures in the blind arcades between the lancets which form the central feature of the composition, but the suggested relation of the figures to the arcades recalls Lincoln and Peterborough, where the figures form incidents in a linear pattern rather than the all-over high relief of Wells, though there is no provision of canopies above the figures at York as in the lower row at Lincoln.

On the Wells west front, precocious as it is as an example of the use of the arch-gable motif, it is used so tightly packed and with such a quantity of other devices, shafting, vertical lines of crockets, arcading, and spandrels enriched with foliage sculpture, that it has little of the implication of a localized ornamental feature with defined boundaries such as it has at Salisbury a generation later, and even possibly at York. The arch-gable motif takes its place with all the others in a general all-over effect. This attitude to ornament of all kinds is never completely abandoned in England throughout the thirteenth century and endures beyond it. It can be seen in a specialized form in the development of the stiff-leaf capital. The differentiation of the height of the foliage enrichment according to the diameter of the shaft or pier, which has been noticed as a French trait at Canterbury, Chichester, and elsewhere, was not a fashion of long duration in England, where almost at once the foliage capital tends to become a band of sculptured enrichment, a decorated impost moulding rather than a capital, and our use of the word, with its classical and Renaissance associations, tends to obscure this. From the nature of its position in the structural scheme, the stiff-leaf capital has a special typological history, and there are other fields in which the use of sculpture as an all-over surface enrichment can be observed, notably spandrel decoration.

The outstanding early thirteenth-century examples of sculptured, rather than moulded, spandrel decorations are in the eastern extensions of Worcester and Ely; the former is a work of the 1220s finished in 1232, and the latter was begun in 1235. At Worcester the spandrels of the wall arcades are filled with figure groups, and the tympana of the triforium arches, that is the common spandrels to the sub-arches, have single figures.[7] At Ely the combination of an enriched hood-mould and a very tall vault shaft corbel ornamented with elaborate foliage carvings only leaves a very small space to be filled with moulded trefoils. Other early examples of spandrel decoration can be found on ecclesiastical tomb slabs, including a few which date to the twelfth century; these show a similar treatment with either leafage or figure carving in the areas left by the arch enclosing the effigies; examples in Purbeck marble are at Exeter and Ely and in freestone at Wells. The east end of Ely can hardly have been finished [8] when the ambulatory and transept at Westminster Abbey were begun, and Westminster, as already suggested, may be held to inaugurate a new treatment of architectural enrichment. The wall arcades of the ambulatory and transept chapels at Westminster have, for the most part, been damaged or obscured by the insertion of later wall tombs, but enough remains to show that both foliage and figure sculpture were employed in the spandrels, and indeed elsewhere, with a freedom unequalled before that time.

One of the themes of the new chapter inaugurated at Westminster can be claimed as that of the predominance of the illuminator in the sense of the man responsible for the colour decoration of the building. The most striking examples of this influence on sculptural decoration are in the treatment of the chapter-house doors, both the outer one towards the cloister and the door of the octagon itself, and very probably the treatment of the tympana of the north transept doors, as far as these can be recovered. The outer door

Figure 57. Westminster Abbey: Diagram of chapter-house door

of the chapter-house has a tympanum framed in an arch with an elaborate sculptured moulding representing the ancestry of the Virgin. The figures embedded in leaf carving follow the line of the arch moulding in a manner more common in France than in England, though an earlier example is at Malmesbury in the twelfth century, and thirteenth-century examples are at York and Lincoln, the latter almost certainly deriving from Westminster. The field of the tympanum is covered with low relief scroll work of a kind which is well known in painted architectural examples.[9] Against this background the images of a Virgin and Child flanked by angels were set, standing boldly forward on leaf-carved bracket corbels. The door from the octagon itself (Figure 57) was similarly surrounded by a figure-sculptured moulding, representing prophecies of the birth of Our Lord, and instead of a tympanum the door-head was filled with open tracery so as to give light to the stairs where corbel brackets for figures were also provided.[10] The whole doorway composition was flanked by the well-known figures of the Virgin and Gabriel standing before arcades, but these were linked to the doorway by diapered spandrels, including trefoils, framing censing angels which face outwards towards the Virgin and the archangel. Both these doorway compositions show the painter's approach to sculpture and its architectural setting, and indeed the whole composition of the side of the octagon containing the door is, in addition to its iconographical unity, held together by its surface treatment. The evidence accumulated by Professor Lethaby shows that the tympana of the north transept doors at Westminster were treated with a pattern of foiled figures, presumably containing reliefs.

At Crowland a somewhat similar treatment is used, except that, instead of a series of quatrefoils, one large one containing reliefs of scenes in the life of St Guthlac occupies the main space of the tympanum with relief scroll-work filling up the corners. The tympanum of the west door of Higham Ferrers church may be taken to illustrate the descent of this sculptural treatment from painted motifs; in this composition the centre was formed by an image, possibly of the Virgin, set before a diapered background, while on either side are a series of roundels containing low relief scenes, which with relief motifs in the spaces between them maintain an even texture over the whole area of the tympanum. This use of roundels containing relief groups links very directly with the fashion for painted scenes in roundels which is a commonplace of manuscript illumination of the first half of the thirteenth century, and also appears in large-scale painting at Romsey where the resemblance to Higham Ferrers (Plate 104B) is noticeable, at Winchester, and, as Dr James pointed out, on a major scale on the presbytery and choir vault at Salisbury, where the arrangement is almost certainly authentic though the details have been entirely over-painted.

A good example of decoration, both in relief and paint, and dating from about 1230, is in the chapter-house of St Frideswide's (Christ Church), Oxford, where the lancet composition of the east end shows good examples of foliage carving in the spandrels, and the severies of the vault are painted with large-scale roundels with figure subjects. An obvious link between the manuscript fashion for scenes in roundels and the same practice in wall painting and sculpture is glass painting, where the motif is almost universal from the twelfth century, and its employment on walls may well be taken as an attempt to give a certain consistency to the whole interior scheme.

The loss of so much painted decoration makes it difficult to appreciate the effect intended in many designs of the first half of the thirteenth century. Prior has pointed out that the desire to fill in the spaces between the main moulded or arcaded lines of the composition extended even to the elaboration of the iron-work hinges at the doors, in imitation of the usual painted scroll-work patterns (Plates 105 and 117). Undoubtedly the white-washing and lining out in red of plain masonry surfaces, as at Byland in the twelfth century, was a simple device for effecting this organization of the bare areas between motifs in relief, but there were other more complex patterns, as the lined squares with roses inside, of which Lethaby found examples in the parts of the early thirteenth-century Lady Chapel which had survived the sixteenth-century reconstruction at Westminster, and even more complicated patterns, such as those of which we have fragments at Norwich, and that illustrated by Prior from Wellow near Romsey.

Even where there is little or no evidence of an attempt at filling the spandrels and other blank areas with carvings or moulded figures, and we can at most guess at the presence of some simple linear treatment, as in many of the north-country designs, there is a marked tendency as the thirteenth century advances to vary the linear treatment of roll and hollow arch-mouldings with various forms of carved enrichments of the mouldings themselves. Of these the dog-tooth is the most frequent and one of the earliest, and in its more developed form this decorative enrichment of the hollow moulding on the splay almost loses its early geometrical character, and the component parts take on a leaf-like form. Though the dog-tooth in all its varieties of elaboration is much the most common, there are a number of other kinds of enriched mouldings of which the great arches of the Peterborough west front show a remarkable assemblage. This includes a formalized rose in the hollow mouldings of the central opening as background to the shafts of Alwalton marble, and a number of different enriched mouldings in the great side arches, including one with bold foliage enrichment, almost a midway term between the late twelfth-century sculptured mouldings at Malmesbury and Glastonbury and the Westminster examples which we have been discussing. At Peterborough there is also a remarkable ringed roll moulding, a motif deriving from the ringed shafting of the end of the twelfth century (cf. the upper parts of Ely west front) and an interesting instance of the persistent English disregard of structural propriety, for it is as if a slender ringed shaft had been bent to follow the curve of the arch; other examples of which are the free use of the mouldings of cusped arches handled with complete disregard of their structural sense, as on the Beverley staircase, at the east end of Wimborne, or on the eastern clerestory of Salisbury.

It would be hard to exaggerate the importance of Westminster Abbey in the history of English architecture.[11] It has been considered almost as a revolutionary building, and it does show on a grander and more consistent scale certain characteristics which can only be found occasionally and fragmentarily before it was built, though afterwards some of these became governing factors in English design. This is natural enough from the size and splendour of the building put up, as it was, under direct royal patronage, and from its position at the centre of government where it became familiar to men from all over the country. If the most remarkable innovation at Westminster is the character of the decorative treatment, the next most striking is the plan: this is a return to the apse and ambulatory plan, which had almost ceased to be used since the early twelfth century (Figure 58). One of the few examples that we know in the early thirteenth century was the Cistercian Abbey of Beaulieu, founded by King John in 1204, and there the form of apse and ambulatory employed was derived from later Cistercian practice rather than from a general knowledge of north French architecture of the time. The royal work at Westminster Abbey was begun in July 1245. The plan was certainly governed by two fixed points: one, the position of the dormitory on the eastern side of the cloister buildings, which fixed the position of the south transept; and the other the new Lady Chapel which had been begun in 1220. The position of this Lady Chapel, of which some slight evidences remain near the entrance to Henry VII's Chapel, seems to have been well to the east of the apse of the eleventh-century presbytery, and this strongly suggests that a scheme for rebuilding had been initiated some years before 1245. This is reinforced by a Papal letter which commends the King's intention to take over the cost of the new building and makes the point that the monastery had embarked on a scheme which was more costly and ambitious than it could afford. This sounds rather peculiar when applied to one of the richest abbeys in England but, however that may be, the main point is hardly affected. How much the monastery may have achieved before 1245 is a matter of speculation: possibly only the foundations, possibly enough to provide a means of access from the aisles of the old presbytery to the new chapel.[12] It is

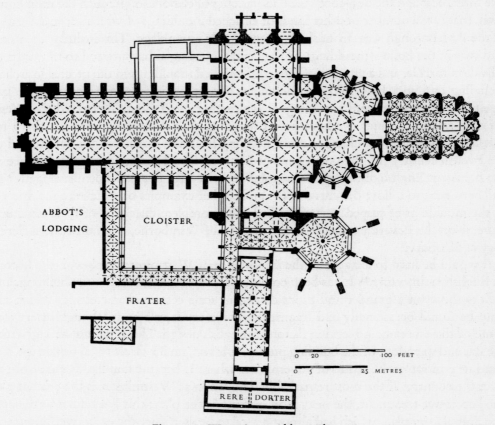

Figure 58. Westminster Abbey: Plan

worth remarking in this connexion that the pulling down of the eleventh-century pres-bytery was started in 1245, and that the earliest work of the King's undertaking seems to be at the extremity of the north transept where, moreover, the design of the tribune storey seems to be slightly earlier and more experimental than the corresponding part of the new presbytery. The extreme inference might be drawn that the aisles and the eastern chapels may have been completed some time before 1245, and this would mean that two of the most important architectural innovations of the building – the form of the plan and the use of naturalistic foliage carving – must be ante-dated by some years.

The form of the eastern limb of Westminster is a presbytery with two bays east of the crossing, east of which was one straight bay before the springing of the apse. In this the altar was placed where it is now, at the east end of the second bay, and behind it was the shrine of St Edward. The form of the apse itself is, however, rather different from the normal French practice; though the fourth bay from the crossing is canted inwards, it is only slightly so, and the general effect of the apse is almost three-sided. This means that the difference in width between the easternmost straight bays and the canted bays is not very marked, and in consequence the rhythm of the vertical divisions of the internal elevation is not quickened in the way which was customary in France, where the plan of the apses is often in the form of half a regular decagon. A precedent for this arrangement can be found in France, but one is naturally reminded of the three-sided apse and ambulatory systems of Gloucester and Tewkesbury. There are four polygonal chapels set radially to the ambulatory, and at the east there was a junction with the Lady Chapel. The transepts have both eastern and western aisles, and are actually a little wider than the nave. The western aisle of the south transept, which conforms to the northern in its upper parts, forms a part of the cloister and is, therefore, exterior to the church up to the height of the springing of the main arches. The nave, including the western towers, is of twelve bays of which the four easternmost belong to the thirteenth-century building.

The design of the internal elevation of the main vessels of the church consists of a tall, acutely pointed arcade, a tribune with its own external windows, and a clerestory (Plate 102). In the choir the vaulting is quadripartite and has a longitudinal ridge rib and also wall ribs. These latter are very stilted, in the French fashion, so as to narrow the bearing surfaces of the mass of the vault on the clerestory wall. This makes

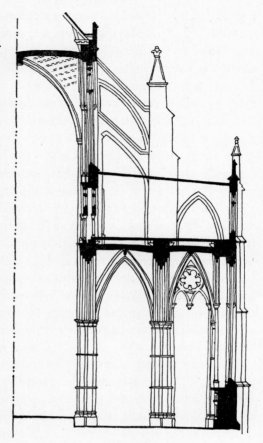

Figure 59. Westminster Abbey: Section of presbytery

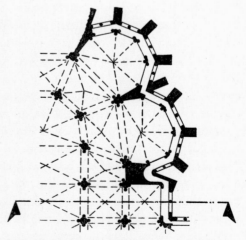

Figure 60. Westminster Abbey: Vaults of ambulatory and chapels

it possible to have wide clerestory windows, but is inconsistent with the system of the thick wall and galleried clerestory, and implies an elaborate external buttressing system. The clerestory walls are built in two planes of masonry, and the windows, in consequence, have rear-arches (Figures 59 and 60). It is curious to note that though the French characteristic of the stilted wall rib is present at Westminster, the mass of masonry at the springing of the vault is much greater than would normally be the case in France, and the whole system, including its very French-looking flying buttresses (Plate 103), is French architectural practice but with a strong English accent. One constructional trait, however, is extremely French, and that is the construction of the springing of the vault in large blocks of carefully wrought stone on the system known as *tas de charge*.

Another important innovation at Westminster is the character of the window treatment, both in the aisles and the clerestory. This consists of two foiled lights of lancet proportions, surmounted by a round foiled figure. The actual handling of the stonework is what is known as bar tracery as opposed to plate tracery, that is to say that the design is not made by piercing apertures in the stone in-filling of the window, but by filling the head of the window opening with a skeleton construction of arches or curved members, parts of arches, or parts of circles. This method of constructing tracery had been brought to maturity in France and appears at Rheims about 1212 or shortly after, and the design of the Rheims windows, which were indeed much admired,[13] is very close to that used at Westminster.

The most important of the Westminster windows are not, however, in the great church itself. On a site east of the south transept a great octagonal chapter-house was built as part of the first building campaign of Henry III. This was almost completed by 1253, and its windows, which consist of four main lights with an elaborate geometrical design of foiled figures above them, must have been in existence by then. There can be no doubt that the example of the great windows of Westminster chapter-house was an important – possibly the most important – factor in setting the fashion for the great many-lighted tracery windows which was to oust from favour the lancet compositions popular in the first half of the century and to dominate the character of English architecture till the end of the Middle Ages. They are not, however, the first examples of big tracery windows, for we have it on the authority of Matthew Paris that the west front of Binham Abbey in Norfolk was built in the time of an abbot who died in 1240 (Plate 104A). Binham was a dependency of St Albans, and Matthew Paris was a St Albans man, and so likely to be well informed on this point. The Binham window, therefore, should antedate the chapter-house at Westminster, and certainly shows the system of the great geometrical window already fully developed.

The detail treatment of the interior of Westminster Abbey is extremely remarkable. The piers are entirely of Purbeck marble and have moulded caps, the main arches of the arcade are elaborately moulded in the normal English manner, and the spandrels between them are covered with diaper. The arches of the tribune storey, which have two sub-arches and traceried heads, are built double with two complete planes of arches, sub-arches, and tracery, in order to carry the very thick wall of the clerestory level we have already mentioned. The mouldings of the tribune arches are even more elaborately treated with decorative carving than those of the main arcades, and the spandrels again are filled with diaper. From the clerestory string the small areas of wall on either side of the springing of the vaults are the first areas of plain ashlar to be found in the elevation, and these are hardly visible from the floor of the church by reason of the exaggerated height of the proportions of the main vessel.

These proportions are another trait which suggests the strength of the French influence on Westminster, and in some degree this French taste for height in proportion to width remains in the later thirteenth and in the fourteenth century as an abiding influence of the Westminster way of work. Recent scholars, studying the documents of the dispute between the Italian builders and the imported French and German masters at Milan in the later fourteenth century, have shown that the French and German masters were contending with the Italians over a system of internal proportions which they expressed in mathematical terms. Whether the French formula was introduced in England at Westminster for the first time we do not know; it is certain that the French master at Milan cited the English masters as familiar with this system of proportions, as contrasted with the Italians who were ignorant of it.[14] It is possible that the French formula was known and used in England, at any rate from the end of the first quarter of the thirteenth century if not before, but the circumstance that most of our important early thirteenth-century works took the form of additions to Romanesque buildings largely prejudiced their proportion and may have disguised this fact. It is certainly interesting in this connexion to note that the eastern parts of Beverley, which seem to have been untrammelled in this respect, have also a rather French proportion internally.

The character of the internal decoration at Westminster, which seems to concern itself more with effects of surface textures than of line, is the most complete and advanced example of a taste which we have seen coming gradually in the works of the 1230s, notably the eastern parts of Ely. Some of the work executed in the early 1240s at Lincoln (Plate 107), in particular the lower stages of the lantern tower and the treatment of the central gable of the west front, show quite clearly, however, the same preoccupation with surface texture as Westminster. The great spread of trellis diaper which has always been taken as the distinguishing mark of the work done in the episcopate of Grosseteste is an outstanding example.[15] At Westminster the same preoccupation with decorative effects can be seen in the treatment of the transept aisle walls, and the walls below the windows of the radiating chapels; these have blind arcading with diaper or foliage sculpture, and occasionally figure sculpture, though many examples in the earliest and most richly decorated part of the church have been damaged, destroyed, or hidden by the multitude of later tombs which have accumulated. The treatment of the walls of the radiating chapels above the arcade and below the windows is with an internal gallery. This has been cited as another link between Westminster and Rheims, where similar galleries appear internally, but it should be borne in mind that wall galleries are a very favourite device in this country, and they are employed at the same level in the building in the eastern parts of Worcester, an enterprise of the earlier part of Henry III's reign and one in which the King was particularly interested as Worcester was the burial-place of his father. Moreover, at Westminster the wall gallery round the radiating chapels turns eastward at the point of junction with the Lady Chapel, and it is more than possible that that building, which was contemporary with Worcester, also embodied this feature.

Westminster Abbey is of special importance not only in itself but also because it is the first great medieval building in England for which we have a very full documentation, including large parts of the building accounts. We are therefore in a position to know the names and a good deal about the actual masons and officials employed there. Of recent years great attention has been paid to the study of medieval building accounts, and we have gone a long way to breaking down the anonymity which the nineteenth century claimed as one of the characteristics of medieval building. From Westminster Abbey onwards our information is fairly full, especially as far as buildings put up by the Government are concerned, and a number of great monastic and cathedral churches have also retained a considerable quantity of their building documents from the later Middle Ages. Before Westminster we have to rely on the evidence of chroniclers who are not always as interested in the processes of building as was Gervase at Canterbury in the late twelfth century. But in various documents recording gifts in money or kind from royal or ecclesiastical benefactors, it is sometimes mentioned that they are intended for architectural purposes, and occasionally documents authorize special steps to be taken to raise money for the benefit of the fabric. In addition there are occasionally the names of masons, which can sometimes certainly, and in other cases possibly, be associated with particular buildings. Such are Master Robert at St Albans in the eleventh century – incidentally Robert seems to have been a favourite name in the building trade in earlier times, as there are sculptures at Romsey and at St Augustine's, Canterbury, signed with that name – or Adam Lok, who is known to have been a mason who was granted a house by the authorities at Wells at a date which is consistent with his having something to do with the west front. The name of Alexander occurs in the second quarter of the thirteenth century at both Worcester and Lincoln, though whether we can be as optimistic about identifying these two Alexanders as Mr Harvey seems to be is more questionable.[16] But from the time of Westminster Abbey one begins to get a rather clearer picture of how a great medieval building came into being, though even to-day the matter is obscure enough. Professor Lethaby in his two great books has traced the names of the craftsmen employed at Westminster in detail, being able to assign to them with considerable probability the parts of the work which they actually executed, and he has in a number of cases been able to find other references to them in documents relating to Windsor and elsewhere, besides those immediately connected with Westminster, and his work has been continued by later scholars.

There has been much discussion as to whether the chief master mason employed by Henry III at Westminster from 1245 was or was not a Frenchman. It is a mistake to be too impatient with those nationalistic debates which occur from time to time in the history of medieval architecture, for in cases such as this they do reflect real problems of the nature of the process by which such a building as Westminster came into being. The name of the mason first employed by the King at Westminster was Henry de Reynes. It has been claimed on the one side that this quite certainly means that he came from Rheims, and the analogies between Westminster and Rheims have been called in evidence to support this; on the other hand those critics who have tended to emphasize the English characteristics of the building have pointed out that the name is perfectly consistent with an English origin, that the name Reynes is well known in other contexts in England, and that there was a place in Essex called Reynes. The difficulty of such speculation as to the names and origins of masons responsible for particular parts of the building is well illustrated by this, for if we do not know exactly how far the building had got in 1245, the question of Henry de Reynes's nationality takes on a very different significance. That there was a very strong French influence on the design of Westminster Abbey is beyond all question at whatever time it appeared; it is present in the plan of the east end, in the use of the constructional device of the *tas de charge*, in the stilting of the wall ribs, and in the management of the flying buttresses. It also appears in the tracery, which, as we have said, is very close to Rheims, and in the other masonry details, notably the appearance for the first time in England of really naturalistic leaf carving. One can go even further and say that it is certain that some French masons must have been employed on the work, but to suggest that Westminster Abbey is a French church of its age transplanted to London would be a gross simplification of the problem. In some respects the French characteristics are extremely up-to-date, notably in the treatment of the rose windows of the north and south transepts. At the same time there is, for example, a hesitancy about the handling of the buttress system which does not suggest a master fully abreast of the French developments of the middle years of the thirteenth century.

Professor Lethaby suggested that the mason at Westminster had certainly been abroad and made notes of things which struck him, or would be useful to him, at various places in France, including Rheims and, perhaps even more important, Amiens. It is interesting to note in this connexion that as late as the first half of the seventeenth century, when there were considerable remains of medieval building practice still current in England, Mr Townshend took his master mason with him to Holland to look at buildings preparatory to setting about the erection of Raynham Hall. That the master mason at Westminster was sent to look at the more important recent buildings in France is almost more than a possibility, but it is very unlikely that he was as independent a designer as the architect in the modern sense of the word; for the profession of architect only differentiated itself from that of the mason in the course of the seventeenth and eighteenth centuries. It is true that William of Sens at Canterbury as early as 1174 had shown many of the characteristics of the modern architect in the diplomatic way in which he handled his clients, who were reluctant to face the expense of pulling down most of the east end of the church and completely rebuilding it. Architecture, however, even in the hands of the most individualistic of post-Romantic architects, is always a matter of compromise between the architect and his clients, and there is good reason to suppose that the client counted for even more in this compromise in the Middle Ages than he has done since.

We know that behind Henry de Reynes at Westminster there was Odo the goldsmith, who acted for the King in the matter of the financing of the building, and later Odo's son Edward. Moreover, the letters from the King to Odo suggest that this important official was very much concerned in advising the King on matters to do with the arts.

We also know that even in the case of buildings of great importance and expense, it was often the custom to instruct the mason that he should take some existing building as a model, and we find a case of this when Henry VI was building Eton College. The modern tendency has been to identify the medieval master mason almost too closely with the modern architect, in reaction against the nineteenth-century acceptation of the ascription by medieval writers of the authorship of great buildings to the patrons for whom they were built. It is gracious and proper to remember the names of craftsmen who can be associated with fine buildings, but, except at Westminster, we are hardly doing more than a gracious act when we record that such and such a church was built by such and such a mason. Where we have other evidence of the activities of the mason than the association of his name with one particular building the matter is different. There are cases in the fourteenth century where a whole series of works can be associated with one particular master and one begins to get some idea of his personal style; but that is rarely so, even with as well-documented persons as Henry de Reynes and his successor John of Gloucester. This is not to denigrate in any way the study of medieval building documents; not only are they of immense use in accurately dating important buildings, but by their intensive study we may ultimately obtain an understanding of medieval building processes and the organization of the building trade which will greatly increase our understanding of the architecture, and contribute to the solution of the fundamental everlasting question of art history, 'Why does the object look like that?' Admittedly some attempts to present a history of the organization of the building trades in the Middle Ages and to show the changes which came in chronologically have been premature, but ultimately this task must be attempted, and is likely to be the most profitable way in which economic history can be applied to architectural and art historical studies.

CHAPTER 7

THE DECORATIVE CONSEQUENCES OF WESTMINSTER ABBEY

THERE are a number of buildings which show the immediate influence of Westminster Abbey but, with the exception of Salisbury chapter-house, it is rather a matter of individual features, such as the distinctive curvilinear triangle windows to the tribunes which appear in Lichfield nave and Hereford north transept (Plates 114B and 132A) – where there are also diaper spandrels in the triforium – or the angel spandrels of Lincoln presbytery, than major architectural forms. The Frenchified chevet found hardly any imitators, for Hailes, the Cistercian Abbey founded by the King's brother, though begun a year later than Westminster was completed sooner. The Salisbury chapter-house is, however, very close to Westminster and differs chiefly in the treatment of the entrance side, which, as the building is not raised on an undercroft and approached by steps, presented a different problem. There was no need to borrow light for the vestibule, and the doorway has a solid sculptured tympanum instead of open tracery and the figure composition does not cover the whole width of the bay. Indeed, the whole treatment is less pictorial than at Westminster. There are also differences in the wall arcading, which has a faster rhythm: there are seven cinquefoil arches to the bay instead of the five broader trefoil arches at Westminster. The spandrels of the wall arcading are filled with figure sculpture instead of diaper, but the buildings are of nearly the same dimensions and the *ensembles* resemble each other very closely. It seems a likely case of the well-known custom of requiring that a building should be 'like' another one, a common clause in building agreements in the Middle Ages.

The most striking example of an individual feature deriving from Westminster was the east-end treatment of St Paul's Cathedral, London. This, as we know from Hollar's engravings, consisted of a large and intricate rose window above a horizontal member, as it were a great transom, supported on seven tall cusped lancet lights. The horizontal member (in fact a gallery) seems to have been kept sufficiently slight to maintain the effect of one great window divided by a transom, to a much greater degree than in the Westminster transepts or in most contemporary French examples. The lower spandrels of the rose were pierced with tracery, as at Westminster, where this development is well abreast of the latest Parisian fashions, being almost exactly contemporary with the south-transept rose of Notre Dame. The St Paul's [1] eastern rose seems to have enjoyed a great popular success and was imitated as a pattern on tiles and even, it is said, on articles of clothing, but it found no architectural imitators. It is possible, however, that its influence may be found in the exploitation of the largest circular member of a many-lighted geometrical window as an almost independent rose, which is sometimes found as for example at Merton College Chapel east window in the thirteenth century, Tilty in Essex and, above all, the west window of Exeter in the fourteenth century. In those windows where there is an uneven number of lights, and therefore no central mullion such as one finds at Lincoln and almost always in France, the circle in the arch head gains a special importance and independence, which is enhanced when the heads of the sub-arches at the sides are filled with patterns of trefoils or other non-circular motifs and the central figure is the only circular form in the pattern. The effect of a rose dominating subordinate tracery forms is then very marked (Plate 142).

The nineteenth-century historians of English Gothic rightly paid great attention to the traceried window, even going so far as to divide all our later medieval architecture into two periods, the curvilinear and the rectilinear, preceded by the geometric and lancet periods, basing their classification entirely on the character of window design. Having in mind the importance attached to decorative effect in all English medieval architecture and the revolution – which is hardly too strong a word – occasioned by the introduction of the bar tracery window, there is considerable justification for this; for the English seized upon this device and exploited it beyond anything to be seen in the land of its origin up to that time. The traditional English square east end, and the importance given to transept ends, both gave opportunities for windows of great size which are rarely offered abroad. The Binham window is only some 16 feet wide by 31 feet high, for the church is quite small, but the Lincoln east window, begun not long after 1256, is some 59 by 29 feet, and this is only the first of a series of such features which continue to be popular in England to the end of the Middle Ages (Plates 108 and 109A).

These great windows, splendid as they are and bringing about an entirely new kind of façade design, which, especially in the north, is developed with much skill and invention, were hardly as important as the effects of the introduction of the new fashionable windows for clerestories and aisle bays. To get the maximum spread of tracery the English builders were compelled to attempt something more like the skeleton construction of the French, and to develop their buttress system beyond anything that they had attempted hitherto. The earlier lancets, even when grouped in twos or threes, left enough masonry between the groups to form an adequate support for the upper works, but as the windows absorbed more of the bay, the necessary mass had to be provided by a more boldly projecting buttress. This is perhaps more marked in the smaller churches with wooden roofs than in the great vaulted buildings, for the only restraining influence on the effect of the new craze for the great window was found in the English tradition of vaulting which continued to develop in this period.

English vaulting, which had started a very special development from the choir vault of Lincoln, had attained by the middle of the century to a type of vault where, by the increase in the number of ribs springing from the same point, it already showed signs of becoming almost a series of solid stone-built brackets rather than a series of arched vaults. This system of vaulting had developed naturally out of the thick-wall method of construction, and implied a broad bearing surface where the vault met the clerestory wall. At Westminster the French system was employed, whereby the wall rib of the vault was markedly stilted in order to narrow the mass of the vault masonry against the clerestory. This device is an essential part of the French system of building out the necessary mass in a direction at right angles to the main line of the building by means of buttresses, including fliers.

The English vaulting tradition, however, was so developed, and its decorative possibilities were so agreeable to the general intentions of the English designers, that the example of Westminster made very little effect. At Lincoln, where the presbytery vaults have a broad bearing surface to the clerestory, four-lighted tracery windows are set in a thick-wall galleried clerestory of the normal Anglo-Norman type and the traceries are duplicated (Plate 115B): on the outer face of the clerestory they are glazed and the duplicate on the inner face is open. This is the simplest compromise solution of the problem of the inherent incompatibility between the traditional method of vaulting, which satisfied the desire for decorative linear continuity, and the new fashion for wide traceried windows. It produces a special and indeed very successful effect, for the inner grille of tracery in the clerestory, being in the same plane as the traceried openings of the middle storey below, greatly enhances the effect of an all-over filigree box which so often seems to be the ideal of the great English church interior. It is interesting to see that a similar treatment of double traceries was introduced into the eastern transept at Durham in the course of its building. This remarkable work was begun in the early 1240s with the most advanced and elaborate design of lancets (Plates 109B and 110). The building, however, was not completed till nearly 1280, by which time the new type of tracery window had become the fashion, and this is introduced in the double traceried form we find in the Lincoln clerestory. This straightforward acceptance of a compromise solution does not occur very frequently, and a different method is found at Exeter (Plate 112), in the choir of Lichfield, and later at Winchester, where the thick wall is retained but a transition is made by moulded splays from the inner face of the clerestory to the plane of the glazed and traceried windows. This produces an effect of movement in and out of the plane of the clerestory, and a wavy rhythm down the length of the church.[2] The adoption of this wavy rhythm in these fourteenth-century clerestories takes its place in a general fashion for weakening the strength of the straight line and exploiting the possibilities of a play of recession and projection, which can be found in other architectural features of the time but must be further discussed later.

Another effect of the new fashion for large tracery windows was the disturbance of the old balance between verticals and horizontals in the internal composition of the great churches. The earlier thirteenth-century buildings had relied very strongly on the form of their lancet windows to emphasize their vertical lines. The new fashion deprived them of this resource, and it is curious to observe the various expedients to which the builders resorted to restore this vertical emphasis. In some cases the vault shafts are given a length and importance almost comparable to that which they had in France. In others – and this is the more general method – the importance of the middle storey is reduced and it becomes either a low triforium, as at Exeter (Plate 112) and Chester, or a frankly two-storeyed elevation is adopted. There was of course precedent for this last solution in the series of buildings which can be traced back from Southwell, through Pershore and Christ Church, Dublin, to Llanthony in the very first years of the thirteenth century and beyond. This two-storeyed system redresses the balance between verticals and horizontals

Figure 61. Guisborough Abbey, bay design of choir

by eliminating the strong horizontal emphasis of the normal middle storey, and be-comes perhaps the favourite solution towards the end of the thirteenth century. Good examples are at Guisborough (Figure 61) and Bridlington in Yorkshire, and in the nave of York itself. At York the vestiges of the triforium remain, but the main lines of its design are linked with those of the great windows above them, and the effect of height is also stressed by the massive vault shafts which descend from the vault springing to the pavement. At Guisborough and Bridlington the triforium is only represented by an inner plane of traceries, through which the bottom of the great clerestory windows can be seen. This last solution is also an example of the taste for open-work effects, whereby one system of lines is seen through another, a popular device both in England and in France at this period.

Yet another way of restoring the vertical lines to their former importance is to be found in the treatment of the Lady Chapel at Lichfield in the early fourteenth century (Plate 113). This takes the form of an eastern extension of the church rising to the full height of the main vessel. It is apsidal and lighted by tall traceried windows of three lights each, which rise the whole height of the church above the wall arcading. An earlier example of such windows occurs in the tall three-light windows of the Hereford north transept, which was built in the 1260s (Plate 114A). This type of tall tracery window is very uncommon in England and almost certainly of French derivation; it was particularly exploited by the German architects of the fourteenth century, who equally derived it from France. The proportions of the Lichfield Lady Chapel suggest French influence also, and may be an example of the adoption of a French system of arithmetical proportion such as we have mentioned above. These expedients to restore the importance of the vertical line were not always exploited: a notable case is Exeter, where the effect of the broad traceries in diminishing the apparent height of the building is frankly accepted, for, though the middle storey is reduced in importance, the width of the windows and the strong lines of the decorative parapet at the base of the clerestory, together with the importance given to the ridge rib of the vault, make the horizontal lines very strongly marked.

The two great enterprises of the second half of the thirteenth century – Lincoln presbytery and the beginnings of Exeter – illustrate very clearly two aspects of that change in the character of decoration which is first shown on a large scale in the treatment of the interior of Westminster. At Lincoln the multiplication of decorative forms and the extensive use of figure sculpture, notably in the spandrels of the middle storey which are filled with the angels which give the choir its name, produce an effect of great splendour and one in which, from the evidence of vestiges which remain, colour must have played a very large part, but which is still predominantly of linear conception (Plates 115B, 116, A and B).

At Exeter (Plate 112; Figure 62), which was begun about the time that Lincoln was finished, i.e. c. 1280, the emphasis on surface texture and colour is developed far beyond anything to be seen at either Westminster or Lincoln. The piers are of Purbeck marble and many-shafted, but the shafts, though numerous, are not boldly detached from the core, and an almost rippling surface which exploits the character of the material is produced. The arch mouldings, by the multiplicity of their small members, also gain a breadth of effect, but the most striking feature of the interior is the vault. This employs a greater number of ribs springing from the one source than in any previous example, no less than eleven. But in addition to this multiplicity of ribs, the ribs themselves are given an unusually strong projection from the surface of the vault, and this surface, so broken up and so recessed, appears almost less as a surface proper than as a series of pockets of shade between the lines of the ribs.

One of the great deficiencies in the technique of art history is our inability to describe colour with any accuracy, or to reproduce it in a book.[3] This is a platitude, and because of that we are perhaps inclined to put it out of our minds, but the effects of this deficiency are particularly important in relation to medieval architecture. Many writers have ignored this problem altogether, though all scholars are aware of its importance, and the evidence of colour on medieval buildings, both documentary and actual remains, is in the aggregate considerable. The actual remains are, of course, extremely fragmentary; most of it has perished naturally, much of it has been scraped off in the restorations of the nineteenth century; and where it has survived it is often a repainting which reflects the taste of a later age than that of the work which it is adorning. In consequence very little attempt has been made to distinguish the colours available at any particular period, except perhaps by the students of stained glass. Unquestionably this neglect of the colour treatment of medieval buildings has a more disastrous effect on our understanding of the architecture of the period beginning about the middle of the thirteenth century than at any time before.

Professor Lethaby has left some valuable notes on the evidence of colour in the interior of Westminster Abbey. First of all the stonework (as opposed to marble) of the building must be considered as having been lime-washed all over. There was a resident whitewasher employed with his man consistently throughout the later stages of the work. It is reported that the diaper work in parts of the choir was gilded on a red ground, and certainly evidence of red used as a background to gilded carving does exist in other parts of the building, such as the foliage carving in the spandrels of the south-eastern chapels. The plain stone surface where it existed at Westminster seems to have been whitened and marked out in red masonry lines, in some parts certainly with a little formal red flower in the middle of each rectangle. This practice, with and without the flowers, and sometimes in conspicuous positions with small scrolls branching from the lines of the fictitious masonry joints, has been found in a variety of places, including Byland the great Cistercian house in the north, and dates back to an early period. It seems that a usual way of filling up a blank space was by fairly elaborate scroll-work, lined out in colour on white, and Professor Prior has pointed out that this way of filling in the interspaces between architectural features was equally applied to the openings of doors, where the iron-work of the hinges and of the straps which strengthened the wood-work of the door are elaborated in imitation of the painted scroll-work which can be observed elsewhere. The most remarkable remaining example of this is perhaps the splendid door made for Henry III's Chapel at Windsor, presumably just before the work was begun at Westminster. The woodwork of the door was covered with scarlet gesso, and the close-mesh pattern of iron scrolls [4] may well have been gilded. This must have been an exceptionally splendid example (Plate 117).

Colour has been observed also on the figure sculpture of the transepts at Westminster, and it seems that the draperies were not only coloured but elaborately patterned. It is possible that the broad areas of diaper in the transept, and in the church generally – except, as we have said, the presbytery – may have been merely whitened, and bright colour have been confined to important mouldings and sculptures; this would accord with what we know of the stained glass of the Abbey, which seems to have been largely grisaille, with colour confined to small areas such as heraldry and particular figures. The whitening of the carved diaper work would produce a silvery-greyish effect by reason of the broken surface, and would accord well with the predominating silver colour of the grisaille. The fittings of the Abbey were, however, much more elaborately coloured than this suggests, notably the canopies of the tombs. Besides the gilding of metal-work, the presence of a technique of decorative colouring involving transparent varnished colours on gold, the use of glass with coloured foils behind it, and of gesso, are known from existing remains, especially the great retable, the Coronation Chair, and some of the more important tombs. These of course would be the stronger accents of the whole colour scheme, but there is every reason to believe that there were a great many of them.

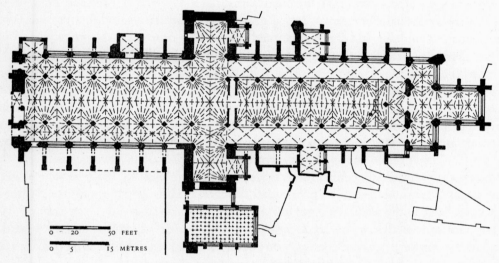

Figure 62. Exeter Cathedral: Plan

The documents bear out the importance of all this paint-work and colour decoration by the large sums of money paid out to the painters on a medieval enterprise. These may sometimes appear disproportionately large in comparison with payments to other craftsmen, but this may in part be explained by the costliness of the materials used, which the painters frequently supplied themselves.

All our evidence goes to show that the elaborate character of the colour decoration of Westminster set a fashion which continued with undiminished vigour for two centuries and more. One of the governing factors in this taste must have been the new fashion for large windows. The greater amount of light that they admitted encouraged experiments in broad effects of colour on the moulded work of the interior, and the importance of the large window, as itself providing a patterned and coloured enclosure in lieu of a wall, set a standard to which the solider part of the building had to approximate. It does not seem possible to relate the technical advances in the making of stained glass with the progress of this taste, which is well advanced before the most important of these, the use

of silver stain, becomes at all frequent, and the lightness of the effect of the great windows of the later thirteenth and early fourteenth century must be attributed to the extensive use of grisaille, the colours themselves remaining, for some time at least, fairly
heavy. We are very fortunate in this country in that a number of large fourteenth-
century windows have survived with their complete glass, notably at York, Wells,
Tewkesbury, and Gloucester. Unfortunately we do not know what the first of the really
large-scale windows – that of the eastern end of the Lincoln presbytery – looked like
from the point of view of colour, and that would have been one of the most important
links in our train of evidence on this subject.

The change in mouldings in the later thirteenth century seems to be affected by considerations of the incidence of light, and the suitability of the shapes to painting. This
change in taste first shows in a breaking away from the simple rolls and hollows of
approximately equal dimensions, and a great increase in the use of fine lines derived
from small mouldings and sharp edges and fillets. This makes for the softening of the
earlier forms by breaking them up into a multitude of small lines. With the fourteenth
century the large moulding returns, but with flatter curves and sometimes with double
curvature. These latter reflect a general taste for double curved effects – the ogee, in short
– which is found in all branches of decoration in the early years of the fourteenth century. The first signs of the ogee curve in England are said to be on the Eleanor Crosses,
the monuments erected in the 1290s at the points where the cortège of the body of King
Edward's Queen rested on its journey from Lincoln to London. The ogee was a device
which greatly assisted that movement which is perceptible in the last years of the century to do everything to break up, or rather dissolve, the lines of a composition, whether
the main lines of the whole of a great building or the individual lines of a feature. We
have already seen this in the handling of the thick-walled clerestory at Exeter in the
fourteenth century, but it is conspicuous about the 1290s in the handling of the stall
canopies which form a continuous band round the great octagonal chapter-house at
York. These canopies project from the plane of the wall as three-sided bows, and are
set so close together that they give the effect of a rippling line of decoration all round
the building immediately below the great windows (Plate 118B).

Another example of the desire to break up the line is to be found in the use of ball-
flower ornament. This small formalized rosebud form of decoration is used particularly
by some west-country masons with a profusion which is quite astonishing. The most
remarkable examples are the central tower at Hereford (Plate 114A), the south aisle of the
nave of Gloucester Cathedral, and the windows of the south aisle of Leominster, but
these instances hardly give us as good evidence of the purpose of this form of decoration
as the interior of the chapter-house at Wells (Plate 120). In this building the ball-flower
does not, as at Gloucester and Leominster, creep up the sides of the mullions of the windows, but is used with considerable profusion in the jambs. The effect is to dissolve the
lines in a sort of spotty glitter, and in this one can see a direct link between the colour
decoration and the carved form. The ogee curve finds its greatest use in window tracery,
and though purely geometrical forms maintain themselves right into the fourteenth
century, and by multiplicity and variety considerably soften the effect of the earlier

uncompromising lancet and foil circle compositions, it is only in the free patterning of the curvilinear windows that the full effect of this taste for lines in dissolution can be seen.

Another expedient of the greatest importance for dissolving the strong lines of the earlier thirteenth-century compositions is the niche. This becomes one of the favourite motifs out of which the fourteenth-century designer composed his effects. The outline of the niche is most frequently finished with an ogee arch, but the change from a linear moulded frame related to the Romanesque wall arcade, which is a stock device of the early thirteenth century, to a niche, resides in the actual depth of the recession of the niche itself, which thereby breaks up the surface of the wall in which it is set. The most remarkable examples of niche composition of this kind are perhaps the middle storey of the remodelled choir at Wells (dating from the 1320–30s) (Plates 119 A and B and 124), and the east front of Howden in Yorkshire, where the buttresses, the spandrels of the great east window, and the small areas of wall which flank the window are all broken up in this way (Plate 141B).

The west-country masons showed a special appreciation of the possibilities of this new fashion and applied it to works of very different scale. The sedilia of the Lady Chapel at Bristol Cathedral are, as we see them now, a reconstruction from the small fragment which remained when the great sixteenth-century tomb was moved from before them (Plate 122A). The details of much of the composition are therefore nineteenth-century, but the main lines are certain, and it is in these that the most remarkable quality of the composition consists. The sedilia are covered by arched canopies, the lines of which are carried up as reversed curves to form pinnacles above each support. Immediately above the intersection of these reversed curves figures are placed in the plane of the pinnacles, and behind both pinnacles and figures are a series of deeply hollowed niches which have little more relation than that of a vague shadow background to the objects standing before them.

Another example of this three-dimensional quality in design is the tomb-chest and canopy of Edward II at Gloucester (Plate 122B). There has been considerable tinkering with the upper parts of this object, but again the most striking example of the characteristics under discussion is established beyond question. The tomb-chest is of Purbeck marble, and the lines of the little buttresses at its sides are carried on in the small free-standing buttresses of the canopy. The little marble buttresses on the tomb-chest are set, not at right angles to the chest, but splayed outwards. Their free-standing continuations have springing from them a series of miniature fliers to the inner plane of the canopy work. As a result of the outward splay of these buttresses, the fliers are seen from in front moving diagonally into the depth of the monument, thereby linking intimately the different planes of the canopy work. Whatever may have been done to pinnacles and other details of the upper part of Edward's canopy, it is hard to believe that this extraordinary baroque device can be anything but original.

At Wells and Bristol this new taste for three-dimensional effects is found applied to the planning of buildings themselves. The two outstanding examples are the remodelled treatment of the east end of Wells and the porch at St Mary Redcliffe, Bristol. The work at Wells began at the east end in the last decade of the thirteenth century, and there is reason to believe that the Lady Chapel was finished by 1306 (Plate 121). The original east end of Wells had an aisle returned as an ambulatory round the east of the presbytery (Figure 52). The new work involved the extension of the presbytery further to the east, the prolongation of the aisles, and the building of a new ambulatory with transeptal chapels from which projects further to the east a new Lady Chapel, actually the first part of the scheme to be undertaken. The Lady Chapel is in the form of an irregular octagon, the three short sides towards the east forming an apse, the corresponding sides to the west being open arches interpenetrating into the space of the ambulatory. This produces a very remarkable effect, owing to the unexpected positions of the piers of the Lady Chapel arches in relation to the piers of the ambulatory vault, an effect the full quality of which can only be appreciated from a variety of view-points, including a diagonal one.

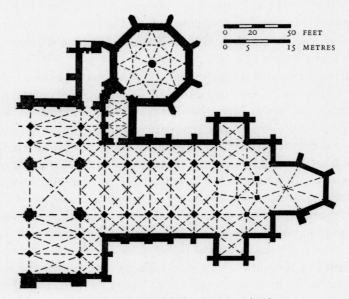

Figure 63. Wells Cathedral, east end: Plan

The whole arrangement is greatly enhanced by the difference in the height of the vault of the Lady Chapel and that of the ambulatory, so that a true effect of the interpenetration of two volumes is achieved. It is the most complete and complicated example of what a generation or so later in Germany would be described as *Sondergotik* (Plate 119A; Figure 63).

The fourteenth-century additions to the porch of St Mary Redcliffe, Bristol, though smaller in scale, are hardly less remarkable than the *tour de force* at Wells which we have been discussing (Plate 125A). This fine church had a north porch of the early thirteenth century, itself a design of some ambition. It was a plain rectangle in plan with elaborately moulded and shafted outer arch and doorway; on to this was built an outer porch, hexagonal in plan and covered by an almost domical vault. The north face of the hexagon has the main outer door, but two subordinate doors are placed in the canted sides to the east and west. Again a curious relationship is set up between the volume of the interior of the hexagon and the tunnel-like effect of the original porch to which it is attached, but this seems much less considered than the relationship of the ambulatory and the Lady Chapel at Wells. The decorations of the hexagon porch [5] are of an extraordinary complication and unlike anything else surviving in this country, though nearest to the remarkable tomb embrasures in the walls of the almost contemporary choir of the Augustinian Priory, now the Cathedral, at Bristol. These west-country examples should not necessarily be taken to represent a regional school, as it is most likely that the tomb of Edward II represents the grand London work of its time, and it may be some degree of coincidence that many of the most advanced examples are to be found in the west.

The other great assemblage of early or mid fourteenth-century architecture which exemplifies the tendencies under discussion is to be found at Ely, where the whole plan of the great octagon, which replaced the central lantern tower which fell in 1322, is an example of the new breakaway from the orthodox straightforward arrangement of rectangular spaces meeting at a rectangular top-lighted lantern crossing (Plate 123, A and B). Again one is in the presence of a design which invites one to view-points other than from the obvious central position. In the details of the Ely [6] work, not only the octagon, but the reconstructed choir of the same date and the Lady Chapel completed a few years later, are equally interesting (Plates 125B and 126). It has been claimed that the octagon and the Lady Chapel represent different traditions of mason-craft; if this is so, either one school of masons imitated the other or one controlling designer dictated to both, for a highly individual motif is found both in the octagon and the Lady Chapel, and again in the private chapel of the Prior, which dates also from the 1320s. This is a variant of the open-work device which we have noticed in relation to the traceries at Lincoln and the middle storeys at Guisborough and Bridlington. It consists in a three-sided bowed feature, the ogee arches of which suggest the outlines of niches. These are, as it were, drawn over and across the main vertical lines of the vaulting shafts which appear rising through and behind them. The same motif appears between the windows of the Lady Chapel. The ogee heads of the niches of the Lady Chapel wall arcades not only have the double curve the name implies, but project forward as well as upward from their springing – a device known as the nodding ogee – and this gives an extraordinarily subtle, three-dimensional quality to the composition. The Ely Lady Chapel is perhaps the most elaborate example of this type of decoration, for this elaborate three-dimensional ogee arcading is combined with a wealth of figure sculpture, both in relief and in the round, unequalled in any other building of the time. Considerable remains of the paint-work of this decoration survive, and it is noticeable that some of the wall arcade supports which were carried out in Purbeck marble are completed in clunch (a soft white chalk stone), which clearly had to be coloured to match the marble mouldings immediately below them and with which they are continuous.

The development of the buttress system, which came with the fashion for the great traceried window, led also to the exploitation of the pinnacle in the late thirteenth century and thereafter. The pinnacle had always been in use to flank a gable, and can be traced back into the twelfth century in such compositions as the Lady Chapel of Glastonbury, the transept ends of St Frideswide's, Oxford, and the west fronts of Hereford and

Rochester. In the early thirteenth century a type of treatment with an acutely pointed gabled weathering is applied to buttresses, and is particularly noticeable at Southwell and, to a lesser extent, at Lincoln, but a great composition like Beverley (Plate 127A) only employs the pinnacle flanking a main gable, though the number of gable ends, which includes those of both transepts, naturally gives a very strong vertical emphasis to the exterior of the building. The French use of the pinnacle in conjunction with the flying buttress is found at Westminster, but naturally is not normally necessary in English churches, where the double-aisled plan hardly ever obtains. The English use of pinnacles is therefore very largely a matter of aesthetic preference, and may be another symptom of the desire to give due emphasis to the vertical lines of the exterior in view of the breadth of effect of the new window treatment, and also to counteract the strong horizontal lines of the elaborate open-work parapets which became the fashion in the course of the fourteenth century. Frequently these open-work parapets were interrupted by small pinnacles, which at once linked them to the building below and helped, by the elaboration of the upper line of the building, to dissolve the uncompromising line which bounded the main mass, and in many of these buildings this aesthetic preference is the only reason for employing a pinnacle which has little or no structural function. It is noticeable in this connexion that pinnacles are as frequently employed, and as elaborately, in wooden-roofed buildings even of quite small size as in the greater vaulted structures.

A very remarkable variety of invention is shown in the fourteenth-century pinnacle, though perhaps the favourite form is that of a spirelet rising from a four-sided lower part which is itself finished with miniature gables. The surface of the lower member of the pinnacle is frequently enriched with tracery motifs, and sometimes with niches. An interesting example of the latter is at Boston in Lincolnshire, where a three-sided pinnacle consists entirely of deeply hollowed niches forming a curious complex three-dimensional composition.

This development of the pinnacle, as a means of vertical emphasis and of breaking up the strong lines of the upper part of the building, is in some degree reflected in one of the most remarkable developments of later medieval architecture, the attention that was given to the design of towers and spires. From the twelfth century, as we have seen, the normal design of a great church implied a finishing of two or more towers, and from what we know of early examples on the continent and at such places as Southwell, these towers would have been finished with pyramidal wooden roofs.[7] Only one great English church has its complete set of three towers with spires – Lichfield Cathedral – and these belong to the fourteenth century. Many more churches are known to have possessed spires, but they were often constructed in timber and have frequently perished, as the celebrated spire on the top of old St Paul's or that of the central tower of Lincoln. Good examples of timber spires do, however, exist, notably Sutton St Mary in Lincolnshire, which is an example of the middle of the thirteenth century. Of surviving early examples of stone spires nearly all are to be found in two main groups: the Oxfordshire group, of which that of St Frideswide's (Plate 127B) is one of the earliest surviving, and the Northamptonshire group, in which a continuity of tradition in spire design can be traced down from almost the end of the twelfth into the elaborate examples of the four-teenth and fifteenth centuries. It is very noticeable, however, that the later Northampton-shire spires are far more sophisticated and elaborate and show the effects of experiments in spire design derived from outside their own region.

The spire of St Frideswide's is the nearest thing we have to the great early spires of France, especially Normandy. Transition from the four-sided tower to the octagonal spire which completes it is made by four pinnacles rising from the angles of the tower oppo-site the diagonal faces of the octagon, and four tall gabled windows standing bold from the cardinal faces. The Northamptonshire tradition was to cover in the spaces left in the angles at the top of the tower by the change from square to octagon plan with a simple ridged and sloping weathering. This latter device is known as a broach (Plate 128B). Where the tower has pronounced angle turrets in lieu of buttresses, as in many Lincoln-shire and Fenland examples, such as that at Sutton St Mary, these are carried up to form pinnacles the lines of which are a prolongation of the buttress turrets of the tower itself. The Northamptonshire broach spire, though capable of great refinement, hardly gave the opportunity for elaboration and enrichment to be found in the Oxfordshire or Lin-colnshire types with their angle turrets and pinnacles, and in the course of the fourteenth century the latter type of design began to prevail over a large part of the country, to-gether with a strong tendency to give to the top of the tower a definite parapet line which often was combined most ingeniously with the broaches and pinnacles. Two of the most remarkable examples of this are the tower of the University Church at Oxford, which dates from 1310–20, and the important fourteenth-century spire finish to the small north-western angle tower of the west front of Peterborough (Plate 128A). In these ex-amples the transition from the tower to the spire is made by a multiplication of angle pinnacles mounting up towards the face of the spire, three in the case of the Oxford church and two at Peterborough. Other ingenious experiments appear from the four-teenth to the end of the fifteenth century, such as the use of small flying buttresses from the angle pinnacles to the face of the spire, of which notable examples are Kings Sutton, Oxfordshire, Patrington in Yorkshire (fifteenth-century), and St Michael's, Coventry (begun 1442). At St Michael's, Coventry, the spire surmounts an octagonal lantern on the top of the tower with its own angle treatment and parapet; at Patrington, though the spire rises direct from the tower, an effect similar to that at St Michael's is gained by a skeleton arcade, crowned with a parapet of pinnacles, which stands round the base of the spire and through which the tapering lines of the angles of the spire are clearly visible.

The concentration on the design of towers and spires in the fourteenth century arises naturally, as these luxurious finishings had been left to the last by the builders of the great thirteenth-century churches. There is no doubt, however, that in carrying on the general intentions of their predecessors and improving on them, the fourteenth-century designers were moved by an aesthetic motive, the desire to pull together the complicated elaboration of masses which often formed the legacy of their thirteenth-century predecessors. A most notable case of this is at Salisbury, where the tower and spire were added in the middle years of the fourteenth century (Plate 90). This justly celebrated feature is far greater in height and far more striking in character than anything contemplated by the thirteenth-century masters of the building. The original design seems to have implied a lantern tower over the crossing for internal effect, and a pyramidal or spire finish, presumably in wood, above that – that is to say a further storey above the point where the thirteenth-century work now finishes, and above that a relatively light timber structure. The fourteenth-century builder, a man by name Richard of Farleigh,[8] went far beyond this suggestion. His tower rises two tall storeys above the thirteenth-century masonry and is then crowned with a stone spire treated with angle pinnacles, the outer ones being prolongations of the angle treatment of the tower itself, the inner ones rising from the space between the diagonal faces of the octagon and the corners of the tower. Richard of Farleigh employed a wealth of ball-flower ornament in the upper storeys of the tower: a circumstance which may link him with the western school of masons we have mentioned who were certainly responsible for a similar treatment of the central tower of Hereford Cathedral about the same time (Plate 114A). The size and weight of the tower and spire raised on the crossing at Salisbury led to a need for strengthening the building internally with stone arches across the openings from the crossing into the transept, though these were not inserted till the fifteenth century. At Wells, where a massive central tower was added above the early lantern, the remarkable cross arches to strengthen the crossing piers were inserted almost immediately, if they are not actually contemporary with the tower itself. In the case of both Salisbury and Wells the lantern effect of the central tower was abandoned, and the space of the crossing covered by a vault to ceil off the tower.

There is a tendency in the fourteenth-century designs to abandon the conception of a central lantern, which it may be supposed arises from two sources: the desire for unity of space effect which was interrupted by this upward extension of the crossing, and secondly from the circumstance that the great enlargements of the eastern limbs of the more important churches, which had been made in the late twelfth and early thirteenth centuries, had tended to diminish the importance of the crossing as the spatial climax of the interior: indeed in some cases, notably at Gloucester and Sherborne which are both monastic churches, an effect of unity was given to the choir and presbytery by carrying the vault of the eastern limb uninterrupted to the western side of the crossing; this in turn involved supporting the eastern face of the tower on a large arch concealed above the vaulting.[9] In many cases, however, of which Ely, York, and Lincoln are the most notable, the lantern is retained and even employed on a scale never previously attempted. In this respect the York central tower, built in the first years of the fifteenth century, is the most triumphantly successful, with the exception of the special case of the Ely crossing. The reason for this is the great width of the main vessels of the York design, and the consequent large volume of the crossing space itself. The Durham lantern (Plates 31 and 42B), which belongs to the last quarter of the fifteenth century, is externally a splendid example of this late medieval feeling for the use of a central feature to give unity to a complex and spreading plan, which is the primary function of the tower, but the actual dimensions of the crossing itself are not large, and the internal effect is not therefore very far removed from the original conception of the Romanesque master. At Lincoln, where a central lantern tower had been carried up one whole storey above the ridge-line of the main roof in the thirteenth century, a further additional storey was added in the first years of the fourteenth century, and this we know to have been completed with a timber spire; the western towers, of a slightly later date, are equally works of the fourteenth century (Plate 129A). Their design is to some extent determined by the pre-existing octagonal angle turrets of the Romanesque towers, and in this way they form a connecting link between the mid twelfth century and the octagonal buttress turrets which became prevalent at the end of the Middle Ages and pass into the repertory of early Tudor designers. The central tower at Canterbury, which was built between 1490 and 1497, also adopts the octagonal angle turret. In this instance the lantern effect is retained and, though small in comparison with the main volumes of the church, produces an effect of climax to the western parts of the interior before the main entry into the eastern limb.

CHAPTER 8

THE GENESIS OF ENGLISH LATE MEDIEVAL STYLE

THE foliage carving of the period from 1250 to 1350 shows a development which, though not parallel in all respects with other aspects of architecture, can be reasonably related to them. By the middle of the thirteenth century the stiff-leaf convention had by no means exhausted its possibilities and the new attitude towards decoration, with its interest in effects of light and shadow, and its flirtation with the possibilities of colour had already begun to affect the forms of the carved leaves. What has been described as the 'blobby stiff-leaf' indicates an interest in the movement of the surface of the leaves as well as in the pattern made by their silhouettes, and the carvers were showing considerable powers of invention in exploiting this type of foliage decoration. At Westminster, in the eastern chapels and in the diaper of the chapter-house, there are definite indications of a new naturalism in the handling of plant forms. This had already appeared in France, notably at Rheims, and is almost certainly one of the French traits visible in the Westminster work. The naturalistic foliage, however, did not oust the traditional stiff-leaf suddenly and completely, but in monuments such as the Angel Choir at Lincoln and the nave of Lichfield the stiff-leaf foliage adapts itself to the new fashion and wears a more naturalistic air.

The supreme examples of naturalistic foliage carving are to be found at Southwell[1] in the chapter-house and its vestibule (Plate 129B), and in the choirs at Exeter and at Lincoln, all examples dating from the late 1280s or 90s (Plate 116B). But already there are signs at York and elsewhere of a new invention in foliage carving in which those leaf forms most suitable to slight variation of surface treatment begin to become popular. In some of the naturalistic capitals of Southwell a very nice balance is maintained between the interest of the surface and that of the outline of the leaf pattern, and there is great subtlety in the relation established between the plane of the leaf decoration and the shadowed background against which it is set. In this the decoration has almost ceased to be sculptural in the full sense of the word and has become illusionistic in a painter's way.

The new development that we have mentioned at York and Wells is rarely illusionistic, and though these carvings depend on painting effects it is decorative colouring rather than illusionism which conditions them. It is curious to note in an interior such as that of the Lady Chapel of Ely (Plate 125B), dating in the main from the 1330s, that while a vast preponderance of the foliage decoration is of this developed fourteenth-century type, using rippling seaweed motifs calculated to make the most of the glitter of the gilding, occasional passages of purely naturalistic carving are to be found; notable examples of this naturalism are to be seen in two tympana of the wall arcading, one on each side of the chapel, which are treated in this way and contrast very markedly with their neighbours.

In the late thirteenth and early fourteenth century the regional divisions that we have used in discussing the architecture of the earlier periods are still useful. Indeed, when dealing with lesser buildings, particularly parish churches, a strong case can be made for much more numerous and closely defined regional schools than is warranted in discussing the major buildings. This is natural enough; parish church work is liable to be done by local men, and a system frequently obtained whereby a mason was required to build a church or some new feature of a church after the manner of some well-known local example. Moreover, the nature of the available local materials gave a strong unity to the architecture of some districts. The greater buildings, partly by reason of the less provincial outlook of the patrons for whom they were erected, are less easily divided into geographical groups. But still the north has a character of its own, and the interaction of the style of south and south-east England with that of what may be described as the middle west, that is the counties in touch with the Severn Basin, provides one of the most interesting problems of the architectural history of this period. Until recent years attention had largely been concentrated on the middle western region owing to the almost complete disappearance of all buildings in London dating from between the time of the completion of Henry III's work on Westminster Abbey in the time of his son and the resumption of work on the same building in the time of Richard II. This gap of nearly a hundred years in our knowledge of the architecture of the richest and most advanced centre in the country has been liable to distort gravely the historical picture of English architectural development at one of its most interesting periods. The researches of modern scholars have done much to remedy this, and in the course of these researches it has become almost possible to see much of the architectural history of the fourteenth century in terms of actual named building masters.

The London building of this period seems to have been dominated by three important kinds of work. First of all the rebuilding of the eastern parts of St Paul's, secondly the erection of the Friars' churches, especially that of the Grey Friars in Newgate Street, which was begun in 1306, and thirdly the building of the new chapel of the King's Palace at Westminster, which was begun in 1292 and continued, though at considerable intervals, until its final finishing in the third quarter of the fourteenth century. None of these three major buildings survives, though we have some visual record of the work at St Paul's, we know the plan of the Grey Friars, and we have a large if not sufficient body of evidence for the character of the design of St Stephen's Chapel, Westminster.[2] It has often been remarked that English art of the late thirteenth and early fourteenth centuries shows a more immediate awareness of contemporary French art than at any other time during the Middle Ages. At first sight this suggestion appears to the architectural historian to be fantastically untrue. The whole character of English fourteenth-century architecture is so very individual and in some ways, as compared with continental architecture, so very precocious that the suggestion of a dependence on Paris seems almost less apt at this moment than at any other. Nevertheless the fascination of the study of our evidence of London building during this time may well consist in noting the process whereby very up-to-date Parisian ideas are imported, only to be used and exploited in a context totally different to that in which they were originally born.

The Royal Chapel at Westminster, which survived to become the Chamber of the House of Commons in the sixteenth century, was gravely mishandled in its adaptation to its new use, notably at the hands of Sir Christopher Wren who greatly reduced the total height of the building, and it was finally almost totally destroyed by fire in 1834. All that now remains is the undercroft known as the crypt, though it is nowhere below ground level. This undercroft has been much restored in the nineteenth century, but it retains its vault, and the forms of the windows seem broadly to follow the original design. As completed, the building consisted of the lower chapel (the surviving undercroft) and the main chapel on the first floor (measuring some 90 by 28 feet). Owing to Sir Christopher Wren's alterations we do not know in detail how the upper part of the main chapel was treated. It seems certain, however, that there were two tiers of windows divided internally by a strongly marked horizontal cornice, and the chapel was covered with a wooden vault in imitation of masonry. The internal elevation consisted of five bays divided by piers with canted sides; on the ground level were very elaborate wall arcades surmounted by a complicated cresting, and above this was an enriched zone of paintings in each bay divided by three vertical mouldings which were the prolongations of the mullions of the windows above them: this painted wall was in approximately the same plane as the glazing of the windows (Plate 130, A and B). The tracery in the window-heads has been plausibly reconstructed by reference to Hollar's engravings of the chapter-house of St Paul's, a building carried out at almost precisely the same time as the work on the upper chapel of St Stephen's by a mason closely allied with those responsible for the chapel design. This tracery appears to have been a network of foiled figures, possibly with straight vertical sides and ogee tops and bottoms. Above the apex of the window arches the great horizontal cornice passed from bay to bay enclosing the composition in a rectangular frame; the spandrels so formed were filled with vertical panelling with cusped heads surmounted by a band of trefoils. What there was above the great cornice, which survived until 1834, we have very little evidence, but it seems likely that the clerestory windows had elaborate traceried rear-arches of the type still to be seen in the clerestory of the choir of Ely.[3] Externally the upper chapel had the spandrels above the main windows filled with geometrical tracery very similar in character to that shown by Hollar in the gables surmounting the windows of the St Paul's chapter-house. The mullions of these upper chapel windows were carried down and interpenetrated with the hood-mouldings of the windows of the undercroft. The interior of the chapel was finished in the most highly coloured and sumptuous manner. Some few fragments of the paintings below the windows and at the east end behind the altar have survived and are now in the British Museum, and copies of other figure paintings were made for the Society of Antiquaries in the early years of the nineteenth century together with elaborate notes of the colour decoration of the main mouldings. A very large proportion of the building accounts of the chapel have survived, and from these much evidence can be gathered of the nature of the painted decoration. The wall arcades were painted with angels holding elaborately patterned cloths before them; the cresting was treated with heraldry having elaborate grotesques, often of an indecent character, in the position of supporters. The main zone of painting below the windows contained an elaborate iconographical scheme of which part of the story of Job has survived. On the eastern wall below the window the King and Queen and their family were represented together with the Adoration of the Magi and the Good News told to the Shepherds. The panels in the spandrels above the windows were filled with single figures, and all the mouldings were not only coloured but adorned with relief stars and other devices in lead or gesso, and much use was made of glass and foils such as we have mentioned in connexion with the Westminster Abbey tombs. Indeed, the interior of St Stephen's, which was finished in the 1360s, seems to have been the culmination of this particular type of illuminated architecture.

The precedent for this remarkable work was above all the Sainte-Chapelle in Paris, which, apart from its associations with St Louis, on its own merits as architecture struck the imagination of succeeding generations almost more than any single medieval building. The general arrangement of such two-storeyed chapels followed a well-established tradition, and early French examples have survived at Laon and elsewhere. The immediate English predecessor of St Stephen's is the chapel of the London residence of the Bishops of Ely in Holborn, and this also stands, like the Sainte-Chapelle, on an undercroft. The immensely rich colour decoration of the Westminster Chapel was unquestionably inspired by the example of St Louis's work in Paris, but there are other more detailed traits at St Stephen's which are of French derivation. The motif which dominated the effect of the chapel was that of the arch framed at the top in a rectangle and having vertical traceried panels in the spandrels. This motif is a very favourite one among the masons working in London in the first half of the fourteenth century, and is used in a variety of scales. In the internal elevation of St Stephen's the scale is large, whereas on the doors leading into the westernmost bay, which formed the ante-chapel, it is used on a small scale; in the arches opening into the undercroft of the chapter-house of St Paul's it is used on an intermediate scale.[4] In the upper parts of the chapter-house the window is surmounted by a gable in the tympanum of which are tracery motifs like those found externally at St Stephen's. This gable rises between the angle pinnacles of the octagonal chapter-house in front of an arcade finishing in a strongly marked horizontal line. This motif of the gable backed by an arcade is quite definitely traceable to French practice of the later thirteenth century. It is related to, and is possibly the origin of, the motif inside the chapel which we have been discussing. A further French motif is the prolongation of the mullions externally till they interpenetrate with the hood-moulds of the windows of the lower chapel. Something of this kind is found at the Sainte-Chapelle, but it belongs to a whole category of motifs whereby a plane of open-work tracery of strongly vertical character is established in front of the main lines of an architectural composition. A good instance can be seen in the designs, both projected and executed, for the west front of Strasbourg Minster.

St Stephen's Chapel was measured and drawn by various scholars in the early years of the nineteenth century; first when Wyatt enlarged it after the Act of Union with Ireland, and again after the fire of 1834. The former occasion gave us our record of the painting and colour decoration of the building, the latter very accurate measurements of mouldings and details. St Paul's chapter-house is less well known, but the Hollar engraving is a very good one and quite convincing. The foundations remain in the angle of the nave and south transept of the existing church, and some fragments which may belong to the chapter-house have been preserved. The detailed treatment of the two buildings seems to have been very close, and we have evidence that William de Ramsay, the master mason in charge of the chapter-house in 1332, had formerly worked at Westminster and was to work there again when he succeeded Thomas of Canterbury, under whom work in the chapel had been resumed in 1330 after a short pause. Similar details to those of the chapel and chapter-house can be found at Windsor, dating from the middle years of the century, and in a number of tombs and other decorative works at Westminster, Canterbury, and elsewhere. From these a convincing picture can be built up of a school of designers sharing a repertory of motifs, which can be traced in its formative stage and later settling down into a recognizable set of mannerisms which endure throughout the century, though this never becomes stereotyped and new motifs are added to the repertory or old ones re-used in new ways.

Many of these motifs can be traced in buildings directly under the influence of Court fashion throughout the fifteenth century and beyond. The outstanding characteristic of this Court manner is its fondness for geometrical forms; the bands of trefoils above the cusped panels in the spandrels of the main windows at St Stephen's; the quatrefoils in rectangles above the arches into the undercroft of the chapter-house at St Paul's, and between the two storeys of the cloister which surrounded it; the quatrefoil in a rectangular frame or a foiled rectangle, often with a shield of arms, which became extremely common on tomb chests and is found below the niches that flank the west door of Canterbury Cathedral (dating from the end of the century) and in a similar position at Westminster Abbey and Westminster Hall, where, though they are nineteenth-century 'reconstructions', they probably reflect the original forms. The gables that surmount tomb canopies such as those of John of Eltham (1334), which is known to us from Stothard's drawings, and Edward III (Plate 131B) (1377) have their tympana filled with foiled circles and other geometric motifs, which contrast markedly with such treatments as that of the gables above Prior Sutton's tomb at Oxford (Plate 131A) (c. 1300), with its wealth of ball-flower and its reliance on a shallow shadowed recession of the planes of the tympana, giving the effect of a gently modelled surface. It is not suggested that London or the Court had any exclusive use of geometric forms, but only that in the aggregate a taste for them characterizes their works, and this impression is strongly reinforced by Hollar's plates of the tombs which once existed in old St Paul's Cathedral. The most characteristic motif of the school is, as already mentioned, that of the arcaded or panelled spandrel of the arch-head or gable, and it is in this motif that the Court masons made the boldest use of the ogee. Occasionally an arch set in a rectangular frame was given a double curve to its extrados, which was carried up to meet or cut the horizontal line above. The gables on Edward III's tomb tester are good miniature examples, or those above the niches on either side of the west door of Canterbury. Sometimes the sides of the gable are given an inward curve as though they were the completion of an ogee of which the lower curve had been omitted. The tomb of Rahere at St Bartholomew's, Smithfield (c. 1400), is a good late instance. The ogee line is also found used with more subtlety to break up the outline of the foiled rectangles containing shields of arms on the tomb-chest of John of Eltham and in the cusps of the canopy of Aymer de Valence's tomb, both of which are at Westminster. These show how the desire to break up the line is present even when geometrical forms are used.

The tracery suggested by Hollar's engraving of St Paul's chapter-house and its cloister seems to have been very close to the work at Windsor on the Dean's cloister and its entry (c. 1350). The actual tracery at Windsor has been much restored, but the blind tracery in the entry is untouched; it shows a system of reticulation consisting of quatre-foils, the upper and lower lobes of which were ogeed, set between vertical mullions rising from the apexes of the lower lights. A similar motif is found in the tracery of the cloister itself.

Throughout the fourteenth century there is a very close connexion between Canterbury and the Court school. The names of the early master masons at Westminster suggest it: Michael of Canterbury, Walter of Canterbury, Thomas of Canterbury, and later the work of Henry Yevele both in London and on the nave of Canterbury is fairly established. An early and interesting example is Prior D'Estria's screen in the Cathedral, which, in its use of elaborate diapers with geometric tracery motifs softened by the use of double curves in the foiling and the strong horizontal line of its cornice, seems to form a link between the style of the Eleanor Crosses of the 1290s (Plate 113A) and the later Court manner we have been discussing.

Though plenty of examples of the use of the ogee curve can be cited from works of the Court school, and its use persisted longer in that school than almost any other, it was never exploited quite as wholeheartedly as in other parts of the country, and the affection for geometrical forms remains the most distinctive characteristic of this school. This is itself a symptom of the link between the Court circle and France, and it is possible that the whole fashion for panelled effects which characterizes the later phases of English medieval architecture may be due to the knowledge by the Court masons of French late thirteenth- and early fourteenth-century precedents; for cusped wall panelling is to be found in a number of French buildings dating from the last years of the thirteenth century. Most of these buildings are at some distance from Paris, even as far as the extreme south, but they are recognized as being the work of Parisian masters called in by provincial centres.

The early years of the fourteenth century have left an extraordinary number of major architectural works in the west and middle-western counties of England: Exeter,[5] which from 1280 to the middle of the fourteenth century was in almost continual building; Milton Abbas, Dorset, begun about 1310; the reconstruction of the east end of St Augustine's which is now the Cathedral at Bristol [6] and which seems to have been nearing completion in the early 1320s; the great rebuilding scheme of the eastern parts of Wells [7] which may be considered to have been begun with the staircase to the chapter-house (probably about 1285) and continued till the choir was ready to be glazed in 1332; the remodelling of the eastern parts of Tewkesbury, the glazing of which is believed to date from between 1340 and 1344. To these may be added the building of the Lady Chapel of Lichfield (about 1320–35) and the remodelling of the choir which followed immediately after (Plate 132A). These are all major works, and together form one of the most interesting and important groups of English medieval building.

At Wells a process can be traced which appears rather as a sequence of tastes reflected in the employment of masters belonging to slightly different groups or schools than as a continuous development in architectural style or technique. To take the window tracery only, the sequence begins with the almost standard geometrical traceries of the chapter-house staircase windows with their lancet and foiled circle motif (1285 *et post*); and continues with the curious reticulated windows of the Lady Chapel (Plate 121), reticulations which consist almost entirely of trefoils (*c.* 1300); the next stage is the elaborate late geometric designs in the chapter-house (Plate 120) (finished *c.* 1319), followed by the aisle windows of the choir in which, though the forms are still largely geometrical, the ogee line is used with some freedom; the last stage is the great east window of the choir clerestory, where strong emphasis is given to the middle area by carrying up the mullions which define it unbroken to the top of the window, and where the five central foiled figures of the tracery lights are straight-sided. This last characteristic of the great east window seems to recall one of the types of tracery which we associate with the exactly contemporary London work, and is possibly an example of the invasion of the west by new ideas deriving from the Court school of masons. It is a motif found a year or two later in the south transept at Gloucester, the remodelling of which was begun in 1331, and the Wells window may therefore be the first example of this London influence in the west.

The historical importance of these works at Wells and Gloucester, and especially the later work in the choir at Gloucester, resides in the fact that from the time of Professor Willis in the nineteenth century it has been held that Gloucester shows the first development of an architectural manner which reacts against the decorative freedom of early fourteenth-century architecture as we know it in the north, at Ely, at Exeter, and elsewhere, and shows a manner at once more rigid in its effects, more given to the employment of geometrical forms, and to the covering of large areas with a system of cusped panelling applied equally to plain wall-spaces and to the in-filling of great windows, a system, moreover, in which, though the vertical lines are the much more strongly stressed, the horizontal lines are allowed a full measure of emphasis, from which characteristics the nineteenth-century authorities derive their names Rectilinear and Perpendicular. This view of the stylistic changes of the fourteenth century maintained that at Gloucester the south aisle of the nave (1318–29) was carried out by a school of masons whom we have already noticed at work at Hereford, Leominster, and elsewhere, whose designs were characterized by a profuse use of ball-flower, and that these men were superseded in the south transept work (begun in 1331) by another school whose earlier work could be seen at St Augustine's, Bristol. There, indeed, the window traceries do show an unusual emphasis on the horizontal line, each side window being divided by a transom into two systems of lights with two systems of tracery, the upper one occupying the window head as usual, the lower forming a band of decoration immediately below a transom. There is also evidence of a taste for straight lines at Bristol in the curiously original tomb embrasures below the windows of the projecting presbytery and in the treatment of the vaults of the side aisles. The forms, however, of the work of St Augustine's, Bristol, have little in common with the work at Gloucester, except the traits just mentioned, whereas the Gloucester south transept shows forms of tracery light which seem very close indeed to those used in contemporary work in London.[8]

The more recent view of the origins of the Perpendicular style maintains that it was developed gradually by the masons working for the Court and was carried by them to the west country, notably to Gloucester, a quite likely suggestion as the Court in the second quarter of the fourteenth century frequently visited that centre, and it is in this connexion that the burial of Edward II at Gloucester has its importance, perhaps more than by any wealth which the cult of that dubious monarch may have brought to the monastery. This theory would allow for the suggestion that the strictly geometrical elements in the early Perpendicular, including the panel system, might derive ultimately from French practice through London, and suggests a process, the importation and assimilation of foreign motifs, rather different from that more local evolutionary development envisaged by the earlier architectural historians.

The eastern end of St Augustine's, Bristol (Plates 132B and 133), is, however, a work of the greatest interest and importance in its own right, quite apart from its position in any historical development or its relation to Gloucester choir. In plan it consists of a transept, crossing, and choir of five bays, the central vessel of which projects two bays further to the east. This is a plan-form with which we are familiar, which seems to have been particularly popular with houses of Augustinian Canons, to which Order the Bristol church belonged. The originality of the Bristol design consists, however, in the relation of its aisles to the central vessel; this latter has no clerestory and is lit exclusively by tall windows in the aisle bays. The main arcades are some 50 feet in height, and the vaulting of the aisles is of a highly original description. The aisles are spanned by a series of arches, across the tops of which are substantial horizontal moulded members, as it were stone beams, the spandrels so formed being filled with leaf-shaped foiled figures. In the middle of these beams above the apex of the arches the vaults spring in all four directions, forming pairs of minor vaults to the north and south which interpenetrate with the major vaults over the adjoining bays of the aisles; the beams themselves thus act as internal buttresses to the main arcades, and the springing of the aisle vaults bears a curious resemblance to king-posts rising from the tie-beams of a timber roof. The only precedent for this extraordinary device seems to be the small horizontal members to be found in a similar position in the undercroft of the Sainte-Chapelle, but the Bristol example is on so much larger a scale and so much further developed that it is questionable whether there is any connexion between the two. The effect of this scheme at Bristol is that of a hall church, and it is unquestionably a reflection of that desire for the effect of unity of space which is to be found in the work of this age. The mouldings at Bristol show an interesting mingling of broad surfaces calculated to exploit the incidence of the side lights of the windows, set off by extremely delicate fine sharp mouldings to give a strong linear contrast to the easy-moving surfaces of the larger mouldings. In each bay of the aisles and of the projecting presbytery are the elaborate tomb embrasures already referred to. The head of each embrasure is framed in three straight mouldings, and from the outside of each and from the vertical sides of the embrasure spring in-curving mouldings terminating in leaf-carved finials: the head of the embrasure is further enriched within by mouldings forming trefoils with elaborate cusping. These tomb embrasures are among the most complex and original of fourteenth-century decorative designs. The south-eastern bay of the presbytery also contains the remarkable sedilia already described.

Perhaps the most outstanding feature of the Bristol design is the treatment of the vault of the main vessel. From each pier seven vault ribs spring, two to the side compartments of the vault, the other five, including the transverse and diagonal ribs, following the main vault surfaces. There is, however, no longitudinal ridge rib, and instead of it are contrived a series of foiled figures, and irregular (kite-shaped) lozenges; the transverse ridge ribs also terminate in such lozenges. The intermediate ribs reach only to the outer angles of the lozenges, while the diagonal and transverse ribs meet at the points of junction of the lozenges. The effect of this is to reduce the importance of the division into bays and to stress the unity of the space. The new feeling for effects of depth, as compared with the simple linear pattern of vault ribs against vault surface, is shown in the handling of the cusps of the lozenges which stand out at right angles to the ribs from which they spring and bold from the retreating surfaces of the vault behind them, producing almost an open-work effect. This search for open-work effects in the vaults, of which the aisle vaults are even more pronounced examples, is also found in the sacristy attached to the south aisle of the church, where the main vault ribs are completely detached from the vault surface and form a series of slender curved stone struts springing from the walls and meeting the vault only at its apex. A similar conceit is found some years later in the choir vault of St Mary's at Warwick, which dates from the 1380s. The main vault at Bristol is an example of these new tastes in design applied for the first time to a tradition of vault building which can be traced in the west to the vault built over the choir of Pershore shortly after 1288. The example at Pershore, however, still relies in the main on an intricate linear pattern of vault ribs, and shows no sign of the spatial subtleties attempted in the handling of the cusping at Bristol and in a more developed form in the vaults of the aisles and sacristy. The choir vault at Wells, which is possibly slightly later than Bristol, makes an even more remarkable use of foiled figures (Plate 124). They are again lozenges, regular and irregular, so disposed as to interrupt the lines of all the vault ribs except the transverse. The total effect is to suggest that the ribs themselves are purely a surface patterning and that the vault is essentially a pointed barrel interpenetrated by similar vaults over the windows, and indeed structurally this seems to be the case. It is equally a striking example of the tendency to break up the structural line which has been noticed in other connexions. This vault has met, as can be well imagined, with much abuse from nineteenth-century historians of Gothic, as it certainly is a complete denial of the rigid principles of Gothic vaulting maintained by the strictest sect of pharisees.

The experiments in vault patterning which appeared first at Bristol found their most complete development at Tewkesbury (Plate 134), where the fourteenth-century alterations consisted of an elaborate remodelling of the eastern limb and the provision of vaulting throughout the building, which entailed in the nave a considerable modification to the proportions of the clerestory. The work, however, at the east end was of a very drastic character. In the eleventh-century church, as at Gloucester, there was an apse of three bays, and the ambulatory of this was greatly enlarged at the reconstruction, when a series of chapels were formed; those opposite the canted bays were set north and south so as to prolong the aisles and form a larger ambulatory space to the east, from which two chapels were set diagonally and one, the now-vanished Lady Chapel, axially to the east. The effect is extraordinarily spacious and varied. The main vessel of the choir, which had been treated with a colossal order, was cut down so as to become a simple pointed arcade on short cylindrical columns surmounted by seven great five-light windows. The triforium was replaced by a simple unemphasized gallery crossing the bottoms of these windows. The windows retain their original glass, including a series of figures of the Clare and Despenser families and their ancestors in the two westernmost, from the heraldry of which Mr Rushforth has determined the date of the glazing as 1340-4. The most distinguished thing, however, about the Tewkesbury choir is the nature of its vault. This is very steeply pitched, and the side bays slope up sharply towards the crown. The rib system is extraordinarily elaborate, great use being made of short lierne ribs of intricate patterned forms and of cusping in the spaces so formed. By these devices the pattern is so disposed as to concentrate the interest on the centres of the bays rather than on their junctions, and so emphasizes the unity of the space of the eastern limb. In this vault the possibilities of exploiting the relation of rib and surface have been explored very fully. The varying treatment of the ribs themselves and the steeply inclined surfaces of the vault give great variety of light and shade. Exeter shows the beginning of this tendency, and Bristol is an intermediate stage to the full development of Tewkesbury. The Tewkesbury nave vault, however, is altogether simpler in construction. This vault is much less steeply pitched, and the side bays giving on to the clerestory windows interpenetrate with the main vault at a comparatively low level. The centre of the vault is treated with three longitudinal ridge ribs and these strongly emphasize the unity of the vault and tend to obliterate the separation of the bays; both choir and nave vaults make great use of sculptured bosses at the main intersections of the ribs.

The work on the eastern limb of Gloucester (Plates 135 and 136A) must have been begun before Tewkesbury was finished and was completed by about 1357, the glazing of the great east window being finished by about 1350. As at Tewkesbury it was a case of modifying an eleventh-century structure. At Gloucester the clerestory only of the early building was removed, leaving the aisles and tribunes intact, but the whole of the apsidal end of the main vessel was taken down (it originally had a three-sided apse and ambulatory as at Tewkesbury), a new and very tall clerestory was built, and with extreme ingenuity the last bay to the east was splayed outwards and a great east window constructed, in plan like a very shallow three-sided bow, so that the effect as seen down the main axis of the church is as if the whole eastern wall of the building was glazed. To give unity to the new interior elevations the builders adopted the device, used on the exterior of St Stephen's, of carrying a web of open-work tracery down from the lines of the new clerestory over the whole internal face of the earlier building. This is the grandest example of the application to an English building of this ultimately French motif. As at St Stephen's, this open-work web of tracery at Gloucester lays great emphasis on the vertical line; not only are the vaulting shafts carried down right to the ground, but the lines of the mullions of the clerestory windows are equally carried down to just above the tombs and screens which line the sides of the choir. The distinction of Gloucester, however, is the breaking up of these vertical lines within the bays by frequent horizontals, thus forming a panelling system. The motifs used in these panels and to reinforce these horizontal lines are strongly suggestive of Court influence. The panels are provided with cusped arch heads, generally of ogee form, and in the spandrels of these are geometrical figures or, in those immediately below the sills of the clerestory windows, foiled arcading, a miniature version of the motif so often found in London, and in the lower part of the tribune level is a band of quatrefoils set in rectangular frames. These are not the only Court motifs in the Gloucester choir, for the traceries of the heads of the clerestory windowsthemselves are very close to the traceries indicated by Hollar in the cloister of St Paul's chapter-house, though, being larger in scale, they are rather more elaborate.

The vault which surmounts this central vessel is a little less complex than that of Tewkesbury. It is ingeniously designed to unify the space of the main vessel and counteract the strong effect of division set up by the unbroken verticals of the vault shafts. This is achieved by three devices: the intermediate ribs are prolonged so as to intersect at the centres of the transverse ribs, thereby uniting each bay with its neighbours; the vault is steeply pitched, and the side bays over the clerestory windows interpenetrate well below the crown, leaving room for three longitudinal ridge ribs which further tend to unite the bays; the last unifying characteristic is the multiplicity of short liernes turning the whole design into a close-mesh network of lines over the vault surface. This vault is carried westwards uninterrupted by any arch on the east side of the crossing, so as to incorporate the crossing space containing the choir stalls with the space of the eastern limb itself. The east side of the central tower is ingeniously carried on a great arch concealed above the surface of the vault. The outstanding characteristic of the Gloucester work is its extraordinary ingenuity, and in this it seems to relate to the choir at Bristol which nineteenth-century historians regarded as its parent. Certainly there are strong west-country characteristics in this work, and it is not to be regarded as an example of wholesale importation of Court fashions into an alien territory. The characteristic quality of ingenuity set a standard at Gloucester which was maintained in the later fourteenth and fifteenth centuries in the rebuilding of the cloister of the central tower and of the Lady Chapel. These two last have a unity of feeling with the work of the choir which gives to the Gloucester work of the fourteenth and fifteenth centuries a special quality of continuity, and it is interesting to see in some parish church work in Gloucestershire a reflection of the masonic virtuosity of which the Cathedral is the outstanding example. The treatment of the interior elevations with a net of open-work tracery was imitated in the fifteenth century at Glastonbury, but only small fragments remain.

The west-country contribution to the Gloucester design is strongly suggested by the character of the vault, which, as we have seen, seems to belong to a group of vaults which include Exeter, Wells, Bristol, and Tewkesbury. We have very little evidence of the Court masons' handling of ambitious vaults. The undercroft of St Stephen's Chapel has a complex vault with elaborate patterns formed with liernes which dates from about

1320 or even earlier; but the only other important vault which we can definitely associate with a Court mason is that of the choir of Lichfield Cathedral, where William de
Ramsay, the master of the St Paul's chapter-house, is known to have been employed in
the late 1330s. This is an accomplished version of the Lincoln presbytery vault in which
the ribs all rise to a strongly marked single ridge rib. It is of course possible that the
presbytery vault at Lichfield is merely a continuation of that erected for the Lady Chapel
of c. 1320, but this is somewhat unlikely. Certainly the next great work undertaken at
Gloucester after the completion of the choir – the rebuilding of the cloister of the monastery – shows a further and final step in the development of west-country vaulting. The
cloisters are the earliest example that we have of a fully developed fan vault, and indeed
it was some time before this form was used to cover really wide spans. The cloisters
themselves date from about 1370 and were not completed until about 1412.

The south-eastern bays, however, between the chapter-house entrance and the church
itself, are specially recorded as having been finished in Abbot Horton's time, that is, before 1377, and in these bays the new system is fully developed. The innovation consisted in making the vault conoids – i.e. the great bracket-like masses formed by the ribs
and their in-filling – regular both in plan and section: the ribs are spaced at equal angles
and at least every alternate one is of the same curvature.[9] In most bays the conoidal
brackets of the Gloucester cloister only just meet tangentially, leaving a flat spandrel to
be filled in the middle of the vault. This clearly limited the use of the new system to
relatively small spans (the cloister is 12 feet wide). One bay, however, is oblong rather
than square, and in this the conoids intersect, thus forming the ultimate solution of the
problem of large-span fan vaults. It was not, however, exploited for the main spans of a
large church for some considerable time after the completion of the cloister, as far as we
know, and the choir vault at Sherborne Abbey, which was planned before the fire of
1437 but not carried out till after, is the earliest surviving large-scale example.

It seems likely, however, that a very early fan vault on a fairly large scale was built
over the chapter-house of Hereford 1360–70 (Plate 136B), and this would have been contemporary with or even possibly earlier than the Gloucester cloisters. We know it only
from Stukeley's drawings and description of 1721, but comparison of the drawing with
the actual remains confirms the reliability of the antiquary. The chapter-house was a decagon of 45 feet diameter vaulted to a central pier. A specially interesting feature of this drawing is the character of the tracery pattern covering the vault surface. This is markedly
'geometrical' and strongly suggests London with its French Rayonnant affinities: it is
quite unlike the standard panel effects which we normally associate with fan vaults and
which first appear in the Gloucester cloisters. It is particularly unfortunate that we have
no remains of the great Abbey churches of Winchcombe or Evesham, where the other
early examples might have been found. It is possible to see indications of the early experiments which led to the Gloucester cloister vaults in some of the tomb canopies at
Tewkesbury, notably that of Sir Hugh le Despenser, which dates from 1350 or shortly
after. This canopy is ceiled in six bays formed of miniature conoids or part conoids supporting a flat ceiling. The conoids are perfectly regular and without ribs, which were
added in paint. There are signs also in the transept vaults at Tewkesbury that the form of

the transverse ridge ribs has been dictated by the requirements of the arched ribs, and this is an essential condition for the development of the fan system. The tendencies, to be seen at Tewkesbury and elsewhere, to treat the spaces between ribs as panels with foiled heads or cusping, and to increase the number of ribs as the vault gets higher also suggest the new kind of effect. These characteristics of the advanced fourteenth-century lierne vaults of the west country, which foreshadow the fan system, must not lead one to consider these vaults as incomplete stages in an evolutionary process which only completed itself in the great vaults of Sherborne and those that followed after. The elaborate distortions of the Tewkesbury vault surfaces were accepted and exploited, as suggested above, to gain effects of light and shade and depth with which the middle fourteenth century was deeply concerned. The flexibility of the lierne vault and the variety of patterns it made possible ensured that it should continue in favour, and great lierne vaults continued to be built right on into the sixteenth century. The fan vault gave the effect of unity mainly by the repetitive nature of its tracery patterns; the lierne vault offered a variety of ways of achieving that effect.

Of the great architectural enterprises of the second half of the fourteenth century at Canterbury, Winchester, and York, the two first can reasonably be called works of the Court school, and the eastern limb of York is clearly influenced by it. Canterbury nave, begun in 1379, and the series of smaller works that followed it there are almost certainly due to Henry Yevele and his partner Stephen Lote, both masons known as working for the Crown at Westminster, and William of Wynford, named as the mason in charge of the Winchester nave in Bishop William of Wyekham's will, is known to have worked earlier at Windsor. The Bishop had been much concerned with the administration of the royal works earlier in his career, and his own great enterprises, including the colleges at Oxford and Winchester, gave to his favourite mason unrivalled opportunities. These two masons, Yevele and Wynford, can be traced through documents and surviving buildings so as to stand out as far more solid and appreciable personalities than any of their predecessors, with whom, except for William de Ramsay, it is generally a case of associating a mason's name with only a single work, often an interesting fact and one worth noting but not in the present state of our knowledge usually very illuminating. Yevele is known to have worked on the continuation of the nave of Westminster Abbey from 1362, but his most important work is certainly at Canterbury.

The new nave at Canterbury replaced that of Lanfranc and is of the same length, nine bays including the western towers; the early north-western tower survived until 1834. The design (Figure 64) is an outstanding example of that desire to gain an effect of unity of space that has been noticed as a characteristic of so many buildings of the age. At Canterbury (Plate 137) this is achieved by heightening the aisles in relation to the main vessel and relying on the aisle windows as the main source of light for the church. The middle storey and the clerestory windows, which are both rather modest in size and in treatment, play little part in the effect which depends on the design of the piers and the vaults, both the main and the aisle vaults. The piers have three vaulting shafts which rise unbroken, except for two sets of rings, from their bases on the pavement to the capitals from which the vault springs. They are widely spaced, and the centre one is boldly projecting. A double ogee or wave moulding is carried without any interruption from the floor to the apex of the clerestory window, and behind this the main arcade with its traceried spandrels bounded by a bold horizontal string, the plain panelled middle storey and the clerestory window are all set in one plane, forming as it were one tall panel divided into three unequal parts. The whole is extremely elegant and accomplished, the effect of the curved profiles being subtly enhanced by slight but very sharp and clean

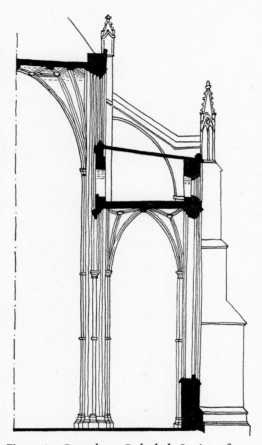

Figure 64. Canterbury Cathedral: Section of nave

linear accents. The vault, although a relatively simple lierne design, when compared with the extravagant ingenuity of some of the west-country examples, is no less accomplished, and shows equally with the western vaults much concern with the management of the curvature of the ribs to obtain an ordered and regular form to the vault conoid. The whole design, with its strong vertical emphasis, its dependence on geometrical forms, and its spare almost over-elegant quality, has a very French flavour, and shows how abiding this continental influence was on the Court school, though any less general word than flavour would be overstating the case. The effect of setting back the whole bay design framed in an uninterrupted suite of mouldings is very marked and recalls

Gloucester choir: it was later to be carried out in a different but equally effective manner in the choir of Sherborne, where the middle storey, the arcade, and the clerestory windows are framed in a deep-panelled splay which is also uninterrupted from the floor to the apex of the clerestory windows.

The Winchester (Plate 138) nave design is very different from this, partly because it is a remodelling, drastic but without involving complete rebuilding, of the Romanesque structure. Moreover, it is a nave of twelve bays as compared with nine at Canterbury, and though in height the naves are almost equal (78 feet at Winchester and 80 feet at

Figure 65. Winchester Cathedral, bay of nave: (*left*) original, (*right*) existing

Canterbury), the Winchester design is much less concerned to exploit that dimension. The bays at Winchester are divided by single large half-round shafts almost as large as their Romanesque predecessors (Figure 65). They seem, indeed, in some cases to be the earlier shafts pared down. The main arcades are low compared with Canterbury, their tops rising only to about the height of the springing of the Romanesque tribune arches: they have elaborately moulded arches supported on two substantial shafts. Above these the arcade is framed by a heavy enriched string surmounted by another string with a band of closely set trefoil-headed arcade panels between them: together they form an emphatic division of the bay into two parts. The spandrels of the main arcade are filled with large single trefoil-headed panels in rectangular frames. The treatment of the clerestory is very ingenious: the remains of the Romanesque thick-wall structure have been used to produce a series of recessions which give an undulating effect down the length of the church in striking contrast with the single-panel effect of the bays at Canterbury. This recession is effected by keeping the window tracery in the outer wall of the clerestory as in the Romanesque building, and managing the recession from the plane of the main arcade in two broadly moulded transitions, the first taking the eye back to a section of panelled wall flanking the window, and the second to the plane of the window tracery itself. The vault is a very high-pitched lierne design with the lateral cells interpenetrating with the main vault well below the crown: this scheme, together with a boldly treated ridge rib, gives a strong longitudinal emphasis to the vault. Throughout the design of the nave there is a consistent quality in the way the massive character of the early Romanesque building has been interpreted in terms of the subtly graduated light-and-shade effects of the fourteenth century. The other buildings on which Wynford is known to have worked, including the south-west tower of Wells, all share something of this breadth of treatment, though not of course in so marked a way as the nave of Winchester.

Two minor decorative works further illustrate the virtuosity of these great masons of the fourteenth century: William of Wykeham's chantry, which belongs to the first years of the fifteenth century, and the Neville screen at Durham, which is dated some twenty-five years earlier (1372–80) and is known to have been made in London and shipped in boxes to the north. The Neville screen is perhaps the finest piece of church furnishing of the age and one of the most remarkable pieces of stone tabernacle work in the country (Plate 140, A and B). It consists of five spires of four storeys, separated by four of three storeys; the spires are flanked by pairs of diagonal double buttresses which greatly enhance the vertical effect. The major spires are part octagon in plan and so have three-sided bow fronts towards the choir; the smaller spires are four-sided and set diagonally. Originally these spires formed housings for images and were filled with alabaster figures painted and gilded. In detail the composition can be seen to be largely made up of variations on the favourite Court motif of the niche framed in an arch, the extrados of which is prolonged upwards in an ogee to form a kind of gable with incurved sides and having a clearly defined tympanum filled with some geometrical motif. Sometimes only the vestiges of such a motif are used, i.e. just the upper part giving an effect of a pendant gable with curved sides.[10] On the west side, where the screen forms the reredos of the High Altar, these niche and gable forms are of open-work skeleton construction, and on the side towards the shrine of St Cuthbert, where some solidity was needed, the design is made up of smaller true niches with ogee tops, but of similar basic form. The screen makes an interesting comparison with the tomb canopy of Edward II of a generation earlier. The tomb shows the designer attempting to improve on the early kind of open-work effect in parallel planes by managing his miniature flying buttresses so as to lead the eye inwards to the successive storeys of the tabernacle work. A similar result of an effect in depth is achieved at Durham by the use of the octagon and square set diagonally for the plan of the spires.

The Wykeham chantry (Plate 139) is formed out of one bay of the south arcade of Winchester Cathedral nave. The two main piers are linked by a tall screen rising the full height of the arcade in the form of a three-sided bow with narrow canted sides. The canted sides are solid and adorned with a tier of three boldly designed housings for images. The broad middle side consists of three tall arches with very slender mullions and elaborately cusped heads. These arches are treated at the top with a bold version of the typical Court motif of the ogee extrados forming a gable set against arcade-panelled spandrels. The lower parts of the arches are filled with close-mesh traceried screens. Inside there is a complex little lierne vault and a reredos of tabernacle work which recalls in its detail some of the motifs of the Neville screen. The canopies of the housings on the canted sides are of special interest, for they have the ogee gable form boldly corbelled out from the wall on short canted segments of arches, giving the effect of a 'three-dimensional' cusp. The tympana of the gables of these canopies are filled with free sculptured motifs, except for one which is geometrical. The insides of the canopies are treated with miniature ribbed vaults so tilted as to display their rib patterns towards the front. This is a trick which came into fashion in the second half of the fourteenth century; the niches containing musician figures on the Singing Gallery at Exeter are a well-known example. This device not only makes the best of the decorative effect of the miniature vault patterns but also gives a sort of false perspective effect. It is used on a large scale in the western porches of Westminster Abbey and Westminster Hall, where the spatial effect is clearly a large part of the intention.

The series of building campaigns which transformed York Minster (Plates 111B and 144), except for the transepts, into a late Gothic church, continued at intervals for over two hundred years until, with the finishing of the north-west tower in the 1470s, there was no major work left to be done. The eastern limb was built in two main efforts: the four eastern bays begun in 1361 and said to have been finished in twelve years, and the five western in the last quarter of the century. Internally the bay design gives an effect of uniformity throughout the two works, except where it is interrupted above the main arcade by the eastern transepts. This is attained by the similarity of treatment of the main arcades and of the middle storey in both parts, which, like Guisborough and Bridlington, consists in a scheme of open-work traceries the verticals of which correspond with those of the clerestory windows above them. At York the tracery consists of a parapet of blind quatrefoils surmounted by open-work tracery which is an adaptation of the tracery heads of the aisle windows framed into a series of rectangular panels. The most important difference between the two works is in the handling of the clerestory windows, which in the later part are set back in the outer plane of the thick double wall, while in the earlier part these are in the inner plane and only slightly recessed behind the plane of the tracery of the middle storey. This important difference is much lessened in its effect by the interruption of the eastern transepts. These curious features are said to reflect similar transepts or even towers of the twelfth-century church. They are true transepts, and not transeptal chapels, in that, while they do not project to the north and south of the line of the aisle walls on the ground level, they are carried up the whole height of the building. They are also rather puzzling as to date as they have a rather later look than the rest of the eastern limb, and their great north and south windows (80 feet high) were not glazed until c. 1420 and 1430 respectively. They are most effective both inside and out, and with the great east window (glazed 1400–5) are the most striking features of the eastern parts of the building.

It is, however, the exterior of the four eastern bays which is the most notable aspect of this part of York Minster. In these the placing of the window traceries, in the inner plane of the double wall, has allowed for the provision of an elaborate traceried external gallery of three tall cusped arches with very slender dividing mullions and finished at the top by a strong horizontal line into which the mullions are framed, leaving traceried spandrels; all this is in marked contrast with the plain areas of ashlar in the spandrels of the aisle windows below them and throughout the work of both storeys to the west of the eastern transepts (Plate 111B).

The management of the eastern front of York is one of the triumphs of this four-teenth-century rebuilding (Plate 145B). It is the last and by no means the least of the great series of north-country east fronts – at Ripon, Guisborough, Selby, Howden (Plate 141, A and B), and the south transept of Melrose – and it is to Howden that it seems most closely related. The centre bay of the York design is almost entirely filled by the great window, except for a narrow line of image housings which rise to the springing of the window-head, where they pass imperceptibly into a system of panels which fill the spandrels and whose verticals rise to form an elaborate pinnacled cresting. This middle bay is framed by two rather slender buttresses, which are still further lightened in effect by being divided for the greater part of their height into pairs of image housings with projecting canopies and octagon image pedestals. The side – i.e. aisle – bays are flanked by octagonal turrets with buttresses projecting from their cardinal faces and surmounted by spirelets of considerable size. The plain ashlar of the plinth is in these bays carried up to the top of the spandrels of the aisle windows except on the faces of the buttresses. Above, a tall band of close-set arcading in high relief is carried round the buttresses and canted sides of the octagon towers and across the ends of the aisles. The depth of shadow in this arcading contrasts effectively with the shallow relief panelling of the upper parts of the towers and their buttresses. It is interesting to compare the subtle and unemphatic way in which an effect of depth and a play of light and shade is achieved in this predominantly linear composition with the bold, deep-set niches of Howden, whether on the buttresses or in the spandrels of the great window, and to note the rever-sion to an all-over linear effect as against a concentration of richness in the earlier design. The comparison is as good an illustration as one could wish of the fact that, though the latest development of English Gothic is indeed a reversion to that taste for all-over linear pattern effects which is so constant a quality in the architecture of medieval England, yet there can be no going back in history, and the art of the late fourteenth century and after never loses the recollection of the three-dimensional effects which were developed so boldly by the designers of the early part of the century.

Of the other great façade designs of the fourteenth century, two – Winchester and Exeter west fronts – belong to the category of the York east front, that is the high clerestoried middle bay formed by the end of the main vessel of the church flanked by two lower bays, the aisle ends; three – the west fronts of Lichfield, York, and Beverley – are two-towered compositions of more or less the orthodox continental type.

The Lichfield front in its general lines is the most complete façade composition of the early fourteenth century that we have, including as it does both towers and their spires.[11] The detail is almost entirely of the nineteenth century, but the general lines, including the disposition of the ornament, can be accepted as evidence of the original intention. The most striking characteristic of the design is the completeness with which the spread of decoration ignores the divisions between the main vessel and the flanking towers, and the way it is carried round the octagon corner turrets at the north-west and south-west angles of the composition. There are plenty of precedents for this reaching back into the twelfth century, but in earlier examples the designers were not faced with the problem of absorbing into their composition one of the new-fashioned great windows, and it is at this point that the tragic history of this building inhibits us from judging it. It is hard to imagine that the original design of the window got over this difficulty, but we cannot now be sure, for the existing window is a nineteenth-century replacement of the one made in the late seventeenth-century restoration after the devastation of the civil war. The York west front, with its boldly projecting buttresses and deeply recessed windows at clerestory height, is completely successful in solving this problem of absorbing a great traceried window as part of a two-towered western composition.[12] The character of the decoration of this front is no less successful than the scale of the main parts, and angular and flowing lines are most ingeniously mixed in the niche forms, arcading, and window traceries to set each other off.

At Beverley the western towers and front were begun in the last twenty years of the fourteenth century (Plate 127A). They were completed to one consistent design, unlike York, where the upper parts of the towers are about a hundred years later than the main design of the front. The proportions of the church at Beverley had from the beginning been very tall for its width, again in contrast to York, and this is maintained in the design of the front, where the buttresses of the towers maintain an unusually bold projection right up to the level of the tops of the belfry windows. The surface decoration of the front consists of tiers of image housings and arcade panelling, skilfully graduated from the bold relief of the lower parts to shallow relief at the tops of the buttresses. The Beverley towers certainly owe something to the lower parts of the York design in the management of their buttresses, but their most notable quality – the success with which the unity of the composition has been maintained in the vertical sense – is something of which we have little or no evidence to judge at York. The two towerless west fronts – Winchester and Exeter – have little in common except the similar fundamental problem of handling the relation of the aisles to the mass of the main vessel and combining this with some sort of entrance porch. The Winchester front has been much decried as unimaginative and mechanical (Plate 145A). It is almost certainly a design initiated in the middle years of the fourteenth century, and altered and completed in the early part of the fifteenth century as part of the finishing of the nave under the terms of William of Wykeham's will. The management of the aisle ends, with their raking arcades and substantial parapets, is skilful and successful enough in helping to concentrate attention on the main vessel. This effect is furthered by the handling of the porches, those to the aisles being kept well back from the plane of the main porch and made considerably lower. It is also notable that both at Exeter and Winchester little importance is given to the outer angles of the aisles, in contrast to the normal practice in north-country façades of this type. The result of all this is to require a considerable climax in the upper part of the main vessel, and this is hardly provided. The parapet above the great west window, the main gable which surmounts it, and the treatment of the upper parts of the octagon turrets which flank it, are all very sober, and though the proportions are admirable this is not what the critics of fourteenth-century Gothic have learnt to expect on such an occasion, hence possibly the unpopularity of this design.[13]

The Exeter west front is the most complete example we have in this country of a façade composition of the late Middle Ages combining architectural forms and figure sculpture (Plates 142 and 143). It was in building from 1346 to 1375. The elements of the composition are the gable end of the nave roof, the great west window of the nave, the ends of the aisles, and the screen. It is arranged in three bays of which the middle one, containing the main west window, is finished at the top with two bold string courses and a plain battlemented parapet wall, above which a comparatively small and simple gable with a traceried window to light the space above the nave vault and a pinnacled niche just appear from behind the parapet. The upper string course and the parapet wall are continued down the raking screen walls above the aisle ends. The lower string meets the shallow buttresses which frame the middle bay, forming a rectangular panel. The main emphasis of this upper part of the façade is given by the traceried head of the great window of nine lights, framed by these buttresses and strings; the tracery is of the type embodying a main circular figure of great elaboration. It forms a very close mesh pattern, and the scantling of the main order of tracery is sufficiently large to make a more than usually telling effect as an area of patterned enrichment set off by the plain wall areas of the spandrels. Below the parapet wall and strings which finish the tops of the raking screen walls of the side bays, is a zone of gabled arcading diminishing with the rake of the screens and returned round the small octagon corner turrets at the angles of the aisle walls. These turrets are kept very low, and at the top hardly disengage themselves from the raking screens. Beneath this relatively simple scheme of contrasted surfaces a sumptuously enriched sculptured screen in two storeys stretches right across the end of the building and stands well in front of it.

In this, as in the treatment of the walls above the ends of the aisles, the contrast with the Winchester front is very marked. At Winchester, where everything is done to enhance the impression of the height of the middle bay, the porches are treated separately, and those leading to the aisles are set well back from the plane of the central porch; at Exeter everything is done to strengthen the effect of breadth rather than height, and the strong horizontal line of the top of the screen is one of the most effective of the devices employed. The screen is contrived in two main storeys of niches: there is some variety in the design of the canopies of the lower storey, which are mostly broad, low, nodding ogees with very elaborate gables and pinnacles above, while the upper-storey niches have taller nodding ogees with simpler traceried gables above; the lower-storey niches have two tiers of figures, the upper single figures. The niches are separated by slender rectangular piers set diagonally so that the images themselves and their housings establish the main surface continuity of the screen. Everything is done to exploit the effect of rippling continuity of surface; the buttresses on either side of the middle bay, which are of considerable bulk and projection and have pinnacles and short strong flyers to buttress the ends of the main arcades of the nave, are almost completely absorbed into this surface continuity, for the niches and figures are returned round them; those which abut on the western ends of the aisle walls are almost completely masked, the niches passing in front of them uninterrupted and returning round the north and south ends of the screen, the angles of which are canted. The treatment of the doorways, which in the tradition of Wells, Salisbury, and Lichfield are not large, is also kept subdued in relation to the complicated play of light and shade of the surface in which they are set. The division into bays is, however, recognized in the design, not only by the presence of the two buttresses flanking the centre part, but also by a fascinating variation in the design of the cresting which surmounts the screen. In the middle and on the buttresses this is a boldly designed system of battlements pierced and filled with tracery motifs: [14] over the side bays there is a double line of smaller-scale battlements rising one behind another, their embrasures peopled with figures, a motif that suggests the illustrations to a romance of chivalry; but these are the ramparts of Heaven, and the religious application of the conceit was of long standing.

The screen contains within its depth a tomb chapel for Bishop Grandison slightly to the south of the main doorway, just as Bishop Gower's splendid contemporary pulpitum at St David's is provided with a place for his tomb to the right as one passes into the choir. They give to both monuments a very personal quality; they are early but typical examples of this individualist spirit of the later Middle Ages. The later works at Exeter are very well documented and the names of the masons are known; Richard of Farleigh, the mason of the tower and spire of Salisbury, and William Joy, whose name occurs in connexion with the choir of Wells, were both associated with this west front. Both names have Somerset associations, and there are interesting links between the Exeter front and the work at the east end of Wells. The treatment of the gable of the nave roof, cut off from the lower part of the composition by a strongly marked parapet standing bold before it, recalls a similar trick at Wells: it was to become a cliché in Somerset and Dorset in the fifteenth and sixteenth centuries. There is an interesting stylistic connexion between the lower storey of the screen and the design of the middle storey of Wells choir, which is by way of Christchurch in Hampshire where the tabernacle work has affinities with Wells, and where both the images and their housings have much closer affinities with the Exeter work.

CHAPTER 9
DEVELOPED GOTHIC BUILDINGS OTHER THAN CHURCHES

THE fashion of the large traceried window and the developed type of late thirteenth- and fourteenth-century vaulting, had as great an effect on the design of chapter-houses and cloisters as on any other type of medieval building. The octagon form of chapter-house naturally lent itself to the exploitation of the great traceried window, and the first and most influential example was almost certainly the great work at Westminster, which was nearing completion in 1254. The Westminster chapter-house (58 feet across) was the model for Salisbury, which followed some ten years later, and differs from it mainly in being placed on the ground level and not upon an undercroft, which greatly simplifies the character of the approaches. On the other hand, the absence of a dormitory range makes possible the opening up of the eighth window, above the entrance. The decoration of the Westminster chapter-house has been discussed above, and indeed Salisbury is less interesting in this respect, though the treatment of the spandrels and the zone between the wall arcades and the window-sills with a running frieze of figure sculpture is notable. The influence of the Westminster chapter-house extended far outside the range of such buildings themselves: it became, owing to its use as a meeting-place for Parliament and other national assemblies, one of the best known buildings in medieval England, and unquestionably the great four-light geometrical windows were a major factor in spreading the fashion for such features in all forms of architecture.

In the late thirteenth century two remarkable chapter-houses were begun at Southwell and at York. The Southwell example, which is relatively small (only 31 feet diameter), is covered by a stone vault without the usual central support. The York example (58 feet across) has an elaborate timber roof ceiled in imitation of vaulting. Southwell is approached by a passage leading from the north side of the choir and ending in a vestibule from which the chapter-house itself opens to the east (Plate 129B). The passage and vestibule are elaborately arcaded, and the wall arcade of the chapter-house shares with them the distinction of having the finest assemblage of naturalistic carved foliage in the country, generally dated to the early 1290s. The passage leading to the vestibule was originally open, in the manner of a cloister, to the east, and this must have considerably increased the effect of contrast in the sequence of passage, vestibule, and the octagonal building itself. The traceried windows are of an elaborate late geometrical character of three lights, the centre one rising so that its apex interpenetrates with a quatrefoil at the extreme top of the window-head, the upper part of this light being flanked by two large trefoils. The character of the vault, which has five ribs springing from each corner of the octagon – the centre ones meeting at a boss in the middle of the vault, the others rising to bosses on ridge ribs which radiate also from the great main boss in the middle – is of an elaborate patterned ceiling; it combines with the richness of the window traceries, the shafted window-splays, the sumptuous wall arcade topped by crocketed gable mould-ings and with elaborate foliage carvings in their tympana, and the celebrated naturalistic carved capitals, to make an interior of extraordinary richness and delicacy. The York chapter-house (Plate 118B), which is only a few years later than Southwell–it was begun just before 1300–is approached by a passage leading from the north transept (Figure 66); this extends two small bays and one large bay to the north, and then turns at right angles for two more bays towards the east, to the door of the chapter-house itself. The windows of the chapter-house are of five lights with elaborate geometrical heads; seven of these are glazed and the eighth on the entrance side has blind tracery of the same pattern. The

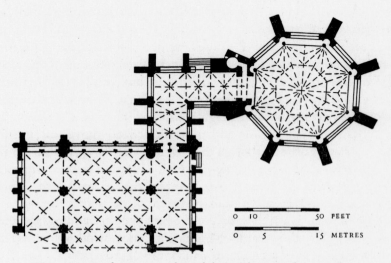

Figure 66. York Minster: Plan of chapter-house and approaches

most distinguishing features of the York design, however, are the great effect of the un-broken space of the interior achieved by the timber vault, which dispenses with the need of a central support, and the character of the canopies above the stalls which surround the building below the level of the windows. These are bowed outwards with two canted sides, and each side is crowned with an acutely pointed gable moulding with a bold finial. Above these finials is a band of decoration following the line of the bowed cano-pies and forming the front of the window-sill. The effect is to give a rippling line to the seven sides of the building. It is a good example of the tendency of that age to dissolve the logical structural lines of a building and to produce an indeterminate sense of space. The vestibule is lighted with four- and five-light windows and is very high for its width. The vestibule and the chapter-house both retain a very large part of their original glazing.

The history of the building of the Wells chapter-house is more complicated than any that we have hitherto considered. As mentioned above, the intention to build a chapter-house of octagon plan dates back to the first building period of the existing church. The work was abandoned, however, and not taken up again until the 1280s, when it was re-sumed on the chapter-house approaches. These are by way of the celebrated staircase (Plate 146) leading northwards from the angle of the north transept, and turning at right angles to the door of the chapter-house itself. It is lit by two geometrical traceried win-dows which follow the slope of the stairs, and originally a third similar window lit the half-landing at the point where the stairs turn to the east. The present picturesque treat-ment, whereby the stairs turn and at the same time continue in a northerly direction to the bridge over the chain gate, dates only from the fifteenth century. The chapter-house itself (Plate 120) is a work of the first years of the fourteenth century, and it was in use by 1319. The windows are of four lights with elaborate late geometrical traceried heads, and the decoration of the rear-arches and splays of the windows is distinguished by the quantity of ball-flower employed, a decoration which is also found in the zone beneath the windows and above the arches of the wall arcade. But the most characteristic feature of the Wells chapter-house is the treatment of the vault. Nine ribs spread from every corner, the four outermost rising to ridge ribs set radially to the centre of the building, the other five to a ridge rib placed intermediately between the central column and the outer wall. No less than thirty-two ribs spring from the central column to meet those from the angles of the building at this intermediate ridge rib in a series of carved bosses. The effect is extremely sumptuous, but the building is saved from too great heaviness of decoration by the elegance and glitter of the treatment of the windows and the wall arcades, an effect which is dependent on the profuse use of ball-flower. Wells is the latest of the great polygonal chapter-houses which survives in anything like completeness; but we have evidence of others, notably the one at Hereford (some 45 feet in diameter) which, as already mentioned, was completed by 1370 and was apparently vaulted to a central column with fan vaults (Plate 136B). The fashion for polygonal chapter-houses spread also to Scotland, where there are a number of examples, including the small one at Inchcolm on the Firth of Forth (dated 1265, and 24 feet in diameter), and another at Elgin, a building probably set out c. 1270 but not given its present form until the later fifteenth century, to which period both the system of window tracery and the vaulting seem to belong; the vaulting, however, follows the type evolved in England in the late thirteenth century.

From the thirteenth century onwards the great churches of secular canons not only imitated the monastic houses by building such splendid accommodation for chapter meetings, but added to their great churches cloisters which equally derived in essential idea from monastic usage. The secular cloisters being built solely for architectural effect and unrestricted by any traditional relation to surrounding buildings, such as prevailed in a monastic layout, vary very considerably in their arrangement but are often of great splendour. The earliest are at Salisbury (Plate 147, A and B), where the building began with the chapter-house about 1263 and was finally completed in 1284. Here the cloister forms a square of ten bays, each inner side measuring 130 feet, the cloister walks themselves being some 18 feet broad. Each bay contains a four-light window with an elaborate geometrical traceried head. The cloisters are placed on the south side of the nave, and to avoid obscuring the windows of the south aisle a long, narrow court is left between the north wall of the cloisters and the south wall of the church. They are entered from the south-west bay of the nave through a vaulted passage of three bays in line with the west walk of the cloisters; and from a doorway in the south-west bay of the main south transept. They are vaulted with plain, simple quadripartite vaults, and give an effect of great breadth and spaciousness (Figure 56).

The cloisters at Lincoln (Plate 115A), which were occasioned by the placing of the chapter-house north of the north-east transept, extend from the vestibule of the chapter-house to about the middle of the north main transept. They are on a much smaller scale than those of Salisbury, the internal court measuring only some 90 by 60 feet. They were completed in the last years of the thirteenth century, each bay containing a four-light geometrical window of a far more developed type than those at Salisbury. At Wells the existing cloister, which measures about 155 feet square, took on its character in a fifteenth-century rebuilding, though it seems that the outer walls may date back to the thirteenth century or earlier. The cloister is three-sided only, and is entered from the south-west angle of the south transept and the south-west tower; the width of the cloister walk is only some 14 feet. Other secular cloisters were built at Chichester and Hereford, the latter a work of the early fifteenth century, probably, as far as the east walk is concerned, being on the site of an earlier covered way leading from the Bishop's Palace to the nave of the cathedral. The south walk, which was of nine bays, is covered with a fine vault with intermediate and ridge ribs and good carved bosses. It is lit with four-light windows with tracery in four-centred heads.

It was not only the great establishments of secular canons that built cloisters in the later Middle Ages; many of the larger monastic houses remodelled their own cloisters in accordance with the new fashions. At Westminster itself (Plate 148) the first few bays of the eastern walk were rebuilt as part of the scheme which included the south transept and chapter-house in the mid thirteenth century, though the whole cloister was not finished until Abbot Litlington's time under Richard II. Other great houses, however, such as Norwich, Worcester, Gloucester, and Canterbury all rebuilt, or began to rebuild, their cloisters in the course of the fourteenth century. All these cloisters are distinguished for the size and splendour of their traceried windows, often repeated as blind tracery on the inner walls of the walks. The size of these monastic cloisters was largely determined by the pre-existing buildings dating back to a much earlier age. They often contain individual features of the greatest interest, such as the main door into the south-east bay of the nave at Norwich (Plate 149B), a remarkable piece of fourteenth-century design in which the lines of the arch mouldings can be seen passing behind the figures which, with their canopied frames, are set radially to the arches. The Norwich cloisters are also distinguished for the elaboration of their sculptured bosses. The vaulting of these later cloisters is often their finest feature, notably at Worcester (Plate 149A), which dates from the third quarter of the fourteenth century, where in the west walk a broad, low-pitched lierne vault springs from supports which are without capitals and produces a notably spacious effect. But perhaps the most remarkable of these fourteenth-century cloister vaults, not excepting those at Norwich, are at Canterbury and Gloucester. The Gloucester vault has already been discussed as an early example of fan vaulting, but the

Canterbury vault (Plate 149C) is in its way equally remarkable; it dates from the very last years of the century, and is possibly the work of Henry Yevele and his partner Stephen Lote. It has a lierne vault of extraordinary complication for its size, the longitudinal emphasis being given by a concentration of heraldic decoration at the main junctions of the ribs. The windows of the Canterbury cloister are of four lights with traceried heads of the straight-sided foiled figure type that we have discussed in connexion with the Court school of that age. They are typical of that school also in that on the outside the extrados is carried up in an ogee curve to form a gable above the window arch, the tympanum of which is filled with a foiled figure. The apex of this gable is carried so high as to cut the parapet of the cloister roof, so forming a series of intermediate pinnacles alternating with those over the buttresses between the bays. It is, indeed, the largest and most ambitious example of this typical Court motif that we have.

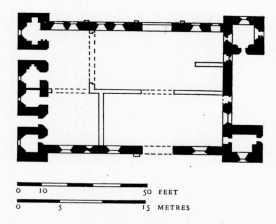

o   10   50 FEET

o   5   15 METRES

Figure 67. Acton Burnell, Bishop's Palace: Plan

Heraldic decoration appears for the first time on a large scale in the spandrels of the wall arcading of the later parts of Henry III's work at Westminster Abbey. It is a symptom of the growth of a new taste, rooted in the ideals and the way of life of the layman as contrasted with the ecclesiastic, which was gradually emerging as a conscious system. From the time of Westminster Abbey onwards this layman's taste becomes more and more a factor affecting the architecture not only of churches, chantries, chapels and tombs, for which the layman often paid, but gradually of domestic architecture which hitherto had been purely practical, either in the nature of a grandiose centre for the administration of an estate or practical in a purely military sense. At Acton Burnell (Plate 150A), in Shropshire, the Bishop of Bath and Wells, Chancellor of Edward I, built himself a grand country house, for which the licence to crenellate was granted in 1283. The building is a rectangle with four tall corner towers, and the centre parts of the short ends, also built up as towers, rather shorter and broader in proportion (Figure 67). The main body of the rectangle contained, on the first floor, a great hall and another large chamber running parallel with the hall, as well as smaller rooms arranged on two floors, thus making a block two rooms thick. This uncommon disposition of rooms may well derive from the early thirteenth-century Palace at Wells, and Bishop Burnell was certainly in a position to command the best architectural advice. The general external appearance of Acton Burnell is faintly military with its towers, but the building was not intended in any serious way for defence; the walls are only some 3½ feet thick, and the arrangement of windows and doors is not particularly defensible. It is perhaps the oldest surviving domestic building in the country in which a self-conscious composition has been adopted, with the intention of giving an impression of dignity and splendour simply as the dwelling-place of a great man. The inside of the building has been almost completely wrecked, and there is little by which one can judge of its architectural effect, though it is possible to be fairly certain about the nature of the accommodation provided. Bishop Burnell also added to the early thirteenth-century Palace at Wells a new chapel and a great hall (some 115 by 59 feet), which even in its ruined state remains one of the most impressive English domestic buildings of the Middle Ages. This hall is placed at ground level, and the butteries etc. and a passage, leading presumably to a detached kitchen, are contained within the same block as the hall itself, with above them a large solar, an arrangement similar to that of the upper plans at Acton Burnell. The window traceries, both at Acton Burnell and at Wells, are very advanced for their date, a point which is of some interest, as there are some indications that domestic building had been early in adopting this new fashion of window design.[1]

The type of domestic building in which the great hall was placed above an undercroft, often vaulted, a system of domestic arrangement which can be traced back to the earliest medieval times, continued in use in the fourteenth and even in the fifteenth century, though the hall built on the ground level unquestionably became the more general in the later Middle Ages. The type of quasi-military composition, of which Acton Burnell is a very splendid and complete example, continued into the fourteenth century and is found at Woodford Castle in South Dorset, again a rectangle with four corner towers; and a later example is Nunney in Somerset. Woodford and Nunney are rather more military in appearance than Acton Burnell, but still essentially domestic buildings given a military look. The nature of dissension in the later Middle Ages, both political and private, was not such as to involve sieges, though it was as well to be able to defend one's house against the casual assault of bad characters; such buildings, however, can hardly be dignified by the description of serious military engineering. Amongst the most remarkable surviving examples of this ambiguous type of architecture is Wardour Castle (Plates 150B and 151A), a building of the second half of the fourteenth century, built round a small hexagonal court, the proportions of which are very confined for the height of the building surrounding it. Indeed, it would be fairer to describe it as almost a light-well in a solid block of building, rather than to suggest that the Castle consists of a number of buildings disposed about a central space. The external effect of Wardour is difficult to appreciate owing to the loss of the elaborately corbelled-out corner turrets of which unquestionable traces can be found, but it seems certain that this building presented the appearance that we associate with continental castles of the late Middle Ages to a greater degree than almost any English building of which we have evidence.[2]

All these buildings share with Acton Burnell the characteristic of having their main apartments on the first floor, but this arrangement was not confined to the class of semi-military domestic buildings we have been discussing. In the course of the fourteenth century the lodgings of the Prior at Ely were greatly enlarged with a series of splendid apartments, in addition to the original great hall of his house which was also remodelled.[3] These are now known as the Guest Hall and the Queen's Hall, though these names are probably somewhat deceptive. In addition to these main apartments the Prior built for himself a smaller square room, fitted with a rather elaborate fireplace, and the chapel,

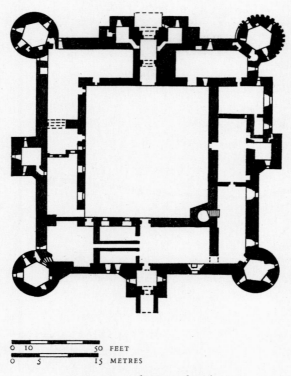

O 10   50 FEET
O   5   15 METRES

Figure 68. Bodiam Castle: Plan

which is well known for its tiled floor and in which the decorative detail clearly relates to that employed in the octagon and Lady Chapel of the monastic church hard by. All these new and splendid apartments were built on the first floor above undercrofts. Externally their effect is of a picturesque disorder, for it was almost impossible to obtain any monumental effect, such as that to be found in the important laymen's houses, as the architect's problem was one of adaptation to the existing buildings of the great institution. Their interest resides very largely in their size and proportions, the character of their open timber roofs, and the survival in some cases of features such as fireplaces. Perhaps the most splendid of all surviving palatial buildings are those parts of the castle at Kenilworth provided for John of Gaunt towards the end of his life; probably built from 1390 to 1393 (Plates 151B and 152A).[4] This work consisted of a great hall entered by a porch

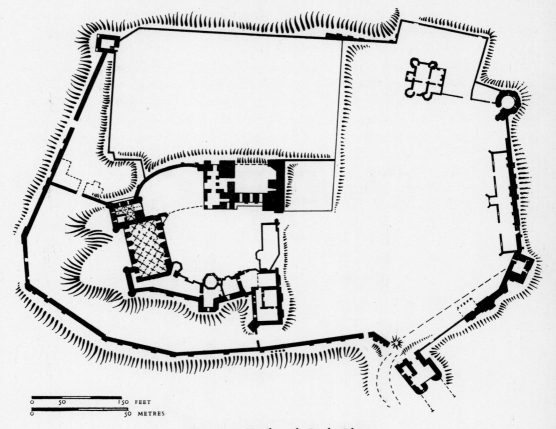

0 50 150 FEET
0 50 METRES

Figure 69. Kenilworth Castle: Plan

from the inner courtyard, flanked to the north by a tower with octagonal buttress turrets at the outer angles, and a similar tower built so as to overlap the other end of the hall, the two towers with the hall space between presenting a symmetrical façade as seen from the west on the outside of the building (Figure 69). The hall itself was some 90 by 45 feet and roofed in a single span. The building has long been in ruins, but enough remains for us to appreciate the intention of the designer in his elevations, and the fine quality of the detail of the interior work, notably the deep window recesses and the fireplaces. In addition the Prince remodelled the south range of the court to provide a great suite of state apartments, though these are less regular in their disposition and were probably conditioned by the sub-structures of earlier works. They included a very large oriel window at the point of junction of the hall range and the state apartments on the court side; this oriel formed a room of some pretensions in itself and was equipped with a fireplace. It is a remarkable development of one of the functions of these deep window embrasures in halls and other large rooms, as places where a group of people could obtain some degree of privacy within the common space of the great apartment.[4a] It is a conception of practical space organization to be found in other buildings than grand houses in the Middle Ages, notably schools, of which Wainfleet School in Lincolnshire is a good

160

example, and continued as a legacy from the Middle Ages to the great chambers and long
galleries of the Elizabethan and Jacobean age.

One of the most remarkable of the palatial buildings of the fourteenth century is that
of Bishop Gower at St David's in South Wales.[5] This complex of buildings (Plates 152B,
153, A and B) contains two great halls, a feature which it shares with the Palace at Wells
after Bishop Burnell's additions, and which can be found elsewhere both in palaces and in
some of the big Edwardian castles such as Harlech. The household of an important Bishop,
such as Gower or Burnell, provided a considerable administrative staff for his diocese as
well as those functionaries necessary to the way of life of a great man in the Middle Ages,
and presumably a second great hall was added nearby for business and ceremonial purposes rather than for domestic use. The Palace at St David's is somewhat irregular in the
disposition of its parts (Figure 70), but the group is dominated by the great ceremonial
hall, which is built above an undercroft and forms a solid rectangular block *c.* 115 by 30
feet. The outstanding feature of the palace is its decorative character. The walls are
crowned by a parapet pierced with a row of wide pointed arches corbelled out from the
wall top. These are carried out in a polychrome masonry of gold or violet coloured stones,

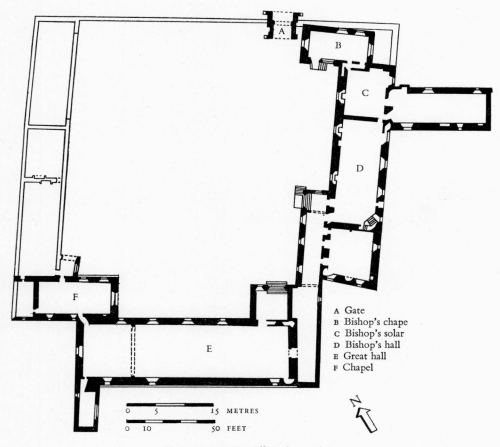

A Gate
B Bishop's chape
C Bishop's solar
D Bishop's hall
E Great hall
F Chapel

0   5   15 METRES
0   10   50 FEET

N

Figure 70. St David's Palace: Plan

and have delicate little shafts in the jambs of the arches. Other features of the hall block show equal attention to decorative effect. Apart from these important examples, which show domestic design almost untrammelled by any other consideration than conveni- ence and effect, examples can be found of improvements to existing buildings, or of a greater attention to these two considerations in new buildings the general character of which was dictated by a military necessity. A good instance is at Goodrich Castle, where most of the existing buildings date from about 1300.[6] Here the solar takes the form of a great state apartment entered at one end from the hall, the entrance being separated from the main space of the apartment by a handsome arcade of two tall arches; the antechamber thus formed also leading to a room in an adjacent tower. The search for monumental effect in domestic and palace buildings, of which John of Gaunt's hall at Kenilworth is the outstanding example, is seen some years earlier in the

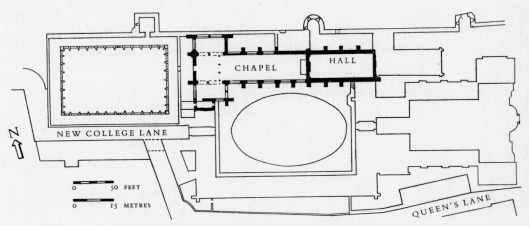

Figure 71. New College, Oxford: Plan

design of New College, Oxford.[7] William of Wykeham, who had himself in earlier days been intimately associated with the royal works, could command the best archi- tectural skill of his age, and his mason, William of Wynford, here inaugurated a type of composition which was at once successful in giving consistent monumental character to the buildings of the College and had a profound effect on the subsequent collegiate architecture of Oxford. The College buildings consist of a quadrangle (Figure 71), com- pleted in 1386, on the north side of which is placed a great unified block, which con- tains to the east the hall raised upon an undercroft, and to the west the chapel which is T-shaped in plan, having a transept which is aligned on its outer front with the west- ern range of the court. In consequence there is no window in the eastern wall of the chapel, which was instead treated as a reredos with tiers of figures in elaborate niches. Westwards from the whole of this group a cloister court was laid out having on its north side a bell-tower built up against the town wall. The type of T-shaped chapel established at New College, and which presumably derives from the unfinished chapel at Merton College, where a nave was certainly intended though never built, was adopted in the fifteenth century at All Souls and Queen's Colleges, and the whole scheme of uniting the hall and chapel in one monumental block was repeated on a grand scale at Magdalen, which was begun in 1474.

The normal plan of the medium-size country house assumed in the fourteenth century the standard form which was to persist to the end of the period covered by this book. This was the ground-floor hall, having at one end the offices – buttery, pantry, and kitchen – and at the other end a parlour on the ground level, and a solar, the second most important room of the house, on the floor above it, the hall itself rising internally to the full height of the building. Houses of all degrees of architectural importance adopted this scheme, though there was considerable variety in the way of placing the offices, and the tradition of the detached kitchen persisted till quite a late date. Some of these halls are apartments of fine architectural quality, and the improvements in the design of open timber roofs and the new varieties of roof trusses can be found well represented in the more ambitious examples. An interesting variation of the normal plan is to be found mainly in western England, where the entrance passage is separated from the main space of the hall by a structural feature consisting of a special roof-truss supported on two large wooden posts set well in from the long walls of the hall. This feature is known as a speres truss, and has been considered to represent a survival of the tradition of the aisled hall which gradually became obsolete in the fourteenth and fifteenth centuries. The York Guildhall, destroyed by fire in 1940, was an unusually late example. A good surviving example of a timber hall of the fourteenth century where the speres truss scheme was adopted is at Amberley, in Herefordshire. At Ockwells, in Berkshire (Plates 154 and 155), a remarkable timber ensemble of the 1460s (it was still uncompleted in 1465) survives, and retains much of its original character both inside and out. The hall, which measures some 40 by 20 feet and 36 feet in height, is a particularly interesting example of the exploitation of the special properties of timber. The walls, which are constructed of timber framing with brick in-filling between, rise to a height of 18 feet, the upper third of which is formed of two five-light windows which are separated only by one of the main verticals of the framing. At the high table end of the hall an oriel projects boldly, to finish flush with the solar wing. There are three window lights in the upper part of the oriel on the projecting side, and twelve lights, six above and six below, on the main front; thus, except for the more substantial structural posts dividing the windows on the long side of the hall and at the corners of the oriel, the whole of the upper part of the wall is window. The long sequence of nineteen lights has retained almost all its original heraldic glass, and the decorative effect of such a great state apartment can be better appreciated at Ockwells than almost anywhere in the country.

The taste for heraldic decoration and for giving a somewhat military look to buildings which were essentially of a non-military character, is found in its most developed form in the gatehouses of the fourteenth century and after. The tradition of the gatehouse seems to derive from two sources; the monastic gateway tower, of which that at Bury St Edmunds of the middle twelfth century is the most complete surviving early example, and the developed military gatehouse of the great castles of the second half of the thirteenth century. The Bury St Edmunds gate and its successors took the form of a simple square tower having the gate itself on the ground level and two storeys above, which at Bury served as a belfry. There is a second gateway to the monastic precinct at Bury, dating from the early fourteenth century (Plate 156A); here the plan is still a simple rectangle with the sides considerably longer than the inner and outer fronts. It is of two storeys only, having a large apartment, the purpose of which is obscure, on the first floor. The later Bury gate has on the courtyard side boldly projecting buttresses at the angles, adorned with elaborate niches and a three-light traceried window in the upper storey. On the outer front the place of the three-light window is taken by an elaborate composition of niches with nodding ogee heads. Later examples of the tower gate, such as that at St Augustine's, Canterbury, which is also of the fourteenth century, have at the angles small octagonal or part octagon buttress turrets which are carried up above the main block of the tower. This is a motif which was to have a great future in late fifteenth- and sixteenth-century building. It seems to have attained popularity first in the region where the influence of Lincoln was strong, and square towers with their angles treated as octagons, deriving presumably from the Romanesque western towers of Lincoln Minster (Plate 129A), are to be found in Lincolnshire and in the Fen country in the thirteenth century, and became gradually more formalized and decorative in character in the same areas in the fourteenth century. The gate of St Augustine's, Canterbury, is an early example outside this district. Among other early examples are the angle treatments of the great hall block that Bishop Burnell built at Wells in the late thirteenth century, and, perhaps almost more striking, the treatment of all the buttresses as part octagons on the south side of the church of Sutton-in-the-Isle in Cambridgeshire, which dates from the 1370s (Plate 166B). Elsewhere the fashion for splayed angles to gatehouse towers in particular can be found in serious military works in the thirteenth and early fourteenth centuries, but these are generally bolder in scale and less decorative in effect, and the Lincolnshire tradition seems to be a more probable source for this very influential motif.

From the late thirteenth century a number of great abbey gatehouses were built on a rather different system. These gatehouses consist of a long rectangle set transversely to the direction of the entrance. This sometimes gives space for a double gate, that is, a large main arch with a small arch for foot-passengers to one side. The gateway passage has on one side of it accommodation for a porter, and on the other a room and sometimes a staircase leading to the rooms on the floors above. The broad front of such a building offers special opportunities for decorative treatment, and from Kirkham Abbey gatehouse, finished in 1296, onwards this decoration is very liable to take the form of elaborate displays of heraldry (Plate 156B). Kirkham, though very much ruined, is an extremely grand example of this, and a somewhat later gateway at Butley Priory, in Suffolk (c. 1336), has a remarkable panel of heraldic devices carved in low relief alternating with small fleur-de-lis set in flint. At St Osyth, in Essex (Plate 157), is a fine gatehouse of the late fifteenth century in which the elaborate flint and stone panelling, well known in the East Anglian churches, is carried out on an unsurpassed scale. All these gatehouses provided considerable accommodation either for domestic or business purposes on the floors above the entrance. The grandest examples of these later gatehouses, in which the secondary uses have become almost more important than the function of a state entrance, are at Thornton Abbey in North Lincolnshire (dating from the 1380s, licence to crenel-late granted in 1382), and Ely (1396–7).

The Thornton gatehouse is perhaps the grandest example of its kind remaining. The outer front (some 65 feet across) stands flush with a great towered wall, and the main body of the gatehouse, which is some 40 feet thick, projects into the courtyard of the monastic precincts. The outer front is framed by two part-octagon turrets, and two intermediate buttresses, also with splayed angles, are corbelled out to become part octagon turrets in their upper parts. The three bays so formed have, on the ground floor, the main gate arch in the middle and blank walls with only narrow slit windows in the side bays. The outer turrets and the buttresses are linked by four-centred arches just below first-floor level, and these support a gallery across the front of the building. On the two top floors, above this gallery, the bays are filled with niche compositions in tiers, single in the outer bays and a group of three in the middle bay. Some of the figure sculpture of these niches still survives. The decorative work and main features of the front are car-ried out in stone, the walling in the upper parts is mainly brick. The effect of this grand composition has been to some extent spoiled by the addition of an elaborate brick bar-bican in the first half of the sixteenth century. The front towards the courtyard is again divided into three bays by four bold part-octagon turrets rising the whole height of the composition (Plate 158A). The centre bay, which on this side is given greater breadth by the larger dimensions of the intermediate buttress turrets, also rises to a greater height than the side bays. On the floor above the gateway arch, the centre bay has a three-sided oriel window standing out on corbelling, and above it a two-light traceried window in the top storey. Smaller two-light windows also appear on the first floor in the side bays. The accommodation provided by this grandiose building consists of the central gateway passage which is ceiled with an elaborate vault; on the south side is a passage leading to a secondary gateway arch in the southern bay of the courtyard front, which leaves room also for a considerable porter's lodge; at the north end is a single large room with smaller closets opening from it into the octagonal turrets. On the first floor is a very splendid apartment, about 48 feet long by 20 feet wide, having on the courtyard side a very elaborate recess which includes the oriel above the inner gate. There is evidence that this apartment, which still retains great dignity, had originally a timber ceiling of some pre-tensions, the boldly carved corbels for which survive; there is also a fine broad fireplace at one end of the room, and the oriel bay contains a prettily carved washplace. The top floor of the building is said to have been divided into a number of rooms, but it is diffi-cult to determine their arrangement; they were, however, of a comfortable size to judge from the character of the surviving windows.

The Ely gatehouse, which is almost as large as Thornton, is much less sumptuously fitted. It seems to have served for the office accommodation of the steward of the monas-tic estates, and possibly for his living accommodation as well. The building is not only less elaborate internally but, though nobly proportioned and of great size, is plainer out-side. It is a rectangular block with two main storeys, the lower containing a double gate-way, the smaller one for foot-passengers; the main block is flanked by square towers at the outer angles, and the upper floor, which contains the steward's accommodation, has

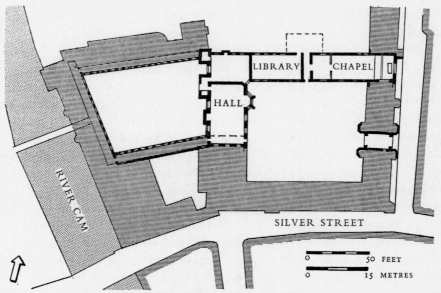

Figure 72. Queens' College, Cambridge: Plan

windows of some elaboration and four finely carved niches, one on each side of the main window feature. The building is of well-coursed rubble with freestone dressings. Apart from the extra accommodation provided by these later monastic gatehouses, there can be little question that one of their main functions was display. Even the comparatively severe treatment of the Ely gate enhances rather than detracts from the impressive quality of this entrance to the great institution, and Thornton is one of the most splendid pieces of pageant architecture that an age which specialized in sumptuous effects of that kind is known to have produced. The contrast in the treatment of the inner and outer fronts is quite striking; the outer front being paradoxically more delicate, and at the same time more ecclesiastical in its character, than the frankly military reminiscences of the front towards the courtyard.

Queens' College, Cambridge, begun in 1444 (Figure 72), is an example of the adaptation to a special purpose of the normal plan of a great house, carried out on a new site and under direct royal patronage, so that, apart from the provision of a library on the first floor of the range adjoining the hall and a comparatively large chapel, it represents almost an ideal standard arrangement. Considerable care has clearly been taken to make this building, if not symmetrical, at any rate orderly in its disposition of parts. There is a gatehouse tower of the normal Cambridge type – that is, with polygonal corner turrets – and opposite this is the entrance to the hall, at the high table end of which is the President's lodging and the library, with the kitchens reaching to the angle of the court from the other end of the hall. A chapel and the library range together formed one side of the court, and the gatehouse tower itself was used to provide, above the actual entrance, an elaborately vaulted apartment to contain the charters and muniments of the institution. It is worth considering whether the provision of carefully isolated towers in some great medieval houses may not have been as much for the preservation of legal documents and such valuables as for a refuge for the owner against the turbulence of his hired retainers, and this example of Queens' College may well be significant in this respect. The symmetrical and orderly appearance of Queens' College was emphasized by rectangular corner turrets at each external angle of the original court. Not long after the building of this first compact entrance court, the buildings were increased by the addition of a range of chambers on the river bank, and this was linked to the screens passage and to the high-table end of the hall by two covered walks built in brick. The new range of chambers has on its internal front a similar covered walk, the whole forming a sort of three-sided cloister. Though the term 'cloister' was applied to this court from comparatively early times, it is quite clear that this arrangement has little or nothing to do with the normal monastic cloister, which implied not only a set arrangement of buildings round it, but also sufficient space within its walls to provide living and working space for the inmates. The Queens' College 'cloisters', though built solidly with brick arches, are really a more substantial variation of the wooden covered walks which connected scattered parts of many great houses in the later Middle Ages, and are called pentices. The form of Queens' College, allowing for the special circumstances of the foundation – i.e. the size and importance of the chapel and the provision of a library – is an early example of the standard layout of the great houses of the late fifteenth and early sixteenth centuries.

Most early purely secular examples, such as Haddon Hall, with which Professor Willis compared the plan of Queens', are adaptations of earlier houses, and the sites being encumbered have not quite the regularity and finish of the Queens' College design. From the provisions of the document known as the Will of Henry VI, relating to King's College, it is clear that a similar ordered arrangement, deriving from the ideas evolved in domestic buildings, was intended in the case of this very grandiose royal foundation, the only part of the scheme to be realized being that whole of one side of the main court-yard which was given up to the great chapel. Of the other great houses of the first half of the fifteenth century, two particularly call for notice: one is Herstmonceux (Plate 158B), where an elaborate fortified wall with a great tower gatehouse enclosed originally a series of small courts (Figure 73) laid out on a scheme conditioned by the traditional arrangement of hall, upper-end chambers and offices, such as can be paralleled in many more modest examples.[8] The scheme also included a courtyard surrounded with covered walks, such as that added to Queens' College. A later example of the same kind of planning was at Shelton, south of Norwich, known to us only from an early and rather inadequate drawing.

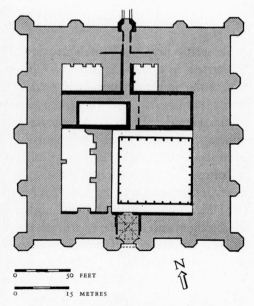

Figure 73. Herstmonceux Castle: Plan

The other type of early fifteenth-century great house which shows any considerable architectural pretension is that best exemplified by Tattershall [9] in Lincolnshire (Plate 159), where the Lord Treasurer Cromwell remodelled an earlier house in the years 1431–9. His establishment consisted of a large collegiate church with accommodation for the chantry priests attached to it, and the great house itself, surrounded by elaborate water defences. Within these defences there were, apart from offices and ranges of accommodation for the household and retainers, a great hall, and adjoining it at the high table end a splendid tower of five storeys with large polygonal angle turrets and elaborate machicolated galleries on the top storey (Figure 74). All the lower storeys have large traceried windows, including the ground floor, so that the superficial analogy with the early medieval keep or defensible strong tower is hardly tenable. The great tower at Tattershall contains a series of very splendid state apartments, approached by a grand staircase in one of the angle turrets and vaulted corridors on the upper floors, the other

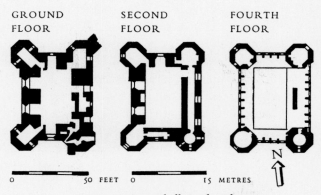

GROUND FLOOR   SECOND FLOOR   FOURTH FLOOR

0   50 FEET   0   15 METRES

N

Figure 74. Tattershall Castle: Plans

angle turrets providing smaller rooms. The reasons for building the state apartments at Tattershall in this special form are probably twofold at least: one, the space available within the water defences may well have been restricted and therefore a vertical disposition of the state apartments the most practical, as contrasted with their development round one side of the inner courtyard at Kenilworth; and secondly, a matter of semi-military fashion. An early engraving of the castle at Poitiers, which dated from the late fourteenth century, shows a similar arrangement. Only the great hall now survives at Poitiers, but the state apartments attached to its upper end were built in the form of a massive rectangular tower with four angle towers rising above its main structure. The Lord Treasurer Cromwell built another great house at South Wingfield in Derbyshire, the arrangements of which are much more like those of a normal manor house, but which embodies on one side of its main courtyard a strong tower, much less clearly differentiated from the surrounding buildings, however, than that at Tattershall. Lately Mr Douglas Simpson has suggested that these great houses of the later Middle Ages, especially those which appear to revert to the isolated keep tradition of the twelfth century, were occasioned by the nature of the households of the great nobility of that period, including as they did considerable numbers of hired mercenary soldiers – 'gangs of toughs', as he expresses it – whom it was necessary to exclude from the private apartments of the owner. He points out that in many of these later castles, beginning with Bodiam in Sussex of the later fourteenth century, elaborate pains have been taken to make the private apartments inaccessible from the main parts of the house except by controllable entrances (Figure 68). This theory is almost certainly sound, but, as usual with problems of domestic arrangements, is not, as suggested above, the whole story, and it is more than possible that the separation of one part of the building from the rest may be as much a form of insurance of valuables against *inter alia* fire as of the personal safety of the lord and his family against the violence of his hired soldiery. The nature of the design of the great tower at Tattershall, and the use of the gatehouse at Queens' College as a strong-room down to the present day, suggest that there may have been a variety of motives for the adoption of this arrangement. One of them is probably the emergent desire to gain an effect of military splendour suitable to the rank and dignity of the owner. The defences of Bodiam were, however, seriously meant, and the danger of French raids in the phase of the Hundred Years War, after we had lost command of the seas, is specially mentioned in the licence to crenellate of 1385.

CHAPTER 10

THE PARISH CHURCH

THE late thirteenth century saw the beginnings of a great change in the character and importance of the parish church. Early parish churches are not often buildings of much architectural ambition, though there are often individual features of very great interest and architectural merit. Inevitably, however, in buildings of such small scale the range of such features is limited. Exceptional parish churches from as early as the mid twelfth century do exist, however, such as Melbourne in Derbyshire with its handsome two-towered façade, New Shoreham in the south, and Darlington in the north, both of them fine buildings of the later twelfth and earlier thirteenth centuries. Some of the parish churches of the great seaport towns, such as Rye, Yarmouth, and Hedon near Hull, were buildings of considerable size and fine quality from quite an early date. There are, moreover, a number of parish churches with central towers, such as Poterne in Wiltshire, which are buildings of great quality, while fine western towers to parish churches can be found at almost all times in the Middle Ages. Nevertheless the generalization will hold, and the later thirteenth century saw a revolutionary change in the scale and character of these buildings. Two forces making for this change may be distinguished. The establishment of the Orders of Preaching Friars in the course of the century led to an increasing importance being attached to popular preaching, and this was ultimately reflected in the design of parish churches. Far more important was the rise of the custom of the foundation of chantries at the existing altars of parish churches, or in special buildings erected for the purpose. A chantry may be defined as a foundation and endowment for the celebration of masses for the soul of the donor, and sometimes for his relations also. The custom of establishing such masses reaches back to an earlier period than the middle of the thirteenth century, but from that time onwards the practice of establishing these foundations in parish churches, rather than in the churches of monastic houses, became increasingly popular.[1] A chantry might range in importance from a small endowment for a parish priest to say mass at the main altar of the church, to elaborately organized institutions in the form of colleges of priests with a special church such as those established in the fifteenth century at Tattershall or Fotheringay. Several intermediate stages of elaboration can be met with, and in many towns the endowment of a number of individual chantry foundations led eventually to the incorporation of all these additional clergy attached to a parish church into a special college. Later in the fourteenth and fifteenth centuries a third force, which strongly affected the architectural importance and plan of the parish church, began to make itself felt. This was the great importance and popularity of religious guilds. These societies interpreted their purpose of mutual benefit not only in the worldly sense of the care of their members in sickness, or of their widows in hardship, but included among their benefits those of masses for the welfare of the souls of the deceased members. Their activities centred often in an altar in the parish church, and the guilds

formed a vehicle directing the stream of benefactions towards the maintenance, adornment, and even on occasion alteration and rebuilding of the church to which they were
attached. It is difficult to over-estimate the effect of the growth and popularity of chantry
foundations and religious guilds on the purely architectural aspect of the parish church.

The Orders of the Preaching Friars hardly seem to have established an architectural
manner peculiar to themselves before the end of the thirteenth century. This is natural
enough, as the benefactions which would make possible building on an ambitious scale
naturally did not come in at once, but gradually grew in size, and the churches grew
with them as the popularity of the Mendicant Orders became firmly established. The
greatest of the Friars' churches [2] – those in London – have, now that the Dutch church
of Austin Friars has been destroyed, left no trace except in documents, and Friars'

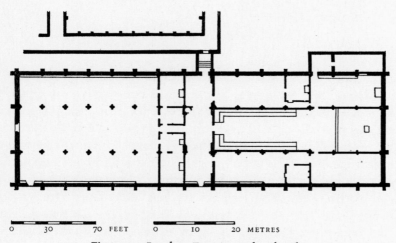

O   30   70 FEET   O   10   20 METRES

Figure 75. London, Franciscan church: Plan

churches in other important cities had been specially marked out for destruction in the
years following the religious changes of the sixteenth century. It seems, however, that
by the early fourteenth century a plan had been established, at any rate at the Franciscan
house in Newgate Street (begun in 1306), which was to be very generally adopted
(Figure 75). This church consisted of two great aisled rectangles each of seven bays,
divided by a passage-way between solid walls which led from the outside world to the
cloister and domestic buildings which were situated to the north of the church. The eastern rectangle formed the church of the community itself, the western a large open nave
with four chapels flanking an entrance in the centre giving into the cross passage, and so
to the choir. The distinguishing characteristic of this plan – the division into two almost
independent spaces combined with the extraordinary lightness of construction and open-
ness of the planning of the two rectangles – is found in other great Friars' churches and
their derivatives in a variety of plans throughout the country. The Franciscans' and
Austin Friars' churches in London both had aisled choirs as well as aisled naves, but even
such a great example as the Dominican church at Norwich [3] had only aisles to the nave,

N   171

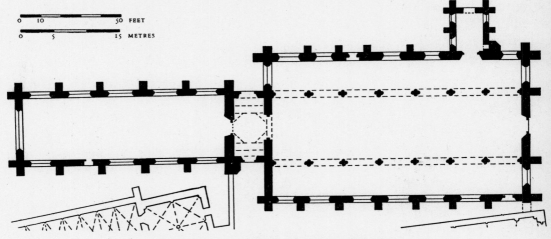

Figure 76. Norwich, Dominican Church: Plan

while the great choir of five bays was aisleless (Figure 76). The cross passage leading to the domestic parts of the institution at Norwich was surmounted by a central tower and both have now disappeared, leaving the two parts of the church almost as separate buildings. At King's Lynn the Franciscan church which also exemplified this plan has lost both the nave and choir, and only the central tower and its substructure survive as an isolated feature in the public gardens (Plate 160A). It is known that the great London churches also had towers above the central passage-ways dividing the two parts of their churches. Perhaps the example from which we can get the best idea of the effect of one of these churches is Holy Trinity, Hull.[4] This was not a Friars' church, but in the course of the fourteenth century certainly assumed the form made popular by the Friars. The earliest part of the surviving building dates from the last twenty years of the thirteenth century, and was built as a transept rather than a cross passage, and there was provision for a central tower, the upper stages of which were added in the early sixteenth century. The choir and nave buildings date from the second quarter of the fourteenth and first quarter of the fifteenth century respectively, and are rectangles with all the characteristics associated with the Friars' churches in London and Norwich. Hull seems an early example ot the influence of the Friars' churches on the architectural character of the parish church.[5] That influence is in the main to be found in the character of the naves of the churches, which tend in the fourteenth and fifteenth centuries increasingly to become simple aisled parallelograms with arcades of extraordinary lightness of construction. Undoubtedly the aesthetic preference for unity of space effect, which we have seen exemplified in important cathedral and monastic churches, seized upon the plan-forms initiated by the Friars because these expressed the new taste so admirably. In extreme cases, such as North Walsham in Norfolk, of the fourteenth century, and St Nicholas, King's Lynn,[6] of about 1400, the search for unity of space effect is carried to its logical conclusion, and there is no structural division between the chancel and nave of the church which almost becomes one single-aisled parallelogram (Figure 77). Though the influence of the Friars' churches was confined in the main to the form and plan character of the naves, these are of special importance in the later Middle Ages, as the system whereby the care of the chancel of a parish church devolved upon the appropriator of the living while the nave was the responsibility of the parishioners, often led to the reconstruction of the nave on a grand scale while the chancel remained unaffected. Where the authority responsible for the chancel was a great monastic establishment or other institution with a strong sense of continuity and a well-developed organization for the care of its outlying properties, the chancels were often kept for generations in at any rate reasonable repair, whereas the nave, as the parish responsibility, was allowed to fall into decay until pressure of conscience or of outside authority compelled rebuilding on a grand scale. Moreover, the guilds, as part of the organized life of the parish, were often concerned to lavish their benefactions on the nave, which was more particularly the concern of their members.[7]

The earliest effect of the vogue for chantry foundations in parish churches is to be seen in the fine chancels which were built to churches in the north and the eastern midlands in the course of the second half of the thirteenth century and the first years of the fourteenth. A notable example is Cherry Hinton near Cambridge (Plate 160B), a rectangular building lighted by seven lancet windows adorned on the inside with cusped rear-arches supported on slender shafting. But the new movement for a large chancel coincided very nearly in date with the fashion for great traceried windows, and these, divided externally by boldly projecting buttresses, are the elements out of which a number of very noble architectural designs were made in these areas. These new and more ambitious chancels, depending as they do on the management of their windows, are as good a field for the study of the development of tracery patterns in the late thirteenth and early fourteenth centuries as the great churches themselves. The chancel of Fenstanton church in Huntingdonshire is a suitable example and closely dated to the years about 1350 (Plate 161A); it is 50½ by 25 feet, as compared with the nave of 44½ by 15½ feet, exclusive of the aisles, and its great east window of seven lights with reticulated tracery in the head which is varied by a very complex circular motif in the middle, is the dominating feature both inside and out.[8] The side windows of three lights take up the reticulated motif. Internally the contrast between the open spaciousness of this chancel and the

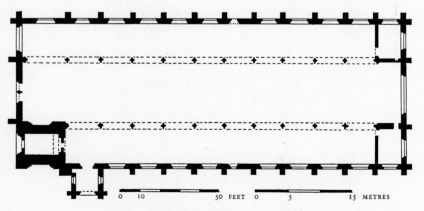

Figure 77. King's Lynn, St Nicholas: Plan

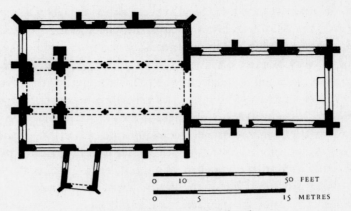

Figure 78. Fenstanton church: Plan

comparatively broken spaces of the rest of the church, consisting of nave, aisles, and a western tower, the lower space of which is open to both nave and aisles, is architecturally very dramatic (Figure 78). It is not suggested that this contrast was anything more than an acceptable by-product of the intentions of the builders, but to suppose that the medieval builders were unconscious of such matters is inconsistent with the general evidence of the buildings of the time. Cotterstock in Northamptonshire is a similar example dating from the late 1330s, and another even more elaborate is Lawford in Essex (Plate 161B), where the internal effect of the windows is enhanced by a wealth of decorative carving of un-paralleled magnificence in the splays and rear-arches. The whole interior effect of this chancel (36 by 20 feet) is immensely rich. These examples are all chosen from churches where the rebuilding of the chancel was a separate undertaking and not part of a general rebuilding.

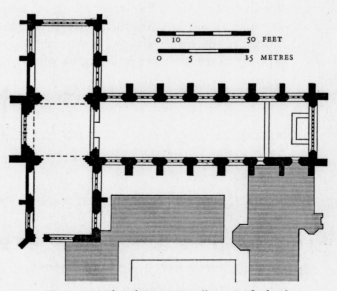

Figure 79. Chapel, Merton College, Oxford: Plan

Throughout the later Middle Ages there are occasional examples of complete re-building, and in these the chancels are often just as splendid; Uffington in Berkshire in the mid thirteenth century, Heckington in Lincolnshire, and Patrington in Yorkshire in the fourteenth century are outstanding examples. A stress has been laid on these parochial chancels as they are something new in the thirteenth century, but smaller monastic establishments can show similar developments, except that monastic churches tended to preserve the central tower and cross-plan with transepts which was traditional with them. A good instance of the mid thirteenth century is what is now the chapel of Jesus College, Cambridge. The first parish church where the design is consciously

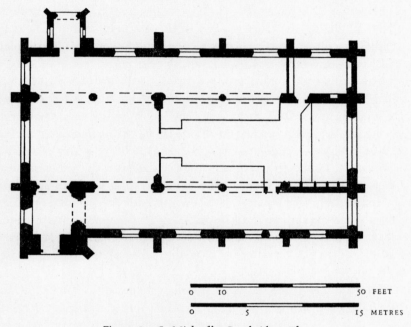

O   10   50 FEET

O   5   15 METRES

Figure 80. St Michael's, Cambridge: Plan

adapted to the special character of a University College is St Michael's, Cambridge, of the late 1320s. The plan (Figure 80) is an aisled rectangle of five bays, of which the three easternmost are the collegiate chancel, divided from the aisles by walls and screen, and from the two westernmost bays by a stone-built chancel arch which has a purely functional not a structural purpose. Rather earlier (1289–94), the chapel at Merton College, Oxford, shows a fine chancel with remarkable traceried windows which all retain their original coloured glass. As it survives at present, Merton chapel consists only of the chancel, crossing, and transepts, but a nave was certainly intended (Figure 79). The building was to serve as a parish church as well as a chapel for the newly-founded College. Essentially such a building differs in no way from examples such as Cotter-stock, which we have been discussing; for Cotterstock was equally a collegiate found-ation, differing only from that in Oxford in the special nature of the constitution and duties of the collegiate body in the university town. The Merton choir and chancel are of unusual length and splendour (102 by 28 feet) with seven three-light windows on the north side and five on the south, the two easternmost southern bays giving on to the sacristy; the east window is of seven lights with elaborate geometrical traceries in its head, the lower lights having a motif of a cusped sub-arch enclosed in a gable form and the head of the window filled with a complicated circular motif.

Some interesting examples of mid thirteenth-century aisleless chancels, of a comparable scale to the English ones we have been discussing, exist in a fragmentary state in Scotland and Ireland. At Brechin (Plate 11) there are the remains of the western part of a chancel with fine many-shafted rear-arches to the lancets in the north and south walls; the chancel was 23 feet in width and is said to have been some 84 feet long. The eastern limb of the cathedral of Dunblane (Plate 163), though flanked on the north by a two-storey building like a hall, is in fact a chancel of this character but of a later date in the thirteenth century; its dimensions are 81 by 28 feet, and the south wall is divided into six bays containing two- and three-light windows, the existing traceries of which seem to be of a later character than the clerestory windows on the north side, and are presumably insertions. The eastern part of the Augustinian Priory church at Inchmahome near Stirling, which measures some 66 by 23 feet 8 inches, though it lacks the distinguishing window treatment in its north and south walls, has some of this character, its chief feature being a fine five-light east window of grouped lancets. Of the Irish examples, Ardfert (Plate 162A) measures 25 feet in width and was originally possibly as much as 65 feet in length. It has a fine three-lancet east end and nine surviving southern lancets with delicately shafted rear-arches. The remains of the enigmatical eastern building at Ferns (Plate 162B) (36½ by 22½ feet) is similar to the work at Ardfert and even more delicate in the effect of its shaftings and mouldings, and shows a distinctive handling of the rows of lancets which has great charm. The eastern limb of the cathedral of Cashel (1235) belongs to the same type.

The architectural effects of adaptations and accretions as time or the incidence of benefactions made them necessary or possible, makes the study of parish churches one of the most complicated and fascinating branches of medieval archaeology. Moreover, it is not confined to the study of small and modest buildings. Fine churches such as St Michael's and Holy Trinity, Coventry, and Cirencester and Grantham parish churches, owe their character not only to the gradual additions and alterations of features at different periods – this is true of most of the great monastic and cathedral churches – but almost more to the individualism of benefactors, whether expressed directly in the building of personal or family chantry chapels, or through the agency of a religious guild of which the benefactor was a member. This individualist spirit is in general stronger than any aesthetic feeling for architectural unity of effect. This is not to say that such a feeling is not perceptible in many important parish churches; indeed, the skill of such enlargements or additions of aisles, naves and chancels is often admirable. It is possible to see the history of later medieval church building in England as a continual struggle between centripetal and centrifugal forces resulting in every degree of compromise. The centrifugal forces were not only those already mentioned as specially affecting parish churches, the particularism of individuals or corporations, but the example of the great churches themselves with their spreading transepts and, as compared with many continental schools, their dispersed plans.

The two main traditional types of parish church plan, as developed in the later twelfth and earlier thirteenth centuries, the cross-plan with an important central tower, and the longitudinal plan of chancel, aisled nave, and tower at the west, were both difficult to discipline in accordance with a desire for unity of effect. The cross-plan, which when used on a sufficient scale can give a considerable sense of unity to the building externally by the dominating feature of the central tower itself, and internally by the sense of climax given by the upward extension of the crossing space, was, when used on a normal parochial scale, inclined to divide up the four main limbs of the cross into almost completely separate spaces, and this may well have been a factor in the gradual disuse of the cross-plan in later churches. Examples can be cited, as St Cuthbert's, Wells (Plate 164B; Figure 82), where a new tower has been built to the west and a central tower removed, though the original cross-plan has left traces of its former presence in the eastern bays of the nave arcade and the transeptal extensions immediately to the west of the chancel arch.[9] The plan so developed was also adopted in some new churches from the outset, and not necessarily arrived at by a process of adaptation. Yeovil in Somerset (c. 1380) is a particularly fine example, and the height and splendour of the transeptal extensions give to it a great part of its quality both inside and out.[10] There are plenty of transeptal extensions which are in fact merely chapels built out to the north and south at the eastern end of the nave aisles, and have no implication of the existence of a former cross-plan or even, as they certainly have in Yeovil, implications that they were inspired by true cross-planned examples. They vary from places where the extensions are architecturally oriented, that is their roofs run north and south and their end walls have large window features, to a simple doubling of the end bays of the aisles. These can be found at almost all dates, and seem to belong to a tradition of enlargement of the nave by annexes, as and when required, which is distinct from the developed plan with a true crossing and, in ambitious examples, a lantern tower. Where care has been taken to make these extensions symmetrical the two traditions seem to coalesce; they are nevertheless quite different, and an almost bewildering variety of examples of the sporadic growth of such chapels can be cited from all periods.[11]

The addition of chapels east of the chancel arch, or sacristies, was equally likely to happen as and when benefactors came forward, and on occasion consideration was given to matching up such extensions on each side of a chancel to produce a symmetrical effect. A good instance is Lavenham church in Suffolk, where the original fourteenth-century chancel has been flanked by important early sixteenth-century chantry chapels, given by different donors, opening into it with two arches on each side and giving the effect almost of aisles. At Lavenham the chancel is further compassed about by a sacristy built up against the east wall and kept low so as not to interfere with the main east window. A curious effect is produced externally, as these very late additions have the low-pitched roofs concealed by parapets of their own age, whereas the original chancel retains the form of its high-pitched fourteenth-century roof which rises boldly in the middle.

The western parts of the parish church were equally liable to piecemeal enlargement,

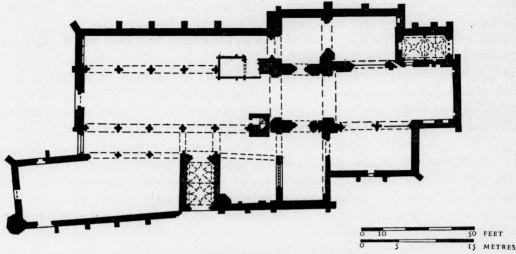

Figure 81. Burford church: Plan

whether by transeptal chapels as discussed above, by porches, by chapels placed at al-most any point along the length of the nave aisles, by western towers, or by enlargement to provide further windows and more light (Figure 81). On occasion aisles of the late thirteenth or early fourteenth centuries are heightened in the fifteenth or early sixteenth centuries in order to improve the size of the windows, and even more frequently, espe-cially in eastern England, the improvements carried out by the parishioners consisted in the addition of a fine many-windowed clerestory, and these alterations inevitably en-tailed a renewal of the roofs. Where the enlargement of an aisle involved the heightening of its outside walls to accommodate taller windows, it was often accompanied by the heightening of the nave arcades to correspond. Examples can be found in Cambridge-shire, as at Chesterton, where this process seems to have preceded the alterations to the aisles and, very remarkably and successfully, at St Cuthbert's, Wells, where the piers of a fine early thirteenth-century arcade have been heightened so as to give an effect en-tirely alien to the ideas of their original builders. The nave of St Cuthbert's is seven bays in length, of which the easternmost embodies the remains of the former crossing (Figure 82). The heightened piers, with their early thirteenth-century bases and capitals, are sur-mounted by arches in four orders having hood-moulds with sculptured stops; above these are figure corbels supporting shafts from which eventually spring the main timbers of the roof (Plate 164B). In each bay there is a fine five-lighted clerestory window. St Cuthbert's is an altogether exceptional building in that, while no expense has been spared and the later work – tower, roof, clerestory, aisles, transeptal chapels, and chancel chapels – is all carried out in the finest manner, conservatism, or sentiment, or some other motive that we do not know, has brought about the retention of earlier medieval features and, that rather rare phenomenon in medieval buildings, the deliberate imitation of the moulded forms of one generation by its successors.

It is tempting to treat later parish church architecture on a regional basis, and indeed the variety is so bewildering that some such system must needs be adopted. At the same time examples are so numerous, running into several thousands, and the diversity so extraordinary that without very considerable further study regional differences can only be distinguished in broad terms. The factors making for these differences are of course primarily economic, generally in the sense that certain areas in the fourteenth, fifteenth, and early sixteenth centuries enjoyed special periods of prosperity, and the expression 'a wool church' is often used to describe buildings in Somerset, East Anglia, and the Cotswolds; more particularly economic, in the sense of the availability of materials, was the effect on architecture of the costs of carriage in certain areas such as East Anglia, where good building-stone is extremely rare. Beyond these two very general factors, which themselves have been hardly sufficiently studied, is the further complication of the influence of local centres such as York, where undoubtedly the great building enterprises of the fourteenth and fifteenth centuries brought a concentration of the building and church-furnishing trades to the city, so that the influence of a York school can be traced far and wide over the north midlands and Yorkshire itself. It seems likely that other centres, possibly at Norwich, Bristol, Bury St Edmunds, Exeter, or Coventry, could also be recognized, though in all these cases the evidence seems harder to come by than at York. A further complication is added by the common practice, of which there is abundant evidence in contemporary documents, of requiring a medieval builder to model his work on some well-known local example, and in consequence features or whole churches which appear to have a family resemblance are not necessarily built by the same masons, though they may be, but may have been examples where one mason has been required to form his design on the work of another. Clearly this last practice was powerful enough to bring about such local specialities as the clerestories of south Lincolnshire and the Fen country, where from the mid fourteenth century a type of many-windowed clerestory, having two windows to each bay of the nave, became

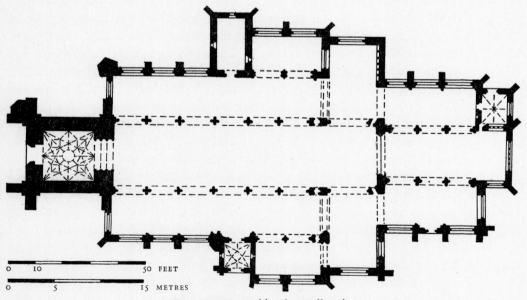

Figure 82. St Cuthbert's, Wells: Plan

extremely popular and was developed with extraordinary refinement. Another district where the fashion for fine clerestories was presumably spread by this process of prescribed imitation is the Cotswolds, where the clerestories are distinguished not only for the size of their windows – single many-lighted windows, not pairs as in the east – but also by their being raised well above the chancel arch, and the eastern end of the clerestory itself glazed with a many-lighted window even larger than those above the main arcades. The result is to produce a lantern-like quality which is very distinctive.

The policy of prescribing one or more well-known local examples as models to be copied when new work was being undertaken is, of course, responsible for much closer resemblances than is implied in these general remarks about clerestory treatment. As we know from the Eton College documents, different buildings may be prescribed as models for different features in the same contract; in the work at Eton the rood-loft was to be made like the rood-loft at Winchester College, and the stalls like those of a London church. The study of building documents, accounts, and agreements has so far rather enabled us to understand the general conditions in which the churches were built than to tie down particular resemblances between buildings to particular causes, the employment of the same craftsmen, or the prescribed imitation of particular features. The mass of surviving documents is very large and very varied; the number of major buildings even more so, and though much progress is being made along these lines we have still a long way to go.

Of the regional schools, that of Somerset and the south-west is one of the most distinguished and the most varied. The two examples already cited at Yeovil and Wells represent early and late examples of the great building period which stretched from the later fourteenth to well into the sixteenth century, when the dates of the Acts of Parliament dissolving chantries and guilds (1545–7) may be taken as terminal dates as close as can be defined at all narrowly, though even these are not absolute, and in Devon men went on spending money on parish churches for some years after the machinery for the direction of benefactions to church building and adornment had been officially stopped. The chronology of the west-country churches has hardly been systematically worked out. The indications are, however, that, though examples can be found fairly evenly spaced over the hundred years 1375–1475, it is the seventy years after that which saw the greatest church-building activity in the west, and all the dated woodwork known in Somerset is of that time. The piecemeal way in which churches came to be built – here an aisle, there a chapel or a porch or a tower added, here a partial rebuilding, there an adaptation – makes the study of the chronology of the style extremely complicated; but some movement can be traced, as in the gradual establishment of characteristic pier-forms, or the trick of using an easily recognizable type of cusped panelling all round the jambs and soffits of arches, especially tower arches, uninterrupted by any impost moulding. The monumental example of this trick is in Sherborne Abbey, notably in the nave arcades and the bay design of the presbytery, but this is not to suggest that the motif originated there, merely that Sherborne is the most sophisticated and elaborate example of its use. The standardization of pier-forms, and perhaps the pierced or battlemented parapets, may often be due as much to the practice of having the stone prepared at the quarry as to prescribed imitation or the influence of the same masons on the spot. We know that this practice was common throughout the country, at any rate in the fifteenth century, and there is an apt illustration in the Sherborne Almshouse chapel (finished 1442), where the windows were bought ready cut from the Ham quarries and set up by a 'Rough Mason', the two transactions being entered separately in the accounts. Eastern and southern Somerset and north Dorset is a country of fine building stone in considerable varieties of colour and texture, including the red stone of the Quantocks, the blue lias of central Somerset, the fine grey Doulting stone of which the great works at Wells and Glastonbury are made, and, perhaps most important of all, the golden stone of Ham Hill and its related quarries. A comparison of the work at Yatton, where the Doulting stone is exploited with an extreme delicacy, with the broader effects of the Ham stone at Sherborne is instructive (Plates 164A and 180A); the use of the continuous panel soffit in the arch to the north chancel chapel at Yatton is especially interesting in this respect; but though this factor of the imaginative exploitation of the qualities of the local material is one of the most fascinating and important aspects of late medieval parish church building, it is possible to overstress it, and it is certain that the same masons were ready to work in a great variety of materials.

There are two quite distinct types of church prevalent in Somerset, the one to which both the examples we have already cited belong, that of the tall arcaded church with clerestory, distinct chancel, and on occasion even transeptal extensions to the aisles, which is found mainly in the eastern and south-eastern parts of the county; this type of church has affinities with the work of Gloucestershire and the Cotswolds and indeed with the manner of church building which spreads broadly over central England.[12] The other type, in which an aisled rectangle is formed of three broad parallel spaces divided by wide, and often comparatively low, arcades, is to be found commonly in Devon and in such churches as Hinton St George, and Dunster, in Somerset. In general these spaces are covered with tunnel-like timber constructions of the type known as wagon roofs.[13] There is no clerestory, in the developed examples no chancel arch, and the division between the eastern and western parts of the church is made by a very splendid wooden screen stretched right across the church. Halse and Dunster have both retained their screens with a good deal of the upper parts (so often destroyed) still remaining. Both these examples are fine ones, though the greatest are to be found in Devon in such churches as Swymbridge (Plate 167A), Dunchideock, and Atherington, the last example so well advanced into the sixteenth century that the ornament includes motifs ultimately of Italian derivation, though probably reaching Devon through French sources.

The towers of Somerset churches have long been rightly famous, and since the youth of Professor Freeman in the middle of the nineteenth century have attracted the attention of historians. They have been analysed with great acumen and subdivided into types and schools. The latest critic, and one of the most knowledgeable and acute, has accepted the division into schools as set out by Dr Allen in 1932, but with very serious detailed modifications.[14] Here it will be enough if we mention the two chief types: that which seems to derive through the south-western tower of Wells Cathedral, built by the mason William of Wynford in 1395 and ultimately deriving from the central tower of the

Cathedral of the early 1330s. In this the distinguishing characteristic seems to be the prolongation of the lines of the belfry windows downwards to include the middle storey of the tower in a single enriched upper area: examples are the towers of St Cuthbert's, Wells (Plate 165), naturally close to the prototype, Wrington (1420–50) (Plate 166A), and Evercreech (c. 1450). In addition to the features mentioned, all these towers show an extraordinary subtlety in the handling of their corner buttresses and pinnacles; all of them have large and well-designed west windows to light the ground storey of the tower, and in all of them their staircase turrets are ingeniously exploited as part of the general composition. These last characteristics are common to almost all Somerset towers. Another recognizable group appears as that of which Bishop's Lydeard (also c. 1450) may be taken as an early type. The whole tower is divided into four stages, the topmost set back on all four faces, so that the corner buttresses finish as pinnacles at that level. The top storey has two grouped three-light windows on each face, whereas the two storeys immediately below have one two-light window on each face; the western face of the bottom storey has a broad five-light window surmounting the west door; the window on the south face of the third storey is flanked by niches for images. Variations on this scheme can be found in a number of churches, such as Ile Abbots and Kingston St Mary. One of the most distinguished features of the Somerset towers of almost all types is the treatment of the parapets and pinnacles forming the upper finish of the tower. There is evidence that a spire was originally intended on some early examples; indeed at Shepton Mallet it was carried up to a height of 8 feet and is clearly visible above the parapet at the belfry stage. But this is almost the last indication of a desire to build spires in Somerset, and thereafter the flat-topped tower enriched with a crown formed of elaborate pinnacles and pierced parapet becomes the rule.[15] Shepton Mallet is claimed as the prototype of a special group of towers, having three windows – the two outer ones, however, being blind – on each face of the belfry stage. Other examples of the group may be Axbridge, also an early tower, and Wedmore.

The broad-aisled type of church plan, without clerestory, is found in Cornwall as well as in Devon and western Somerset. It occurs also in Kent, and in that county it seems to be associated rather with town churches. There are a number of examples, as at Rye, Sandwich, Westerham, and New Romney (Plate 167B), where churches of a scale suitable to the importance of the town were built in this fashion, or assumed it as the result of a process of modification. The Kentish churches are particularly distinguished for the size of their eastern windows rather than of the side windows of their aisles. An inland example at Westerham has three five-light windows in its three broad eastern gables. Examples such as this at Westerham and the church at New Romney, where there is no structural division between the chancel and the nave, approximate very closely to the south-west England type.

The Gloucestershire–Oxfordshire area – the part which is the Cotswold country – fulfilled both the necessary conditions for the development of remarkable local building traditions. There was abundance of fine building stone, and the district became one of the great centres of the wool trade in the later Middle Ages. The area may be said to lie between two important centres from which architectural ideas might readily be derived·

Gloucester itself in the west and Oxford towards the east. The parish churches of the Cotswolds are distinguished as far back as Romanesque times for the quality and ingenuity of their stone-cutting, and even quite small churches of the early twelfth century contained features of extraordinary interest as examples of the developing techniques of stone-cutting. The outstanding characteristic of the later churches, however, is the developed clerestory with its great windows returned on the eastern side above the chancel arch to which we have already referred, but in churches such as Northleach (Plate 170) and Chipping Campden, both good examples of this typical clerestory treatment, the handling of the piers and arcades is quite as remarkable as any other feature of the church. In both these churches, which are indeed very closely related, the piers are octagonal in plan with shallow concave sides and moulded capitals adapted to this form. The arcades above these piers have notably broad and low four-centred arches. This is a form of arch which had already begun to be exploited in the mid fourteenth century, e.g. in the chapter-house and cloisters of St Paul's, and was to be one of the determining motifs of the final development of Gothic in the first half of the sixteenth century. In contrast to the normal medieval pointed arch, with its strongly emphasized upward movement, the four-centred arch, especially when combined with an almost flat ceiling, introduces an entirely new type of space composition of which the Cotswold churches appear to be early examples. It seems that the origins of this type of space organization may possibly be traced in the Bristol, Gloucester, and Severn area buildings of the early fourteenth century, and especially in the vaulting treatment which we have discussed in a previous chapter. Another interesting connexion between the Cotswold parish churches and the monumental stonework of the Gloucester masons is to be found in the tower of Chipping Campden church (Plate 171), which has that same quality of displayed virtuosity that characterizes the work at Gloucester from the moment when the transformation of the eastern parts of the great abbey church was undertaken.

The regions to which the stone was supplied from the Northamptonshire and Lincolnshire quarries had a certain unity of manner in spite of the great extent of the area, which includes south-east Yorkshire, the eastern midlands, Lincolnshire, the Fen country, Norfolk, Suffolk, and in some degree Cambridgeshire. The fine freestones of the Ketton, Weldon, and Ancaster areas were distributed largely by water carriage throughout these regions, and the fine Lincolnshire stone which was used in Holderness is also quoted in the surviving contract for the clerestory of Wingfield church in southern Suffolk. Naturally within these regions there are considerable local variations. Lincolnshire itself develops in the fourteenth century a style which eventually becomes extremely influential, a style well exemplified by the great church at Boston, of which the main body dates from before 1350. Boston church is an early example of the elaborate clerestory having two windows to a bay which eventually became the fashion far and wide over these regions. In East Anglia, where there was little good building stone, the cost of transport compelled a rigid economy in the use of freestone, and the great churches built in flint or flint-rubble are distinguished for their size and the delicacy and elegance of their supports, notably their pier designs (Figure 83). The same economic causes gave to the Norfolk and Suffolk towers their character, which contrasts so markedly with those of the stone-building districts further to the west. The flint towers, such as the great unfinished work at Lavenham in Suffolk or the extraordinarily slender and lofty tower at Winteringham in Norfolk, depend almost entirely on their main proportions for their effect, and their windows are not exploited on the scale of those in Somerset. In later examples in flint-building districts a very decorative effect was obtained by patterned work of cut freestone inlaid with specially split flints, to obtain a contrast in colour and texture between the smooth stone and the dark, glittering, vitreous effect of the flint. This was in some cases carried to great lengths, as the crown and initials of the Virgin which are found on many churches, e.g. Lavenham, where the trademark of Thomas Spring, the celebrated early sixteenth-century wool millionaire, also appears carried out in this technique on the tower, to the cost of which he so largely contributed. This elaborate flint-and-stone decoration was not confined to towers and is found in great splendour in the clerestory of Long Melford church in Suffolk, and the remarkable Lady Chapel which is built on an interesting centralized plan at the east end of the church, and perhaps most remarkably of all in the great gatehouse of St Osyth's Abbey in Essex.

The aisled rectangular plan without structural division between chancel and nave appears early in the east at North Walsham and King's Lynn in Norfolk, and grows in popularity with the fifteenth and early sixteenth centuries. Long Melford, where the presbytery projects one bay to the east of the aisles, is an outstanding example. The naves of these East Anglian churches, and also of those in the East Riding and generally in this region, seem clearly to reflect the influence of the 'large and wyde chirchis whiche religiose persoones, namelich of the begging religiouns, maken, that therebi the more multitude of persoones mowe be receyved togidere, for to here theryn prechingis to be mad in reyne daies'.[16] The origins of this later East Anglian manner seem to be traceable through southern and western Lincolnshire in the fourteenth century, but in Cambridgeshire, where much fine building was done also in the fourteenth century, a series of remarkable buildings carried out in the local soft, chalk-like building stone known as clunch have survived which have a rather different character. In these the clerestory, though exploited decoratively, is not over-lit, and sometimes consists of circular foiled windows and normal two-light windows alternating. In contrast to the freestone-built churches, these Cambridgeshire examples have their arcades rather close-set (good examples are St Edward's in Cambridge and Sutton-in-the-Isle (Plate 169)), but the type of composition evolved in Cambridgeshire at this time was superseded by the end of the fifteenth century by the standard eastern type carried out in Northamptonshire stone, and with a developed, almost lantern-like clerestory. Throughout the eastern counties it is clear that to build a new clerestory to the nave was a favourite form of benefaction, and there are plenty of examples in which one of the new fashionable clerestories has been added to an earlier arcade; March church, in the Fens, is an outstanding example. This way of enlarging and enriching the building in its upper parts naturally gives great importance to the character of the roof, and rich as are the roof designs of Somerset and Devon they cannot compare for variety of invention and splendour with those of eastern England (Plates 172 and 173B).

The timber roofs of parish churches of the fifteenth and early sixteenth centuries represent the culmination of a development the earlier phases of which are far from clear, and further study of the very elusive evidence of early timber building is one of the tasks which is crying out for the attention of architectural historians. The importance of timber building in early times is beyond doubt but, except for a few survivals on the continent, notably in Norway, almost all the evidence is by inference, and we have little surviving material to work on. The earliest timber structures of any size, such as the hall of the Bishop's Palace at Hereford, are recognizable as to date mainly because the carpenters have imitated forms with which we are familiar in stonework. The Hereford

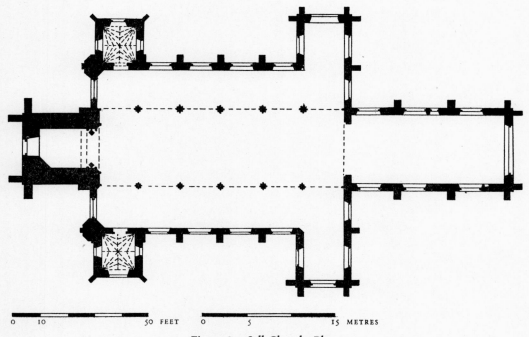

Figure 83. Sall Church: Plan

work has round Romanesque arch forms and scalloped capitals of the familiar twelfth-century type cut out of blocks of wood. This imitation of stone-forms in wood can be found in a number of examples throughout the thirteenth and in the early fourteenth centuries; there is the wooden stiff-leaf capital of the back of the great west door of Peterborough, and the wooden-shafted window arch with moulded capitals at Slough in Buckinghamshire, also of the thirteenth century, and later there is the elaborate window with reticulated tracery, from Prior Crauden's study, preserved in the cloister at Ely. All these are comparable examples to the well known late thirteenth- or early fourteenth-century joinery in the stalls at Winchester Cathedral and the screen-work at St Margaret's, King's Lynn, in which the craftsmen in wood are certainly following fashions set by the masons. Even clearer instances of this are the great series of wooden vaults at

Warmington (Plate 173A), York, Selby, St Albans, and above all in the octagon at Ely. All these examples date from the second half of the thirteenth or the first half of the fourteenth century, a time when there seems to have been a fashion for such wooden imitations of stone vaults. Other examples are known from documents to have existed at Lichfield, Windsor, and, by inference, at St Stephen's, Westminster. It is, however, paradoxical that our earliest great timber-roofed treatments should be those which display their builders' skill by the ingenuity of their imitation of the more costly and difficult technique of stone-built vaulting, whereas we know that great buildings of the highest imaginative ambition had been constructed with timber roofs, and some perhaps entirely of timber, from very early times.

There are numerous examples of primitive timber construction to be found in small domestic buildings in various parts of the country. Lately this subject has attracted much attention, and a survival of early techniques of timber construction has been established in some districts well into post-medieval times. There is every reason to believe that the simpler forms of what is called cruck construction, which consists of supporting the ridge with trusses formed of two large pieces of timber like an inverted V but generally curved and giving the effect of an arch, is an extremely early form of timber building and may well be considered as the basic type from which more elaborate roofs were developed. But hitherto the study of the simple forms of domestic timber building has not thrown any light on the handling of the roofs of such designs as the great Romanesque churches. The only surviving example of the treatment of the timber roof of a building of the first order in Romanesque times is that of the nave of Peterborough.[17] There a tie-beam roof is ceiled underneath with a boarded ceiling made in rows of panels running the length of the nave, and having the outer rows canted where they meet the tops of the clerestory wall. The boarding of the panels of this ceiling is set diagonally, and the lozenge-shaped painted pattern reflects the actual setting of the wood-work; in detail the painting of the ceiling has been much renewed in the fourteenth century and later, but it is generally accepted as the most striking example of how the roof of a great Anglo-Norman Romanesque building was finished internally. A similar system of boarded ceiling is implied by the treatment of the upper masonry of the west end of Llandaff Cathedral, and though the nave and transept ceilings at St Albans are comparatively late in date there is no reason to doubt that they carry on a tradition from the earlier form of the building. The roof of the nave at Ely, now hidden by the nineteenth-century boarded and painted ceiling, appears in engravings as of trussed rafter construction; that is there is no tie-beam at the level of the top of the walls, but the rafters are prevented from spreading out laterally by a system of struts and collars, these horizontal pieces joining the rafters at about three-quarters of the way up their height; the struts and collars at Ely were so placed as to give a five-sided effect internally. The roof over the vault of the eastern limb of Ely is a similar construction to that over the nave, and it is assumed that both are of the thirteenth century.[18] There seems little or no evidence of the survival of such roofs from earlier than the thirteenth century, though it seems extremely likely that they existed. In the open unboarded form, as the Ely nave roof appears in engravings, the roof does not seem a very appropriate internal finish to the structure it covers, but

186

boarded in, to give the effect of a tunnel of polygonal section, it seems quite an appropirate treatment for a Romanesque or early Gothic building.

In the absence of datable early timber buildings, either in England or on the continent, we are left with inference only from buildings which are almost certainly late yet seem to perpetuate constructional schemes of an earlier time. Notable among these are the timber bell-towers already mentioned. Of these there are a number of remarkable examples in Essex, such as Blackmore (Plate 174, A and B), West Hanningfield, and Stock. All these are western towers, in the case of Blackmore built against a twelfth-century façade of some pretension. They are all built with massive vertical posts set on great horizontal baulks of timber which form their sills. The vertical posts rise the full height of the belfry itself, and are buttressed by similarly constructed outbuildings forming aisles to the north and south at Blackmore and Stock, and square extensions like the arms of a cross-plan at Hanningfield. These outbuildings have lean-to roofs giving a three-tiered effect at Blackmore, and a two-tiered effect at Hanningfield. At Blackmore the resemblance to a small independent aisled church is increased by the presence of intermediate posts between the main verticals. The main timbers in all these belfries are elaborately strengthened with cross-bracing and curved struts. These Essex examples immediately recall the mast churches of Norway, and very strongly suggest a type of church building which may well have prevailed widely in this country in early times. The very similarly constructed free-standing belfry tower at Pembridge in Herefordshire suggests rather the type of lantern tower in timber which we know surmounted the crossing spaces of tenth- and eleventh-century churches, both here and on the continent, though we should translate the detail handling into something more like the timber forms suggested by the tenth-century towers at Earls Barton and Barton-on-Humber. On the Welsh border there are examples of such wooden belfry structures placed inside and above stone towers, e.g. Llanthewy Rytherch in Monmouthshire, which may give us some idea of the upper finish of the more ambitious early buildings we have lost. All these considerations, vague as they are, strongly suggest that the great achievements of medieval timber construction were founded on a long tradition of constructional skill and enterprise, and that the variety and ingenuity of early roof forms may have been greater than has often been acknowledged.[19] It cannot, however, be too clearly stated that we have little or no real evidence on this subject and all is inference and speculation. But there can be little doubt that the carpenters and military engineers who seem to have been largely recruited from the carpenters' trade had a long tradition of great constructional skill.

The great age of monumental timber construction opens with the late thirteenth and early fourteenth centuries. The roof of the chapter-house at York, an octagonal building of 59 feet internal diameter, is one of the earliest surviving examples of this period. It dates from about 1300, and is followed some twenty-five years later by the most remarkable of all English timber building, the roof and lantern tower of the octagon at Ely. The Romanesque lantern tower at the eastern crossing of Ely fell in 1322 and was replaced in the years immediately following by the existing ingenious centrally planned space. One bay of each of the four limbs of the church was incorporated into the crossing space, which was formed into an irregular octagon, the arches into the choir, transept, and nave forming the cardinal sides, and low arches with large windows above forming the diagonals. From the angles of the stone octagon elaborate timber brackets of great size (Plate 123A) carry eight tall posts which form the angles of the central octagon lantern, which was designed to act also as a bell-tower, and indeed the work is always referred to in the documents as the 'campanile'. The under-sides of the great timber brackets are ceiled with boarding and ribs contrived to give the appearance of stone vaulting. The diameter of the space is 70 feet (Figure 84). The author of this remarkable design is almost certainly William Hurley, the King's Master Carpenter, the first known name of a dynasty of great engineers in timber whose successor two generations later

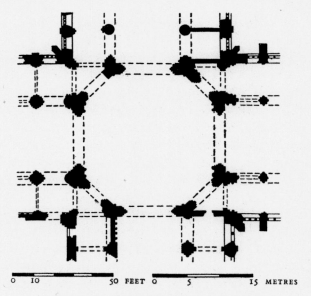

O   10   50 FEET   O   5   15 METRES

Figure 84. Ely Cathedral, Octagon: Plan

designed and built the roof of Westminster Hall with an internal span of 67½ feet. Hurley is also recorded as concerned in a great circular building at Windsor, built in the 1340s, not long after the Ely work was completed. This building, which is said to have had a diameter of 200 feet, was erected for a great feast of the type known as a Round Table. This form of entertainment seems to have implied that the guests sat round the perimeter of a circle of tables in the middle of which *artistes* and acrobats entertained them during their dinner. The Round Table building at Windsor is recorded as being built chiefly of stone, but from the prominence given to the Master Carpenter's name and other indications it seems likely that the carpenter's part was at least equal to the mason's. A design of two concentric masonry circles with a clear span of about 100 feet in the centre would not seem impossible to the Master of the Octagon at Ely.

Except for Edward III's Round Table pavilion we know of nothing else comparable to the Ely octagon, but the kitchen of the Bishop's Palace at Chichester, of about the same date or a little earlier, suggests that the system of construction that made possible the great *tour de force* at Ely was not without precedent. The Bishop's kitchen is a large square building about 40 feet across, covered with a central wooden lantern supported on timber brackets simpler than those at Ely but basically of the same type. The great kitchen at Dartington Hall in Devon, built for Lord Holland the half-brother of Richard II, is as large or larger than Chichester and was presumably covered in a similar way. The Chichester kitchen was a severely practical building, impressive only in its scale and structural ingenuity, and it has not attracted the attention of historians as have the more elaborately finished stone-roofed kitchens, such as those at Glastonbury and Durham, but in the scarcity of early examples of important carpenters' work it deserves study. William Hurley is also known as the carpenter at St Stephen's Chapel, Westminster, which from the evidence of the accounts seems to have had a wooden vault. One of the latest of these wooden vaults, and one of the finest, is over the eastern limb of Peterborough Cathedral and dates from the first half of the fifteenth century (Plate 175A). It is a most interesting and unusual combination of imitation vaulting in timber and the flat ceiling, for the wooden vault conoids at the sides are of a comparatively small size and the main span of the roof is covered by a flat ceiling decorated with ribs and bosses. The handling of the vault conoids and their size recalls, though the scale is much larger, the treatment of certain East Anglian parish church roofs, which had small cornices in wood in imitation vaulting which themselves seem related to the treatments of the upper parts of late medieval rood-screens (Plate 173B). The whole system at Peterborough was, of course, a new fashionable variant of the earlier ceiling of the nave with its canted sides. The effect of the whole design is to accentuate the feeling of breadth of space in a way familiar in the timber-ceiled parish-church designs of the later phases of Gothic (Plate 163), of which an early example has been noticed at Northleach, where the use of the four-centred arch is an even more striking evidence of the emergence of the new taste. The great west-country vaults, notably Bristol and Tewkesbury, have shown the way, and the latest Tudor vaults, such as those of St George's, Windsor, and the choir of St Frideswide's, Oxford, carry the effect as far as seems possible in stone.

The most striking development in the timber-work of the fourteenth century is the appearance of the hammer-beam roof. In this form of roof the arch braces, which rise either to the ridge or to a collar, spring from brackets projecting from the wall top, and these are in turn sustained by curved struts springing from wall posts resting on corbels. This system, once invented, was capable of extreme elaboration and was used in combination with a variety of other forms of truss. An early example of the principle on which the hammer-beams support posts rather than arch braces, is found in a drawing in the handbook of Villard d'Honnecourt dating from about 1240. The French mason describes it as a good light roof for placing above a stone vault. It seems, however, that the device never became current in France, and it is in fourteenth-century England that its real development took place. The earliest example is said to be that of the so-called Pilgrims' Hall at Winchester, a roof of no great size and extremely plain character, which may date from as early as the first half of the fourteenth century. The earliest known dated example is the splendid roof of Westminster Hall, begun in 1394 (Plate 176). Most historians have, with reason, considered it frankly incredible that such an elaborately developed example should be the origin of the type. It seems extremely likely that a hammer-beam roof of some 45 feet span was used for the great hall of Lord Holland's house at Dartington some years before the Westminster roof was begun. This roof no longer exists and has been replaced by a modern copy, but that it was of hammer-beam type is known, for the shadow of the original truss up against the end wall of the hall was clearly visible when the new roof was made some twenty-five years ago. In the course of the fifteenth century this form of roof attained to an extraordinary development, especially in East Anglian parish churches, where every variety can be found, including the double hammer, in which the lower set of brackets projecting from the top of the clerestory wall supports on posts and curved struts a second set of brackets projecting from the middle of the principal rafters, from which arch braces mount to the collars. Several varieties of roof form in which hammer-beam trusses alternate with plain arch braces, or even with king-post and tie-beam trusses, are also found in East Anglia. The projecting hammer-beams were frequently adorned with figures of angels with spreading wings, and so lent themselves to a great elaboration of the decorative character of the whole roof, the hammer-beam and figures acting as a *repoussoir*, i.e. a boldly shaped feature past which, or through which, one looks with an increased sense of the space beyond – a well-known trick in stage scenery. Perhaps the most striking example of the great East Anglian hammer-beam roofs is that at March in Cambridgeshire (Plate 172), a double hammer-beam where the whole space of the roof appears to be filled with the outspread wings of the angel figures, which are placed below the corbels taking the wall posts which support the first row of hammers, on the ends of the hammers them-selves of both rows, and again in pairs facing east and west on the middles of the collars. Knapton in Norfolk has another variation of the double hammer-beam system also adorned with angels, but these are not exploited to the degree of those at March, and the effect is gained more by the cusped silhouette of the trusses themselves. In the late fifteenth and early sixteenth centuries the royal carpenters produced a series of magni-ficent hammer-beam roofs which had pendants hanging from the ends of the hammer-beams of which the roof of the Great Hall of Eltham Palace (nearing completion in 1479) is the earliest example (Plate 177A). Later roofs of a similar type were made by Henry VIII's carpenters at Hampton Court and elsewhere. The decorative possibilities of the new form of roof may have been a factor in prolonging the fashion for high-pitched roofs in face of the evident tendency in the fifteenth and early sixteenth cen-turies to lower the pitch of all roofs, both for practical reasons as more suited to the use of lead covering, and also in accordance with the taste for the broad, low treatments of the spaces of buildings that we have noticed already.

Unquestionably the most splendid example of late medieval timber-work after the octagon at Ely is the new roof at Westminster Hall, and like the Ely work it is an out-standing instance of the exploitation of the possibilities of timber to obtain a spatial effect of great breadth. At Westminster the effect is of a very special kind; for the greater part of the total volume of the building is in the roof, the main trusses of which spring from about half-way down the side walls in a way which enhances this pre-dominance of the timber-work over the stonework in the building. Westminster Hall as

it exists to-day is the result of the happy collaboration of two great masters, Hugh Her-
land the carpenter, and Henry Yevele the mason, and probable author of the nave of
Canterbury Cathedral. The detail of this roof is of considerable interest. The elaborate
traceries which fill the spandrels between the main timbers show geometrical motifs,
ultimately of French derivation, but modified by the use of the ogee curve which we
have noticed already as one of the characteristics of the Court school of that age. The
Westminster work was finished by 1402. An early example of the geometrical tracery
motif of the Court carried out in timber, is in the fine arch-braced roof of the guard
room at Lambeth Palace. This roof is said to have been re-set when the room was reconstructed in the nineteenth century, but in its details dates from the middle of the
fourteenth century.

Two smaller buildings further illustrate the way in which timber-work could be used
to gain novel effects of space; Chartham church in Kent,[20] and Needham Market in
Suffolk.[21] Chartham is a church which has been dated as early as the last quarter of the
thirteenth century, and it contains the celebrated brass of Sir Robert de Septvans, who
died in 1306-7, and who presumably was in part responsible for the rebuilding of the
church. It is a cruciform building with a large chancel, a very wide aisleless nave, and wide
shallow transepts. The roofs (Plate 175B) of all four limbs are of wagon form and meet at
the crossing, where two great timber arches spring diagonally from piers set slightly in
from the angles of the transepts and nave to the angles of the chancel and transepts. The
two diagonal timber arches have a large carved wooden boss at the intersection.[22] Between
the inset piers and the nave walls are small arched openings which have been described
as squints. The whole church seems to be of one date, except the western tower, which
is of the fifteenth century. The fourteenth-century stonework is celebrated for the
specially complicated form of tracery known as Kentish. The work throughout is of
the highest quality and the effect of the broad, unbroken spaces is very impressive. This
system is also found at Luppitt in Devonshire, and there is a fifteenth-century variation
at Ilsington and formerly one existed at Honiton in the same county. Chartham and
Luppitt represent a natural development of the wagon-roof tradition which obtained
both in Kent and Devon, in the direction of the new fashion for broad, low effects with
the emphasis on spatial unity.[23] The Needham Market church, which dates from the
third quarter of the fifteenth century, has also a broad aisleless nave, but being an East
Anglian church is not to be denied a clerestory. This feature was achieved by a remarkable variant of the hammer-beam roof in which the posts rising from the inner ends of
the hammer-beams are of unusual height, and are secured half-way up by light ties and
again at the top by slightly cambered timbers supporting an almost flat ceiling. In the
upper part of the structure, between the level of the lower ties and the ceiling, clerestory
windows are contrived in the roof itself. Externally, while the main span of the roof is
very low-pitched and covered with lead, there are steeply sloping lean-to roofs from the
tops of the walls to the level of the lower ties. The great hammers have angels with outspread wings at their ends and the whole effect is of a curiously elegant lantern. The span
is 30 feet. The church is otherwise remarkable for its decoration in stone and flint, including inscriptions carried out in this technique.

In some of the few surviving roofs of the middle of the fourteenth century it is clear that the designers are much concerned with making their trusses into a pattern of large foiled figures, often employing the ogee curve; recently an example has been discovered in Dorset of a king-post roof in which the king-post is shaped into large cusps so as to form foiled figures with corresponding cusps on the principal rafters. This roof has also longitudinal braces springing from the king-post to the ridge purlin, and horizontal braces from the base of the king-post to the purlins at the sides. These last form foiled figures in the horizontal plane through which, as it were through an open-work ceiling, the elaborate decorative forms of the upper parts of the roof can be seen. This Dorset roof seems to date from about 1360 and is the most elaborate example of the taste for one set of decorative forms seen through another which we have noted as a characteristic of early fourteenth-century design in stone applied to roof construction.

CHAPTER 11

THE LAST PHASE

THE latest phase of medieval architecture in England may be taken to begin with the re-establishment of orderly government under Edward IV and to continue over the reigns of the first two Tudors, the period, that is, of the last quarter of the fifteenth and first half of the sixteenth centuries; a good terminal date is that of the dissolution of chantries and guilds in the years 1547–8. It is a period in which the two major tendencies of the fourteenth century, the layman's taste expressed in the pageantry of romantic chivalry and the new conception of space, pass beyond the stage of creative experiment to one of assured accomplishment which at times appears almost facile, but it is difficult to name any one great revolutionary development comparable to the introduction of the great window in the mid thirteenth century, or the new techniques of vaulting or of open timber roofing in the fourteenth century. Certainly the introduction of exotic elements into the decorative repertory of the later masters cannot claim to be such a revolution, though the ultimately Italian sources of these elements and their antique reference have given them a special prominence in the retrospective views of historians.

England had been very precocious in the development of the pageant chivalry taste and of its expression in art and policy, and circumstances combined to encourage Edward IV to exploit it. His revival of the Order of the Garter combined to recall the glories of his great namesake in the fourteenth century, after the humiliations of the reign of Henry VI, and provided a ceremonial framework for his relations with the Burgundian Court, where the Order of the Golden Fleece flourished as the great exemplar of this tradition in the Europe of the fifteenth century.[1] The effects of this policy are perceptible in other fields than those of the visual arts, and Malory's *Morte d'Arthur* is the greatest work of a revival of earlier medieval literature of chivalrous adventure, re-modelled in the form of prose narrative from the epic verse romances of an earlier age. Its nearest cousins are the pageant chivalry romances produced for the Burgundian Court. Henry VIII, physically and in other ways an even more formidable edition of his Yorkist grandfather, maintained and enlarged this tradition with resources that Edward could not command. The pages of Hall's *Chronicle* abound in evidence of the importance of the millinery of jousting, and the elaboration of the arts of display as an instrument of government.

Only fragments of Edward IV's own building have come down to us, the Great Hall of Eltham Palace [2] (Plate 177B; Figure 85) and the beginnings of St George's Chapel, Windsor, which Henry VIII was to finish. The Eltham Hall (101½ by 36 feet) is in six bays, the upper end bay having spacious oriel windows on both sides; there are pairs of two-light windows in the upper part of each of the other bays. Both inside and out the building has a certain severity, and the most important remaining feature of the interior, the great hammer-beam roof, though elaborately moulded and

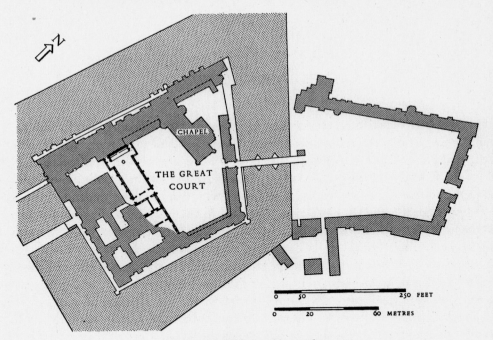

Figure 85. Eltham Palace: Plan

composed of trusses with a novel and complex internal silhouette attained by carrying the hammer posts down beyond the ends of the hammer-beams in the form of pendants, preserves this building's monumental scale (Plate 177A). The Eltham roof is the earliest surviving large-scale example of the roof with pendants, though the fact that the effect appears in stone at the Divinity School at Oxford almost at the same moment suggests that earlier examples may have been lost, for it is a device which seems likely to have been tried first in timber and to come more naturally in that material. Edward IV's other great building, the Chapel of the Order of the Garter, St George's, Windsor, remained a fragment for some years, and its final effect is due to Henry VIII's completion.

The most complete work of the first importance belonging to Edward IV's time is the main building at Magdalen College, Oxford, begun by an eminent Oxford mason-contractor for Bishop Waynefleet in 1474[3] (Plate 178B). This consisted of a hall and chapel, united in one monumental block after the fashion of New College (Figure 86). On the north side of this was a quadrangle having covered walks on all four sides at ground level, the upper floors of the ranges of chambers being built over the walks in a manner found also in the river-side building of Queens' College, Cambridge, and which is known to have been used in a number of Friars' buildings from whose practice it probably derives, as distinguished from the orthodox monastic cloister[4] with its greater width which was always separately roofed within the enclosure of the surrounding buildings. The quadrangle at Magdalen is entered by a splendid four-storeyed gatehouse on the western side, the most remarkable features of which are the fine flatly bowed oriel windows to the two middle storeys. These are treated as a single composition. The arches lighting the covered walks are four-centred and the upper windows have flat heads. Below the battlements is a bold string course enriched with sculptured bosses, and there is thus great emphasis on the horizontal lines of the ranges in contrast with the strong verticals of the hall and chapel buttresses. Sumptuous as the effect is, and there is no lack of carved and moulded decoration, it is the flat stretches of fine ashlar and the bold scale of the detail that gives this building its solid and monumental character.

The work at Magdalen was carried out by William Orchard,[5] a mason-contractor and quarry owner, the earliest important personality known to us in a group of master masons who can be traced working both at Oxford and for the Court until about 1530. Two other families of masons, the Janynses and the Vertues, can be traced for two generations and more. The earliest member of the Janyns family was Robert Janyns, employed on the building of Merton College tower in 1448–50: he worked later at Eton, where Henry Janyns appears as an apprentice. Henry later appears at St George's, Windsor, in Edward IV's time, and a later member of the family was prominent among the leading masons of the earlier part of Henry VIII's reign. The Vertue family are not traceable for quite so long. Robert Vertue, who died in 1506, is first heard of as an apprentice working with another mason, Adam, of the same surname, at Westminster Abbey before 1480, and he is mentioned later with William Vertue, a younger man, in a letter of Bishop King's about the new building of Bath Abbey in 1503. William Vertue lived

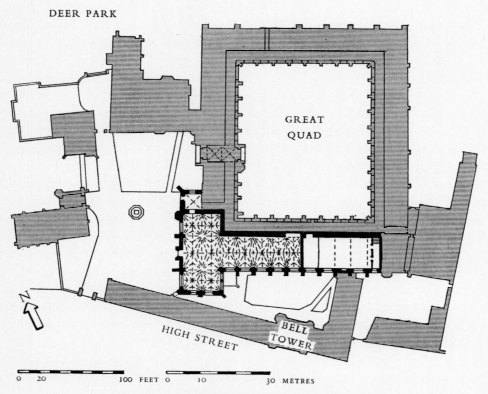

Figure 86. Magdalen College Chapel, Oxford: Plan

until 1527, having accomplished a series of great works at Oxford as well as in London, latterly in conjunction with another mason, Henry Redman, who died a year later. Two other important masters must be mentioned: Humphrey Cook, a carpenter, who died in 1531, and who worked in close collaboration with Vertue and Redman both in London and at Oxford. The two fine roofs of Corpus Christi and Christ Church Colleges were made by him in the finest tradition of timber design. The other eminent master was John Wastell, whose two important documented works are the Bell Harry tower at Canterbury (1490–1503) (Plate 179), and the finishing of King's College Chapel, Cambridge (1508–15) (Plate 180B). These two achievements are sufficient to place him extremely high among the masters of his or any other time. These men, who are known to us mainly through the archives of the central Government, or the records of bodies such as colleges at Oxford or Cambridge, the founders or benefactors of which were closely connected with the Court, have a recognizable character at least as a group and almost as individual architects. There are others, such as Christopher Scune, said to be the mason of the new nave of Ripon Minster, who are much more shadowy figures.

The survival of building documents in greater quantity than from any earlier period gives the impression that we know more than in fact we do about these late medieval masters, and it is possible that further study will make clearer that changes were taking place in the structure of the building trades, comparable in importance to the more obvious changes in the incidence of patronage. Certainly the system of contract work which can be traced back to the twelfth century seems to have been growing in popularity from the fourteenth century onwards, and we have evidence that masons such as Orchard or Wastell were prepared to undertake bigger jobs than any that we know of as being done by contract at an earlier date.[6] It is important, however, to notice that Wastell's contract for finishing King's College Chapel did not include the supply of materials. Nevertheless important works were still often carried out by the old system of direct labour, and it is difficult to establish any principle as to what determined the choice of one system rather than the other in any particular instance, except that any very big rush jobs, such as Henry VIII's work at Hampton Court or Nonsuch Palace, were too large for any mason-contractor to undertake.[7] There are also signs in the royal accounts of a tendency for masons to be separated into two diverging categories, one being assimilated to an administrative and designing class (and there are increasing references to drawing and devising), and the other depressed (their real wages seem to have sunk) into artisans. These are signs only; for the type of sculptor-mason who also contracted for large buildings, for the designs of which he was often mainly responsible, certainly survived throughout the seventeenth century as the names of Stone, Pierce, Marshall, the Stantons, and the Grumbolds of Cambridge bear witness. In the fourteenth century Yevele and Lote seem to have been tomb sculptors as well as mason-designers; Wastell is known to have made a tomb, and it seems that it would be very easy to overstress the evidence of change in the structure of the industry at this time.

Two of the most admirable illustrations of the type of internal architectural effect which the late fifteenth and early sixteenth centuries aimed at, and achieved with such apparent mastery, are the nave of Sherborne [8] (1475–90) (Plate 180A), and the eastern extension of Peterborough (*c.* 1500) (Plate 181A). The Sherborne work consists of the recasing of the lower parts of an early Romanesque – perhaps even a pre-Conquest – building, and the addition of a large windowed clerestory and a fan vault above. The builder has exploited the need to make use of the earlier structure by clothing it with a skin of panelling, which increases its appearance of sturdiness and helps the effect of subordination to the clerestory and vault to which it acts as a sort of podium. The independence of the two storeys is emphasized by the strong horizontal line dividing them, no vertical shafts or mouldings being carried up to unite the two.[9] The Peterborough work consists of a broad transverse hall of four bays by two, approached by two bay extensions of the north and south aisles of the eastern limb so as to embrace the Romanesque apse, which was left standing with a minimum of ingenious adaptation. The effect

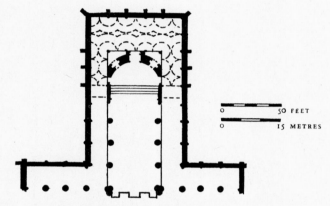

Figure 87. Peterborough Cathedral, east end: Plan

of a returned aisle with eastern chapels, which is what, in fact, seems to have been provided, is lost in the unity of space enforced by the splendid span of the fan vault, the axis of which is north and south; if there were indeed altars with low screens between them against the eastern wall, a curious ambiguity as between the units of the space of the transverse hall and the functional variety of the aisles and chapels, with their east–west axis, would have been set up. It is an effect that certainly existed in the octagon at Ely, where the choir stalls extended across the octagon in the line of the nave and presbytery ignoring the plan-form at ground level.

The Peterborough[10] eastern chapels have long been attributed to Wastell on the grounds of style (Figure 87). The vaults seem, indeed, to be close in detail to those of King's College Chapel (Figure 88), but the most marked characteristic which distinguishes the Cambridge vault from any other of its time is the separation of the bays by strongly emphasized transverse arches, which divide each conoid into two segments, an effect not attempted elsewhere, and certainly not at Peterborough where it would have profoundly changed the effect as we now see it. The vault at King's College, in spite of its separation into bays, emphasizes the unity of the interior space by sheer force of repetition, a unity which is sufficiently strong to overcome the profound change in character between the western ante-chapel and the chapel proper in point of detailed handling. The ante-chapel has a wealth of heraldic decoration exalting the Tudor family and its Beaufort connexions, and stone screens separating the side chapels from the main vessel. These have four-centred arches with geometrical traceried heads, recalling the Court style as it evolved in the fourteenth century, and the whole contrasts strongly with the earlier manner of the chapel proper. The exotic character of the pulpitum, which Henry VIII gave in the 1530s [11] to divide the two parts, only served to make this transition more easy. The whole of this interior, being complete with its stained glass, is the best evidence that we possess of the total effect intended by a great monumental interior of the early sixteenth century, in spite of the detail alterations of the seventeenth century and more recent times, important though these are.[12] Wastell's other authenticated work, the central tower, Bell Harry, at Canterbury, is a very understandable precursor of the finishing work of King's Chapel. The subtlety with which the sumptuous surface

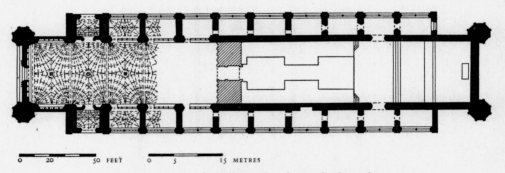

0   20   50 FEET   0   5   15 METRES

Figure 88. King's College Chapel, Cambridge: Plan

pattern is managed, and the strengthening of the angles of the octagon corner turrets with slender but well-defined buttress projections, both suggest the same hand in the design as the angle towers at King's Chapel, and they are managed in rather a different way from anything attributable to other members of the group of royal masons that has come down to us from just that moment. The choir of Bath Abbey, of which the masons Robert and William Vertue assured Bishop King on the subject of the fan vault that 'there should be none so goodly neither in England nor in France', and which dates from just between Wastell's Canterbury and Cambridge works, emphasizes this sense of kinship between his two buildings.

Robert and William Vertue's work at Bath was far surpassed by William's completion of St George's Chapel, Windsor (Plate 181B), where the choir vaults date from 1506 to 1511, the nave vaults about 1503, the crossing vault being carried out by Redman after William Vertue's death in 1528.[13] Except for the crossing, the St George's vaults are of the lierne type and among the most elaborate and successful that were ever built; for, whatever the intentions of the earlier masters of St George's may have been, it is the character of the nave and choir vaults, with their astoundingly flat pitch, that gives the quality to the interior as we see it. This is not to decry the interest of the handling of the piers which belong to the building of Edward IV. The easy mastery with which the suites of delicate narrow mouldings – bowtells – are contrasted with fuller rounded forms, the descendants of the earlier Gothic shafts but without capitals, and with the broad, shallow casement mouldings, makes this one of the finest of all English late medieval arcades. Equally remarkable are the ingenious interpenetrations by which these complex mouldings are brought to rest in the simpler forms of the arcade bases. Forerunners of these complex and ingeniously designed piers can be seen in the earliest parts of the Divinity School at Oxford, built by Richard Winchcombe in the 1430s before an excess of Puritanism, or possibly merely parsimony, required their simplification in the parts carried out in the next decade by a new master mason. The magnate benefactors in 1439 had said that 'abundance of curious works were unsuitable to poor scholars'. But at St George's, a royal work and the Chapel of the Order of the Garter, nothing was to be restricted. It is curious how completely the earlier work at St George's is masons' rather than sculptors' architecture. There is an almost complete absence of sculpture and decorative carvings, and even the exception to this, the remarkable string course carved with innumerable angels, is no real exception; for by multiplication the angels are reduced almost to an architectural rather than a sculptural motif. St George's is the outstanding example of the triumph of the mason-constructor over all the other ancillary building crafts; this predominance is perceptible in almost all the important buildings of this age, but never to quite the same degree as at St George's. In other respects St George's, as befits the purpose for which it was built and which it still serves, embodies the taste of its age in a quite unexampled perfection, including the incorporation in the south transept chapel of a type of glazed terra-cotta detail of egg and tongue mouldings,[14] which is among the earliest Italian Renaissance motifs to be found in English architecture.

The other great achievement of the Court school is the magnificent chantry chapel which, under the will of Henry VII, replaced the early thirteenth-century Lady Chapel at the east end of Westminster Abbey (Plate 182, A and B). The plan of this building (Figure 89), which is aisled and has an apsidal east end, is particularly remarkable for the treatment of the outer walls of the aisles and apsidal chapels: the former are constituted of a series of trefoil-planned oriel windows, and in the latter the central lights are canted outwards to form an acute-angled projection. It is possible that these elaborate window forms are in part a device to overcome the deadness of stained glass as seen from the outside, by presenting their surfaces at a variety of angles to the light. Between the aisle windows of Henry VII's Chapel the wall piers are in the form of solid octagonal turrets, which appear free-standing above the parapets of the aisles and finish in ogee cupolas. These cupolas were originally crowned by sculpture representing the king's beasts (a select troupe of heraldic animals), each carrying a gilded vane on a rod between its paws. The vanes were contrived to turn in the wind and, as Professor Lethaby pointed out, gave a final touch of twinkling life to the whole elaborately carved, gilded and painted substructure.

Internally the fanciful pageant character of Henry VII's Chapel is consummated in the extravagantly ingenious vault over the main span (Plate 183). This is the finest and most elaborate of the pendant vaults, though not the earliest. That distinction belongs to

William Orchard's vault at the Divinity School at Oxford of 1479 (Plate 178A). Orchard's scheme involved the building of massive four-centred transverse arches, and springing the vault from voussoirs in these arches about one-third of the distance in on each side. The stones forming these voussoirs, which are of enormous size, are continued downwards to form lantern structures containing figure sculpture. The vault of Henry VII's Chapel is an improvement on this. Again the actual vault itself is sprung from voussoirs of big transverse arches, and the springing is placed in about the same relative position on the arches as at Oxford. But at Westminster the vault-springing comes from the pendant part of the voussoir and not from the top of it, so that the larger part of the transverse arch is concealed above the surface of the vault. A further refinement at Westminster is that much of the elaborate panelling of the vault surface is in fact open-work, and a careful study from the ground enables one to see faintly in the gloom the great transverse arch passing above it. This must surely be William Vertue's masterpiece. The other re-markable example of a pendant vault of the early sixteenth century is at St Frideswide's, Oxford, where the character of the vault was largely conditioned by the need to adapt it to the Anglo-Norman galleried clerestory. Here, as at the Divinity School, the ribbed pattern of the vault is of lierne, and not fan type as at Westminster. In addition to these major examples there are also vaults over the eastern chapel at Christchurch in Hamp-shire, where there are pendants from the main transverse arches but hanging only a short distance in from the wall.[15] In a number of cases – at St George's, Windsor, and Henry VII's Chapel – the central spandrel, where the conoids of the fan or similarly formed vaults meet, is treated with a pendant. These central pendants, being structural elaborations of the spandrel stone, are constructionally a much simpler phenomenon than those ingeniously suspended from the side voussoirs of transverse arches.

The origins and architectural justification of these constructional fancies pose some in-teresting and very difficult problems. It seems clear that they are related to the type of pendant hammer-beam roof truss that appears at Eltham Palace Hall and is continued in the great roofs of Christchurch, Corpus Christi at Oxford and at Hampton Court (Plate 188). One of the most interesting examples of a pendant vault is in the ceiling of the chapel at Hampton Court, where the effect of a stone vault of this type is imitated in wood (Plate 184B). It is one of the most remarkable pieces of joinery ever achieved. The translation into masonry of a form originally developed in carpentry is certainly not the whole story; for in a sense these late Gothic pendant vaults are descendants of the west-country open-work vaults of the fourteenth century, such as those at Bristol, St David's, and in the chancel at Warwick church. There are, moreover, examples in canopy work, both in wood and stone, in which elaborate superstructures are raised above over-hanging pendants, a notable example being at Long Ashton in Somerset, dating from the 1480s, above the tomb of Sir Richard Choke, where the upper part of the canopy is formed by a series of pendant angels with upraised wings. The Long Ashton tomb (Plate 184A) is a piece of purely decorative fantasy, but it seems possible that the monumental use of pendants was a device to give depth and movement to the upper parts of build-ings, in view of the tendency both of the stone and wooden roofs to lose the quality of depth as they became flatter in pitch. The vaults of Henry VII's Chapel again exemplify the desire to combine such an effect of depth and movement, with a quality of breadth and space, which the fan and late forms of lierne vault could give. In the Westminster vault every device is employed that can mitigate the broad-panelled ceiling effect of the fans, which is so uncompromising at Peterborough and Bath and in the aisles of St George's. These devices include not only the main pendants and the way the fans spring from them, but spandrel pendants in the middle of the vault, and a fantastic series of pendant cinquefoils that follow the line of the transverse arches from which the vaulting springs. A simpler example of the use of pendant forms to give depth to a flat ceiling is

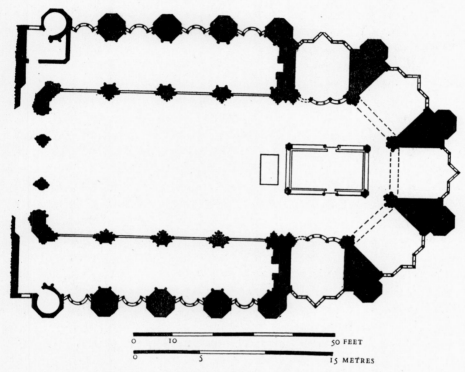

O   10   50 FEET
O   5   15 METRES

Figure 89. Henry VII's Chapel, Westminster Abbey: Plan

the remarkable timber roof of St David's Cathedral made at about this time (Plate 85A). In this example the ceiling is divided into square panels, which are enlivened by pendants attached to the beams by four curved braces at every alternate intersection. The tradition of the pendant continues beyond the confines of the period covered by this book as a legacy to the plasterers of the late sixteenth and early seventeenth centuries.

A large part of the surviving work by the Court masons of this age is either domestic or college buildings that are in the main domestic. The latter are the visual evidence of that change in the incidence of patronage, from the great ecclesiastical institutions to the endowment of learning which had been growing ever since the fourteenth century, and produced an extraordinary outpouring of benefactions both at Oxford and at Cambridge in the fifteenth and sixteenth centuries. It is, perhaps, one of the more practical aspects of that zeal for the founding of chantry and guild chapels which was transforming the parish churches of the country in the same period. These learned foundations were in the main the work of bishops such as Waynefleet, Fox, Alcock, and Wolsey himself – and perhaps Fisher, as adviser to the Lady Margaret, mother of Henry VII – most of them men in touch with the Court circle, and the two universities contain a large proportion of the finest examples of the domestic building of the time. Henry VIII, in addition to benefactions at Oxford as the successor of Wolsey, and at Cambridge as heir to his father's interest in Henry VI's foundation, King's College, also built new cloisters for the collegiate body at St Stephen's, Westminster, between 1526 and 1528. These were built by William Vertue and Henry Redman and, though very much restored after the severe damage they sustained in the fire of 1834, are one of the most sumptuous examples of the Court style that we have. The cloisters are two-storeyed and have a chapel projecting from the western walk. They are fan-vaulted, and the tracery of their window openings shows the same fondness for quatrefoils that appears in the ante-chapel at King's College. It seems like a lingering memory of the French sources of the Court style of two hundred years earlier.

Of the purely domestic building by the Court school comparatively little has survived. The Court works of Greenwich, Whitehall, Richmond, and Nonsuch are only known to us from early pictures; and even Hampton Court, except for the hall and chapel, has lost its most splendid early sixteenth-century parts, the state apartments which were rebuilt by Wren for William and Mary. The loss of these palace buildings is the more grievous in that we have little other evidence than the pictures of them, for the tall many-storeyed and towered compositions, which seem to have formed their main living quarters, and to have given them a distinctive character quite different from the low two-storeyed ranges which made up the larger part of the college buildings and indeed of the surviving great country houses of the time. In these palaces the pageant chivalry taste seems to have produced architecture the only examples comparable to which, allowing for all differences of national tradition and materials, are the great contemporary French palaces, such as Chambord, with their tall main blocks and fantastically elaborate skylines. The most precious remaining fragment to indicate the character of these works, is the building made in the first years of the sixteenth century for Humphrey Stafford, Duke of Buckingham, who was beheaded as an over-mighty subject in 1521. The Duke left his palace of Thornbury [16] in Gloucestershire uncompleted at his death, but even so it survives as the finest example of the taste of the age that we possess in this country (Plates 190 and 191).[17] The building (Figure 90) consisted of at least three large rectangular courtyards, the outer court with its gatehouse surrounded by comparatively low buildings, the stables below and rooms for the Duke's retainers on the first floor; these with the gatehouses occupied three sides of the court. The fourth side is hardly more than a fragment, but consisted of a series of great towers, the two central ones forming an inner gatehouse, the two outermost containing rooms attached to the buildings in the ranges behind them; between these four towers were smaller octagon turrets containing, certainly in one case, a staircase. Opposite this second gatehouse, on the far side of the inner court, was a great hall, a chapel, and, in an arrangement which is uncertain, the apartments for guests. At the high table end of the hall range a state staircase led up to the first floor of one range of the court, which contained the great chamber, and beyond it, forming the side of the court, a series of state apartments devoted to the Duke himself on the first floor, his own room being in the angle tower; beneath, on the ground floor, was a similar suite of apartments for the Duchess, and both suites were lit by a series of elaborate traceried oriel windows, polygonal or trefoil in plan, and sometimes changing in plan from the ground to the first floor. The nearest analogies to these windows are in the state apartments of Henry VII at Windsor Castle, and in the form of the windows of

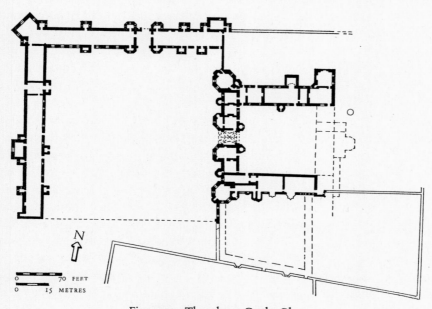

Figure 90. Thornbury Castle: Plan

the side aisles of the apsidal chapels of Henry VII's Chapel at Westminster. At Thornbury the splendidly lighted state apartments looked out upon a side court, which was enclosed by covered walks in two storeys and had a garden in the middle. The covered walks provided access from the two floors of the state apartments to the churchyard of the parish church adjoining. Two qualities stand out in this design; first of all the conscious splendour of the Duke's apartments with their state entrance up a magnificent staircase which anticipates the suites of splendid entertaining rooms, which are a distinguishing feature of the planning of great houses in the post-medieval world; and secondly the completely unmilitary character of the south front towards the cloistered garden. Here the big oriel windows of the Duchess's apartments come right down to the ground level, and completely contradict the exaggerated military appearance of the main approach to the second court from the first or retainers' court. A third and very interesting point about the plan is its close connexion with the royal buildings which were contemporary, particularly the handling of the windows themselves, which we have already mentioned, and the existence of the two-storeyed cloister garden which seems also to have formed part of the scheme of Richmond Palace, to judge from a picture in the Fitzwilliam Museum at Cambridge. There can be little doubt that Thornbury was devised by the Officers of the Royal Works.

The fragment of the second court at Thornbury, especially the towered front through which it is entered, suggests that it was not only in details that this Gloucestershire building reflected the London taste of its time. Thornbury, however, as becomes a building on the edge of the Cotswold district, is built of fine ashlar masonry; both Richmond Palace and Hampton Court were built mainly of brick, a material that had been steadily growing in popularity throughout the fifteenth century. The use of brick at Richmond and especially at Hampton Court, where no expense is likely to have been spared, is the culmination of a long process by which this material became a way of building valued for its own qualities, instead of being merely a substitute for stone in such districts as East Anglia or the Humber Basin where stone had to be imported from a distance; and the example of North Germany and the Low Countries was strong, through an active commercial connexion.

The beginnings of brick-making in medieval England are still obscure, and it is possible that they may be found much earlier than the early thirteenth century, when the evidence from the Hull–Beverley district becomes clear. Naturally enough the early evidences are almost all from eastern England, and it is at Coggeshall in Essex that the earliest examples of specially made brick for window details, etc., have been found. Though late fourteenth- and fifteenth-century brick buildings of considerable ambition have survived, such as the gatehouse at Thornton Abbey, Herstmonceux, Tattershall Castle, or Queens' College, Cambridge, it is not until this last phase of medieval architecture that the material makes a really important contribution to the range of architectural effects. It seems likely that one of the causes of the increased use of brick by the Court architects and, deriving from them, by fashionable patrons all over the country, was the greater economy of skilled labour that it made possible. This was an important point where rush jobs were concerned, and there is plenty of evidence that King Henry VIII was sometimes a very impatient patron, and possibly the great Cardinal himself may have been in a hurry for his new palace at Hampton Court. A major factor in the popularity of brick as a material for the most splendid buildings was, however, its colour and the possibility of varying the colour with diapers, that is, patterns formed of darker burnt bricks. These, with the use of stone for specially elaborate detail features, or specially made bricks which when employed were usually painted to resemble stone, were capable of great richness of effect of just the kind that the pageant taste of the time required.

In the buildings of the sixteenth century, special details made of very refined clay, i.e. terra-cotta, and making use of exotic Franco-Italian or Flemish-Italian decorative motifs began to be employed. The most interesting examples, except for Sutton Place near Guildford, are in East Anglia, where Layer Marney in Essex (Plate 185), East Barsham and Great Snoring in Norfolk are outstanding. Cressingham, also a Norfolk house, has one side entirely faced with enriched terra-cotta, but in this instance traditional Gothic forms were used. The early sixteenth-century bricklayers exploited most admirably the octagon and part octagon forms for which their material was specially adapted, and showed great virtuosity in the design of elaborate chimneys to form parts of the complicated silhouette treatments then in vogue, both cut brick-work and specially moulded bricks being used for these features. The crow-stepped gable was presumably an importation from Flanders, and was sometimes used in combination with elaborate cusped corbel tables in cut brick. Early sixteenth-century brick-work is generally laid with a thick mortar joint to take up the inequalities in the bricks, and in this shows itself related to the rubble or flint walling of the districts where good freestone was an expensive luxury. As with brick-work, these designs in small unit materials sometimes achieve a modelled or plastic quality, which suggests quite a different architectural ideal from that of the linear pattern-making which is so constant a factor in English medieval art. It is possible that, had the rendering and colour-washing survived of such buildings as the tower of Stoke-by-Nayland Church, or St Botolph's, Cambridge – two outstanding examples where the play of surface seems to be the governing quality in the design – this effect would be less remarkable, and with some brick buildings if the colouring and gilding had survived, the contrasts thereby being sharpened would emphasize the linear qualities more than appears at present. A number of Late Gothic buildings are extant in which the polychrome materials are used with astonishing variety of effect, notably at St Osyth's, where the mid sixteenth-century additions employ chequer-work in flint and chalk as well as brick-work both plain and diaper; and early pictures show that the Holbein Gate at Whitehall Palace employed both flint and white stone as well as the terra-cotta roundels of the Caesars which are now at Hampton Court. A curious minor example of the same use of varied materials to produce an effect of polychromy is in the exterior treatment of the arches of the clerestory window at March church in the Fens, where brick voussoirs are used in combination with flint and light-coloured stone.

The developments in domestic planning, and indeed in domestic interior arrangement generally in this age, are important, though it would be difficult to point to any obviously revolutionary changes. Considerable importance has been attached to the appearance of symmetrical effects in domestic elevations, but all medieval building tends towards a symmetrical arrangement, or at least an orderly balance of features whenever it is considered desirable to give an impressive or formal effect. There are plenty of examples dating back to the thirteenth century and beyond, apart from the obvious instances of great church façades. Certainly in the fifteenth and sixteenth centuries this tendency seems more marked as the proportion of monumental building that we have left increases, and becomes more domestic or collegiate, and this impression is not only an accident of survival; for certainly more domestic buildings of a consciously splendid character involving a higher degree of formality were being built. Moreover this increased formalism develops markedly in the later sixteenth and early seventeenth centuries, in a way that is clearly in part a continuation of an existing tendency, though admittedly also in part due to renewed influence from the continent, particularly France. In detail features, however, the signs of the development of a domestic style are more readily definable. The great suite of state apartments at Thornbury does seem to point the way to the mansions of the latter part of the century, though the introduction of such arrangements may have been anticipated at Kenilworth and elsewhere in the fourteenth and early fifteenth centuries. The galleries surrounding the garden courts at Thornbury and Richmond may also be the forerunners of features which were to remain popular in English domestic architecture until the eighteenth century. It has often been suggested that the long gallery derives from the monastic cloister, and these two-storeyed cloister galleries lend some support to this view. It is, however, probable that the long gallery developed naturally from the medieval conception of the great single space from which smaller spaces led off or were isolated in other ways, as we have noticed in connexion with the great oriel at Kenilworth and in such buildings as the schoolroom at Wainfleet, and in a narrow range of one-room-thick building down the side of a courtyard this development appears a very natural one. The Galérie de François Premier at Fontainebleau, for all its Giulio-Romano derived detail, is no more than this, and that long galleries seem to have developed at the same time both in England and France tends to support this suggestion. Henry VIII certainly erected a long gallery at Whitehall in the 1530s, which in fact had originally been built for Cardinal Wolsey's house at Esher and was taken to pieces, being a timber building, and re-erected by the King in London. The addition of deep bay window embrasures to provide focal areas for social groups, withdrawn from the main space of the apartment, which is a feature of so many later galleries, can be compared with the deep window embrasures leading off the main spaces of tower halls, a good example of which is at Borthwick, in the Scottish Lowlands (Plate 186), where the main space of the apartment can hardly have been more than a general assembly area except at night time.

In the later years of the fifteenth and the early part of the sixteenth century a number of ecclesiastical dignitaries improved their private lodgings, and examples have survived at Muchelney in Somerset, Castle Acre in Norfolk, Thame in Oxfordshire, and Much Wenlock in Shropshire. These are all the private apartments of the heads of monastic establishments, and in them are to be found some of the best examples of sets of rooms having qualities of privacy and intimacy, which can scarcely be paralleled in the royal residences of the time, though this is almost certainly due to accident of survival, especially of the detail fittings in some of these late monastic examples. At Muchelney [18] there is a staircase which shows a quality of architectural effect on a moderate domestic scale which it would be difficult to parallel, and more impressive still is the Abbot's Parlour (Plate 189B) to which the staircase leads, with its fitted wooden seating, and particularly its small and elaborate chimney-piece which forms the focal point of the room. Chimney-pieces of considerable elaboration can be found in much earlier buildings, such as Tatter-shall Castle, but at Muchelney the extension upward of the angle moulding of the chimney-breast defined, with the carved lions at the top, a space presumably intended for a picture or a tapestry panel, and suggests the first of these two-tiered chimney-pieces that were to form the main features of so many English living-rooms for generations to come. The Abbot's Lodging at Muchelney also includes fragments of a great hall in which the characteristic late Gothic details of the Ham stone building district are seen applied to domestic use. At Thame the Abbot's Parlour retains its panelling and frieze of Franco-Flemish antique work panels and medallion heads. This room also includes an internal porch to exclude draughts, of a kind that was to become very popular in the latter part of the century, and of which we have evidence of another early example in Holbein's famous drawing of the More family sitting in their parlour. The domestic buildings added by the Prior of Much Wenlock (Plate 187; Figure 91) and the Abbot of Forde to their respective houses are both outstanding works of their time. The Much Wenlock example, though less interesting from the point of view of internal fittings than the house already cited, has again a suggestion of intimacy and moderate scale, but its really distinguishing quality is the ingenuity with which the mason has exploited the long two-storeyed glazed corridors which run the whole length of one side of the range,

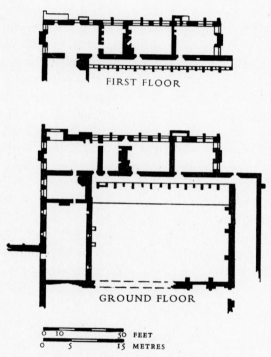

FIRST FLOOR

GROUND FLOOR

Figure 91. Much Wenlock, Prior's Lodging: Plan

like two-decker pentices in stone rather than wood. In so doing he has produced one of the most exciting domestic elevations of the late fifteenth century that we know. The Abbot's Lodging at Forde (Plate 192), almost a generation later, is a more normal composition of the great hall approached by a towered porch, but the quality of the work, both inside and out, and the character of the accommodation produced in the two upper storeys of the porch with its fine oriel window, are outstanding. The decoration of this building includes a bold use of detail of French Renaissance type.

At Lyddington in Rutland there is a small house built as a country retreat for the Bishop of Lincoln in the last years of the fifteenth century. It is a two-storeyed block, with the hall and main rooms on the first floor, and is complete with its garden layout, including a small garden house or gazebo of octagonal form standing at the corner of the garden looking out on to the village street. The hall itself (Plate 189A), though comparatively low proportioned, has retained the remarkable treatment of its ceiling, which is boarded and divided into small panels by applied wooden mouldings. It seems very clearly the anticipation of the moulded plaster ceilings of the latter part of the century.[19] Even more remarkable, however, than the ceiling itself is the treatment of the cornice forming the transition between wall and ceiling. This is treated as the underside of the gallery of a rood-screen in miniature, and is extremely elaborately enriched with traceried arches in wood, open-work forms suggesting vaulting, and little pendant fretwork arches. It is the prettiest piece of domestic interior fitting that we have remaining from this time.

In all these domestic examples qualities are to be found looking forward to the new age which opens with the second half of the sixteenth century. In some districts, however, the date 1550, which has been chosen as the limit of the period covered by this book, has little or no meaning, and it is possible to find examples in Dorset of tricks and habits of design which can be traced from the great towers of Somerset of the early sixteenth century applied to domestic features such as façades or oriels in domestic buildings of the second part of the century. Binghams Melcombe is a notable example, and further west still, in Devon, the closure which was applied to parish church enrichment by the dissolution of chantries and guilds hardly seems to have been regarded. Though the religious changes of the middle of the century are indeed the most important factors in the discontinuance of church building and church furnishing in its later years, one is sometimes tempted to speculate whether the immense output of the first half of the sixteenth century in church building did not overreach itself, and even without the Protestant Reformation whether there would not have been a considerable slackening in the production of church building, at any rate in the years following 1550.

NOTES

CHAPTER I

p. 1 1. The recent discovery of the stone and clay foundations of a church possibly dating from the time of St Ninian (fifth century) in Galloway, does not seriously affect this generalization.

2. For Tara see R. A. S. MacAllister, *Tara*, 1931.

3. The most easily available discussions of these churches are in A. W. Clapham, *English Romanesque Architecture before the Conquest*, 1930, and G. Baldwin Brown, *The Arts in Early England: Architecture*, 1925.

p. 2 4. For Reculver see C. R. Peers in *Archaeologia*, LXXVII, 1927.

p. 4 5. For Jarrow see C. A. R. Radford in *Archaeol. Jnl*, CXI, 1954.

p. 5 6. The discoveries which were made during the nineteenth century were not properly planned and it is impossible to be sure whether the walls which seem to indicate a transept are not of a later Anglo-Saxon date.

p. 6 7. For Brixworth see A. W. Clapham and Baldwin Brown *op. cit.*, and C. A. R. Radford, *Archaeol. Jnl*, CX, 1953.

p. 7 8. For Llantwit Major see *Arch. Camb.* 6th series, XV, 1915.

9. For Tintagel see C. A. R. Radford, *Ministry of Works Guide*, 1950.

10. For Whitby see A. W. Clapham, *Ministry of Works Guide*, 1952.

11. For Nendrum see H. C. Fowler, *The Monastery of St Machaoi Nendrum*, 1925.

p. 8 12. *Cogitosus vita S. Brigidae virginis*, Migne *P.L.*, vol. LXXII, cols. 788–9.

13. In the later Middle Ages this would almost certainly mean chandeliers, but at this date may refer to that kind of jewelled pendant of which the best known examples are the Visigothic crowns formerly in the Musée Cluny.

p. 9 13a. Since the above was written, the results of the excavations at Yeavering, Northumberland, and Cheddar, Somerset, have been made known, though not yet fully published. At Yeavering they revealed a great hall, one of three successive timber structures of the seventh century on the same site. The Hall of King Edwin (616–32) is described as built of 'squared timbers set upright in a foundation trench but without any sleeper beam: its roof was supported with the aid of external buttresses and its interior was divided by posts into a central "nave" and "aisles". At one end a partition cut off a space for some specialised purpose' (*History of the King's Works*, H.M.S.O., 1963, I, p. 2 ff., which also gives a diagrammatic plan of the buildings excavated). This plan also shows the remarkable structure consisting of a wedge-shaped bank of tiered seats laid out on a curve – 'clearly an assembly place . . . Despite its timber construction its resemblance to the segment of a Roman amphitheatre is obvious.' The *History of the King's Works*, I, p. 5, and II, p. 908, also gives plans of the Royal Residence at Cheddar, a complex of buildings of various dates but including a great timber hall, ninth century or earlier, measuring 78 by 18 feet internally, which appears to have been built in two stories. The plan of this building shows a pronounced taper at each end; it was entered at the centre of each long side.

14. For Glastonbury excavations see *Ant. Jnl*, p. 10
VIII, 1927, and X, 1929; also *Somerset Archaeol. Soc. Trans.*, LXXIV, 1925, LXXV, 1929, and LXXVIII, 1932.

15. It seems likely that the newly discovered church under the nave of Muchelney Abbey may be of the eighth century.

16. Sir Alfred Clapham with whom Professor Brønsted is in agreement assigns these sculptures to the late eighth century and this is generally accepted. See *Archaeologia*, LXXVII, 1928.

17. For Glendalough see publication of the p. 11
Ancient and National Monuments of Ireland, Irish Stationery Office, 1911–12.

18. For Irish Round Towers see H. G. Leask, *Christian Art in Ancient Ireland*, vol. II, 1941.

19. Information from Sir Alfred Clapham.   p. 12

20. See J. Bilson in *Archaeologia*, LXXIII, 1923.   p. 13

CHAPTER 2

1. For excavations at St Augustine's, Canterbury, p. 18
see C. R. Peers and A. W. Clapham in *Archaeologia*, LXXVII, 1927.

2. For Great Paxton see Cyril Fox and L. Cobbett p. 19
in *Camb. Antiq. Soc. Proc.*, XXV, 1924, and R.C.H.M. *Inventory of Huntingdonshire*, 1926.

p. 20   3. It seems that it was so at Sherborne and possibly at Wimborne Minster, and suggests that at the former church the aisles which are implied by the surviving tenth-century north-west door may have been additions to an aisleless nave.

4. For North Elmham see A. W. Clapham and W. H. Godfrey in *Ant. Jnl*, VI, 1926.

5. For South Elmham see *Archaeol. Jnl*, LVIII, 1901, and G. Baldwin Brown, *op. cit.*, and A. W. Clapham, *English Romanesque Architecture before the Conquest*, 1930.

p. 23   6. There are triangular arcades on short pilasters on the front of the well-known gatehouse at Lorsch.

7. See D. Talbot Rice, *Oxford History of English Art*, vol. II, pp. 53 ff.

8. The Hadstock responds have nook-shafts: not a common feature and possibly an imported one, but also believed to have existed at St Alkmund's, Derby, from which two interesting decorated capitals were recorded in the nineteenth century. *Archaeol. Jnl*, II, 1841.

p. 24   9. At Bradford-on-Avon the central figure is missing; at Barton-on-Humber only the head of the central figure survives.

10. For Deerhurst see W. H. Knowles in *Archaeologia*, LXXVII, 1927.

11. *Late Saxon and Viking Art*, 1949, p. 140. Sir Thomas Kendrick, it seems to me, rather exaggerates the architectural discipline of twelfth-century decorative carving, at any rate as exemplified in some monuments (see below on Castle Acre), but as a general statement it can certainly hold and Durham nave is a good example.

12. H. Focillon, *L'Art des sculpteurs romans*, 1931.

13. The evidence for a pre-Conquest origin for these and for the Barnack Majesty seems to outweigh any stylistic arguments in the present state of our knowledge. They must in any case be later than the groups we have been discussing.

p. 26   14. They were not only from Normandy but probably included eastern Frenchmen, such as the Lorrainer bishops who had already appeared in Edward the Confessor's time.

p. 27   15. For pre-Conquest Westminster see Armitage Robinson in *Archaeologia*, LXII, 1911, and A. W. Clapham in *Archaeologia*, LXXXIII, 1933; also R.C.H.M. *Inventories of West London*, 1925.

16. For St Albans see C. R. Peers in V.C.H. *Herts*, vol. II, 1908, and R.C.H.M. *Inventory of Hertfordshire*, 1910.

17. For eleventh-century Lincoln see J. Bilson in *Archaeologia*, LXII, 1911, and F. Saxl, also A. W. Clapham in *Archaeol. Jnl*, CIII, 1947.

18. York and Canterbury are outstanding fifteenth-century examples, though Canterbury is almost sixteenth-century.

19. I know of no satisfactory explanation of this p. 28 architecturally very important phenomenon.

20. It seems that St Albans had always a triforium or narrow gallery rather than a proper tribune for its middle storey.

21. The diaphragm arch may be described as an p. 29 arch supporting a transverse wall, and its purpose has been claimed to be an early means of localizing the effects of fire. No one can question that this was a powerful practical consideration in the minds of early medieval builders, and one of the motives for the pursuit of the ideal of a completely stone-vaulted church. Contemporary writers refer to the need for some such expedient, and the experiences of the ninth and tenth centuries are more than enough to warrant it, but even so it is unlikely to have been the only motive for the desire for high vaults. Such simplified explanations are partial truths which are seized upon (and probably were by contemporaries) and became current because they by-pass the very serious difficulties of appreciating the more profound motives which are sometimes very difficult to analyse or express.

22. J. Bony, 'La Technique Normande du Mur Epais' in *Bulletin Monumental*, 1939.

23. Tewkesbury is a rare instance where both but- p. 30 tresses and attached shafts have been dispensed with.

24. For Winchester see C. R. Peers and H. Brakspear in V.C.H. *Hampshire*, vol. 5, 1912.

25. For Worcester see H. Brakspear in *Arch. Soc. Rep.*, XXXI, 1911, and XXXV, 1926; also R. Willis in *Archaeol. Jnl*, XX, 1843.

26. For Gloucester see A. W. Clapham, *English Romanesque Architecture after the Conquest*, 1932, and R. Willis in *Archaeol. Jnl*, XIX, 1842.

27. There are also crypts of this age at St Augus- p. 31 tine's, Canterbury (excavated), and still buried at Bury St Edmunds and Evesham.

28. See F. Saxl in *Archaeol. Jnl*, CIII, 1946.   p. 32

29. For Tewkesbury see A. W. Clapham in *Archaeol. Jnl*, CVI, Supplement 1952; also W. H. Knowles in *Bristol and Glos Archaeol. Soc. Trans.*, L, 1928; also J. Bony in *Bulletin Monumental*, 1937.

30. W. H. Knowles puts Tewkesbury nave after Gloucester: Sir Alfred Clapham dates the remark-

able west front 1130–40. The central tower is almost certainly mid twelfth century.

p. 33 31. See J. Bony, *Bulletin Monumental*, 1937; A. W. Clapham, *Archaeol. Jnl*, CVI, 1952.

32. The clerestory at Jumièges is similarly very tall but that church seems to owe much to the Romanesque schools further to the east.

33. Monsieur Bony has shown that there was hardly room for such a treatment at Gloucester.

p. 34 34. In repairing war damage at Exeter a large scalloped capital was found, implying that this type of cylindrical pier was also used in the Romanesque cathedral of which only the towers now survive.

35. For Hereford see R.C.H.M. *Inventory of Herefordshire*, vol. I.

CHAPTER 3

p. 35 1. For Durham see J. Bilson in *Archaeol. Jnl*, LXXIX, 1922, and A. W. Clapham, *English Romanesque Architecture after the Conquest*, 1932.

2. Replaced in the thirteenth century.

3. A similar treatment, but with simple unmoulded ribs, appears at Tewkesbury.

p. 37 4. Cylindrical is not an exact term as these piers have shafts towards the aisles.

5. The use of intersecting blind arcading is another instance of the precocity of the Durham architect.

p. 38 6. This is not to suggest that there is no Norman element in the Durham books. The position is complicated by the presence of a strong Anglo-Saxon element in the illumination of Normandy itself.

p. 39 7. I hesitate to say 'logic' in view of the strictest sect of the structural Pharisees.

8. For Ely see A. W. Clapham, *op. cit.*; also Inskip Ladds, *The Monastery of Ely*, 1930.

p. 42 9. It is not certain whether the main apse may not also have been square externally, for only the internal face was seen in the restoration work of 1842–9.

10. Internally the arrangement gives rise to even more curious speculation: was the main altar placed so far to the west as to leave the last bay clear as a means of access to the main apse – a sort of ambulatory? The eastern limb is only three bays long.

p. 43 11. See Armitage Robinson in *Archaeol. Jnl*, LXXXVIII, 1931.

p. 45 12. Fontenay has no clerestory and the main span is covered with a pointed barrel vault. It is extremely dark.

13. In the Kirkstall presbytery the westernmost transverse rib is some little distance to the east of the crossing arch, the vault linking the two being a pointed barrel.

14. See A. W. Clapham in *Archaeol. Jnl*, LXXXVIII, 1931.

15. The factor of increasing and increasingly p. 46 widespread knowledge of geometry may also have to be taken into consideration.

16. Dr Zarnecki dates these about 1140; the Abbey rebuilding began about 1120. Some fragmentary figured capitals at Hereford may date from about 1115.

17. The use of strips at Norwich has a curiously p. 49 tubular effect and reminds one rather of some pre-Conquest motifs.

18. The use of banded shafts is possibly one of p. 50 those tantalizing suggestions of a link with north-eastern France and southern Flanders, as yet insufficiently studied. Cf. Laon and Noyon.

19. Our knowledge of Waterford is based on an p. 51 eighteenth-century painting which, though crude, is clear enough in the main features. See *Archaeol. Jnl*, CVI, A. W. Clapham Memorial Volume, 1952.

20. The hood-moulds at Wimborne Minster are p. 52 perhaps closest to the Malmesbury examples.

21. See also Lindisfarne and Kirkby Lonsdale. At p. 53 Dunfermline the arch mouldings of the arcade are also like those of Durham, but the system is a continuous and not an alternating one.

22. The lower part of the church is carried out in a much richer decorative manner and contrasts strongly with its superstructure.

23. For Kelso see MacGibbon and Ross, *Ecclesiastical Architecture of Scotland*, 1896, and A. W. Clapham in *Archaeol. Jnl*, XCIII, 1936.

CHAPTER 4

1. Palaces similar to Clarendon existed at Gilling- p. 56 ham in Dorset and Geddington in Northamptonshire, but they have not been excavated: sixteenth-century plans exist of Hertford, Havering, and Eltham.

2. See also A. W. Clapham, *Lesnes Abbey*, 1915, plate XXIV. D. Eadmer the Precentor speaks of a cloister at Christchurch, Canterbury, on the north side of the church which was burnt in 1067, and this is taken to date in its main arrangements from the tenth century. The evidence from St Augustine's is too slight to bear any real weight and there is no reason to suppose that the old arrangements were retained.

p. 56   3. We have no traces of the barrel-vaulted cloisters which preceded the ribbed-vaulted types of the later Middle Ages on the Continent.

4. There are also fragments at Kirkstall and Rievaulx.

p. 58   5. For Newminster see *Proc. Newcastle Soc. Ant.*, 3rd series, VI, 1913/14, and 4th series, I, 1923/4.

p. 59   6. For Ely monastic buildings see T. D. Atkinson, *Monastery of St Etheldreda at Ely*, 1933.

p. 60   7. The chapter-house at Gloucester, 72 by 34 feet, is covered with a pointed barrel vault with transverse arches.

p. 62   8. For Worcester chapter-house see R. Willis in *Archaeol. Jnl*, XX, 1843.

p. 64   9. The same arrangement is found at Rievaulx and Kenilworth and elsewhere.

p. 65   10. The difference in treatment is to be explained by the placing of the buildings: Beaulieu being Cistercian and Chester Benedictine, and the consequent difference in the relation of the refectory to adjoining buildings.

11. The halls of the Palais des Papes at Avignon are vaulted as are many monastic refectories in France; in England they are always timber-roofed.

12. A fine refectory dating *c.* 1139–40 at Dover is illustrated in Hudson Turner, vol. I. Here the wall below the windows is plain but the upper wall is treated with alternate blind and window arcades. The dimensions are 107 by 34 feet.

In 1959 a survey of the remains of the Old Deanery at Salisbury by the officers of the Royal Commission on Historical Monuments (England) led to the discovery of an open timber roof over the hall of the house which dates from before 1274 and after 1258 (see *Ants. Jnl*, 1964, part I, pp. 42 ff.). This roof is of 31 feet span. Though there are no intermediate supports the upper parts of the roof rest on longitudinal timbers which recall the wall plates above the internal arcades of such a hall as Oakham. These 'arcade' plates are themselves supported by two trusses consisting of great raking principals with auxiliary struts springing from stone corbels in the walls. It is clearly structurally an intermediate stage between the aisled hall roof and the large single spans of the next century. As compared with the later types of open timber roof, that of the Old Deanery is remarkable in that there are no curved timbers embodied in it.

p. 66   13. For Westminster Hall see W. R. Lethaby in *Archaeologia*, LX, 1907, and R.C.H.M. *Inventory of West London*, 1925.

14. There is another timber aisled hall at Dudley, though even more damaged than Hereford.

15. For Winchester Castle Hall see E. Smirthe. On the Hall and Round Table at Winchester see M. E. Wood, *Archaeol. Jnl*, Supplement to vol. CV, 1950.   p. 68

16. Probably to be dated 1203–4 when John was spending large sums on the Castle.

17. For Palace at Wells see J. H. Parker, *Architecture of the City of Wells*, 1866, and M. E. Wood in *Archaeol. Jnl*, Supplement to CV, 1950. Dr M. E. Wood dates this building 1230–40: the earlier date has been chosen here as a result of comparison with King John's block at Corfe.   p. 69

CHAPTER 5

1. For Canterbury see R. Willis, *Canterbury Cathedral*, 1845.   p. 72

2. E.g. Arras.   p. 73

3. For the problem of the early use of special materials, e.g. marble, for shafts and other details see J. Bony in *Warburg and Courtauld Jnl*, XII, 1944. Dr Zarnecki in *Later English Romanesque Sculpture*, 1953, gives other early examples from Old Sarum, Glastonbury and Lewes. In a more recent paper (*Jnl of the Brit. Arch. Ass.*, 1957–8) M. Barry has discussed the problem of the relation of the eastern limb of Canterbury to North Eastern French buildings, notably Laon.

4. The outer aisle walls at Canterbury are also provided with a galleried passage like a clerestory.   p. 74

5. For Lincoln see J. Bilson, W. R. Lethaby and others in *R.I.B.A. Jnl*, 3rd series, vol. XVIII, 1911.   p. 76

6. Professors Lethaby and Prior both saw the aesthetic purpose of this vault, see *R.I.B.A. Jnl*, vol. XVIII, 1911, and *Gothic Art in England*.   p. 77

7. See J. Bilson in *R.I.B.A. Jnl*, vol. XVIII, 1911. The purpose of these mysterious features seems to be to lighten the structure.

8. For Rochester see W. St John Hope, *Architectural History of St Andrew Rochester*, 1900.   p. 79

9. For Peterborough see C. R. Peers in V.C.H. *Northants*, II, and G. F. Webb in *Archaeol. Jnl*, Supplement to CVI, 1952.   p. 80

10. There is some evidence that such a wooden spire existed until the eighteenth century on the north transept tower.   p. 82

11. For Roche see J. Bilson in *Archaeol. Jnl*, LXVI, 1909.

12. The pointed or keel-shaped roll moulding and shaft had a great future, especially in the north.

At the date of Roche these are almost certainly a French importation, though their function of sharpening the linear effect proved very much to the English taste and was exploited here with a gusto surpassing the country of their origin. See J. Bilson in *Archaeol. Jnl*, LXVI, 1909.

p. 83 13. This criticism is based on an imaginary reconstruction. The actual treatment is now obscured by a nineteenth-century modern vault.

p. 84 14. The analogy of Roche and Ripon though certain enough must not be pressed too far. The group of vault ribs at the latter are not brought lower than the capitals of the arcades.

15. For Arbroath see MacGibbon and Ross, *op. cit.*

16. For Tynemouth see *Ministry of Works Guide*, by R. N. Hadwick, 1952.

p. 87 17. For whole problem see H. Brakspear in *Archaeologia*, LXXXI, 1931. For Wells and Glastonbury see J. Bilson and J. Armitage Robinson in *Archaeol. Jnl*, LXXXV, 1928; for St Davids see Lovegrove in *Archaeol. Jnl*, LXXXIII, 1926.

18. Known also as St Joseph's Chapel and said to have been dedicated by Christ Himself.

p. 88 19. The carving on the Glastonbury doorways is dated by Dr Zarnecki to the early thirteenth century, i.e. some twenty years after the accepted date of the completion of the building.

p. 90 20. Dr Bilson is inclined to date Wells rather later than this, i.e. *c.* 1192, on the grounds of style, but see Dean Robinson, *op. cit.*

p. 92 21. It is possible that a painted pattern on the vault, either intended or achieved, may have softened down this inconsistency.

p. 93 22. Monsieur Bony thinks it was intended and possibly actually built. He advances French parallels to the system of sexpartite vaults over wide arcade bays and suggests a possible Continental prototype. *Warburg and Courtauld Jnl*, XII, 1949.

p. 94 23. For Llanthony see Lovegrove in *Arch. Camb.*, XCIX, 1946–7, and H. Brakspear in *Archaeologia*, LXXXI, 1931.

24. There is evidence of large benefactions to the monastery in the last quarter of the twelfth century. See Lovegrove, *op. cit.*

25. Now in the Museum of the York Philosophical Society.

26. For Southwell see A. Hamilton Thompson in *Thoroton Soc. Trans.*, XV, 1912. Being built in 1233, Southwell was a minster of the Archbishop of York who had close connexions with the west country Severn Basin area.

27. For Abbey Dore see R.C.H.M. *Inventory of Herefordshire*, vol. I.

28. The single eastern arch from the presbytery to p. 95 the Lady Chapel at Llandaff seems to belong to an earlier phase of the school with its disc ornament of the Malmesbury type.

29. A curious example is the absence of necking below capitals in some of the buildings in question.

CHAPTER 6

1. For Winchester see C. R. Peers and H. Brak- p. 96 spear in V.C.H. *Hampshire*, V, 1912.

2. For Salisbury see A. W. Clapham in *Archaeol. Jnl*, vol. CIV, 1947.

3. For Beverley see J. Bilson in *Durham and* p. 100 *Northumberland Arch. Soc. Trans.*, 1896, and *Arch. Review*, III, 1897.

4. For York Minster see R. Willis in *R.A.I. Proc.*, p. 103 1846, and A. Hamilton Thompson in *Archaeol. Jnl*, XCI, 1934.

5. Similar quatrefoils with head sculpture are p. 104 found in the spandrels of the upper windows on the outside of the apse at Peterborough. They are presumably earlier than the west front but must represent a re-embellishment of the east end of the church.

6. Smaller scale examples can be found in the p. 105 twelfth century at Lullington, St Germans and Kelso.

7. If, as seems likely, the figures in a similar posi- p. 106 tion at the east end of Chichester are additions of the later thirteenth century, it is possible that the origin of the motif is to be found at Worcester. Unfortunately the sculptures themselves at Worcester have been very drastically restored.

8. The work was in full swing in 1238–9.

9. Beeleigh Abbey chapter-house is a good p. 107 example and there are plenty more. A number of remarkable survivals are in Sweden, e.g. Västeras.

10. The nineteenth-century relief of Christ in Majesty which now fills the centre of the tracery of the door is an egregious iconographical blunder, as witness the censing angels whose backs are turned towards the figure of Christ. It is a practical blunder also as it darkens the stairway up to the chapter house.

11. For Westminster Abbey see R.C.H.M. *Inven- p. 109 tory of Westminster Abbey*, 1924, and W. R. Lethaby, *Westminster Abbey and the King's Craftsmen*, 1906, and *Westminster Abbey Re-examined*, 1925.

12. The problem of access to the new Lady p. 110 Chapel of 1220 was appreciated by the Editor of the

R.C.H.M. (England) Volume *Westminster Abbey*, in which it is suggested that the eastern limb of the eleventh-century church may have been lengthened in the twelfth century prior to the translation of the Confessor's body in 1163.

p. 112   13. See Villard d'Honnecourt who sketched one for his book.

p. 113   14. For Milan Cathedral see *Art Bulletin*, XXXI, 1949.

15. There seems no evidence that the great Bishop himself was particularly concerned in it – the expression is purely one of date.

p. 114   16. J. Harvey, *The English Cathedrals*, 1950.

CHAPTER 7

p. 117   1. For Old St Paul's see W. R. Lethaby in *The Builder*, CXXXVIII and CXXXIX.

p. 119   2. The extreme examples of this are the clerestories of Wells, *c.* 1330, and of the Cathedral of St Vitus at Prague which was built after 1353 by Peter Parler of Cologne, who is believed by some continental scholars to have been influenced by English examples.

p. 122   3. This is no less true of the more recent art books than of their predecessors: indeed, apart from the fact of reminding one that the pictures are in colour, it is difficult to see what advance there is in the majority of these productions.

4. The iron-work is signed Gilebertus.

p. 127   5. It has a curious Portuguese look, but the date is rather early for anything of the sort in Portugal, though the connexion between Bristol and the Peninsula is well known to have existed.

6. For later work at Ely see F. R. Chapman, *Sacrist Rolls of Ely*, 1907, and Inskip Ladds, *The Monastery of Ely*, 1930.

p. 128   7. The Southwell pyramids were destroyed in the course of the eighteenth century, but have been replaced in accordance with the early engravings of the building.

p. 130   8. Who is known to have done work elsewhere while he was in charge of the Salisbury work.

9. Cf. also Hereford and Malmesbury west towers.

CHAPTER 8

p. 132   1. For Southwell chapter-house see N. Pevsner, *The Leaves of Southwell*, King Penguin Books, 1945.

p. 133   2. For St Stephen's Chapel, Westminster, see M. Hastings, *St Stephen's Chapel, Westminster*, 1955.

p. 134   3. Mackenzie, who prepared measured drawings

from the ruins of the chapel, states that he found on the cornice the bases of marble shafts which can hardly have served any other purpose than as supports for these rear-arches. Moreover the lower chapel has wall ribs to its vault in the form of three cusped rear arches, and there is evidence of some such treatment in the upper part of the great east window of the chapel, but this point is very obscure.

4. It appears again on a small scale in the doors p. 13 leading from the transepts into the choir aisles at St Paul's. It is frequent in tomb niches and canopies.

5. For Exeter see H. E. Bishop and E. K. Prideaux, p. 13 *The Building of Exeter Cathedral*, 1922.

6. For Bristol see N. Pevsner in *Arch. Rev.*, CXIII, 1953.

7. For Wells fourteenth-century work see J. Armitage Robinson in *Archaeol. Jnl*, LXXXVIII, 1932.

8. It must be admitted that our evidence for the p. 13 early use of these tracery forms in London is based in the main on Hollar's engraving of the St Paul's chapter-house.

9. Mr Howard in *Archaeol. Jnl*, 1911, defines the p. 14 fan vault as follows, 'A fan vault is a vault of many ribs spaced at equal angles to one another, the alternate ribs being equal in curvature'.

10. Cf. the tester of Edward III at Westminster. p. 14

11. The Lichfield front was probably set out as p. 15 early as 1280 though the bulk of the work seems to belong to the first half of the following century.

12. A very curious feature; they light no part of the main spaces of the church.

13. The mason who must almost certainly be re- p. 15 sponsible for the finishing of this composition is known from other works, e.g. the western towers of Wells, to have been a man of great qualities. Possibly the explanation may be financial, for the patron was dead.

14. It has been pointed out that there is evidence p. 15 that the central doorway was originally surmounted by a feature distinguishing it from the north and south doors, and that the continuous line of canopied figures owes its present character to alterations of the late fifteenth or early sixteenth century. Information from S. C. Fox, and see also L. Stone, *Sculpture in Britain: The Middle Ages*, 1955, p. 223.

CHAPTER 9

1. The windows of the early thirteenth-century p. 15 hall at Corfe Castle appear to have had traceries of a relatively advanced character for their time.

2. Except possibly Meare Castle, Wilts, built by Richard of Cornwall, King of the Romans. From the nature of its site it is almost certainly of this type.

.159 3. For the monastic buildings of Ely see T. D. Atkinson, *The Monastery of St Etheldreda at Ely*, 1933.

4. For Kenilworth see V.C.H. *Warwickshire*, vol. VI and Ministry of Works Guide.

4a. The best known of these great apartments from both drawings and written evidences was the King's Great Chamber in the Palace of Westminster, later known as the Painted Chamber. It was a re-modelling for Henry III in the 1230s of a building of the time of his grandfather. The Great Chamber was damaged by fire in 1263 and much renovation had to be carried out in the immediately following years. The room measured 80 feet 6 inches by 26 feet and was 31 feet 9 inches high. A small chapel or oratory was added externally at the eastern end of the north wall. This was entered from the Great Chamber by a door at its east end, and just to the west of this was a quatrefoil opening some 4 feet from the floor in order that the King might see the altar from his bed, which stood between the door and a fireplace some 20 feet farther west. The bed itself was a very splendid structure surrounded by posts and surmounted by a 'tabernacle', the decoration of which by a court painter cost £13 6s. 8d. There is plenty of evidence that the whole decorative scheme of the Great Chamber, apart from the great zones of narrative painting reaching to the top of the walls, was of the most sumptuous character. The floor was paved with glazed tiles and the boarded ceiling as replaced after the fire of 1263 was adorned with flat carved bosses with colour inlay, and much painted gesso. The borders of some of the many individual figure paintings were enriched with gold patterns on blue glass, a technique which can be seen on a smaller scale on the well-known retable in Westminster Abbey. In addition to the great bed, the King had two wardrobes; these were separate rooms, not pieces of furniture, as the bed, however large and architectural in character, must be considered; one wardrobe was for the King's clothes and one, with water laid on, is described in 1256, when it was adorned with wall paintings as 'the warbrobe where the King washes his head'. See *History of the King's Works*, 1964, I, p. 494.

161 5. For Bishop Gower's Palace see C. A. R. Radford, *Guide to St David's Palace*, Ministry of Works, 1934.

6. For Goodrich see R.C.H.M. *Inventory of Herefordshire*, I, 1931. p. 162

7. For New College see R.C.H.M. *Inventory of the City of Oxford*, 1939.

8. For Herstmonceux see W. Douglas Simpson in *Archaeol. Jnl*, XCIX, 1942. p. 167

9. For Tattershall see the Marquess Curzon and H. A. Tipping, *Tattershall Castle*, 1929. p. 168

CHAPTER 10

1. Professor Hamilton Thompson points out that, in addition to the declared purpose of such foundations, they provided additional clergy for large parishes, and this motive was certainly an important one. There were other socially useful purposes which could be served by the system, and these factors certainly encouraged the movement. p. 170

2. For Friars' Churches see W. H. Godfrey in *Some Famous Buildings and their Story*, 1913. p. 171

3. For Norwich Dominicans see F. C. Elliston Erwood in *Archaeol. Jnl*, CVI, 1951.

4. For Holy Trinity, Hull, see *Archaeol. Jnl*, CV, 1938. p. 172

5. Holy Trinity, Hull, was not a parish church in the strictest sense of the term but a dependent chapel of the older parish of Hessle.

6. For St Nicholas, King's Lynn, see E. M. Beloe, *Our Churches, our Borough*, 1899; and *Archaeol. Jnl*, LXXXIX, 1932.

7. There are plenty of places where the altar of the saint to whom the guild owed particular devotion was situated in the eastern part of the church. p. 173

8. For Fenstanton and Lawford see R.C.H.M. *Inventory of Huntingdonshire*, 1926, and *Inventory of Essex*, vol. III, 1922. Fenstanton was founded by William de Longthorne, Rector 1345–52.

9. For St Cuthbert's, Wells, see Joan Evans in *Archaeol. Jnl*, CVII, 1952. In this instance there is documentary evidence: in other cases in Somerset (and at Oundle) the process can be deduced from the structure. p. 177

10. The Will of the Rector, dated 1382, left the residue of his estate to the work of the church 'begun by me until it be finished'.

11. Sall Church in Norfolk is a good example of these transeptal chapels; see Joan Evans and A. B. Whittingham in *Archaeol. Jnl*, CVI, 1951. For this whole question see A. Hamilton Thompson, *Historical Growth of the English Parish Church*.

p. 181 12. The churches of this type in general have roofs constructed on a simple tie-beam and king-post principle, though often of extreme decorative elaboration.

13. The wagon roof, though it fits more naturally into a church without a clerestory, is not confined to such buildings, and the most splendid example of such a roof in Somerset is certainly the roof of the nave of Shepton Mallet, dating c. 1500.

14. A. K. Wickham.

p. 182 15. Except for Yatton, exceptional in this as in most other ways.

p. 184 16. Pecock's *Repressor* (Rolls S.), vol. II, p. 553. Quoted G. R. Owst, *Preaching in Mediaeval England*, p. 157.

p. 186 17. The tie-beams of the south transept of Winchester Cathedral are also claimed as of early Romanesque date.

18. The defect of this type of roof, a tendency to movement longitudinally, was by the eighteenth century very marked in the eastern limb of Ely where the gable of the east front was found to be seriously displaced outwards.

p. 187 19. Two recent writers, Mr F. H. Crossley and Mr H. Braun, have called attention to this problem. Mr Braun is unfortunately inclined to date the Essex examples too early, but his suggestion that the system of intermediate posts at Blackmore may give a hint of the origin of the alternate system of supports in Romanesque is a very interesting one.

p. 191 20. For Chartham see A. W. Clapham in *Archaeol. Jnl*, LXXXVI, 1929.

21. For Needham Market see Munro Cautley, *Suffolk Churches*, 1937.

22. Mr Cave compares this boss with those of the Angel Choir at Lincoln.

23. The possibility of actual physical influences passing between Kent and Devon need not necessarily be excluded, sea transport being a closer link than land transport generally in the Middle Ages.

CHAPTER II

p. 193 1. See J. Huizinga, *The Waning of the Middle Ages*, 1924.

2. For Eltham Palace see W. H. Godfrey in *Some Famous Buildings and their Story*, 1913.

p. 194 3. For Magdalen College, Oxford, see R.C.H.M. *Inventory of the City of Oxford*, 1939.

4. Herstmonceux provided originally a good example of this type of 'cloister' as a domestic feature. See Figure 73. The pentice and court of the College of the Vicars Choral at Hereford are a fine surviving example.

5. Probably designed by Orchard; certainly he p. 1 submitted a drawing for the west window of the chapel in 1475.

6. At Queens' College, Cambridge, the contract p. 1 for the principal court provides an interesting example of a carpenter in partnership with a cloth merchant, which is presumably the profits of the great industry of the country being invested in the building trade.

7. Henry had 146 masons at Nonsuch in one month in 1538, and earlier at Westminster, 1531, had 267. At Hampton Court, in the hall, there is evidence of stone corbels imitated in plaster, which testify to the need of haste in carrying out the work.

8. For Sherborne see R.C.H.M. *Inventory of West Dorset*, 1952.

9. The spacing of the arcades being dictated by p. 1 the earlier structure is very irregular, and the vertical line dividing the bays was indeed impracticable.

10. For Peterborough see C. R. Peers in V.C.H. *Northamptonshire*.

11. The decoration includes the cipher of Anne p. 1 Boleyn as Queen.

12. The canopies of the side stalls of the chapel are post-Restoration, and the whole treatment of the Presbytery has been profoundly changed in modern times.

13. It seems that there had been an original intention to have a lantern at the crossing, hence the unusual order in which the vaults were built.

14. Of the kind associated with the name della p. 1 Robbia.

15. A curious derivative of these pendant vaults is p. 2 to be found at Rosslyn Chapel in Scotland, a fantastic example of the combination of ideas derived from the south with Scottish pointed barrel vault construction and Flemish-derived detail, which dates from 1501.

16. For Thornbury see Douglas Simpson in p. 2 *Antiq. Jnl*, XXVI, 1946.

17. Something of the same character seems perceptible at Raglan Castle, but that, as embodying an earlier fortress and by reason of the confinement of the site by water defences, is not quite a just comparison.

18. For Muchelney see P. K. Baillie-Reynolds in p. 2 *Archaeol. Jnl*, CVII, 1950, and H. A. Tipping in *English Homes*, Part I, vol. II, 1937.

19. Similar ceilings are to be seen at Hampton p. Court.

GLOSSARY

ABACUS. The uppermost member of a capital.

ACANTHUS. In Classic or Renaissance architecture, a plant, the leaves of which are used in the ornament of the Corinthian and Composite Orders.

ALTAR-TOMB. A modern term for a tomb of stone or marble resembling, but not used as, an altar.

APSE. The semicircular or polygonal end of a chancel or other part of a church.

ARCADE. A range of arches carried on piers or columns.

ARCH. The following are some of the most usual forms: *Segmental:* a single arc struck from a centre below the springing line. *Pointed or two-centred:* two arcs struck from centres on the springing line, and meeting at the apex with a point. *Segmental-pointed:* a pointed arch, struck from two centres below the springing line. *Equilateral:* a pointed arch struck with radii equal to the span. *Lancet:* a pointed arch struck with radii greater than the span. *Three-centred, elliptical:* formed with three arcs, the middle or uppermost struck from a centre below the springing line. *Four-centred, depressed, Tudor:* a pointed arch of four arcs, the two outer and lower arcs struck from centres on the springing line and the two inner and upper arcs from centres below the springing line. Sometimes the two upper arcs are replaced by straight lines. *Ogee:* a pointed arch of four or more arcs, the two uppermost or middle arcs being reversed, *i.e.* convex instead of concave to the base line. *Relieving:* an arch, generally of rough construction, placed in the wall above the true arch or head of an opening, to relieve it of the superincumbent weight. *Stilted:* an arch with its springing line raised above the level of the imposts. *Skew:* an arch not at right angles laterally with its jambs.

ARCHITRAVE. A moulded enrichment to the jambs and head of a doorway or window-opening; the lowest member of an entablature (*q.v.*).

ASHLAR. Masonry wrought to an even face and square edges.

BALL-FLOWER. In architecture, a decoration, peculiar to the first quarter of the fourteenth century, consisting of a globular flower of three petals enclosing a small ball.

BARGE-BOARD. A board, often carved, fixed to the edge of a gabled roof, a short distance from the face of the wall.

BARREL-VAULTING. See VAULTING.

BEAD. A small round moulding.

BELL-CAPITAL. A form of capital of which the chief characteristic is a reversed bell between the neck moulding and upper moulding; the bell is often enriched with carving.

BOSS. A projecting square or round ornament, covering the intersection of the ribs in a vault, panelled ceiling or roof, etc.

BOWTELL. See ROLL-MOULDING.

BRACE. In roof construction, a subsidiary timber inserted to strengthen the framing of a truss. *Wind-brace*: a subsidiary timber inserted between the purlins and principals of a roof to resist the pressure of the wind.

BRATTISHING. Ornamental cresting on the top of a screen, cornice, etc.

BRESSUMMER. A beam forming the direct support of an upper wall or timber-framing.

BRICK-WORK. *Header:* a brick laid so that the end only appears on the face of the wall. *Stretcher:* a brick laid so that one side only appears on the face of the wall.

BUTTRESS. A mass of masonry or brick-work projecting from or built against a wall to give additional strength. *Angle-buttresses:* two meeting, or nearly meeting, at an angle of 90 degrees at the corner of a building. *Diagonal buttress:* one placed against the right angle formed by two walls, and more or less equi-angular with both. *Flying-buttress:* an arch or half-arch transmitting the thrust of a vault or roof from the upper part of a wall to an outer support or buttress.

CABLE-MOULDING. A moulding carved in the form of a cable.

CAMBERED (applied to a beam). Curved so that the middle is higher than the ends.

CANOPY. A projection or hood over a door, window, etc., and the covering over a tomb or niche; also the representation of the same on a brass.

CASEMENT. (1) A wide hollow moulding in window-jambs, etc. (2) The hinged part of a window.

CHAMFER. The small plane formed when the sharp edge or arris of stone or wood is cut away, usually at an angle of 45 degrees; when the plane is concave it is termed a *hollow chamfer*, and when the plane is sunk below its arrises, or edges, a *sunk chamfer*.

CHANTRY-CHAPEL. A chapel built for the purposes of a chantry (a foundation for the celebration of masses for the souls of the founder and such others as he may direct).

CINQUEFOIL. See FOIL.

CLERESTORY. An upper storey, pierced by windows, in the main walls of a church. The same term is applicable in the case of a domestic building.

COLLAR-BEAM. In a roof, a horizontal beam framed to and serving to tie a pair of rafters together some distance above the wall-plate level.

CONSOLE. A bracket with a compound curved outline.

CORBEL. A projecting stone or piece of timber for the support of a superincumbent weight.

COVE. A concave under-surface of the nature of a hollow moulding but on a larger scale.

CREST, CRESTING. An ornamental finish along the top of a screen, etc.

CROCKETS. Carvings projecting at regular intervals from the vertical or sloping sides of parts of a building, such as spires, canopies, hood-moulds, etc.

CURTAIN. The connecting wall between the towers or bastions of a castle.

CUSHION-CAPITAL. A capital cut from a cube by having its lower angles rounded off to a circular shaft.

CUSPS (*cusping, cusped heads, sub-cusps*). The projecting points forming the foils in Gothic windows, arches, panels, etc.; they were frequently ornamented at the ends, or *cusp-points*, with leaves, flowers, berries, etc.

DIAPER. Decoration of surfaces with squares, diamonds, and other patterns.

DOG-TOOTH ORNAMENT. A typical thirteenth-century carved ornament consisting of a series of pyramidal flowers of four petals; used to cover hollow mouldings.

DOUBLE-OGEE. See OGEE.

DRAWBAR. A wooden bar or bolt, inside a door, fitted into a socket in one jamb and a long channel in the other jamb, into which it slides back when not in use.

DRESSINGS. The stones used about an angle, window, or other feature when worked to a finished face, whether smooth, tooled in various ways, moulded, or sculptured.

EAVES. The under part of a sloping roof overhanging a wall.

EMBRASURES. The openings, indents, or sinkings in an embattled parapet or the recesses for windows, doorways, etc.

ENTABLATURE. In Classic or Renaissance architecture, the moulded horizontal superstructure of a wall, colonnade, or opening consisting of an architrave, frieze, and cornice.

ENTASIS. The convexity or swell on a vertical line or surface to correct the optical illusion of concavity in the sides of a column or spire when the lines are straight.

FAN-VAULTING. See VAULTING.

FASCIA. A plain or moulded board covering the plate of a projecting upper storey of timber, and masking the ends of the cantilever joists which support it.

FINIAL. A formal bunch of foliage or similar ornament at the top of a pinnacle, gable, canopy,. etc.

FOIL (*trefoil, quatrefoil, cinquefoil, multifoil*, etc.). A leaf-shaped curve formed by the cusping of feathering in an opening or panel.

FOLIATED (of a capital, corbel, etc.). Carved with leaf ornament.

FRATER. The refectory or dining-hall of a monastery.

FRIEZE. The middle division in an entablature, between the architrave and the cornice; generally any band of ornament or colour immediately below a cornice.

GABLE. The wall at the end of a ridged roof, generally triangular, sometimes semicircular, and often with an outline of various curves, then called *curvilinear*.

GADROONED. Enriched with a series of convex ridges, the converse of fluting, and forming an ornamental edge or band.

GARGOYLE. A carved projecting figure pierced to carry off the rain-water from the roof of a building.

GROINING, GROINED VAULT. See VAULTING.

HAMMER-BEAMS. Horizontal brackets of a roof projecting at the wall-plate level, and resembling the two ends of a tie-beam with its middle part cut away; they are supported by braces (or struts), and help to diminish lateral pressure by reducing the span. Sometimes there is a second and even a third upper series of these brackets.

HIPPED ROOF. A roof with sloped instead of vertical ends. *Half-hipped*: a roof whose ends are partly vertical and partly sloped.

HOOD-MOULD, LABEL, DRIP-STONE. A projecting moulding on the face of a wall above an arch, doorway, or window; in some cases it follows the form of the arch, and in others is square in outline.

JAMBS. The sides of an archway, doorway, window, or other opening.

JOGGLING. The method of cutting the adjoining faces of the voussoirs of an arch with rebated, zigzagged, or wavy surfaces to provide a better key.

KEYSTONE. The middle stone in an arch.

KING-POST. The middle vertical post in a roof-truss.

KNEELER. Stone at the foot of a gable.

LABEL. See HOOD-MOULD.

LANCET. A long, narrow window with a pointed head, typical of the thirteenth century.

LIERNE VAULT. See VAULTING.

LINEN-FOLD PANELLING. Panelling ornamented with a conventional representation of folded linen.

LINTEL. The horizontal beam or stone bridging an opening.

LOCKER, AUMBRY. A small cupboard formed in a wall.

LOOP. A small narrow light in a turret, etc.; often unglazed.

LOUVRE or LUFFER. A lantern-like structure surmounting the roof of a hall or other building, with openings for ventilation or the escape of smoke, usually crossed by slanting boards (called 'louvre-boards'), to exclude rain.

MASK-STOP. A stop at the end of a hood-mould, bearing a distant resemblance to a human face; generally of the twelfth and thirteenth centuries.

MERLON. The solid part of an embattled parapet between the embrasures.

MISERICORD. (1) A bracket on the underside of the hinged seat of a choir-stall, to be used (when turned up) as a support for the occupant, while standing during a long service. (2) In monastic planning, a small hall, generally attached to the Infirmary, in which better food than the ordinary was supplied for special reasons.

MOTTE (earthworks). A steep mound forming the main feature of an eleventh- or twelfth-century castle.

MULLION. A vertical post, standard, or upright dividing an opening into lights.

MUNTIN. The intermediate upright in the framing of a door, screen, or panel, butting into or stopped by the rails.

NECK-MOULDING. The narrow moulding round the bottom of a capital.

NEWEL. The central post in a circular or winding staircase; also the principal posts at the angles of a dog-legged or well-staircase.

OGEE. A compound curve of two parts, one convex, the other concave; a double-ogee moulding is formed by two ogees meeting at their convex ends.

ORDERS OF ARCHES. Receding or concentric rings of voussoirs.

ORDERS OF ARCHITECTURE. In Classic or Renaissance architecture, the five types of columnar architecture, known as Tuscan, Doric, Ionic, Corinthian and Composite.

ORIEL WINDOW. A projecting bay-window carried upon corbels or brackets.

OVERSAILING COURSES. A number of brick or stone courses, each course projecting beyond the one below it.

OVOLO MOULDING. A Classic moulding forming a quarter round or semi-ellipse in section.

PALIMPSEST. (1) Of a brass: re-used by engraving the back of an older engraved plate. (2) Of a wall-painting: superimposed on an earlier painting.

PATERA, PATERAE. A flat ornament applied to a frieze, moulding, or cornice; in Gothic work it commonly takes the form of a four-lobed leaf or flower.

PILASTER. A shallow pier attached to a wall.

PISCINA. A basin for washing the sacred vessels and provided with a drain, generally set in or against the wall to the south of the altar, but sometimes sunk in the pavement.

PLINTH. The projecting base of a wall or column, generally chamfered or moulded at the top.

POPPY-HEAD. The ornament at the heads of bench-standards or desks in churches; generally carved with foliage and flowers, somewhat resembling a fleur-de-lis.

PORTCULLIS. The running gate, rising and falling in vertical grooves in the jambs of a doorway.

PRESBYTERY. The part of a church in which is placed the high altar, east of the choir.

PRINCIPALS. The chief trusses of a roof, or the main rafters, posts, or braces, in the wooden framework of a building.

PURLIN. A horizontal timber resting on the principal rafters of a roof-truss, and forming an intermediate support for the common rafters.

QUADRIPARTITE VAULT. See VAULTING.

QUARRY. In glazing, small panes of glass, generally diamond-shaped or square, set diagonally.

QUATREFOIL. See FOIL.

QUEEN-POSTS. A pair of vertical posts in a roof-truss equidistant from the middle line.

QUOIN. The dressed stones at the angle of a building.

REAR-ARCH. The arch on the inside of a wall spanning a doorway or window-opening.

REAR-VAULT. The space between a rear-arch and the outer stone-work of a window.

REBATE, RABBET, RABBIT. A continuous rectangular notch cut on an edge.

REREDOS. A hanging, wall, or screen of stone or wood at the back of an altar or dais.

RESPOND. The half-pillar or pier at the end of an arcade or abutting a single arch.

RIBBED VAULT. See VAULTING.

ROLL-MOULDING or BOWTELL. A continuous convex moulding cut upon the edges of stone and woodwork, etc.

ROOD. A cross or crucifix. The *great rood* was set up at the east end of the nave with accompanying figures of St Mary and St John; it was generally carved in wood, and fixed on the loft or head of the rood-screen, or on a special beam (the *rood-beam*), reaching from wall to wall. Sometimes the rood was merely painted on the wall above the chancel-arch or on a closed wood partition or tympanum in the upper half of the arch. The *rood-screen* is the open screen spanning the east end of the nave, shutting off the chancel; in the fifteenth century a narrow gallery was often constructed above the cornice to carry the rood and other images and candles, and it was also used as a music-gallery. The *rood-loft* was approached by a staircase (and occasionally by more than one), either of wood or in a turret built in the wall, wherever most convenient, and, when the loft was carried right across the building, the intervening walls of the nave were often pierced with narrow archways. Many of the roods were destroyed at the Reformation, and their final removal, with the loft, was ordered in 1561.

RUBBLE. Walling of rough unsquared stones or flints.

SACRISTY. A room generally in immediate connexion with a church, in which the holy vessels and other valuables were kept.

SCALLOPED CAPITAL. A development of the cushion-capital in which the single cushion is elaborated into a series of truncated cones.

SCARP (*earthworks*). An artificial cutting away of the ground to form a steeper slope.

SEDILIA (sing. *sedile*, a seat; sometimes called presbyteries). The seats on the south side of the chancel, choir, or chapel near the altar, used by the ministers during the Mass.

SEXPARTITE VAULT. See VAULTING.

SHAFT. A small column.

SHAFTED JAMB. A jamb containing one or more shafts either engaged or detached.

SLIP-TILES. Tiles moulded with a design in intaglio which was then filled in, before burning, with a clay of a different colour.

SOFFIT. The under-side of a staircase, lintel, cornice, arch, canopy, etc.

SOFFIT-CUSPS. Cusps springing from the flat soffit of an arched head, and not from its chamfered sides or edges.

SPANDREL. The triangular-shaped space above the haunch of an arch; the two outer edges generally form a rectangle, as in an arched and square-headed doorway; the name is also applied to a space within a curved brace below a tie-beam, etc., and to any similar spaces.

SPIRE. The tall pointed termination covered with lead or shingles, forming the roof of a tower or turret. A *broach-spire* rises from the sides of the tower without a parapet, the angles of a square tower being surmounted, in this case, by half-pyramids against the alternate faces of the spire, when the spire is octagonal. A *needle-spire* is small and narrow, and rises from the middle of the tower-roof well within the parapet.

SPLAY. A sloping face making an angle more than a right-angle with the main surface, as in internal window-jambs, etc.

SPRINGING-LINE. The level at which an arch springs from its supports.

SQUINCH. An arch thrown across the angle between two walls to support a superstructure, such as the base of a stone spire.

SQUINT. A piercing through a wall to allow a view of an altar from places whence it could otherwise not be seen.

STAGES OF TOWERS. The divisions marked by horizontal string-courses externally.

STANCHION, STANCHEON. The upright iron bars in a screen, window, etc.

STOPS. Projecting stones at the ends of labels, string-courses, etc., against which the mouldings finish; they are often carved in various forms, such as shields, bunches of foliage, human or grotesque heads, etc.; a finish at the end of any moulding or chamfer, bringing the corner out to a square edge, or sometimes, in the case of a moulding, to a chamfered edge. A splayed stop has a plain sloping face, but in many other cases the face is moulded.

STRING COURSE. A projecting horizontal band in a wall; usually moulded.

STRUT. A timber forming a sloping support to a beam, etc.

STYLE. The vertical members of a frame into which are tenoned the ends of the rails or horizontal pieces.

TABLE, ALABASTER. A panel or series of panels of alabaster carved with religious subjects and placed at the back of an altar to form a reredos. The manufacture was a distinctively English industry of the fourteenth, fifteenth, and early sixteenth centuries, centred at Nottingham.

TIE-BEAM. The horizontal transverse beam in a roof, tying together the feet of the rafters to counteract the thrust.

TIMBER-FRAMED BUILDING. A building of which the walls are built of open timbers and covered with plaster or boarding, or with interstices filled in with brick-work.

TOUCH. A soft black marble quarried near Tournai and commonly used in monumental art.

TRACERY. The ornamental work in the head of a window, screen, panel, etc., formed by the curving and interlacing of bars of stone or wood, and grouped together, generally over two or more lights or bays.

TRANSOM. A horizontal bar of stone or wood across the upper half of a window-opening, doorway, or panel.

TREFOIL. See FOIL.

TRIBUNE. A gallery forming a complete storey above the aisles and lit by its own windows in addition to arcaded openings to the central vessel. A 'false tribune' is only lit by this latter opening, and the roof descends as a lean-to springing from just above the aisle windows.

TRIFORIUM. An arcaded gallery contrived in the thickness of the wall of the middle storey between the arcades and the clerestory.

TRUSS. A number of timbers framed together to bridge a space or form a bracket, to be self-supporting, and to carry other timbers. The trusses of a roof are generally named after a peculiar feature in their construction, such as *king-post, queen-post, hammer-beam,* etc. *(q.v.)*.

TYMPANUM. An enclosed space within an arch, doorway, etc., or in the triangle of a pediment.

VAULTING. An arched ceiling or roof of stone or brick, sometimes imitated in wood or plaster. *Barrel-vaulting* (sometimes called *wagon-head vaulting*) is a continuous vault unbroken in its length by cross-vaults. A *groined vault* (or cross-vaulting) results from the intersection of simple vaulting surfaces. A *ribbed vault* is a framework of arched ribs carrying the cells which cover in the spaces between them. One bay of vaulting, divided into four quarters or compartments, is termed *quadripartite*; but often the bay is divided longitudinally into two subsidiary bays, each equalling a bay of the wall-supports; the vaulting bay is thus divided into six compartments, and is termed *sexpartite*. A more complicated form is *lierne vaulting*; this contains secondary ribs, which do not spring from the wall-supports, but cross from main rib to main rib. In *fan-vaulting* numerous ribs rise from the springing in equal curves, diverging equally in all directions, giving fan-like effects when seen from below.

VESICA PISCIS. A pointed oval frame generally used in medieval art to enclose a figure of Christ enthroned.

VOLUTE. A spiral form of ornament.

VOUSSOIRS. The stones forming an arch.

WAGON-HEAD VAULT. See VAULTING.

WALL-PLATE. A timber laid lengthwise on the wall to receive the ends of the rafters and other joists.

WAVE-MOULD. A compound mould formed by a convex curve between two concave curves.

WEATHER-BOARDING. Horizontal boards nailed to the uprights of timber-framed buildings and made to overlap; the boards are wedge-shaped in section, the upper edge being the thinner.

WEATHERING (to sills, tops of buttresses, etc.). A sloping surface for casting off water, etc.

BIBLIOGRAPHY

THE decision to exclude from this bibliography all works published in learned periodicals and confine these to the notes inevitably gives a very misleading impression. From Professor Willis, the greatest of nineteenth-century medieval archaeologists, onwards much of the most important work has been published in periodicals, and such names as Bilson, Brakspear, St John Hope, and Peers hardly appear, or occupy so modest a place as to give no indication of the importance of their work to the study of the subject as a whole. *The Antiquaries Journal, The Archaeological Journal, Archaeologia, The Journal of the British Archaeological Association, The Journal of the Royal Institute of British Architects*, and those of many local archaeological societies, together with the great topographical collected works such as the *Victoria County Histories*, the *Inventories of the Royal Commission on Ancient and Historical Monuments*, and the Guides and leaflets issued by the Ministry of Works, have a quite exceptional importance.

GENERAL WORKS

ALLEN, F. J. *The Great Church Towers of England.* Cambridge, 1933.

ATKINSON, T. D. *Local Style in English Architecture.* London, 1947.

BIVER, P., and HOWARD, F. E. *Les Chantry Chapels anglaises.* Caen, 1908.

BOND, F. *Gothic Architecture in England.* London, 1906.

BOND, F. *Wood Carving in English Churches*, Vol. II: *Stalls.* London, 1910.

BOND, F. *An Introduction to English Church Architecture.* Oxford, 1913.

BRANDON, J. R. and J. A. *Parish Churches.* London, 1888.

BRANDON, J. R. and J. A. *Open Timber Roofs of the Middle Ages.* London, 1899.

BRAUN, Hugh. *An Introduction to English Mediaeval Architecture.* London, 1951.

BROWN, G. Baldwin. *The Arts in Early England: Architecture.* London, 1925.

CAVE, C. J. P. *Roof Bosses in Mediaeval Churches.* Cambridge, 1948.

CLAPHAM, A. W. *English Romanesque Architecture before the Conquest.* Oxford, 1930.

CLAPHAM, A. W. *English Romanesque Architecture after the Conquest.* Oxford, 1934.

CLAPHAM, A. W. *Romanesque Architecture in Western Europe.* Oxford, 1936.

CLAPHAM, A. W. *Romanesque Architecture in England.* London, 1950.

CLAPHAM, A. W., and GODFREY, W. H. *Some Famous Buildings and their Story.* London, 1913.

COOK, G. H. *Mediaeval Chantries and Chantry Chapels.* London, 1947.

COULTON, G. G. *Art and the Reformation.* Oxford, 1928.

COX, J. C., and HARVEY, A. *English Church Furniture.* London, 1919.

CROSSLEY, F. H. *English Church Monuments.* London, 1921.

EVANS, Joan. *English Art 1307–1461.* Oxford, 1949.

FOWLER, J. T. (ed.). *The Mills of Durham.* Surtees Society, Durham, 1903.

GARDNER, A. *English Gothic Foliage Sculpture.* Cambridge, 1927.

GARDNER, A. *A Handbook of English Mediaeval Sculpture.* Cambridge, 1935; 2nd ed. 1951.

HARVEY, J. H. *Henry Yevele.* London, 1944.

HARVEY, J. H. *Gothic England.* London, 1947.

HARVEY, J. H. *An Introduction to Tudor Architecture.* London, 1949.

HARVEY, J. H. *The Gothic World.* London, 1950.

HARVEY, J. H., and FELTON, H. *The English Cathedrals.* London, 1950.

HOWARD, F. E., and CROSSLEY, F. H. *English Church Woodwork.* London, 1917; 2nd ed. 1927.

JAMES, M. R., and THOMPSON, A. Hamilton. *Abbeys.* London, 1925.

KENDRICK, T. D. *Anglo-Saxon Art to A.D. 900.* London, 1938.

KENDRICK, T. D. *Late Saxon and Viking Art.* London, 1949.

KNOOP, D., and JONES, G. P. *The Mediaeval Mason.* Manchester, 1933.

LEASK, H. G. Architectural Chapter in *Christian Art in Ancient Ireland*, Vol. II. Dublin, 1941.

LEASK, H. G. *Irish Castles.* Dundalk, 1946.

LETHABY, W. A., *Mediaeval Art.* London, 1904.

MARTIN, A. R. *Franciscan Architecture in England.* Manchester, 1937.

MOORE, C. H. *The Mediaeval Church Architecture of England.* New York, 1912.

PRIOR, E. S. *History of Gothic Art in England.* London, 1900.

PRIOR, E. S. *The Cathedral Builders in England.* London, 1905.

PRIOR, E. S. *Eight Chapters on English Mediaeval Art.* Cambridge, 1922.

PRIOR, E. S., and GARDNER, A. *An Account of Medieval Figure Sculpture in England.* Cambridge, 1912.

RICE, D. Talbot. *English Art 871–1100.* Oxford, 1952.

RICKMAN, T. *An Attempt to Discriminate the Styles of English Architecture.* London, 1881.

SALZMAN, L. F. *A Documentary History of Mediaeval Building.* Oxford, 1950.

SCOTT, G. G. *An Essay on the History of English Church Architecture.* London, 1881.

SHARPE, E. *Architectural Parallels in the Twelfth and Thirteenth Centuries selected from Abbey Churches* (and supplement). London, 1848.

SHARPE, E. *Decorated Window Tracery in England.* London, 1849.

SHARPE, E. *Mouldings of the Six Periods of British Architecture.* London, 1871.

SHARPE, E. *Ornamentation of the Transitional Period.* London, 1876.

STONE, L. *Sculpture in Britain: The Middle Ages* (The Pelican History of Art). London, 1955.

THOMPSON, A. Hamilton. *The Ground Plan of the English Parish Church.* Cambridge, 1911.

THOMPSON, A. Hamilton. *Military Architecture in England.* London, 1912.

THOMPSON, A. Hamilton. *English Monasteries.* Cambridge, 1913.

THOMPSON, A. Hamilton. *The Historical Growth of the English Parish Church.* Cambridge, 1913.

THOMPSON, A. Hamilton. *Cathedral Churches of England.* London, 1925.

TURNER, T. H., and PARKER, J. H. *Some Account of Domestic Architecture in England.* Vol. I: XII and XIII Centuries, 1851; Vol. II: XIV Century, 1853; Vols. IV and V: XV Century. Oxford, 1859.

WEBB, G. F. *Gothic Architecture in England.* London, 1951.

WILLIS, R. *Architectural Nomenclature of the Middle Ages.* Cambridge, 1886.

ZARNECKI, G. *English Romanesque Sculpture, 1066–1146.* London, 1951.

ZARNECKI, G. *Later English Romanesque Sculpture, 1140–1210.* London, 1953.

TOPOGRAPHICAL SERIES

BRITTON, John. *Cathedral Antiquities of Great Britain.* 5 vols. Vol. I: Canterbury, York; Vol. II: Salisbury, Norwich, Oxford; Vol. III: Winchester, Lichfield, Hereford; Vol. IV: Wells, Exeter, Worcester; Vol. V: Peterborough, Gloucester, Bristol. London, 1814–35.

COOK, G. H. *English Cathedral Series* (in process of publication): *A Portrait of Durham,* London, 1948; *A Portrait of Canterbury,* London, 1949; *A Portrait of Salisbury,* London, 1949; *A Portrait of Lincoln,* London, 1950; *A Portrait of St Albans,* London, 1951.

County Churches Series: Isle of Wight, London, 1911; *Norfolk,* London, 1911; *Nottinghamshire,* London, 1911; *Cornwall,* London, 1912; *Suffolk,* London, 1912; *Cumberland and Westmorland,* London, 1913; *Kent,* London, 1913; *Surrey,* London, 1916.

English Cathedral Series. 33 vols. London, 1896–1904. (Uniform with these is a series of 15 volumes on abbeys and other important churches.)

PEVSNER, Nikolaus. *The Buildings of England: Cornwall,* London, 1951; *Middlesex,* London, 1951; *Nottinghamshire,* London, 1951; *Derbyshire,* London, 1952; *Hertfordshire,* London, 1952; *London* (2 vols.), London, 1952 and 1956; *North Devon,* London, 1952; *South Devon,* London, 1952; *County Durham,* London, 1953; *Cambridgeshire,* London, 1954; *Essex,* London, 1954. The series continues.

Royal Commission on Historical Monuments (England). County Inventories: *Hertfordshire,* London, 1910; *Buckinghamshire I,* London, 1912; *Buckinghamshire II,* London, 1913; *Essex I,* London, 1916; *Essex II,* London, 1921; *Essex III,* London, 1922; *Essex IV,* London, 1923; *Westminster Abbey,* London, 1924; *West London,* London, 1925; *Huntingdonshire,* London, 1926; *The City of London,* London, 1929; *East London,* London, 1930; *Herefordshire I,* London, 1931; *Herefordshire II,* London, 1932, *Herefordshire III,* London, 1934; *Westmorland,* London, 1936; *Middlesex,* London, 1937; *City of Oxford,* London, 1939; *West Dorset,* London, 1952; *City of Cambridge,* London, 1959. The series continues:.

Royal Commission on Ancient and Historical Monuments (Scotland). County Inventories: *East Lothian,* Edinburgh, 1924; *Midlothian and West Lothian,* Edinburgh, 1929; *Fife, Clackmannan and Kinross,* Edinburgh, 1933.

TIPPING, H. A. *English Home Series: Norman and Plantagenet*, London, 1921; *Early Tudor I*, London, 1924; *Early Tudor II*, London, 1937; *Mediaeval*, London, 1937.

Victoria County Histories. The following counties have reached a stage where architectural material is treated: Bedfordshire, Berkshire, Buckinghamshire, Hampshire, Huntingdonshire, Kent, Lancashire, Northamptonshire, Rutland, Surrey, Sussex, Warwickshire, Worcestershire, Yorkshire (North Riding).

Works, Ministry of, Official Guides: Only the larger guides have been mentioned and mainly those dealing with ecclesiastical buildings; the leaflets, however, are written with equal authority and in some cases contain accounts of discoveries made by excavation: *Byland Abbey, Yorkshire; Carisbrooke Castle, Isle of Wight; Castle Acre Priory, Norfolk; Dryburgh Abbey, Berwickshire; Dunkeld Cathedral, Perthshire; Easby Abbey, Yorkshire; Elgin Cathedral, Moray; Ewenny Priory, Glamorgan; Holyroodhouse Abbey and Palace, Midlothian; Inchcolm Abbey, Fife; Linlithgow Palace, West Lothian; Melrose Abbey, Roxburghshire; Netley Abbey, Hampshire; Raglan Castle, Monmouthshire; Rhuddlan Castle, Flintshire; St Andrew's Cathedral, Fife; Stirling Castle; Sweetheart Abbey, Kirkcudbrightshire; Thornton Abbey, Lincolnshire; Tintagel Castle, Cornwall; Tynemouth Priory and Castle, Northumberland; Whitby Abbey, Yorkshire;* etc., etc.

PARTICULAR SITES AND DISTRICTS

Cambridge, Architectural History of the University of. R. Willis. Cambridge, 1886.

Canterbury Cathedral, Architectural History of. R. Willis. London, 1845.

Canterbury, Christchurch, Architectural History of the Conventual Buildings of the Monastery of. R. Willis. London, 1869.

Cheshire Churches, Old. Raymond Richards. London, 1947.

Derbyshire, The Churches of. J. Cox. 4 vols., Chesterfield, 1875–9.

Durham Cathedral. W. A. Pantin. London, 1948.

Ely, An Architectural History of the Benedictine Monastery of St Etheldreda at. T. D. Atkinson. Cambridge, 1933.

Ely Cathedral. Geoffrey Webb. London, 1950.

Ely, The Monastery of. Inskip Ladd. Ely, 1930.

Ely, Sacrist Rolls of. F. R. Chapman. London, 1907.

Exeter Cathedral, The Buildings of. H. E. Bishop and E. K. Prideaux. Exeter, 1922.

Fountains Abbey. W. St John Hope. Leeds, 1900.

Glendalough. Publication of the Ancient and National Monuments of Ireland. Irish Stationery Office, 1911–12.

[King's Lynn] Our Churches and Borough. E. M. Beloe. Cambridge, 1899.

Kirkstall Abbey, Architectural Description of. J. Bilson and W. St John Hope. Leeds, 1907.

Lincoln, Excursion of the Architectural Association. E. Sharpe. London, 1871.

Nendrum, The Monastery of St Machaoi. H. C. Lawlor. Belfast, 1925.

Nene Valley Churches (with others). E. Sharpe. London, 1886.

New Shoreham Church. E. Sharpe. Chichester, 1861.

Northumberland, The History of. Newcastle-on-Tyne, 1893–1940.

Oxford Stone, The Story of Architecture in. E. A. Greening Lamborn. Oxford, 1929.

Rochester, St Andrew's, Architectural History of. W. St John Hope and A. W. Clapham. London, 1900.

St Albans, Guide to the Cathedral of. Royal Commission on Historical Monuments. London, 1952.

Shropshire, An Architectural Account of the Churches of. D. H. S. Cranage. Wellington, 1894–1912.

Somerset, The Churches of. A. K. Wickham. London, 1952.

Southwell, The Leaves of. N. Pevsner. London, 1945.

Suffolk Churches. H. Munro Cautley. London, 1937.

Suffolk and Norfolk. M. R. James. London, 1930.

Tattershall Castle. The Marquess Curzon and H. A. Tipping. London, 1929.

Waverley Abbey. Harold Brakspear. Guildford, 1905.

Wells, Architecture of the City of. J. H. Parker. Oxford, 1866.

Westminster Abbey and the King's Craftsmen. W. A. Lethaby. London, 1906.

Westminster Abbey Re-examined. W. A. Lethaby. London, 1925.

Windsor Castle. W. St John Hope. London, 1913.

THE PLATES

St Peter-on-the-Wall, Bradwell-juxta-Mare, Essex. From the north-west. *c.* 660

(B) Escomb church, Co. Durham.
Late seventh or early eighth century

(A) Monkwearmouth church, Co. Durham.
From the west. c. 675

Brixworth church, Northants. c. 670

3

(A) Brixworth church, Northants. *c.* 670

(B) Brixworth church, Northants. Detail of exterior

(A) The Oratory of Gallerus, Dingle, Co. Kerry. Possibly sixth or seventh century

(B) Bench-end. Monkwearmouth church, Co. Durham. Late seventh century

(C) Throne. Hexham Priory, Northumberland. Late seventh or early eighth century

(A) Fragments of early screen. South Kyme, Lincs. Late seventh century or early eighth century

(B) Arch. Britford church, Wilts. *c.* 800

Round tower, Glendalough, Co. Wicklow. *c.* 900

St Columba's house, Kells, Co. Meath. *c.* 800

St Kevin's kitchen and house, Glendalough, Co. Wicklow. From the south–east.
Mid ninth century

(A) Church at St Macdara's Isle, Co. Galway, showing anta detail. *c.* 700

(B) Detail of capital. South side of chancel arch. Rahan, Co. Offaly.
Early tenth century

Round tower and church, Brechin, Angus. Round tower tenth century

(B) St Rule's church, St Andrews, Fife. Detail

(A) St Rule's church, St Andrews, Fife. Mid twelfth century

(B) Chancel arch. Wittering church, Northants. Tenth century

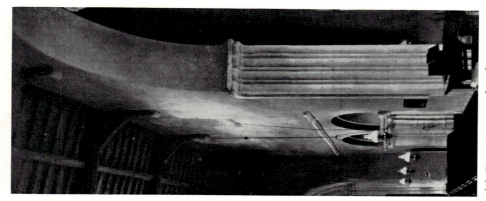

(A) Great Paxton church, Hunts.
From the east.
Mid eleventh century

West tower. Sompting church, Sussex. Early eleventh century

West tower. Earl's Barton church, Northants. *c.* 1000

West tower. Deerhurst church, Glos. Early tenth century

Early church. Bradford-on-Avon, Wilts. From the north-west. Probably a tenth-century remodelling of an eighth-century building

(B) Chancel arch. Bosham church, Sussex.
Early eleventh century

(A) Bradford-on-Avon church, Wilts.
From the west

18

Crypt. Worcester Cathedral. *c.* 1085

(A) West porch. Headbourne Worthy church, Hants. Late tenth century

(B) Great Paxton church, Hunts. Looking east. Mid eleventh century

Nave. St Alban's Abbey, Herts. *c.* 1080–90

(B) Nave. Blyth Priory, Notts. From the north-west. c. 1090

(A) Transept and crossing. St Alban's Abbey, Herts. From the south-west. 1080–90

22

Transept, with nave shown in section. Winchester Cathedral, Hants. c. 1090

23

North transept. Winchester Cathedral, Hants. From the south-east

West front. Lincoln Cathedral. *c.* 1090

South transept. Tewkesbury Abbey, Glos. *c.* 1090-1100

Nave. Tewkesbury Abbey, Glos. Early twelfth century

Nave (after disaster of 1806). Hereford Cathedral. First half of twelfth century

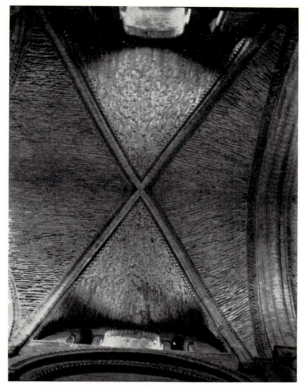

(A) Nave vault. Durham Cathedral. *c.* 1130

(B) Tribune vault. Gloucester Cathedral. 1090–1100

29

Nave. Durham Cathedral. From the west. First quarter of twelfth century

Transept and lantern. Durham Cathedral. Transept early twelfth century; lantern late fifteenth century

Detail of nave and tribune. Durham Cathedral. First quarter of twelfth century

(A) Intersecting arcading. Choir aisle. Durham Cathedral. Late eleventh century

(B) Interior of tribune, showing abutment of high vaults. Choir. Durham Cathedral.
Late eleventh century

33

(B) Detail of nave arcade and triforium. Gloucester Cathedral.
Early twelfth century

(A) Nave. Gloucester Cathedral. From the west.
1090–1100

(B) South-western transept from the western crossing. Ely Cathedral. Late twelfth century

(A) Detail of nave. Ely Cathedral. Mid twelfth century

Nave. Ely Cathedral. From the west. Mid twelfth century

Norwich Cathedral. From the west. Early twelfth century

(B) Arcading in nave. Ely Cathedral.
Mid twelfth century

(A) West side of south transept. Norwich Cathedral.
Early twelfth century

38

Nave. Fountains Abbey, Yorks. From the north-west. *c.* 1140

39

(A) Re-used capital. Crypt. Canterbury Cathedral. *c.* 1075

(B) Capital. Crypt. Canterbury Cathedral. First quarter of twelfth century

40

(A) Capital. Crypt. Canterbury Cathedral.
First quarter of twelfth century

(B) Angle ornament. Kilpeck, Herefordshire

(B) Durham Cathedral. From the south-west

(A) West front. Castle Acre Priory, Norfolk. Mid twelfth century

42

(B) West front. Rochester Cathedral, Kent.
Mid twelfth century

(A) West front. Malmesbury Abbey, Wilts. From the
south-west. c. 1160–70

43

Tower and steeple. Norwich Cathedral. From the south-west. Tower first half of twelfth century; steeple late fifteenth century

44

Central lantern. Norwich Cathedral. Early twelfth century

(B) Central tower. Tewkesbury Abbey, Glos. From the north-west.
c. 1150

(A) Central tower. St Alban's Abbey, Herts.
Late eleventh century

(B) South-west tower and return gable of earlier west front.
Lincoln Cathedral. Mid twelfth century

(A) South transept and south-west tower. Southwell Minster, Notts.
From the south-east. First half of twelfth century

47

West front. Ely Cathedral. Late twelfth century

North transept. Oxford Cathedral. From the south-east. Late twelfth century

(B) Nave. Malmesbury Abbey, Wilts. From the north-west.
c. 1160

(A) Nave. Worksop Priory, Notts. From the south-west.
c. 1180

50

(B) Nave. Dunfermline Abbey, Fife. North side looking east.
Late twelfth century

(A) South side of choir. Jedburgh Abbey, Roxburghshire.
Late twelfth century

51

(A) Nave. Southwell Minster, Notts. From the north-west. Mid twelfth century

(B) Detail of nave. Dunfermline Abbey, Fife

52

Kelso Abbey, Roxburghshire. From the south-west. Late twelfth century

(A) Kelso Abbey, Roxburghshire. Interior. Late twelfth century

(B) Arcaded walk. Canterbury Cathedral.
Mid twelfth century

54

(A) Reconstructed fragments of cloister arcade. Bridlington Priory, Yorks.
Mid twelfth century

(B) Cloister. Newminster Abbey, Northumberland. Early thirteenth century

55

Gatehouse. Bury St Edmunds Abbey, Suffolk. *c.* 1130

Chapter-house. Bristol Cathedral. Mid twelfth century

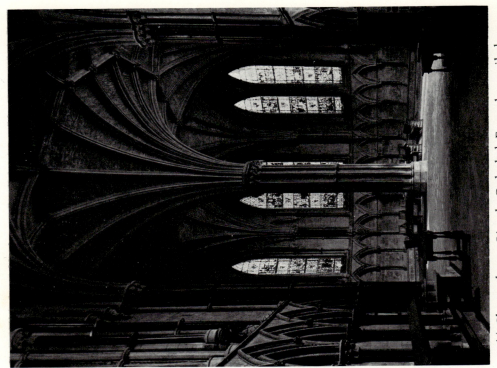

(B) Chapter-house. Lincoln Cathedral. From the vestibule.
Second quarter of thirteenth century

(A) Chapter-house. Worcester Cathedral. First half of
twelfth century

58

Staircase leading to chapter-house. Beverley Minster, Yorks. Second quarter of thirteenth century

(A) Pulpit in refectory. Beaulieu Abbey, Hants. Mid thirteenth century

(B) Pulpit in refectory. Chester Cathedral, Cheshire.
Mid thirteenth century

Aisled hall. Oakham Castle, Rutland. Late twelfth century

(B) Doorway to Bishop's Hall. Durham Castle.
Late twelfth century

(A) Window arcade. Constables' Hall. Durham Castle.
Late twelfth century

(B) Great chamber. Keep. Castle Hedingham, Essex.
Late twelfth century

(A) Detail of doorway to Bishop's Hall. Durham Castle.
Late twelfth century

63

(B) Choir. Canterbury Cathedral.
From the west

(A) Choir. Canterbury Cathedral.
From south-east transept. 1175-8

64

(B) Capital. Presbytery. Canterbury Cathedral. 1175–84

(A) St Thomas's Chapel. Canterbury Cathedral. View showing site of shrine. 1175–84

Detail of crossing. Eastern transept. Canterbury Cathedral. 1175-8

East end. Chichester Cathedral, Sussex. From the north-west. *c.* 1190

(A) Choir vault. Lincoln Cathedral. End of twelfth century

(B) Transept. Lincoln Cathedral. From the north. First quarter of thirteenth century

East end of presbytery. Rochester Cathedral, Kent. *c.* 1200

Presbytery. Rochester Cathedral, Kent. From the south-west. *c.* 1200

Section showing internal elevation of west portico and western transept. Peterborough Cathedral, Northants. *c.* 1190–1235

West front. Peterborough Cathedral, Northants. Early thirteenth century

(B) South transept. Roche Abbey, Yorks. From the north-west,
c. 1160-70

(A) Western transept. Peterborough Cathedral, Northants.
From the north-east. Early thirteenth century

73

(A) Nave. Nun Monkton church, Yorks. From the east, before restoration. *c.* 1200

(B) South transept. Arbroath Abbey, Angus. From the south-west.
c. 1200

74

Transept and crossing. Hexham Priory, Northumberland.
First quarter of thirteenth century

East end of church. Tynemouth Priory, Northumberland. *c.* 1200

Presbytery. Tynemouth Priory, Northumberland. *c.* 1200

(A) Lady Chapel. Glastonbury Abbey, Somerset. From the south. 1184-6

(B) Detail of internal wall arcade. Lady Chapel, Glastonbury Abbey, Somerset

Detail of north doorway. Lady Chapel, Glastonbury Abbey, Somerset. 1184-6

South side of nave. Worcester Cathedral. West bays *c*. 1170; adjoining bays to east
fourteenth century

North porch. Wells Cathedral, Somerset. *c.* 1210

(A) Foliage capital. Wells Cathedral, Somerset. *c.* 1200

(B) Foliage capital, with grotesques. South transept. Wells Cathedral, Somerset. *c.* 1200

Detail of north porch. Wells Cathedral, Somerset. *c.* 1210

Nave. St David's Cathedral, Pembrokeshire. From the west. c. 1180

(B) Bay of nave. Llanthony Abbey, Monmouthshire. From the south. *c.* 1190

(A) Detail of nave. St David's Cathedral, Pembrokeshire

Nave. Llanthony Abbey, Monmouthshire. From the west. *c.* 1190

West front. Llanthony Abbey, Monmouthshire. From the north-west. *c.* 1200

Presbytery. Abbey Dore, Herefordshire. Facing east. *c.* 1210

Ambulatory and eastern chapels. Abbey Dore, Herefordshire. *c.* 1210

Salisbury Cathedral. From the north-east. Second quarter of thirteenth century

Salisbury Cathedral. From the south-west. Third quarter of thirteenth century

Lady Chapel and ambulatory. Salisbury Cathedral. From the north-west. 1220-5

Internal bays. Choir and presbytery. Worcester Cathedral. Finished 1231

(A) Elevation of choir and eastern transept. Worcester Cathedral

(B) Nave. Lincoln Cathedral. From the south-west. Second quarter of thirteenth century

(A) Nave vault. Lincoln Cathedral. Second quarter of
thirteenth century

(B) Angel Choir vault. Lincoln Cathedral. *c.* 1270

95

Wall arcade. Choir. Lincoln Cathedral. End of twelfth century

Triforium of choir. Beverley Minster, Yorks. Second quarter of thirteenth century

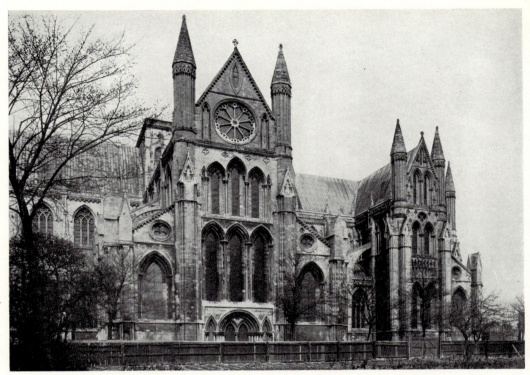

(A) Main and eastern transepts. Beverley Minster, Yorks. Second quarter of thirteenth century

(B) East fronts of church, *c.* 1240, and of Lady Chapel, first half of fourteenth century. Ely Cathedral

Eastern extension of clerestory, and vault detail. Ely Cathedral. *c.* 1240

West front and towers. Lincoln Cathedral. Thirteenth century additions. *c.* 1250;
upper parts of towers fourth quarter of fourteenth century

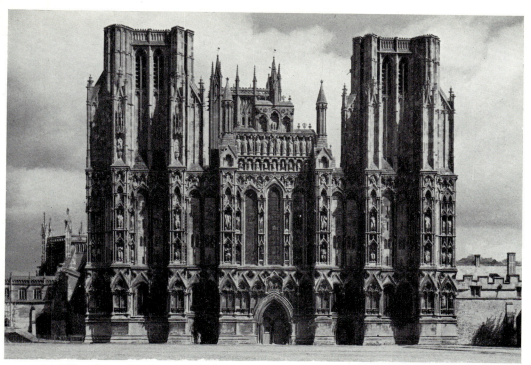

(A) West front. Wells Cathedral, Somerset. Second quarter of thirteenth century

(B) Uppermost part of west front. Wells Cathedral, Somerset

Presbytery bays. Westminster Abbey, London. From the south-west. Mid thirteenth century

South transept and nave. Westminster Abbey, London. From the south-west.
Mid thirteenth century

(A) West front. Binham Abbey, Norfolk. *c.* 1240

(B) Tympanum. West doorway, Higham Ferrers, Northants. Mid thirteenth century

Door of hall. Merton College, Oxford. *c.* 1300

Porch. South transept. Lincoln Cathedral. Mid thirteenth century

Lower storeys of central lantern tower. Lincoln Cathedral. *c.* 1240

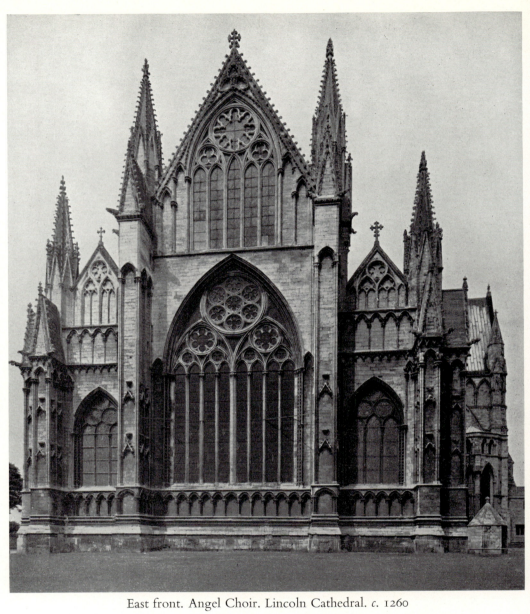

East front. Angel Choir. Lincoln Cathedral. *c.* 1260

(A) Section of eastern part of Angel Choir. Lincoln Cathedral

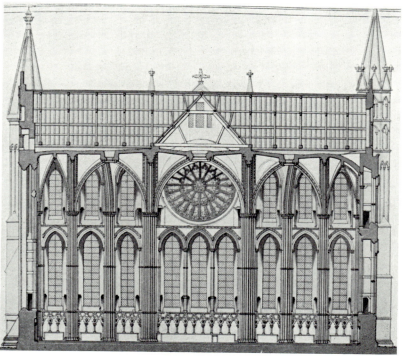

(B) Section of eastern transept (Nine Altars). Durham Cathedral.
Third quarter of thirteenth century

Eastern transept (Nine Altars). Durham Cathedral. From the south-east. Third quarter of thirteenth century

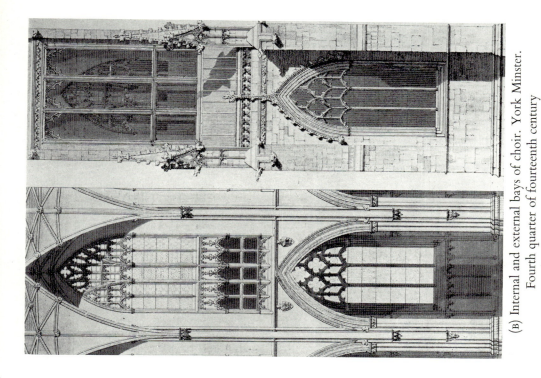

(B) Internal and external bays of choir. York Minster.
Fourth quarter of fourteenth century

(A) Internal and external bays of south transept. York Minster.
Second quarter of thirteenth century

Detail of triforium and clerestory. Choir. Exeter Cathedral, Devon. *c.* 1300

Lady Chapel. Lichfield Cathedral, Staffs. From the south. Second quarter of
fourteenth century

(B) Detail of north transept. Hereford Cathedral

(A) North transept. Hereford Cathedral. From the north-west.
Third quarter of thirteenth century

114

(B) Angel Choir. Lincoln Cathedral. c. 1260

(A) Cloister. Lincoln Cathedral. c. 1290

115

(A) Boss in south aisle. Nave. Lincoln Cathedral. *c.* 1230

(B) Boss in south aisle of presbytery. Lincoln Cathedral. *c.* 1260

Door. St George's Chapel, Windsor, Berks. Mid thirteenth century

(A) Geddington cross, Northants. *c.* 1300

(B) Stalls. Chapter-house, York Minster. *c.* 1300

(A) Longitudinal section. Wells Cathedral, Somerset

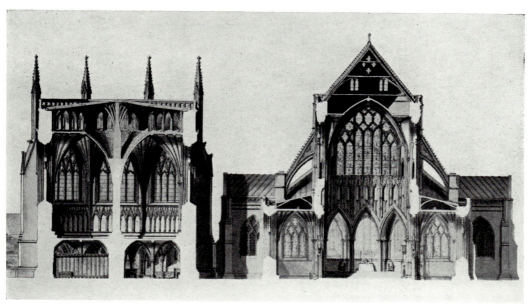

(B) Section of chapter-house and choir. Wells Cathedral, Somerset

Chapter-house. Wells Cathedral, Somerset. First quarter of fourteenth century

Lady Chapel. Wells Cathedral, Somerset. *c.* 1300

(B) Tomb of Edward II. Gloucester Cathedral. *c.* 1330

(A) Sedilia in Lady Chapel. Bristol Cathedral, Somerset.
First quarter of fourteenth century

122

(B) North transept with base of octagonal lantern.
Ely Cathedral. Second quarter of fourteenth century

(A) Constructional model of Octagon. Ely Cathedral.

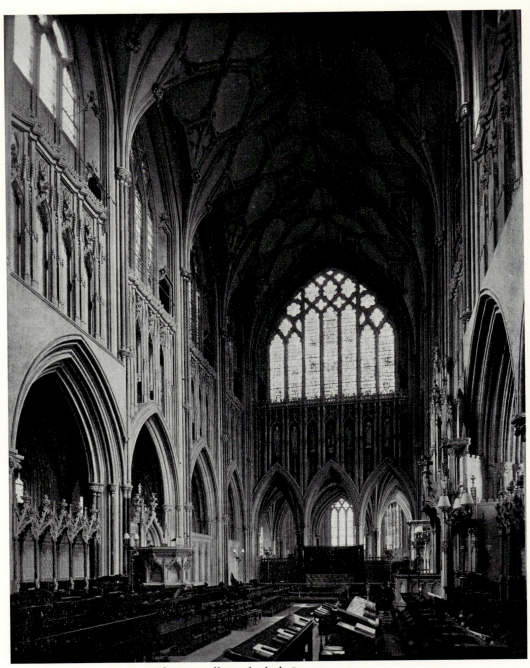

Choir. Wells Cathedral, Somerset. *c.* 1330

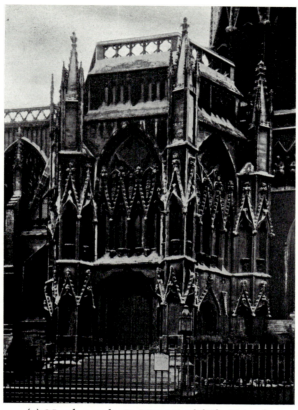

(A) North porch. St Mary Redcliffe, Bristol.
First quarter of fourteenth century

(B) Lady Chapel. Ely Cathedral. Facing east.
Second quarter of fourteenth century

125

Detail of Lady Chapel. Ely Cathedral. Second quarter of fourteenth century

(B) Tower. Oxford Cathedral. Second quarter of thirteenth century

(A) West front. Beverley Minster, Yorks. c. 1400

127

(B) Tower and steeple. Warboys church, Hunts.
Mid thirteenth century

(A) Spire on south-eastern angle tower. Peterborough
Cathedral, Northants. Mid fourteenth century

128

(B) Doorway. Chapter-house. Southwell Minster, Notts. *c.* 1300

(A) West towers. Lincoln Cathedral. Upper parts late fourteenth century

129

(A) Longitudinal section. St Stephen's Chapel, Palace of Westminster, London.
Second quarter of fourteenth century

(B) Detail of spandrel treatment. St Stephen's Chapel,
Palace of Westminster, London

(A) Sutton tomb. Oxford Cathedral.
Mid fourteenth century

(B) Tomb of Edward III. Westminster Abbey,
London. c. 1380

(A) Internal and external elevation of bays of choir and nave. Lichfield Cathedral, Staffs. Nave third quarter of thirteenth century; choir second quarter of fourteenth century

(B) Section showing internal elevation of Lady Chapel. Bristol Cathedral. First quarter of fourteenth century; elder Lady Chapel early thirteenth century

Choir. Bristol Cathedral. From the north-west. First quarter of fourteenth century

Choir. Tewkesbury Abbey, Glos. Second quarter of fourteenth century

Choir and presbytery. Gloucester Cathedral. From the west. Second quarter of fourteenth century

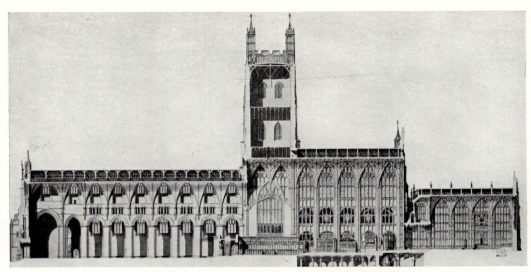

(A) Longitudinal section. Gloucester Cathedral

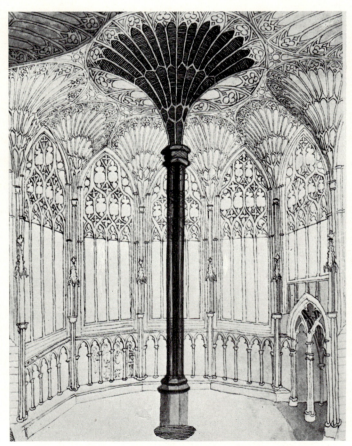

(B) Chapter-house. Hereford Cathedral (after Stukeley).
1364-70

Nave. Canterbury Cathedral. From the south-west. Fourth quarter of fourteenth century

Nave. Winchester Cathedral. Looking west. Late fourteenth and early fifteenth century

Chantry of William of Wykeham. Winchester Cathedral, Hants. *c.* 1400

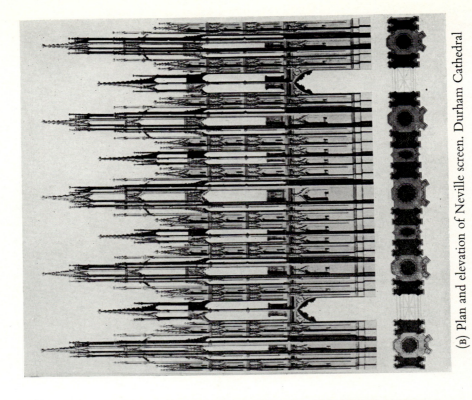

(B) Plan and elevation of Neville screen. Durham Cathedral

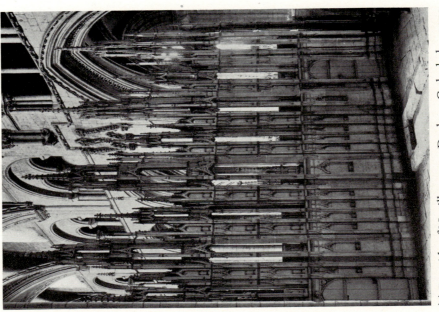

(A) East side of Neville screen. Durham Cathedral. *c.* 1375

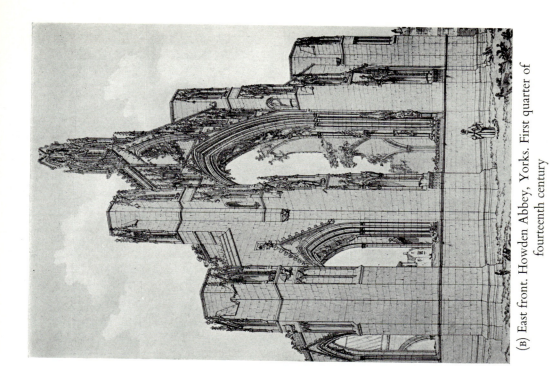

(B) East front. Howden Abbey, Yorks. First quarter of fourteenth century

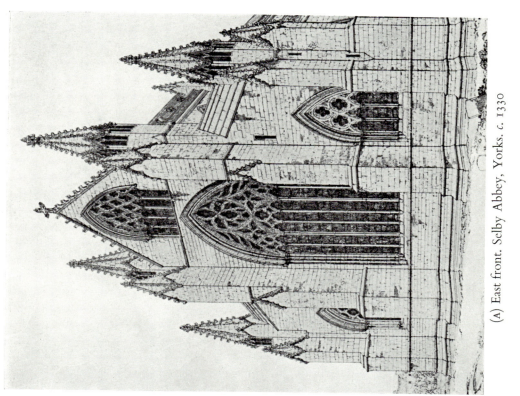

(A) East front. Selby Abbey, Yorks. c. 1330

West front. Exeter Cathedral, Devon. Third quarter of fourteenth century

Detail of west front. Exeter Cathedral, Devon. Third quarter of fourteenth century

York Minster. From the south-east

(B) East front. York Minster. c. 1400

(A) West front. Winchester Cathedral. Third quarter of fourteenth century

Stairway to chapter-house and bridge. Wells Cathedral, Somerset. *c.* 1280;
bridge fifteenth century

(A) Cloister. Salisbury Cathedral. *c.* 1275

(B) Cloister, *c.* 1275, nave clerestory, and return face of west front, earlier.
Salisbury Cathedral.

Cloister garth from the north-west. Westminster Abbey, London. Mid fourteenth century

(c) Cloister. Canterbury Cathedral. *c.* 1400

(B) Doorway from east walk of cloister to nave. Norwich Cathedral. First quarter of fourteenth century

(A) Cloister. Worcester Cathedral. Third quarter of fourteenth century

(A) Bishop's Palace. Acton Burnell, Salop. Fourth quarter of thirteenth century

(B) Entrance front. Wardour Castle, Wilts. Third quarter of fourteenth century

(A) Wardour Castle, Wilts. From the south

(B) John of Gaunt's Hall. Kenilworth Castle, Warwickshire. Fourth quarter of
fourteenth century

(A) John of Gaunt's Hall. Kenilworth Castle, Warwickshire. Interior. Fourth quarter of fourteenth century

(B) Porch of Great Hall and passage linking the two halls. Bishop Gower's Palace, St David's, Pembrokeshire. Mid fourteenth century

(A) Chapel and Great Hall. Bishop Gower's Palace, St David's, Pembrokeshire.
From the east. Mid fourteenth century

(B) Bishop's Hall and kitchen. Bishop Gower's Palace, St David's, Pembrokeshire.
Mid fourteenth century

153

Ockwells Manor, Berks. From the north-east. *c.* 1450 (*Copyright Country Life*)

Ockwells Manor, Berks. Hall. *c.* 1450 (*Copyright Country Life*)

(B) Gatehouse. Kirkham Priory, Yorks. External elevation.
c. 1300

(A) Gatehouse. Bury St Edmunds Abbey, Suffolk. External elevation.
Second quarter of fourteenth century

156

Gatehouse. St Osyth's Priory, Essex. External elevation. Fourth quarter of fifteenth century

(A) Inner front of gatehouse. Thornton Abbey, Lincs. Fourth quarter of fourteenth century

(B) Herstmonceux Castle, Sussex. Second quarter of fifteenth century

Tattershall Castle, Lincs. Second quarter of fifteenth century

(B) Chancel. Cherry Hinton church, Cambs. From the south-west. Second quarter of thirteenth century

(A) Central tower. Friars' Church, King's Lynn, Norfolk. Second quarter of fifteenth century

(B) Chancel. Lawford church, Essex. From the south-west.
Second quarter of fourteenth century

(A) Chancel. Fenstanton church, Hunts. From the north-east.
Second quarter of fourteenth century

(B) East Chapel lancets. Ferns, Co. Wexford. Second quarter of thirteenth century

(A) East end. Ardfert Cathedral, Co. Kerry. Late thirteenth century

162

Dumblane Cathedral, Perthshire. From the south-east. Third quarter of thirteenth century

(B) Nave. St Cuthbert's church, Wells, Somerset. From the east.
Fifteenth century and earlier

(A) South porch. Yatton church, Somerset. c. 1450

164

St Cuthbert's church, Wells, Somerset. Second quarter of fifteenth century

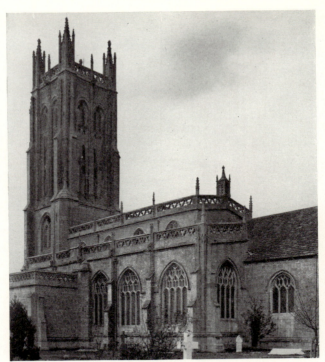

(A) Tower. Wrington church, Somerset. From the south-west. Second quarter of fifteenth century

(B) Sutton-in-the-Isle church, Isle of Ely. From the south-east. *c.* 1375

(A) Nave and screen. Swymbridge church, Devon. First quarter of sixteenth century

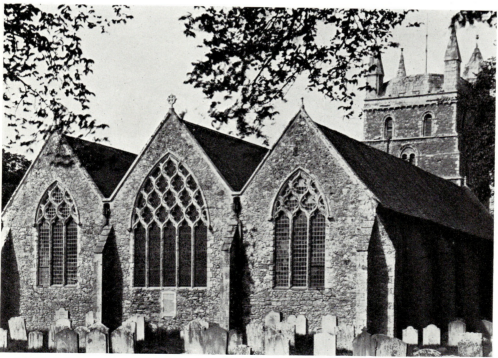

(B) New Romney church, Kent. From the east. Third quarter of fourteenth century

167

Nave. Lavenham church, Suffolk. First quarter of sixteenth century

Nave. Sutton-in-the-Isle church, Isle of Ely. *c.* 1375

Nave. Northleach church, Glos. From the east. First quarter of fifteenth century

Tower. Chipping Campden church, Glos. Mid fifteenth century

Hammer-beam roof. March church, Isle of Ely. *c.* 1500

(B) Roof of nave. Framlingham church, Suffolk. First quarter of sixteenth century

(A) Wooden vault of nave. Warmington church, Northants. Third quarter of thirteenth century

173

(B) Interior of timber-built tower and west front of earlier church. Blackmore, Essex

(A) Timber-built tower. Blackmore church, Essex. From the north. Fifteenth century

174

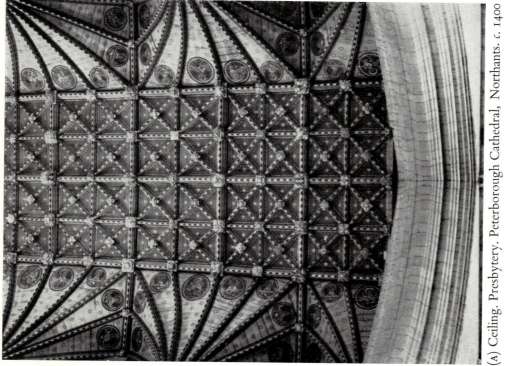

(A) Ceiling, Presbytery, Peterborough Cathedral, Northants. c. 1400

175

Great Hall of Richard II. Palace of Westminster, London. 1394–1402

176

(A) Roof. Great Hall. Eltham Palace, London. *c.* 1475 (*Copyright Country Life*)

(B) Great Hall. Eltham Palace, London

177

(A) Divinity School, Oxford. Looking west. Second and fourth quarters of fifteenth century

(B) Quadrangle. Magdalen College, Oxford. From the north-east. Fourth quarter of fifteenth century

Central tower. Canterbury Cathedral. Exterior from the south-west. *c.* 1500

(B) King's College Chapel, Cambridge. From the screen.
Completed early sixteenth century

(A) Nave crossing and presbytery. Sherborne Abbey, Dorset.
From the west. Fourth quarter of fifteenth century

(B) Bay design. St George's Chapel, Windsor, Berks.
Fourth quarter of fifteenth century

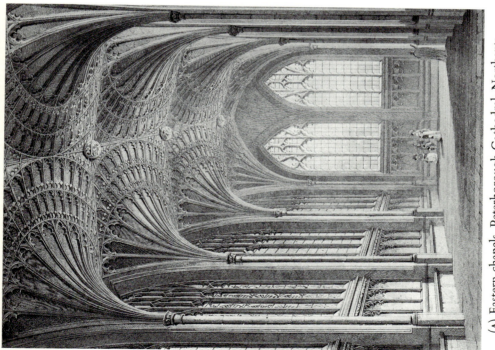

(A) Eastern chapels. Peterborough Cathedral, Northants.
From the north. *c.* 1500

181

(B) Henry VII's Chapel. Westminster Abbey, London.
First quarter of sixteenth century

(A) Henry VII's Chapel. Westminster Abbey, London. From
the north-east. First quarter of sixteenth century

Vault. Henry VII's Chapel. Westminster Abbey, London. First quarter of sixteenth century

(A) Tomb. Long Ashton church, Somerset. Fourth quarter of fifteenth century

(B) Detail of ceiling. Chapel. Hampton Court Palace, Middlesex.
Second quarter of sixteenth century

184

Gatehouse. Layer Marney Hall, Essex. External elevation. *c.* 1520

185

Great Hall. Borthwick Manor, Midlothian. Second quarter of fifteenth century (*Copyright Country Life*)

Prior's Lodging. Much Wenlock, Salop. Fourth quarter of fifteenth century (*Copyright Country Life*)

Hall. Hampton Court Palace, Middlesex. Second quarter of sixteenth century

(A) Hall. Lyddington Bede House, Rutland. Fourth quarter of fifteenth century
(*Copyright Country Life*)

(B) Abbot's Lodgings. Muchelney Abbey, Somerset. From the south-west.
First quarter of sixteenth century

Unfinished front between first and second courts. Thornbury Castle, Glos. First quarter of sixteenth century (*Copyright Country Life*)

Windows of the state apartments. Thornbury Castle, Glos. First quarter of sixteenth century

Porch and hall of Abbot's Lodging. Forde Abbey, Dorset. Dated 1528

INDEX

Numbers in italics refer to plates. References to the Notes are given only where they indicate matters of special interest or importance: such references are given to the page on which the note occurs, followed by the number of the chapter to which it belongs, and the number of the note. Thus 212(4)[11] indicates page 212, chapter 4, note 11.

R   227